healthy
tasteofhome
cooking
annual recipes

tasteofhome
BOOKS

REIMAN MEDIA GROUP, INC. • GREENDALE, WI

healthy *taste* of home cooking
annual recipes

34

113

252

EDITORIAL
EDITOR-IN-CHIEF Catherine Cassidy
CREATIVE DIRECTOR Howard Greenberg
EDITORIAL SERVICES MANAGER Kerri Balliet

MANAGING EDITOR/PRINT & DIGITAL BOOKS
Mark Hagen
ASSOCIATE CREATIVE DIRECTOR
Edwin Robles Jr.

EDITOR Heather Ray
ASSOCIATE EDITOR Amy Glander
ART DIRECTOR Jessie Sharon
LAYOUT DESIGNER Nancy Novak
CONTRIBUTING LAYOUT DESIGNER Holly Patch
EDITORIAL PRODUCTION MANAGER
Dena Ahlers
COPY CHIEF Deb Warlaumont Mulvey
COPY EDITOR Alysse Gear

CHIEF FOOD EDITOR Karen Berner
FOOD EDITOR Peggy Woodward, RD
ASSOCIATE FOOD EDITOR Krista Lanphier
ASSOCIATE EDITOR/FOOD CONTENT
Annie Rundle
RECIPE EDITORS Mary King; Jenni Sharp, RD;
Irene Yeh
CONTENT OPERATIONS MANAGER Colleen King

TEST KITCHEN AND FOOD STYLING MANAGER
Sarah Thompson
TEST KITCHEN COOKS Alicia Rooker, RD (lead);
Holly Johnson; Jimmy Cababa
PREP COOKS Matthew Hass (lead),
Nicole Spohrleder, Lauren Knoelke
FOOD STYLISTS Kathryn Conrad (senior),
Shannon Roum, Leah Rekau
GROCERY COORDINATOR Molly McCowan

PHOTO DIRECTOR Dan Bishop
PHOTOGRAPHERS Dan Roberts,
Grace Natoli Sheldon, Jim Wieland
SET STYLING MANAGER Stepanie Marchese
SET STYLISTS Melissa Haberman, Dee Dee Jacq

BUSINESS
VICE PRESIDENT, PUBLISHER
Jan Studin, jan_studin@rd.com

GENERAL MANAGER, TASTE OF HOME
COOKING SCHOOLS Erin Puariea

VICE PRESIDENT, BRAND MARKETING
Jennifer Smith
VICE PRESIDENT, CIRCULATION AND
CONTINUITY MARKETING Dave Fiegel

READER'S DIGEST NORTH AMERICA
VICE PRESIDENT, BUSINESS DEVELOPMENT
Jonathan Bigham
PRESIDENT, BOOKS AND HOME ENTERTAINING
Harold Clarke
CHIEF FINANCIAL OFFICER Howard Halligan
VICE PRESIDENT, GENERAL MANAGER,
READER'S DIGEST MEDIA Marilynn Jacobs
CHIEF MARKETING OFFICER Renee Jordan
VICE PRESIDENT, CHIEF SALES OFFICER
Mark Josephson
GENERAL MANAGER, MILWAUKEE Frank Quigley
VICE PRESIDENT, CHIEF CONTENT OFFICER
Liz Vaccariello

THE READER'S DIGEST ASSOCIATION, INC.
PRESIDENT AND CHIEF EXECUTIVE OFFICER
Robert E. Guth

COVER PHOTOGRAPHY
PHOTOGRAPHER Dan Roberts
FOOD STYLIST Kathryn Conrad
SET STYLIST Melissa Haberman

PICTURED ON THE FRONT COVER: Honey Wheat Rolls (p. 198), Frosty Mocha Pie (p. 236), Cranberry Walnut Slaw (p. 41), and Makeover Easy Beef-Stuffed Shells (p. 113).

PICTURED ON THE BACK COVER: Orange Beef Stir-Fry (p. 211), Turkey Meatball Gyros (p. 49), Pumpkin Pie Cupcakes (p. 227), and Creamy Spinach & Potato Soup (p. 51).

Contents

Get inspired to try something new, fresh and healthy. With more than 400 satisfying recipes to choose from, you'll find everything you need for casual weeknight dinners, holiday entertaining, vegetarian cooking and more.

Summer Blackberry Cobbler, 251

Real Home Cooking

With the *Healthy Cooking Annual Recipes* collection, you can use what's in your pantry to prepare better-for-you meals.

Let's be real. As a working mother of two, my life can get a little hectic at times. I'd be lying if I said I never took advantage of the convenience of pizza delivery. But as the food editor of *Healthy Cooking* and a registered dietitian, I care about my family's diet and want to be sure they're eating heart-healthy, nutritious meals—at least the majority of the time.

That's why I'm especially excited about this year's collection of *Healthy Cooking* recipes. We set out to prove that eating healthy doesn't mean scouring the store for exotic foods or paying top dollar for fancy products. The recipes that follow come from real home cooks and use practical ingredients in a way that's not only creative but also delicious and good for you.

But there's more to these recipes than simple ingredients and nutrition. Many tell a story, giving us a glimpse into the kitchens of hundreds of home cooks. Jacqueline Correa in Landing, New Jersey, tells us her Cuban mother-in-law makes the best Arroz Con Pollo, but it's too time-consuming for her to prepare. On page 118, she shares her quick weeknight version using ingredients she keeps on hand. In Kearns, Utah, Deonna Weight uses leftover pot roast, potatoes and dried herbs to make a savory soup for her family's Sunday dinner (page 49), and in Hinesville, Georgia, Juli Meyers whips up a simple dip using peanut butter, cream cheese and vanilla (page 11). It's how she gets her kids to eat more apples.

These snapshots bring our recipes to life, and you'll find hundreds more in the next 17 chapters, along with up-to-date health advice, fun facts and cooking tips. And to help you make the best possible choices to meet your dietary needs, we offer Nutrition Facts for every recipe, icons to identify what's low-fat, low-sodium, low-carb and/or meatless, and Diabetic Exchanges for recipes that are diabetes-friendly. Also, rest assured, we test every recipe in the Healthy Cooking Test Kitchen, so we're confident it will turn out as planned.

Now, with hundreds of simple-to-prepare *Healthy Cooking* recipes to choose from, it's easier than ever to serve your family real meals you can feel good about, all year long.

Happy Cooking,

Peggy Woodward, RD

Peggy Woodward, RD
Food Editor, *Healthy Cooking*

P.S. *Want to see your family's favorite healthy dish in an upcoming collection? Submit your recipes at* **tasteofhome.com/submit.**

146

60

Nutrition Fact Nuggets

NUTRITIONAL GUIDELINES

All of the recipes in our *Healthy Cooking Annual Recipes* cookbook fit the lifestyle of a health-conscious cook and family. The recipes represent a variety of foods that will fit into any meal plan that is within the standards of the USDA's "MyPlate Plan" for moderately active adults (see box below).

FACTS

- Whenever a choice of ingredients is given in a recipe (such as 1/3 cup of sour cream or plain yogurt), the first ingredient listed is always the one calculated in the Nutrition Facts.
- When a range is given for an ingredient (such as 2 to 3 teaspoons), we calculate the first amount given.
- Only the amount of a marinade absorbed during preparation is calculated.
- Garnishes listed in recipes are generally included in our calculations.

DIABETIC EXCHANGES

All recipes in *Healthy Cooking Annual Recipes* have been reviewed by a registered dietitian. Diabetic Exchanges are assigned to recipes in accordance with guidelines from the American Diabetic and American Dietetic associations.

The majority of recipes in this cookbook are suitable for diabetics, but please check the Diabetic Exchanges to make sure the recipe is in accordance with your doctor's instructions and fits your particular dietary guidelines.

SPECIAL DIET INDICATORS

To help those on restricted diets easily find dishes to suit their needs, we clearly indicate recipes that are particularly low in fat, sodium or carbohydrates as well as those that contain no meat. You will find these colored special diet indicators directly after the recipe title where appropriate:

F One serving contains 3 grams or less of fat
S One serving contains 140 milligrams or less of sodium
C One serving contains 15 grams or less of carbohydrates
M Recipe contains no meat

POWER IN PAIRS
By Alicia Rooker, RD

Research has found that eating certain foods together can help our bodies absorb more vitamins and reduce the risk of certain diseases. Try these tasty combinations to get the most out of every meal.

Tomato juice, avocado and olive oil: Some nutrients are best absorbed when eaten with healthy fat. Fat-soluble lycopene from tomatoes has been shown to reduce the risk of heart disease and some cancers. Combine it with olive oil and avocado—two excellent sources of monounsaturated fats. Try the **Refreshing Gazpacho** on page 52.

Spinach, salmon and orange: Vitamin C helps increase the absorption of non-heme iron, the kind found in spinach. Eating a heme iron, from animal foods like fish, with a non-heme iron also boosts iron absorption. Try the **Salmon Spinach Salad** on page 168.

Quinoa and black beans: Protein, needed by the body for growth and repair, is made up of building blocks called amino acids. Our bodies produce many of these amino acids but rely on food sources for the rest. Meat, fish, poultry, cheese, eggs, yogurt and milk provide complete proteins, but the right combination of incomplete proteins—from grains, nuts, beans, seeds, peas and corn—can provide all the amino acids we need, too. Try the **Quinoa Tabouleh** on page 183.

DAILY NUTRITION GUIDE

	Women 25-50	Women over 50	Men 50-65
CALORIES	2,000	1,800	2,400
FAT	67 g or less	60 g or less	80 g or less
SATURATED FAT	22 g or less	20 g or less	27 g or less
CHOLESTEROL	300 mg or less	300 mg or less	300 mg or less
SODIUM	2,300 mg or less	1,500 mg or less	1,500 mg or less
CARBOHYDRATES	300 g	270 g	360 g
FIBER	20-30 g	20-30 g	30-40 g
PROTEIN	50 g	45 g	60 g

This chart is only a guide. Requirements vary, depending on age, weight, height and amount of activity.
Children's dietary needs vary as they grow.

12

15

13

Starters
& Snacks

“Here's a lighter version of classic spinach dip, stuffed inside juicy mushrooms and baked. You can also prepare these stuffed mushrooms on the grill. Just be sure to use a grill pan so they don't slip through the grate.”

ASHLEY PIERCE BRANTFORD, ONTARIO
about her recipe, Spinach Dip-Stuffed Mushrooms, on page 12

Strawberry Corn Salsa F S C M

This recipe is art in a bowl! All the colors of summer are captured in this dish with a fresh, light flavor perfect for snacking between swims or to kick off a backyard barbecue. This can be served with chips or alone as a side dish.

—CATHERINE ANN GOZA LELAND, NORTH CAROLINA

PREP: 15 MIN. + CHILLING **MAKES:** 5½ CUPS

- 2 cups fresh strawberries, chopped
- 2 cups grape tomatoes, chopped
- 1 package (10 ounces) frozen corn, thawed
- 2 green onions, chopped
- 3 tablespoons minced fresh cilantro
- ⅓ cup olive oil
- 2 tablespoons raspberry vinegar
- 2 tablespoons lime juice
- ½ teaspoon salt
     Baked tortilla chips

In a large bowl, combine the first five ingredients. In a small bowl, whisk the oil, vinegar, lime juice and salt. Drizzle over strawberry mixture; toss to coat. Refrigerate for 1 hour. Serve with chips.

Nutrition Facts: *¼ cup (calculated without chips) equals 49 calories, 3 g fat (trace saturated fat), 0 cholesterol, 56 mg sodium, 5 g carbohydrate, 1 g fiber, 1 g protein.*

Ants On a Log Spread S C M

PREP/TOTAL TIME: 10 MIN. **MAKES:** 4 SERVINGS

- 1 celery rib, finely chopped
- 2 tablespoons raisins
- 2 tablespoons creamy peanut butter
     Miniature whole wheat bagels or apple slices

In a small bowl, combine the celery, raisins and peanut butter. Serve with bagels or apples.

Nutrition Facts: *2 tablespoons (calculated without bagels and apples) equals 63 calories, 4 g fat (1 g saturated fat), 0 cholesterol, 46 mg sodium, 5 g carbohydrate, 1 g fiber, 2 g protein.* **Diabetic Exchange:** *½ high-fat meat.*

> ❝I make this snack as a protein-packed pick-me-up. It reminds me of 'Ants on a Log' from my childhood, and it's great on an English muffin or apple slices.❞

—LISA HUMMITSCH TINLEY PARK, ILLINOIS

> Thank you for making over my recipe! We tried it with friends and loved it. We barely noticed the difference. Thank you for keeping all of the cheeses.
> —**SONYA LABBE** WEST HOLLYWOOD, CALIFORNIA

Makeover Stuffed Potato Appetizers F S C

PREP: 45 MIN. + COOLING
BAKE: 15 MIN. **MAKES:** 40 APPETIZERS

- 20 baby Yukon Gold potatoes (2 pounds)
- 6 ounces fat-free cream cheese
- ¾ cup reduced-fat sour cream
- 6 bacon strips, cooked and crumbled
- ¼ cup shredded Monterey Jack cheese
- ¼ cup shredded sharp cheddar cheese
- 2 green onions, chopped
- ½ teaspoon salt
- ½ teaspoon pepper

1. Place potatoes in a Dutch oven and cover with water. Bring to a boil. Reduce heat; cover and cook for 8-10 minutes or just until tender. Drain.

2. When cool enough to handle, cut each potato in half lengthwise. Scoop out the pulp, leaving thin shells. Remove ⅓ cup pulp (discard or save for another use).

3. In a large bowl, mash the remaining pulp with cream cheese. Add sour cream and half of the bacon. Stir in the cheeses, green onions, salt and pepper; spoon into potato shells.

4. Place in a 15-in. x 10-in. x 1-in. baking pan. Sprinkle with remaining bacon. Bake, uncovered, at 400° for 15-20 minutes or until heated through.

Nutrition Facts: *1 stuffed potato half equals 35 calories, 1 g fat (1 g saturated fat), 4 mg cholesterol, 87 mg sodium, 4 g carbohydrate, trace fiber, 2 g protein.*

? Did you know?

Baking potatoes, such as russet, have a high starch content that produces a fluffy, dry texture after baking. Waxy potatoes, such as red round, have less starch so they hold their shape after boiling. All-purpose potatoes, such as Yukon Gold, are suitable for both baking and boiling.

Crunchy Peanut Butter Apple Dip SCM

A neighbor gave this peanut butter dip to my mom years ago. She always made it for us in the fall when apples were in season. Now I carry on the tradition and make it for my own kids.

—JULI MEYERS HINESVILLE, GEORGIA

PREP/TOTAL TIME: 10 MIN.
MAKES: 2½ CUPS

- 1 carton (8 ounces) reduced-fat spreadable cream cheese
- 1 cup creamy peanut butter
- ¼ cup fat-free milk
- 1 tablespoon brown sugar
- 1 teaspoon vanilla extract
- ½ cup chopped unsalted peanuts
  Apple slices

In a small bowl, beat the first five ingredients until blended. Stir in peanuts. Serve with apple slices. Refrigerate leftovers.

Nutrition Facts: *2 tablespoons (calculated without apples) equals 126 calories, 10 g fat (3 g saturated fat), 5 mg cholesterol, 115 mg sodium, 5 g carbohydrate, 1 g fiber, 5 g protein.*

Yogurt Dill Dip FSCM

Every person who tries this wants to know what makes it taste special. The secret is the blend of yogurt, sour cream and mayo.

—KRISANN DURNFORD MUSKEGO, WISCONSIN

PREP: 15 MIN. + CHILLING
MAKES: 2½ CUPS

- 1 cup (8 ounces) plain yogurt
- 1 cup (8 ounces) reduced-fat sour cream
- ½ cup reduced-fat mayonnaise
- 2 tablespoons finely chopped onion
- 2 tablespoons minced fresh parsley
- 2 teaspoons dill weed
- ½ teaspoon salt
- ¼ teaspoon pepper
  Assorted fresh vegetables

In a small bowl, combine the first eight ingredients. Cover and refrigerate for at least 1 hour. Serve with vegetables.

Nutrition Facts: *2 tablespoons (calculated without vegetables) equals 44 calories, 3 g fat (1 g saturated fat), 8 mg cholesterol, 121 mg sodium, 2 g carbohydrate, trace fiber, 1 g protein.* **Diabetic Exchange:** *½ fat.*

Iced Lemon Tea FSCM

Sugar-free lemonade drink mix is the perfect ingredient to add to traditional iced tea. It not only tastes cool and refreshing, but also cuts out extra calories. I rely on this beverage during the hot days of summer, but also enjoy it year-round.

—DAWN LOWENSTEIN HATBORO, PENNSYLVANIA

PREP: 15 MIN. **COOK:** 10 MIN. + COOLING **MAKES:** 12 SERVINGS (1 CUP EACH)

- 3½ teaspoons Crystal Light lemonade drink mix
- 4 cups cold water
- 8 cups water
- 8 individual decaffeinated tea bags
- 1 mint-flavored black tea bag
  Ice cubes
  Fresh mint leaves and lemon slices, optional

1. In a 3-qt. pitcher, combine lemonade mix and cold water. Refrigerate until chilled.
2. Meanwhile, in a large saucepan, bring water to a boil. Remove from the heat; add tea bags. Cover and steep for 3-5 minutes. Discard tea bags. Cool; stir into lemonade mixture. Serve over ice with mint and lemon if desired.

Nutrition Facts: *1 cup equals 3 calories, trace fat (0 saturated fat), 0 cholesterol, 1 mg sodium, trace carbohydrate, trace fiber, trace protein.* **Diabetic Exchange:** *Free food.*

Spinach Dip-Stuffed Mushrooms F S C M

Here's a lighter version of classic spinach dip, stuffed inside juicy mushrooms and baked. You can also prepare these stuffed mushrooms on the grill. Just be sure to use a grill pan so they don't slip through the grate.
—**ASHLEY PIERCE** BRANTFORD, ONTARIO

PREP: 25 MIN. **BAKE:** 15 MIN. **MAKES:** 16 APPETIZERS

- 16 large fresh mushrooms
- 2 cups fresh baby spinach, coarsely chopped
- 1 tablespoon olive oil
- 2 garlic cloves, minced
- ½ cup reduced-fat sour cream
- 3 ounces reduced-fat cream cheese
- ⅓ cup shredded part-skim mozzarella cheese
- 3 tablespoons grated Parmesan cheese
- ¼ teaspoon salt
- ¼ teaspoon cayenne pepper
- ¼ teaspoon pepper

1. Remove stems from mushrooms and set caps aside; discard stems or save for another use. In a small skillet, saute spinach in oil until wilted. Add garlic; cook 1 minute longer.

2. In a small bowl, combine the sour cream, cream cheese, mozzarella, Parmesan, salt, cayenne, pepper and spinach mixture. Stuff into mushroom caps.

3. Place in a 15-in. x 10-in. x 1-in. baking pan coated with cooking spray. Bake, uncovered, at 400° for 12-15 minutes or until mushrooms are tender.

Nutrition Facts: *1 stuffed mushroom equals 48 calories, 3 g fat (2 g saturated fat), 8 mg cholesterol, 94 mg sodium, 2 g carbohydrate, trace fiber, 3 g protein.*

Spicy Almonds C M

Our family takes many adventurous hikes in the Selquirk mountain range surrounding our summer lake cabin. These nuts never tasted better than when we enjoyed them together at the peak of an amazing hike. Almonds are extremely nutritious, and, when dressed up with a wonderful blend of spices, they go from ordinary to extraordinary!
—**GINA MYERS** SPOKANE, WASHINGTON

PREP: 10 MIN. **BAKE:** 15 MIN. + COOLING **MAKES:** 2½ CUPS

- 1 tablespoon sugar
- 1½ teaspoons kosher salt
- 1 teaspoon paprika
- ½ teaspoon ground cinnamon
- ½ teaspoon ground cumin
- ½ teaspoon ground coriander
- ¼ teaspoon cayenne pepper
- 2½ cups unblanched almonds
- 1 tablespoon canola oil

1. In a small bowl, combine the first seven ingredients. In another small bowl, combine almonds and oil. Sprinkle with spice mixture; toss to coat.

2. Place in a foil-lined 15-in. x 10-in. x 1-in. baking pan coated with cooking spray. Bake at 325° for 15-20 minutes or until lightly browned, stirring twice. Cool completely. Store in an airtight container.

Nutrition Facts: *¼ cup equals 230 calories, 20 g fat (2 g saturated fat), 0 cholesterol, 293 mg sodium, 9 g carbohydrate, 4 g fiber, 8 g protein.*

> Moderately crispy with a rich and creamy filling, these semi-spicy appetizers taste like they've been fried.
> —**DANIELLE BOOTH** MINNEAPOLIS, MINNESOTA

Southwest Egg Rolls F S C M

PREP: 45 MIN. **BAKE:** 10 MIN.
MAKES: 2½ DOZEN

- 1 **cup fresh baby spinach, chopped**
- 2 **tablespoons finely chopped red onion**
- 2 **tablespoons finely chopped sweet red pepper**
- 1 **jalapeno pepper, seeded and minced**
- 1 **tablespoon canola oil**
- ⅓ **cup frozen corn, thawed**
- ¼ **cup black beans, rinsed and drained**
- ⅛ **teaspoon salt**
  Dash cayenne pepper
  Dash ground cumin
- ¾ **cup shredded reduced-fat Monterey Jack cheese or reduced-fat Mexican cheese blend**
- 4 **ounces reduced-fat cream cheese**
- 30 **wonton wrappers**
  Cooking spray

1. In a large skillet, saute the spinach, onion, red pepper and jalapeno in oil until tender. Stir in the corn, beans and seasonings; heat through. Remove from the heat. Stir in shredded cheese and cream cheese until melted.

2. Position a wonton wrapper with one point toward you. (Keep remaining wrappers covered with a damp paper towel until ready to use.) Place 2 teaspoons of filling in the center of wrapper. Fold bottom corner over filling; fold sides toward center over filling. Roll toward the remaining point. Moisten top corner with water; press to seal. Repeat with remaining wrappers and filling.

3. Place in a 15-in. x 10-in. x 1-in. baking pan coated with cooking spray; lightly coat egg rolls with additional cooking spray. Bake at 425° for 8-10 minutes or until golden brown, turning once.

Editor's Note: *Wear disposable gloves when cutting hot peppers; the oils can burn skin. Avoid touching your face.*

Nutrition Facts: *1 egg roll equals 50 calories, 2 g fat (1 g saturated fat), 5 mg cholesterol, 101 mg sodium, 6 g carbohydrate, trace fiber, 2 g protein.* **Diabetic Exchange:** *½ starch.*

Cranberry Pomegranate Margaritas F S C M

I came up with this beverage to serve at holiday celebrations for a festive twist to a traditional margarita. It's super pretty with frozen cranberries floating in the cocktail. It would also look beautiful with sugar crystals around the rim of glass.

—**MINDIE HILTON** SUSANVILLE, CALIFORNIA

PREP/TOTAL TIME: 5 MIN.
MAKES: 12 SERVINGS (¾ CUP EACH)

- 4½ **cups diet lemon-lime soda, chilled**
- 1½ **cups tequila**
- 1½ **cups cranberry juice, chilled**
- 1½ **cups pomegranate juice, chilled**
  - **Pomegranate slices and frozen cranberries, optional**

In a pitcher, combine the soda, tequila and juices. Serve in chilled glasses. Garnish with pomegranate and cranberries if desired.

Nutrition Facts: *¾ cup equals 97 calories, trace fat (trace saturated fat), 0 cholesterol, 13 mg sodium, 8 g carbohydrate, trace fiber, trace protein.*

Sweet Pineapple Cider F S M

I think the best thing about this recipe is that you can make it hours ahead of time. And you can keep it warm on the stovetop or in a slow cooker throughout the party.

—**MARY PRICE** YOUNGSTOWN, OHIO

PREP/TOTAL TIME: 30 MIN.
MAKES: 12 SERVINGS (¾ CUP EACH)

- 2 **small apples, divided**
- 10 **whole cloves**
- 1 **bottle (48 ounces) unsweetened apple juice**
- 4 **cans (6 ounces each) unsweetened pineapple juice**
- 2 **cinnamon sticks (3 inches)**

1. Core and cut one apple into 10 slices. Insert one clove into each slice. In Dutch oven, combine juices. Add apple slices and cinnamon sticks. Bring to a boil. Reduce heat; simmer, uncovered, for 15-20 minutes or until flavors are blended.
2. Discard apple slices and cinnamon sticks. Core and cut remaining apple into 12 slices. Ladle cider into mugs; garnish with apple slices. Serve warm.

Nutrition Facts: *¾ cup equals 93 calories, trace fat (trace saturated fat), 0 cholesterol, 5 mg sodium, 23 g carbohydrate, trace fiber, trace protein.* **Diabetic Exchange:** *1½ fruit.*

Avocado Bean Dip C M

I love me a good guacamole! I add beans to boost the amount of fiber in this version. It has a similar consistency to hummus and is perfect for dipping chips, pita or veggies.

—**RAQUEL HAGGARD** EDMOND, OKLAHOMA

PREP/TOTAL TIME: 15 MIN. **MAKES:** 2 CUPS

- 1 **can (15 ounces) white kidney or cannellini beans, rinsed and drained**
- 1 **medium ripe avocado, peeled and cubed**
- ½ **cup fresh cilantro leaves**
- 3 **tablespoons lime juice**
- ½ **teaspoon onion powder**
- ½ **teaspoon garlic powder**
- ½ **teaspoon chipotle hot pepper sauce**
- ¼ **teaspoon salt**
- ¼ **teaspoon ground cumin**
  - **Baked tortilla chips**

In a food processor, combine the first nine ingredients; cover and process until smooth. Serve with chips.

Nutrition Facts: *¼ cup (calculated without chips) equals 80 calories, 4 g fat (trace saturated fat), 0 cholesterol, 143 mg sodium, 10 g carbohydrate, 4 g fiber, 3 g protein.* **Diabetic Exchanges:** *½ starch, ½ fat.*

Crab Cucumber Bites F S C

I look for recipes that are deceptively easy. These fancy and fast crab and cucumber appetizers are heavenly, and the standout colors light up any gathering.
—**NANCY CZARNICK** DESERT HILLS, ARIZONA

PREP/TOTAL TIME: 30 MIN. **MAKES:** 4 DOZEN

- 3 **medium cucumbers**
- ⅔ **cup reduced-fat cream cheese**
- 2 **teaspoons lemon juice**
- 1 **teaspoon hot pepper sauce**
- 1 **package (8 ounces) imitation crabmeat, chopped**
- ⅓ **cup finely chopped sweet red pepper**
- 2 **green onions, sliced**

1. Peel strips from cucumbers to create striped edges; cut each cucumber into 16 slices, about ¼ in. thick. Pat dry with paper towels; set aside.

2. In a small bowl, beat the cream cheese, lemon juice and pepper sauce until smooth. Fold in the crab, red pepper and onions. Place 1 heaping teaspoonful onto each cucumber slice. Serve immediately.

Nutrition Facts: *1 appetizer equals 16 calories, 1 g fat (trace saturated fat), 3 mg cholesterol, 41 mg sodium, 1 g carbohydrate, trace fiber, 1 g protein.* **Diabetic Exchange:** *Free food.*

Margarita Granita with Spicy Shrimp F

While tinkering and tuning up recipes for my spring menu, I came up with a snazzy little appetizer that's perfect for Cinco de Mayo. It features two favorites: shrimp and margaritas!
—**NANCY BUCHANAN** COSTA MESA, CALIFORNIA

PREP: 20 MIN. + FREEZING **GRILL:** 5 MIN. **MAKES:** 8 SERVINGS

- 1 **cup water**
- ½ **cup sugar**
- ½ **cup lime juice**
- 3 **tablespoons tequila**
- 3 **tablespoons Triple Sec**
- 4½ **teaspoons grated lime peel, divided**
- 1 **teaspoon ground cumin**
- 1 **teaspoon smoked paprika**
- 1 **teaspoon ground oregano**
- ½ **teaspoon salt**
- ¼ **teaspoon ground chipotle pepper**
- 16 **uncooked medium shrimp, peeled and deveined**

1. In a large saucepan, bring water and sugar to a boil. Cook and stir until sugar is dissolved. Remove from the heat; stir in the lime juice, tequila, Triple Sec and 3 teaspoons lime peel.

2. Transfer to an 11-in. x 7-in. dish; cool to room temperature. Freeze for 1 hour; stir with a fork. Freeze 4-5 hours longer or until completely frozen, stirring every 30 minutes.

3. In a small bowl, combine the cumin, paprika, oregano, salt and chipotle pepper; add shrimp, tossing to coat. Thread two shrimp onto each of eight soaked wooden appetizer skewers.

4. Moisten a paper towel with cooking oil; using long-handled tongs, lightly coat the grill rack. Grill shrimp, covered, over medium heat or broil 4 in. from the heat for 3-4 minutes on each side or until shrimp turn pink.

5. Stir granita with a fork just before serving; spoon into small glasses. Top with remaining lime peel; serve with skewered shrimp.

Nutrition Facts: *¼ cup granita with 2 shrimp equals 110 calories, 1 g fat (trace saturated fat), 31 mg cholesterol, 180 mg sodium, 17 g carbohydrate, trace fiber, 4 g protein.*

My husband and I have a large garden with red potatoes, so I'm always trying to come up with creative ways to use them in recipes. My son calls these tasty noshes "Potato Poppers." They're delicious and low-calorie.
—**KAREN SULAK** LAMPASAS, TEXAS

Sausage-Stuffed Red Potatoes F C

PREP: 25 MIN. **COOK:** 10 MIN.
MAKES: 16 APPETIZERS

- 8 small red potatoes
- 1 pound Italian turkey sausage links, casings removed
- ½ cup chopped sweet red pepper
- 4 green onions, chopped
- 9 teaspoons minced fresh parsley, divided
- ⅓ cup shredded reduced-fat cheddar cheese

1. Scrub and pierce potatoes; place on a microwave-safe plate. Microwave, uncovered, on high for 8-9 minutes or until tender, turning once.

2. Meanwhile, in a large skillet, cook sausage and pepper over medium heat until sausage is no longer pink. Add onions and 4½ teaspoons parsley; cook 1-2 minutes longer. Remove from the heat; stir in cheese. Cut each potato in half lengthwise. Scoop out 1 tablespoon pulp (save for another use).

3. Spoon 2 tablespoons sausage mixture into each half. Place on a microwave-safe plate. Microwave on high for 1-2 minutes or until cheese is melted. Sprinkle with remaining parsley.

Editor's Note: *This recipe was tested in a 1,100-watt microwave.*

Nutrition Facts: *1 appetizer equals 63 calories, 3 g fat (1 g saturated fat), 19 mg cholesterol, 186 mg sodium, 3 g carbohydrate, 1 g fiber, 5 g protein.*
Diabetic Exchanges: *1 lean meat.*

Cook & Carry Appetizers

Bringing bite-size potatoes or stuffed mushrooms to a party or potluck? Use a deviled egg tray to easily transport the goods and keep your apps in tip-top shape.
—**HEALTHY COOKING TEST KITCHEN**

Herbed-Goat Cheese Baguette Slices F C M

This fun appetizer is guaranteed to wow guests! It takes just moments to whip up the herb-infused spread.

— HEALTHY COOKING TEST KITCHEN

PREP: 15 MIN. + CHILLING
MAKES: 4 SERVINGS

  2 ounces fresh goat cheese
  1 teaspoon minced fresh parsley
  ¾ teaspoon minced fresh rosemary
  ¼ teaspoon minced garlic
     Dash salt
     Dash coarsely ground pepper
  8 slices French bread baguette
     (¼ inch thick)
  1 plum tomato, cut into eight thin
     slices
     Additional coarsely ground pepper,
     optional

1. In a small bowl, combine the cheese, parsley, rosemary, garlic, salt and pepper; roll into a 3-in. log. Cover and refrigerate for at least 1 hour.

2. Spread over bread; top with tomato slices. Sprinkle with additional pepper if desired.

Nutrition Facts: *2 appetizers equals 45 calories, 2 g fat (1 g saturated fat), 9 mg cholesterol, 142 mg sodium, 5 g carbohydrate, trace fiber, 2 g protein.*

Pineapple Shrimp Spread C

My aunt used to bring this dish to family gatherings. It brings back childhood memories for me. Today, it's my go-to appetizer for celebrating with others.

—JODI TOMPKINS ELDON, MISSOURI

PREP/TOTAL TIME: 15 MIN. **MAKES:** 1½ CUPS

  1 cup chopped cooked peeled shrimp
  ½ cup unsweetened crushed pineapple, drained
  ½ cup reduced-fat mayonnaise
  ¼ cup chopped pecans
  2 tablespoons minced fresh parsley
  1 tablespoon finely chopped onion
  1 tablespoon lemon juice
  ½ teaspoon salt
  ⅛ teaspoon hot pepper sauce
     Celery sticks and/or crackers

In a small bowl, combine the first nine ingredients. Chill until serving. Serve with celery sticks and/or crackers.

Nutrition Facts: *2 tablespoons (calculated without celery and crackers) equals 70 calories, 5 g fat (1 g saturated fat), 22 mg cholesterol, 197 mg sodium, 3 g carbohydrate, trace fiber, 3 g protein.*

Slim Deviled Eggs F S C M

PREP/TOTAL TIME: 20 MIN.
MAKES: 1 DOZEN

- 6 hard-cooked eggs
- 3 tablespoons reduced-fat mayonnaise
- ½ teaspoon garlic powder
- ½ teaspoon ground mustard
- ⅛ teaspoon salt
- ⅛ teaspoon pepper
- ⅛ teaspoon paprika

1. Cut eggs in half lengthwise. Remove yolks; set aside egg whites and four yolks (discard remaining yolks or save for another use).

2. In a large bowl, mash reserved yolks. Stir in the mayonnaise, garlic powder, mustard, salt and pepper. Stuff or pipe into egg whites; sprinkle with paprika. Chill until serving.

Editor's Note: *Nutrition facts may vary depending on the variation you prepare.*

Nutrition Facts: *1 stuffed egg half equals 40 calories, 3 g fat (1 g saturated fat), 70 mg cholesterol, 85 mg sodium, 1 g carbohydrate, trace fiber, 3 g protein.*

Slim Southwest Deviled Eggs F S C M

PREP/TOTAL TIME: 20 MIN.
MAKES: 1 DOZEN

- 6 hard-cooked eggs
- 3 tablespoons reduced-fat mayonnaise
- 1 tablespoon salsa
- ½ teaspoon chili powder
- ¼ teaspoon ground cumin
- ⅛ teaspoon salt
- ⅛ teaspoon pepper
  Jalapeno pepper slices, optional

1. Cut eggs in half lengthwise. Remove yolks; set aside egg whites and four yolks (discard remaining yolks or save for another use).

2. In a large bowl, mash reserved yolks. Stir in mayonnaise, salsa, chili powder, cumin, salt and pepper. Stuff or pipe into egg whites. If desired, garnish with pepper slices. Chill until serving.

Slim Crab Cake Deviled Eggs F S C

PREP/TOTAL TIME: 20 MIN.
MAKES: 1 DOZEN

- 6 hard-cooked eggs
- 3 tablespoons reduced-fat mayonnaise
- 2 tablespoons crabmeat, drained, flaked and cartilage removed
- 1 tablespoon minced sweet red pepper
- 2 teaspoons sweet pickle relish
- ½ teaspoon reduced-sodium seafood seasoning
- ⅛ teaspoon salt
- ⅛ teaspoon pepper
- ⅛ teaspoon celery seed
  Additional sweet red pepper, optional

1. Cut eggs in half lengthwise. Remove yolks; set aside egg whites and four yolks (discard remaining yolks or save for another use).

2. In a large bowl, mash reserved yolks. Stir in mayonnaise, crab, sweet red pepper, relish, seafood seasoning, salt, pepper and celery seed. Stuff or pipe into egg whites. If desired, garnish with sweet red pepper. Chill until serving.

Slim Asian Deviled Eggs F S C M

PREP/TOTAL TIME: 20 MIN.
MAKES: 1 DOZEN

- 6 hard-cooked eggs
- 3 tablespoons reduced-fat mayonnaise
- ¼ teaspoon reduced-sodium soy sauce
- ¼ teaspoon minced fresh gingerroot
- ⅛ teaspoon salt
- ⅛ teaspoon pepper
- ⅛ teaspoon sriracha Asian hot chili sauce or hot pepper sauce
  Fresh cilantro leaves, optional

1. Cut eggs in half lengthwise. Remove yolks; set aside egg whites and four yolks (discard remaining yolks or save for another use).

2. In a large bowl, mash reserved yolks. Stir in mayonnaise, soy sauce, ginger, salt, pepper and hot sauce. Stuff or pipe into egg whites. If desired, garnish with cilantro. Chill until serving.

Slim Guacamole Deviled Eggs F S C M

PREP/TOTAL TIME: 20 MIN.
MAKES: 1 DOZEN

- 6 hard-cooked eggs
- 3 tablespoons reduced-fat mayonnaise
- 2 tablespoons mashed avocado
- 1 teaspoon minced fresh cilantro
- ½ teaspoon grated lime peel
- ½ teaspoon lime juice
- ⅛ teaspoon salt
- ⅛ teaspoon pepper
  Cherry tomatoes, optional

1. Cut eggs in half lengthwise. Remove yolks; set aside egg whites and four yolks (discard remaining yolks or save for another use).

2. In a large bowl, mash reserved yolks. Stir in mayonnaise, avocado, cilantro, lime peel, lime juice, salt and pepper. Stuff or pipe into egg whites. If desired, garnish with tomatoes. Chill until serving.

Slim Italian Deviled Eggs F S C M

PREP/TOTAL TIME: 20 MIN.
MAKES: 1 DOZEN

- 6 hard-cooked eggs
- 3 tablespoons reduced-fat mayonnaise
- ¼ teaspoon dried basil
- ¼ teaspoon dried oregano
- ⅛ teaspoon salt
- ⅛ teaspoon pepper
  Shredded Parmesan cheese and fresh parsley, optional

1. Cut eggs in half lengthwise. Remove yolks; set aside egg whites and four yolks (discard remaining yolks or save for another use).

2. In a large bowl, mash reserved yolks. Stir in mayonnaise, basil, oregano, salt and pepper. Stuff or pipe into egg whites. If desired, garnish with cheese and parsley. Chill until serving.

Slim Bloody Mary Deviled Eggs F S C

PREP/TOTAL TIME: 20 MIN.
MAKES: 1 DOZEN

- 6 hard-cooked eggs
- 3 tablespoons reduced-fat mayonnaise
- 1 tablespoon reduced-sodium tomato juice
- ¾ teaspoon prepared horseradish
- ¼ teaspoon hot pepper sauce
- ⅛ teaspoon salt
- ⅛ teaspoon pepper
  Crumbled cooked bacon, optional

1. Cut eggs in half lengthwise. Remove yolks; set aside egg whites and four yolks (discard remaining yolks or save for another use).

2. In a large bowl, mash reserved yolks. Stir in mayonnaise, tomato juice, horseradish, pepper sauce, salt and pepper. Stuff or pipe into egg whites. If desired, garnish with bacon. Chill until serving.

SLIM DEVILED EGGS

SLIM GREEK DEVILED EGGS

SLIM ASIAN DEVILED EGGS

SLIM CHUTNEY DEVILED EGGS

SLIM SOUTHWEST DEVILED EGGS

SLIM BUFFALO DEVILED EGGS

SLIM ITALIAN DEVILED EGGS

SLIM CURRIED DEVILED EGGS

SLIM GUACAMOLE DEVILED EGGS

SLIM DEVILED EGGS WITH HERBS

SLIM CRAB CAKE DEVILED EGGS

SLIM BLOODY MARY DEVILED EGGS

❝When you're in the mood for some good finger food, try any one of these sinfully delicious variations on deviled eggs. They're a cinch to fill and make a delightful contribution to a potluck or brunch.❞
—HEALTHY COOKING TEST KITCHEN

Slim Deviled Eggs with Herbs F S C M

PREP/TOTAL TIME: 20 MIN. **MAKES:** 1 DOZEN

- 6 hard-cooked eggs
- 3 tablespoons reduced-fat mayonnaise
- 2 teaspoons minced chives
- 1 teaspoon dried parsley flakes
- ¼ teaspoon dried tarragon
- ⅛ teaspoon salt
- ⅛ teaspoon pepper
  Fresh dill sprigs, optional

1. Cut eggs in half lengthwise. Remove yolks; set aside egg whites and four yolks (discard remaining yolks or save for another use).

2. In a large bowl, mash reserved yolks. Stir in mayonnaise, chives, parsley, tarragon, salt and pepper. Stuff or pipe into egg whites. If desired, garnish with dill. Chill until serving.

Slim Curried Deviled Eggs F S C M

PREP/TOTAL TIME: 20 MIN. **MAKES:** 1 DOZEN

- 6 hard-cooked eggs
- 3 tablespoons reduced-fat mayonnaise
- 2 tablespoons hummus
- ½ teaspoon curry powder
- ⅛ teaspoon salt
- ⅛ teaspoon pepper
  Dash cayenne pepper
  Garbanzo beans or chickpeas, rinsed and drained, optional

1. Cut eggs in half lengthwise. Remove yolks; set aside egg whites and four yolks (discard remaining yolks or save for another use).

2. In a large bowl, mash reserved yolks. Stir in mayonnaise, hummus, curry powder, salt, pepper and cayenne. Stuff or pipe into egg whites. If desired, garnish with garbanzo beans. Chill until serving.

Slim Buffalo Deviled Eggs F S C M

PREP/TOTAL TIME: 20 MIN. **MAKES:** 1 DOZEN

- 6 hard-cooked eggs
- 3 tablespoons reduced-fat mayonnaise
- 2 tablespoons crumbled blue cheese
- 1 tablespoon finely chopped celery
- 1 teaspoon Louisiana-style hot sauce
- ⅛ teaspoon salt
- ⅛ teaspoon pepper
  Celery leaves, optional

1. Cut eggs in half lengthwise. Remove yolks; set aside egg whites and four yolks (discard remaining yolks or save for another use).

2. In a large bowl, mash reserved yolks. Stir in the mayonnaise, blue cheese, celery, hot sauce, salt and pepper. Stuff or pipe into egg whites. If desired, garnish with celery leaves. Chill until serving.

Slim Chutney Deviled Eggs F S C M

PREP/TOTAL TIME: 20 MIN. **MAKES:** 1 DOZEN

- 6 hard-cooked eggs
- 3 tablespoons reduced-fat mayonnaise
- 2 tablespoons mango chutney
- 1 tablespoon chopped green onion
- ⅛ teaspoon salt
- ⅛ teaspoon pepper
  Chopped cashews and additional chopped green onion, optional

1. Cut eggs in half lengthwise. Remove yolks; set aside egg whites and four yolks (discard remaining yolks or save for another use).

2. In a large bowl, mash reserved yolks. Stir in mayonnaise, chutney, green onion, salt and pepper. Stuff or pipe into egg whites. If desired, garnish with cashews and green onion. Chill until serving.

Slim Greek Deviled Eggs F S C M

PREP/TOTAL TIME: 20 MIN. **MAKES:** 1 DOZEN

- 6 hard-cooked eggs
- 3 tablespoons reduced-fat mayonnaise
- 2 tablespoons crumbled feta cheese
- 1 teaspoon dried oregano
- ½ teaspoon grated lemon peel
- ½ teaspoon lemon juice
- ⅛ teaspoon salt
- ⅛ teaspoon pepper
  Greek olives, optional

1. Cut eggs in half lengthwise. Remove yolks; set aside egg whites and four yolks (discard remaining yolks or save for another use).

2. In a large bowl, mash reserved yolks. Stir in mayonnaise, feta, oregano, lemon peel, lemon juice, salt and pepper. Stuff or pipe into egg whites. If desired, garnish with olives. Chill until serving.

Crisp Finger Sandwich C M

PREP/TOTAL: 10 MIN. **MAKES:** 1 SERVING

> 1 slice whole wheat bread, toasted
> 2 tablespoons reduced-fat spreadable garden vegetable cream cheese
> ⅓ cup thinly sliced English cucumber
> 3 tablespoons alfalfa sprouts
>   Dash coarsely ground pepper

Spread toast with cream cheese. Top with cucumber, sprouts and pepper.

Nutrition Facts: *1 sandwich equals 136 calories, 6 g fat (3 g saturated fat), 15 mg cholesterol, 323 mg sodium, 13 g carbohydrate, 2 g fiber, 7 g protein.* **Diabetic Exchanges:** *1 starch, 1 fat.*

❝I love this delicious sandwich, especially with extra-crisp English cucumber. I have made these for parties and showers. I purchase a small party loaf of whole wheat bread or even sourdough—whatever is available—and just downsize the sandwiches.❞

—**MISSI SELIN** BOTHELL, WASHINGTON

Chicken Wonton Cups F S C

These little bites are a great way for my family to enjoy the taste of jalapeno poppers without all the fat and calories. I simply use light mayonnaise and cream cheese to reduce the fat content.
—**NADINE MESCH** MOUNT HEALTHY, OHIO

PREP/TOTAL TIME: 30 MIN. **MAKES:** 3 DOZEN

> 36 wonton wrappers
>   Cooking spray
> 1½ cups shredded cooked chicken breasts
> 1   package (8 ounces) reduced-fat cream cheese
> ½   cup shredded Parmesan cheese
> ⅓   cup reduced-fat mayonnaise
> 1   can (4 ounces) chopped green chilies, undrained
> 1   jalapeno pepper, seeded and minced

1. Press wonton wrappers into miniature muffin cups coated with cooking spray. Spritz wrappers with cooking spray. Bake at 350° for 5-6 minutes or until edges begin to brown.

2. Meanwhile, in a small bowl, combine the chicken, cream cheese, Parmesan cheese, mayonnaise, chilies and jalapeno. Spoon chicken mixture into cups. Bake 8-10 minutes longer or until filling is heated through. Serve warm. Refrigerate leftovers.

Editor's Note: *Wear disposable gloves when cutting hot peppers; the oils can burn skin. Avoid touching your face.*

Nutrition Facts: *1 appetizer equals 62 calories, 3 g fat (1 g saturated fat), 12 mg cholesterol, 126 mg sodium, 5 g carbohydrate, trace fiber, 4 g protein.*

Double-Nut Stuffed Figs F S M

We have a diabetic in the family so we like recipes that everyone can enjoy guilt-free. These figs are healthy and nutritious without compromising all the flavor of a tempting dessert.

—BOB BAILEY COLUMBUS, OHIO

PREP: 20 MIN. **BAKE:** 30 MIN. **MAKES:** 3 DOZEN

- 36 **dried Calimyrna figs**
- ⅔ **cup finely chopped pecans**
- ⅔ **cup finely chopped walnuts**
- 7 **tablespoons agave nectar, divided**
- 3 **tablespoons baking cocoa**
- ¼ **teaspoon ground cinnamon**
- ⅛ **teaspoon ground cloves**
- ½ **cup pomegranate juice**
- 4½ **teaspoons lemon juice**

1. Remove stems from figs. Cut an X in the top of each fig, about ⅔ of the way down; set aside.

2. In a small bowl, combine the pecans, walnuts, 3 tablespoons agave nectar, cocoa, cinnamon and cloves; spoon into figs. Arrange in a 13-in. x 9-in. baking dish coated with cooking spray.

3. Combine the pomegranate juice, lemon juice and remaining agave nectar; drizzle over figs. Cover and bake at 350° for 20 minutes. Uncover and baste with cooking liquid. Bake, uncovered, 8-10 minutes longer or until nuts are toasted.

Nutrition Facts: *1 stuffed fig equals 98 calories, 3 g fat (trace saturated fat), 0 cholesterol, 3 mg sodium, 17 g carbohydrate, 3 g fiber, 1 g protein.* **Diabetic Exchanges:** *1 starch, ½ fat.*

Beef and Blue Cheese Crostini F C

These little gems are easy, impressive and delicious. They're ridiculously easy and inexpensive to make. Seriously, you will look like a total rock star when you serve these!

—MANDY RIVERS LEXINGTON, SOUTH CAROLINA

PREP/TOTAL TIME: 30 MIN. **MAKES:** 3 DOZEN

- 1 **French bread baguette (10½ ounces)**
  Cooking spray
- ½ **teaspoon coarsely ground pepper**
- ½ **cup reduced-fat sour cream**
- 2 **tablespoons minced chives**
- 1 **tablespoon horseradish**
- ¼ **teaspoon salt**
- 1¼ **pounds shaved deli roast beef**
- ⅓ **cup crumbled blue cheese**
  Additional minced chives

1. Cut baguette into 36 slices. Place on ungreased baking sheets. Spritz with cooking spray. Sprinkle with pepper. Bake at 400° for 4-6 minutes or until lightly browned.

2. Meanwhile, in a small bowl, combine the sour cream, chives, horseradish and salt. Top toasts with beef; dollop with sour cream mixture. Sprinkle with cheese and additional chives.

Nutrition Facts: *1 appetizer equals 48 calories, 1 g fat (1 g saturated fat), 11 mg cholesterol, 176 mg sodium, 5 g carbohydrate, trace fiber, 4 g protein.*

Asian Tuna Bites with Dijon Dipping Sauce **F S C**

Big, bold, bright flavors add to the appeal of this healthy dish that's a snap to make and beautiful to serve. It can be made up to 8 hours ahead, and the tuna can be grilled instead of cooked in the pan.
—**JAMIE BROWN-MILLER** NAPA, CALIFORNIA

PREP/TOTAL TIME: 30 MIN. **MAKES:** 2½ DOZEN (½ CUP SAUCE)

- 3 tablespoons Dijon mustard
- 2 tablespoons red wine vinegar
- 2 tablespoons reduced-sodium soy sauce
- 1 tablespoon sesame oil
- 1 teaspoon hot pepper sauce
- 1 pound tuna steaks, cut into thirty 1-inch cubes
  Cooking spray
- ¼ cup sesame seeds
- ½ teaspoon salt
- ¼ teaspoon pepper
- 2 green onions, finely chopped

1. In a small bowl, whisk the first five ingredients; set aside. Spritz tuna with cooking spray. Sprinkle with sesame seeds, salt and pepper. In a large nonstick skillet, brown tuna on all sides in batches until medium-rare or slightly pink in the center; remove from the skillet.

2. On each of 30 wooden appetizer skewers, thread one tuna cube. Arrange on a serving platter. Garnish with onions. Serve with sauce.

Nutrition Facts: *1 appetizer with ¾ teaspoon sauce equals 29 calories, 1 g fat (trace saturated fat), 7 mg cholesterol, 123 mg sodium, 1 g carbohydrate, trace fiber, 4 g protein.*

Blue Cheese-Stuffed Strawberries **F S C**

I was enjoying a salad with strawberries and blue cheese when the idea hit me to stuff the strawberries and serve them as an appetizer. It worked out great, and the flavors blend so nicely.
—**DIANE NEMITZ** LUDINGTON, MICHIGAN

PREP/TOTAL TIME: 25 MIN. **MAKES:** 16 APPETIZERS

- ½ cup balsamic vinegar
- 3 ounces fat-free cream cheese
- 2 ounces crumbled blue cheese
- 16 fresh strawberries
- 3 tablespoons finely chopped pecans, toasted

1. Place vinegar in a small saucepan. Bring to a boil; cook until liquid is reduced by half. Cool to room temperature.

2. Meanwhile, in a small bowl, beat cream cheese until smooth. Beat in blue cheese. Remove stems and scoop out centers from strawberries; fill each with about 2 teaspoons cheese mixture. Sprinkle pecans over filling, pressing lightly. Chill until serving. Drizzle with balsamic vinegar.

Nutrition Facts: *1 stuffed strawberry equals 36 calories, 2 g fat (1 g saturated fat), 3 mg cholesterol, 80 mg sodium, 3 g carbohydrate, trace fiber, 2 g protein.* **Diabetic Exchange:** *½ fat.*

Steamed Turkey Dumplings F C

Here's a great "light" appetizer that tastes wonderful but won't make you feel like you've eaten a meal. They're easy to prepare and a joy to serve—try them at your next party!

—**DONNA BARDOCZ** HOWELL, MICHIGAN

PREP: 30 MIN. **COOK:** 10 MIN./BATCH
MAKES: 20 APPETIZERS (⅓ CUP SAUCE)

- 2 green onions, thinly sliced
- 2 tablespoons cornstarch
- 2 tablespoons minced fresh gingerroot
- 1 tablespoon reduced-sodium soy sauce
- 1 teaspoon sesame oil
- ½ pound lean ground turkey
- 20 wonton wrappers
- 9 lettuce leaves

DIPPING SAUCE
- ¼ cup reduced-sodium soy sauce
- 1½ teaspoons finely chopped green onion
- 1½ teaspoons sesame oil
- 1 garlic clove, minced

1. In a large bowl, combine the onions, cornstarch, ginger, soy sauce and oil. Crumble turkey over mixture and mix well.
2. Place 1 tablespoon turkey mixture in the center of a wonton wrapper. (Keep remaining wrappers covered with a damp paper towel until ready to use.) Moisten edges with water. Fold one corner diagonally over filling and press edges to seal.
3. Line a steamer basket with 3 lettuce leaves. Arrange one-third of the dumplings 1 in. apart over lettuce; place in a large saucepan over 1 in. of water. Bring to a boil; cover and steam for 10-12 minutes or until a thermometer reads 165°. Discard lettuce. Repeat twice.

4. Combine sauce ingredients; serve with dumplings.
Nutrition Facts: *1 dumpling with ¾ teaspoon sauce equals 52 calories, 2 g fat (trace saturated fat), 10 mg cholesterol, 208 mg sodium, 6 g carbohydrate, trace fiber, 3 g protein.*
Diabetic Exchange: *½ starch.*

Southwest Hummus Dip F C M

Not your ordinary hummus, this dip is a combination of two things I love: chickpeas and Southwestern flavor. You can substitute ¾ cup frozen corn, thawed, for the grilled corn.

—**CHERAY BUCKALEW** CUMBERLAND, MARYLAND

PREP: 15 MIN. **GRILL:** 20 MIN. **MAKES:** 2 CUPS

- 1 medium ear sweet corn, husk removed
- 1 can (15 ounces) garbanzo beans or chickpeas, rinsed and drained
- 2 tablespoons minced fresh cilantro
- 1 teaspoon ground cumin
- ½ teaspoon chili powder
- ¼ teaspoon salt
- ¼ teaspoon pepper
- ½ cup chopped roasted sweet red peppers
- ¼ cup fire-roasted diced tomatoes
  Baked pita chips or assorted fresh vegetables

1. Grill corn, covered, over medium heat for 10-12 minutes or until tender, turning occasionally. Meanwhile, in a food processor, combine the beans, cilantro, cumin, chili powder, salt and pepper. Cover and process for 30 seconds or until blended. Transfer to a small bowl. Cover and refrigerate for at least 15 minutes.
2. Cut corn from cob. Add the corn, red peppers and tomatoes to bean mixture; mix well. Serve with pita chips or vegetables.
Nutrition Facts: *¼ cup (calculated without chips and vegetables) equals 68 calories, 1 g fat (trace saturated fat), 0 cholesterol, 223 mg sodium, 12 g carbohydrate, 3 g fiber, 3 g protein.*
Diabetic Exchange: *1 starch.*

Indian Snack Mix

I love the flavor of curry, so I added it to this yummy, crunchy snack mix. The recipe uses the microwave—what a cinch! For a less spicy flavor, use only 1 teaspoon curry and a dash of chipotle powder.
—**NOELLE MYERS** GRAND FORKS, NORTH DAKOTA

PREP: 15 MIN. **BAKE:** 45 MIN. + COOLING
MAKES: ABOUT 3 QUARTS

4 cups Corn Chex
4 cups Rice Chex
3 cups miniature pretzels
1 cup slivered almonds
⅓ cup butter, melted
3 tablespoons Louisiana-style hot sauce
4½ teaspoons Worcestershire sauce
2½ teaspoons curry powder
1 teaspoon onion powder
1 teaspoon seasoned salt
¼ teaspoon ground chipotle pepper
1 cup golden raisins

1. In a large bowl, combine the cereals, pretzels and almonds. In a small bowl, combine the butter, hot sauce, Worcestershire sauce and seasonings. Drizzle over cereal mixture; toss to coat.
2. Transfer to two 15-in. x 10-in. x 1-in. baking pans coated with cooking spray. Bake at 250° for 45 minutes or until golden brown, stirring every 15 minutes. Stir in raisins. Cool completely on wire racks. Store in airtight containers.
Nutrition Facts: ¾ cup equals 172 calories, 7 g fat (3 g saturated fat), 9 mg cholesterol, 360 mg sodium, 26 g carbohydrate, 2 g fiber, 3 g protein. **Diabetic Exchanges:** 1½ starch, 1 fat.

Makeover Creamy Eggnog Ⓜ

I have been making this velvety smooth eggnog on Christmas Day for about 40 years. My family always looks forward to the traditional treat. Feel free to add a little coffee-flavored liqueur.
—**BARBARA SMITH** CHIPLEY, FLORIDA

PREP: 20 MIN. + CHILLING **COOK:** 25 MIN. **MAKES:** 8 SERVINGS

2 eggs, separated
1 can (14 ounces) fat-free sweetened condensed milk
¼ teaspoon salt
4 cups 2% milk, divided
1 teaspoon vanilla extract
⅛ teaspoon ground nutmeg
2 tablespoons sugar
⅛ teaspoon cream of tartar
Additional ground nutmeg, optional

1. In a small heavy saucepan, whisk the egg yolks, sweetened condensed milk and salt until blended. Stir in 2 cups milk. Cook over medium-low heat for 20-30 minutes or until bubbles form around sides of pan and a thermometer reads at least 160°, stirring constantly. (Do not boil.) Remove from heat immediately.
2. Pour into a large bowl. Place bowl in an ice-water bath, stirring frequently until cooled. Stir in the vanilla, nutmeg and remaining milk. Refrigerate until cold.
3. In a small heavy saucepan, combine the egg whites, sugar and cream of tartar. With a hand mixer, beat on low speed for 1 minute. Continue beating over low heat until egg mixture reaches 160°, about 4 minutes.
4. Transfer to a bowl. Beat until stiff glossy peaks form and sugar is dissolved. Gently stir into milk mixture until blended. Sprinkle servings with nutmeg if desired.
Nutrition Facts: ¾ cup equals 232 calories, 4 g fat (2 g saturated fat), 68 mg cholesterol, 203 mg sodium, 40 g carbohydrate, trace fiber, 9 g protein.

41

34

31

Salads & Dressings

66 This dressing is great over greens, pasta salad or summer vegetables. It's a healthy alternative to oil-heavy, store-bought Italian dressings. I think you'll agree it's a slam dunk! 99

SARAH EIDEN ENID, OKLAHOMA
about her recipe, Low-Fat Tangy Tomato Dressing, on page 35

Company Green Salad S C M

For potlucks, I partially put this salad together in advance and take the remaining ingredients (candied nuts, seeds, rice noodles and dressing) to mix in.

—JOAN HALLFORD NORTH RICHLAND HILLS, TEXAS

PREP/TOTAL TIME: 25 MIN. **MAKES:** 12 SERVINGS

- 2 **teaspoons butter**
- ¾ **cup sliced almonds**
- 1 **tablespoon sugar**

DRESSING
- ¼ **cup canola oil**
- 3 **tablespoons rice vinegar**
- 2 **tablespoons brown sugar**

SALAD
- 8 **cups torn leaf lettuce**
- 1 **medium sweet red pepper, chopped**
- 1 **medium sweet yellow pepper, chopped**
- 2 **green onions, chopped**
- 1 **can (3 ounces) crispy rice noodles**
- ⅓ **cup sunflower kernels**

1. In a small heavy skillet, melt butter. Add almonds and cook over medium heat until toasted, about 4 minutes. Sprinkle with sugar. Cook and stir for 2-3 minutes or until sugar is melted. Spread on foil to cool.

2. For dressing, in a small bowl, whisk the oil, vinegar and brown sugar. Chill until serving.

3. For salad, in a large bowl, combine the lettuce, peppers and green onions. Add dressing; toss to coat. Sprinkle with rice noodles, sunflower kernels and almonds. Serve immediately.

Nutrition Facts: *1 cup equals 162 calories, 11 g fat (1 g saturated fat), 2 mg cholesterol, 121 mg sodium, 14 g carbohydrate, 2 g fiber, 3 g protein.* **Diabetic Exchanges:** *2 fat, 1 starch.*

Italian Vinaigrette C M

Ever wonder what all those specks and spices are in your Italian dressing? Well, guess what? You likely have them in your pantry! Now you can create your own signature blend to toss with pasta, greens and fresh spring veggies.

—LORRAINE CALAND SHUNIAH, ONTARIO

PREP/TOTAL TIME: 15 MIN. **MAKES:** 1½ CUPS

- ¼ **cup water**
- ¼ **cup lemon juice**
- ¼ **cup red wine vinegar**
- 2 **garlic cloves, halved**
- 1 **teaspoon sugar**
- ¾ **teaspoon salt**
- ¾ **teaspoon paprika**
- ¾ **teaspoon dried oregano**
- ½ **teaspoon onion powder**
- ½ **teaspoon ground mustard**
- ½ **teaspoon dried thyme**
- ¾ **cup olive oil**

Place the first 11 ingredients in a blender. Cover and process until pureed. While processing, gradually add oil in a steady stream. Refrigerate leftovers.

Nutrition Facts: *2 tablespoons equals 126 calories, 14 g fat (2 g saturated fat), 0 cholesterol, 148 mg sodium, 2 g carbohydrate, trace fiber, trace protein.* **Diabetic Exchange:** *2½ fat.*

Tangy Blue Cheese Dressing C

Caramelized onions add depth of flavor you won't find in a store-bought dressing. As a sandwich spread, crostini topper or celery dip, this mixture is a kitchen staple that adds plenty of zip.
—**ALISHA GOINS** SABIN, MINNESOTA

PREP: 10 MIN. **COOK:** 35 MIN. **MAKES:** 2½ CUPS

- 1 cup chopped sweet onion
- 2 teaspoons canola oil
- 1 cup reduced-fat mayonnaise
- ½ cup reduced-fat sour cream
- ½ cup buttermilk
- 1 teaspoon hot pepper sauce
- ¼ teaspoon Worcestershire sauce
- ½ cup crumbled blue cheese

1. In a large skillet, saute the onion in oil until softened. Reduce heat to medium-low; cook, uncovered, for 30-35 minutes or until deep golden brown, stirring occasionally. Set aside to cool.

2. In a small bowl, whisk the mayonnaise, sour cream, buttermilk, pepper sauce and Worcestershire sauce. Stir in cheese and onion. Store in an airtight container in the refrigerator for up to 2 weeks.

Nutrition Facts: *2 tablespoons equals 70 calories, 6 g fat (2 g saturated fat), 9 mg cholesterol, 156 mg sodium, 3 g carbohydrate, trace fiber, 1 g protein.* **Diabetic Exchange:** *1 fat.*

Grilled Tenderloin Salad S C

I rely on crisp, cool salads during the hot summer months. In this recipe, the pork is grilled so I don't have to turn on the oven.
—**ROBERTA WHITESELL** PHOENIX, ARIZONA

PREP/TOTAL TIME: 30 MIN. **MAKES:** 5 SERVINGS

DRESSING
- ½ cup orange juice
- 2 tablespoons olive oil
- 2 tablespoons cider vinegar
- 1 tablespoon grated orange peel
- 2 teaspoons honey
- 2 teaspoons Dijon mustard
- ½ teaspoon coarsely ground pepper

SALAD
- 1 pork tenderloin (1 pound)
- 10 cups torn mixed salad greens
- 2 seedless oranges, sectioned and cut into bite-size pieces
  Chopped pistachios and cashews, optional

1. In a small bowl, combine all dressing ingredients; cover and chill until serving.

2. Moisten a paper towel with cooking oil; using long-handled tongs, lightly coat the grill rack. Grill pork, covered, over medium heat or broil 4 in. from the heat for 9-11 minutes on each side or until a thermometer reads 145°. Let stand for 5 minutes before slicing.

3. Thinly slice tenderloin. Just before serving, place greens on a serving plate; top with oranges and pork. Drizzle with dressing. Sprinkle with nuts if desired.

Nutrition Facts: *⅕ recipe (prepared without nuts) equals 211 calories, 9 g fat (0 saturated fat), 51 mg cholesterol, 113 mg sodium, 13 g carbohydrate, 9 fiber, 20 g protein.* **Diabetic Exchanges:** *3 lean meat, 1 vegetable, ½ fruit, 1 fat.*

Fiesta Side Salad Ⓜ

PREP: 30 MIN. + CHILLING
MAKES: 8 SERVINGS

- ⅔ cup uncooked long grain rice
- 2 cups frozen corn, thawed
- 1 can (15 ounces) black beans, rinsed and drained
- 6 green onions, sliced
- ¼ cup pickled jalapeno slices, chopped
- ¼ cup canola oil
- 2 tablespoons cider vinegar
- 1 tablespoon lime juice
- 1 teaspoon chili powder
- 1 teaspoon molasses
- ½ teaspoon salt
- ½ teaspoon cumin seeds, toasted and ground

1. Cook rice according to package directions. Meanwhile, in a large bowl, combine the corn, beans, onions and jalapenos. In a jar with a tight-fitting lid, combine the remaining ingredients; shake well.

2. Stir rice into corn mixture. Add dressing and toss to coat. Cover and refrigerate for at least 2 hours.

Editor's Note: *Toasting whole cumin seeds and then grinding them adds extra flavor to this salad. If you don't have whole cumin seeds, substitute ¼ teaspoon of ground cumin—don't toast.*

Nutrition Facts: *⅔ cup equals 206 calories, 8 g fat (1 g saturated fat), 0 cholesterol, 273 mg sodium, 31 g carbohydrate, 4 g fiber, 5 g protein.*
Diabetic Exchanges: *2 starch, 1½ fat.*

Chicken Pasta Salad a l'Orange

I found this recipe in an old cookbook shortly after I got married. Everyone in my large clan likes it—even those who don't usually eat salad!

—ANN BERGER HOWELL, MICHIGAN

PREP/TOTAL TIME: 30 MIN. **MAKES:** 6 SERVINGS

- 2½ cups uncooked bow tie pasta
- 2 cups cubed cooked chicken breast
- 2 celery ribs, thinly sliced
- 1 can (11 ounces) mandarin oranges, drained
- 1 can (2¼ ounces) sliced ripe olives, drained
- ⅓ cup fat-free plain yogurt
- ⅓ cup reduced-fat mayonnaise
- ¼ cup thawed orange juice concentrate
- 1 tablespoon white vinegar
- 2 teaspoons sugar
- ¼ teaspoon salt
- ¼ teaspoon ground mustard
- 6 cups torn mixed salad greens
- ½ cup cubed avocado

1. Cook pasta according to package directions; drain and rinse in cold water. In a large bowl, combine the pasta, chicken, celery, oranges and olives.

2. For dressing, in a small bowl, combine the yogurt, mayonnaise, orange juice concentrate, vinegar, sugar, salt and mustard. Pour over pasta mixture and toss to coat.

3. For each serving, spoon 1⅓ cups pasta mixture over 1 cup of greens; top with about 1 tablespoon avocado.

Nutrition Facts: *1 serving equals 269 calories, 9 g fat (2 g saturated fat), 41 mg cholesterol, 368 mg sodium, 29 g carbohydrate, 3 g fiber, 18 g protein.* **Diabetic Exchanges:** *2 lean meat, 1½ fat, 1 starch, 1 vegetable, ½ fruit.*

top tip — Green Onions

When a recipe calls for green onions, I find it easier and faster to cut them with kitchen scissors rather than a knife. If the recipe calls for quite a few, grab a bunch at one time and snip away. You're done prepping before you know it, and you don't have to wash the cutting board.

—LOUISE B.
COLUMBIA, SOUTH CAROLINA

“Perfect for a buffet, picnic or potluck, this colorful side can be served at room temperature. You'll want to make extra because the flavors only get better the second day.”

—MICHELLE CHICOINE APO, AE

Fresh Broccoli Salad M

This hearty side makes a nice change-of-pace salad. It's crunchy, creamy and simply delicious. You'd never guess it's light!

—DANA HERBERT GOSHEN, UTAH

PREP/TOTAL TIME: 20 MIN. **MAKES:** 9 SERVINGS

- 6 cups fresh broccoli florets
- 1 can (8 ounces) sliced water chestnuts, drained
- ½ cup dried cranberries
- ¼ cup chopped red onion
- ¾ cup reduced-fat mayonnaise
- ¾ cup fat-free plain yogurt
- 1½ teaspoons sugar
- 1½ teaspoons cider vinegar
- 1½ teaspoons Dijon mustard
- ¼ teaspoon salt
- ⅛ teaspoon pepper
- ¼ cup slivered almonds, toasted

1. In a large bowl, combine the broccoli, water chestnuts, cranberries and onion.
2. In a small bowl, whisk the mayonnaise, yogurt, sugar, vinegar, mustard, salt and pepper. Pour over salad; toss to coat. Just before serving, sprinkle with almonds.

Nutrition Facts: *¾ cup equals 144 calories, 8 g fat (1 g saturated fat), 7 mg cholesterol, 272 mg sodium, 16 g carbohydrate, 3 g fiber, 3 g protein.* **Diabetic Exchanges:** *1½ fat, 1 vegetable, ½ starch.*

Strawberry Spinach Salad S C M

This colorful salad is a favorite for my diabetic husband. It's filled with nutritious fruits, topped with heart-healthy nuts and laced with a light-purple yogurt dressing.

—GLADYS NELSON FORT ATKINSON, WISCONSIN

PREP/TOTAL TIME: 25 MIN. **MAKES:** 6 SERVINGS

- 4 cups fresh baby spinach
- 3 cups sliced fresh strawberries
- 1 can (11 ounces) mandarin oranges, drained
- 2 tablespoons canola oil
- 2 tablespoons cider vinegar
- ½ cup fat-free sugar-free raspberry yogurt
- ¼ cup slivered almonds, toasted

1. In a large bowl, combine the spinach, strawberries and mandarin oranges. In a small bowl, whisk together the oil and vinegar. Whisk in yogurt.
2. Divide spinach mixture among six salad plates. Top each serving with dressing and almonds.

Nutrition Facts: *1⅓ cups spinach mixture with 2 tablespoons dressing and 2 teaspoons almonds equals 127 calories, 7 g fat (1 g saturated fat), trace cholesterol, 31 mg sodium, 14 g carbohydrate, 3 g fiber, 3 g protein.* **Diabetic Exchanges:** *1½ fat, 1 vegetable, 1 fruit.*

Almond Coleslaw C M

As a twist to my mother's original recipe, I added toasted almonds to this slaw for extra crunch, flavor and nutrition.

—SARAH NEVIN GILA, NEW MEXICO

PREP/TOTAL TIME: 25 MIN. **MAKES:** 14 SERVINGS

- 2 packages (16 ounces each) coleslaw mix
- 1 cup reduced-fat mayonnaise
- 2 tablespoons cider vinegar
- 1 tablespoon sugar
- ¾ teaspoon seasoned salt
- ½ teaspoon pepper
- ½ cup slivered almonds, toasted

Place coleslaw mix in a serving bowl. In a small bowl, combine the mayonnaise, vinegar, sugar, seasoned salt and pepper. Pour over coleslaw mix; toss to coat. Chill until serving. Just before serving, sprinkle with almonds.

Nutrition Facts: *¾ cup equals 103 calories, 8 g fat (1 g saturated fat), 6 mg cholesterol, 237 mg sodium, 7 g carbohydrate, 2 g fiber, 2 g protein.* **Diabetic Exchanges:** *1½ fat, ½ starch.*

Low-Fat Tangy Tomato Dressing F C M

PREP/TOTAL TIME: 5 MIN. **MAKES:** 2 CUPS

- 1 can (14½ ounces) no-salt-added diced tomatoes, undrained
- 1 envelope Italian salad dressing mix
- 1 tablespoon cider vinegar
- 1 tablespoon olive oil

Place all ingredients in a blender; cover and process until blended.

Nutrition Facts: *2 tablespoons equals 15 calories, 1 g fat (trace saturated fat), 0 cholesterol, 170 mg sodium, 2 g carbohydrate, trace fiber, trace protein.* **Diabetic Exchange:** *Free food.*

❝This dressing is great over greens, pasta salad or summer vegetables. It's a healthy alternative to oil-heavy, store-bought Italian dressings. I think you'll agree it's a slam dunk!❞

—SARAH EIDEN ENID, OKLAHOMA

Cranberry Mandarin Salad with Walnut Vinaigrette S C M

I invented this salad recipe to accompany our Thanksgiving dinner. I love it because of it's versatility—any combination of dried and fresh fruit can be used to suit the season. One of my favorites is dried blueberries and poached pears instead of cranberries and oranges. It also uses walnut oil, which is heart-healthy and something I try to incorporate into our diets.

—HOLLY BAUER WEST BEND, WISCONSIN

PREP/TOTAL TIME: 15 MIN. **MAKES:** 8 SERVINGS

- 1 package (6 ounces) fresh baby spinach
- 2 cups torn red leaf lettuce
- 1 can (15 ounces) mandarin oranges, drained
- ½ cup dried cranberries
- ½ cup chopped walnuts, toasted

DRESSING
- 3 tablespoons walnut oil
- 2 tablespoons plus 1 teaspoon white wine vinegar
- 2 tablespoons canola oil
- 1 tablespoon minced fresh tarragon
- 1½ teaspoons chopped shallot
- 1 small garlic clove, minced
- ¾ teaspoon sugar
- ¼ teaspoon salt
- ⅛ teaspoon pepper

In a large salad bowl, combine the first five ingredients. In a small bowl, whisk the dressing ingredients. Drizzle over salad; toss to coat.

Nutrition Facts: *1 cup equals 178 calories, 14 g fat (1 g saturated fat), 0 cholesterol, 97 mg sodium, 14 g carbohydrate, 2 g fiber, 2 g protein.* **Diabetic Exchanges:** *3 fat, 1 vegetable, ½ starch.*

Sliced Tomato Salad C M

PREP/TOTAL TIME: 25 MIN.
MAKES: 12 SERVINGS

I got this recipe from my grandmother. It's a perfect platter to serve with burgers or hot sandwiches.
—**KENDAL TANGEDAL** PLENTYWOOD, MONTANA

- 8 **large tomatoes, cut into ¼-inch slices**
- 2 **large sweet onions, halved and thinly sliced**
- ⅓ **cup olive oil**
- 2 **tablespoons lemon juice**
- 1 **teaspoon dried oregano**
- ¾ **teaspoon salt**
- ¼ **teaspoon pepper**
- 2 **tablespoons minced fresh parsley**

Arrange tomatoes and onions on a large rimmed serving platter. In a small bowl, whisk the oil, lemon juice, oregano, salt and pepper. Drizzle over top. Sprinkle with parsley.

Nutrition Facts: *1 serving equals 94 calories, 6 g fat (1 g saturated fat), 0 cholesterol, 159 mg sodium, 9 g carbohydrate, 2 g fiber, 2 g protein.*
Diabetic Exchanges: *2 vegetable, 1 fat.*

Mustard Bean Salad F C M

Just a few ingredients are all you need for this tasty side dish. The recipe was inspired by my grandmother and my husband's grandmother—they both used to prepare similar salads.

—**PATRICIA RITTER**
DOUGLASSVILLE, PENNSYLVANIA

PREP/TOTAL TIME: 25 MIN.
MAKES: 8 SERVINGS

- 2 **pounds fresh wax beans, trimmed and cut into 2-inch pieces**
- ¼ **cup finely chopped onion**
- 3 **tablespoons Dijon mustard**
- 2 **tablespoons white vinegar**
  Dash salt

1. Place beans in a steamer basket; place in a large saucepan over 1 in. of water. Bring to a boil; cover and steam for 8-10 minutes or until crisp-tender.
2. Transfer beans to a serving bowl; reserve 2 tablespoons of cooking water. In a small bowl, combine the onion, mustard, vinegar, reserved cooking water and salt. Drizzle over beans; toss to coat. Serve warm or chilled.

Nutrition Facts: *¾ cup equals 44 calories, 1 g fat (trace saturated fat), 0 cholesterol, 167 mg sodium, 9 g carbohydrate, 4 g fiber, 2 g protein.* **Diabetic Exchange:** *2 vegetable.*

Mom's Tangy Potato Salad

This chunky potato salad is a great dish for a family picnic or on a night when you're grilling out. The homemade dressing makes it extra delicious.

—**MICHELLE GURNSEY** LINCOLN, NEBRASKA

PREP: 25 MIN. **COOK:** 20 MIN. + CHILLING **MAKES:** 9 SERVINGS

- 2 **pounds red potatoes, cubed**
- 2 **hard-cooked eggs, chopped**
- 1 **small onion, chopped**
- 1 **celery rib, chopped**
- ¼ **cup reduced-fat mayonnaise**
- ¼ **cup reduced-fat plain yogurt**
- 2 **tablespoons cider vinegar**
- 2 **tablespoons olive oil**
- 1 **teaspoon reduced-sodium soy sauce**
- ½ **teaspoon salt**
- ¼ **teaspoon celery seed**
- ¼ **teaspoon dried basil**
- ¼ **teaspoon dried oregano**
  Dash garlic powder
  Dash ground mustard

1. Place potatoes in a large saucepan and cover with water. Bring to a boil. Reduce heat; cover and simmer for 15-20 minutes or until tender. Drain and cool.

2. Place potatoes in a large bowl. Add the eggs, onion and celery. In a small bowl, combine the remaining ingredients. Pour over potato mixture and toss to coat. Cover and refrigerate for 2 hours.

Nutrition Facts: ¾ cup equals 148 calories, 7 g fat (1 g saturated fat), 50 mg cholesterol, 235 mg sodium, 18 g carbohydrate, 2 g fiber, 4 g protein. **Diabetic Exchanges:** 1 starch, 1 fat.

Mint Watermelon Salad F S C M

I invented this refreshing fruit salad one sultry afternoon while my friends were gathered around my pool. It was quick and easy to prepare and disappeared from their plates even quicker. Even the kids loved it!

—**ANTOINETTE DUBECK** HUNTINGDON VALLEY, PENNSYLVANIA

PREP/TOTAL TIME: 20 MN. **MAKES:** 8 SERVINGS

- 1 **tablespoon lemon juice**
- 1 **tablespoon olive oil**
- 2 **teaspoons sugar**
- 6 **cups cubed seedless watermelon**
- 2 **tablespoons minced fresh mint**
  Lemon wedges, optional

In a small bowl, whisk the lemon juice, oil and sugar. In a large bowl, combine watermelon and mint. Drizzle with lemon juice mixture; toss to coat. Serve with lemon wedges if desired.

Nutrition Facts: ¾ cup equals 56 calories, 2 g fat (trace saturated fat), 0 cholesterol, 2 mg sodium, 9 g carbohydrate, 1 g fiber, 1 g protein. **Diabetic Exchange:** ½ fruit.

To mince or chop, hold the handle of a chef's knife with one hand and rest the fingers of your other hand on the top of the blade near the tip. Using the handle to guide and apply pressure, move knife in an arc across the food with a rocking motion until pieces of food are the desired size. Mincing results in pieces no larger than ⅛ in., and chopping can produce ¼-in. to ½-in. pieces.

Apple Fennel Salad C M

My wife has never been a big fan of fennel, but it's always been a favorite of mine. I was able to successfully sneak it into this salad, and ever since she has given me the green light on dishes with fennel. If you can't find preserved lemon, simply omit it from the recipe.

—**JASON PURKEY** OCEAN CITY, MARYLAND

PREP/TOTAL TIME: 25 MIN. **MAKES:** 9 SERVINGS

- ½ cup balsamic vinegar
- 8 cups fresh arugula or baby spinach
- 1 large fennel bulb, thinly sliced
- 1 large tart apple, cut into julienne strips
- 3 tablespoons lemon juice
- 3 tablespoons olive oil
- 1 teaspoon coarsely ground pepper
- ½ teaspoon salt
- 4 ounces crumbled goat cheese
- 1 cup glazed walnuts

1. In a small saucepan, bring vinegar to a boil. Cook until liquid is reduced to about ¼ cup; set aside. In a large bowl, combine the arugula, fennel and apple. In a small bowl, whisk the lemon juice, oil, pepper and salt. Pour over arugula mixture; toss to coat. Add cheese and walnuts; toss to combine.
2. Drizzle about 1 teaspoon vinegar over each plate. Top with salad mixture.
Nutrition Facts: *1 cup equals 174 calories, 12 g fat (3 g saturated fat), 16 mg cholesterol, 270 mg sodium, 14 g carbohydrate, 3 g fiber, 4 g protein.* **Diabetic Exchanges:** *2 fat, 1 starch.*

Honey-Orange Broccoli Slaw S M

This will be your go-to recipe when you need to whip up coleslaw in a hurry. Flavorful hints of honey and citrus make it stand apart from traditional slaws.

—**DEBBIE CASSAR** ROCKFORD, MICHIGAN

PREP/TOTAL TIME: 15 MIN. **MAKES:** 6 SERVINGS

- 1 package (12 ounces) broccoli coleslaw mix
- ⅓ cup sliced almonds
- ⅓ cup raisins
- 2 to 3 tablespoons honey
- 2 tablespoons olive oil
- 2 tablespoons orange juice
- 4 teaspoons grated orange peel
- ¼ teaspoon salt

1. In a large bowl, combine the coleslaw mix, almonds and raisins. In a small bowl, whisk the remaining ingredients. Pour over salad; toss to coat.
Nutrition Facts: *⅔ cup equals 136 calories, 7 g fat (1 g saturated fat), 0 cholesterol, 103 mg sodium, 18 g carbohydrate, 3 g fiber, 3 g protein.* **Diabetic Exchanges:** *1½ fat, 1 starch.*

Tarragon Lettuce Salad C M

I found this recipe in a packet of materials that came with some butter lettuce seeds several years ago. It is so easy yet so good!

—**DIAN JORGENSEN** SANTA ROSA, CALIFORNIA

PREP/TOTAL TIME: 10 MIN. **MAKES:** 6 SERVINGS

- 3 heads Bibb lettuce, torn
- 4 tablespoons plus 1½ teaspoons olive oil
- 3 tablespoons minced fresh tarragon or 3 teaspoons dried tarragon
- 3 tablespoons minced fresh chives
- 4½ teaspoons red wine vinegar
- 4½ teaspoons Dijon mustard
- ½ teaspoon salt

Place lettuce in a large bowl. In a small bowl, whisk the remaining ingredients. Drizzle over salad; toss to coat.
Nutrition Facts: *1½ cups equals 110 calories, 10 g fat (1 g saturated fat), 0 cholesterol, 293 mg sodium, 4 g carbohydrate, 1 g fiber, 2 g protein.* **Diabetic Exchanges:** *2 fat, 1 vegetable.*

Portobello Gnocchi Salad

Pan sauteing the gnocchi eliminates the need to boil them, while creating a wonderfully tasty, crispy coating on them. The baby bellas lend a real earthiness to this Italian-influenced salad.

—**FRAN FEHLING** STATEN ISLAND, NEW YORK

PREP/TOTAL TIME: 25 MIN. **MAKES:** 14 SERVINGS

- 1 **package (16 ounces) potato gnocchi**
- 2 **tablespoons plus ⅓ cup olive oil, divided**
- ½ **pound sliced baby portobello mushrooms**
- 3 **teaspoons lemon juice**
- 3 **large plum tomatoes, seeded and chopped**
- 1 **can (15 ounces) garbanzo beans or chickpeas, rinsed and drained**
- 1 **package (5 ounces) fresh baby arugula or fresh baby spinach, coarsely chopped**
- ½ **cup pitted Greek olives, cut in half**
- ⅓ **cup minced fresh parsley**
- 2 **tablespoons capers, drained and chopped**
- 2 **teaspoons grated lemon peel**
- ½ **teaspoon salt**
- ¼ **teaspoon coarsely ground pepper**
- ½ **cup crumbled feta cheese**
- ¼ **cup chopped walnuts, toasted**

1. In large nonstick skillet over medium-high heat, cook gnocchi in 1 tablespoon oil for 6-8 minutes or until lightly browned, turning once. Remove from the skillet; cool slightly.

2. In the same skillet, saute mushrooms in 1 tablespoon oil until tender. Place mushrooms and gnocchi in a serving bowl. Add lemon juice and remaining oil; gently toss to coat.

3. Add the tomatoes, garbanzo beans, arugula, olives, parsley, capers, lemon peel, salt and pepper; toss to combine. Garnish with cheese and walnuts.

Editor's Note: *Look for potato gnocchi in the pasta or frozen foods section.*

Nutrition Facts: *¾ cup equals 204 calories, 12 g fat (2 g saturated fat), 5 mg cholesterol, 425 mg sodium, 21 g carbohydrate, 3 g fiber, 5 g protein.* **Diabetic Exchanges:** *2 fat, 1½ starch.*

Strawberry Orange Vinegar F S C M

This light and refreshing strawberry-orange dressing from our Test Kitchen will nicely accent any fresh green salad. Use your favorite salad greens or a ready-to-serve package to keep things simple.

—**HEALTHY COOKING TEST KITCHEN**

PREP: 10 MIN. **COOK:** 10 MIN. + STANDING **MAKES:** 1⅔ CUPS

- 1 **medium orange**
- 2 **cups white wine vinegar**
- 2 **tablespoons sugar**
- 2 **cups sliced fresh strawberries**

1. Using a citrus zester, peel rind from orange in long narrow strips (being careful not to remove pith). In a large saucepan, heat vinegar and sugar to just below the boiling point. Place strawberries in a warm sterilized quart jar; add heated vinegar mixture and orange peel. Cover and let stand in a cool dark place for 10 days.

2. Strain mixture through a cheesecloth; discard pulp and orange rind. Pour into a sterilized pint jar. Seal tightly. Store in the refrigerator for up to 6 months.

Nutrition Facts: *1 tablespoon equals 15 calories, trace fat (trace saturated fat), 0 cholesterol, trace sodium, 4 g carbohydrate, trace fiber, trace protein.* **Diabetic Exchange:** *Free food.*

top tip

Juicy Equivalents

When a recipe calls for fresh-squeezed orange or lemon juice or zest, remember that 1 medium lemon equals 3 tablespoons juice or 1½ teaspoons grated peel, and 1 medium orange equals ⅓ to ½ cup juice or 4 teaspoons grated peel.

—**HEALTHY COOKING TEST KITCHEN**

Homemade Mayonnaise S C M

Pssst! Did you know this top-selling condiment and go-to dressing for chicken, tuna and potato salad can be prepared right in your own kitchen with only a handful of everyday items? It's a cinch with this handy recipe.

—TASTE OF HOME TEST KITCHEN

PREP/TOTAL TIME: 25 MIN. **MAKES:** 1¼ CUPS

- 2 egg yolks
- 2 tablespoons water
- 2 tablespoons lemon juice
- ½ teaspoon salt
  Dash white pepper
- 1 cup olive oil

1. In a double boiler or metal bowl over simmering water, constantly whisk the egg yolks, water and lemon juice until mixture reaches 160° or is thick enough to coat the back of a spoon. While stirring, quickly place the bottom of the pan in a bowl of ice water; continue stirring for 2 minutes or until cooled.
2. Transfer to a blender. Add salt and pepper. While processing, gradually add oil in a steady stream. Transfer to a small bowl. Cover and refrigerate for up to 7 days.

Nutrition Facts: *1 tablespoon equals 84 calories, 9 g fat (1 g saturated fat), 17 mg cholesterol, 50 mg sodium, trace carbohydrate, trace fiber, trace protein.* **Diabetic Exchange:** *2 fat.*

Colorful Garbanzo Bean Salad M

This salad is most flavorful after it chills in the fridge for a few hours. That makes it a nice make-ahead option for lunch.

—DIANA TSEPERKAS NORTH HAVEN, CONNECTICUT

PREP: 30 MIN. + STANDING **MAKES:** 4 SERVINGS

- 1 medium sweet red pepper
- 1 can (15 ounces) garbanzo beans or chickpeas, rinsed and drained
- 6 cherry tomatoes, halved
- 2 tablespoons minced fresh basil or 2 teaspoons dried basil
- 2 tablespoons olive oil
- 1 tablespoon lemon juice
- 1 tablespoon red wine vinegar
- ½ teaspoon salt
- ½ teaspoon grated lemon peel
- ¼ teaspoon pepper

1. Broil pepper 4 in. from the heat until skin blisters, about 5 minutes. With tongs, rotate pepper a quarter turn. Broil and rotate until all sides are blistered and blackened. Immediately place pepper in a small bowl; cover and let stand for 20 minutes.
2. Peel off and discard charred skin. Remove stem and seeds; chop pepper. In a large bowl, combine the pepper, garbanzo beans, tomatoes and basil. In a small bowl, whisk the oil, lemon juice, vinegar, salt, lemon peel and pepper. Pour over bean mixture; toss to coat. Chill until serving.

Nutrition Facts: *⅔ cup equals 174 calories, 9 g fat (1 g saturated fat), 0 cholesterol, 436 mg sodium, 20 g carbohydrate, 5 g fiber, 5 g protein.* **Diabetic Exchanges:** *1½ fat, 1 starch.*

? Did you know?

According to a Harvard study of nearly 89,000 women, those with a family history of cancer who consumed more than 400 micrograms of folate each day lowered their risk of particular cancers by more than 52 percent compared to those who consumed 200 micrograms. If you want to increase the amount of folate in your diet, reach for some chickpeas. One cup of this tasty protein-packed legume contains nearly 300 micrograms.

I make this every year for the holidays. It's a healthy alternative to traditional coleslaw made with mayo. For a different flavor combination, substitute toasted sesame seeds and sesame seed oil for the walnuts and walnut oil, and rice wine vinegar for the white wine vinegar.

—**BOB NOPPER** SALEM, NEW YORK

Cranberry Walnut Slaw CM

PREP: 20 MIN. + CHILLING
MAKES: 12 SERVINGS

- ½ cup white wine vinegar
- 1 tablespoon Dijon mustard
- 1 teaspoon sugar
- 1 teaspoon celery seed
- ¾ teaspoon salt
- ½ teaspoon pepper
- ⅓ cup walnut oil
- 1 tablespoon minced fresh tarragon or 1 teaspoon dried tarragon
- 6 cups shredded cabbage
- 1 cup shredded carrots
- 1 cup dried cranberries
- ¼ large sweet onion, thinly sliced
- 1 cup chopped walnuts, toasted

1. In a blender, combine the first six ingredients. While processing, gradually add oil in a steady stream. Transfer dressing to a small bowl; stir in tarragon.
2. In a large bowl, combine the cabbage, carrots, cranberries and onion. Drizzle with dressing; toss to coat. Refrigerate for at least 1 hour. Just before serving, sprinkle with walnuts.

Nutrition Facts: *½ cup equals 169 calories, 13 g fat (1 g saturated fat), 0 cholesterol, 191 mg sodium, 14 g carbohydrate, 2 g fiber, 2 g protein.* **Diabetic Exchanges:** *2 fat, 1 starch.*

Cucumber and Red Onion Salad F C M

This is one of the first recipes I came up with myself. It's a great salad for picnics or potlucks.

—**BRYNN STECKMAN** WESTERVILLE, OHIO

PREP: 15 MIN. + CHILLING
MAKES: 4 SERVINGS

- 2 small seedless cucumbers, thinly sliced
- 1 cup thinly sliced red onion
- 1 tablespoon white vinegar
- 1 tablespoon white wine vinegar
- 1 tablespoon rice vinegar
- ¼ teaspoon salt
- ¼ teaspoon pepper
- ¼ teaspoon sesame oil

In a small bowl, combine cucumbers and red onion. In a small bowl, whisk the vinegars, salt, pepper and oil. Pour over cucumber mixture; toss to coat. Cover and refrigerate for at least 1 hour. Serve with a slotted spoon.

Nutrition Facts: *¾ cup equals 31 calories, trace fat (trace saturated fat), 0 cholesterol, 151 mg sodium, 7 g carbohydrate, 1 g fiber, 1 g protein.* **Diabetic Exchange:** *1 vegetable.*

58

60

59

Soups &
Sandwiches

66My mom dehydrates the last pick of tomatoes from
her garden each fall—perfect for quick soups like this one.
If I don't have time to prepare dry beans, canned beans
work just as well.99

LORI TERRY CHICAGO, ILLINOIS
about her recipe, Italian Sausage Kale Soup, on page 48

Tangy Beef Chili

Blue cheese is an unusual thing to add to chili, but it lends a creamy, tangy accent. People will be asking you for your secret ingredient.
—LUANN MANER TAYLOR, ARIZONA

PREP: 15 MIN. **COOK:** 35 MIN. **MAKES:** 6 SERVINGS

- 1 pound lean ground beef (90% lean)
- 1 small green pepper, chopped
- 1 small onion, chopped
- 1 can (15 ounces) Ranch Style beans (pinto beans in seasoned tomato sauce)
- 2 cans (14½ ounces each) no-salt-added diced tomatoes, undrained
- 4 teaspoons chili powder
- 1¼ teaspoons ground cumin
- ½ teaspoon pepper
- 6 wedges The Laughing Cow light blue cheese

1. In a large saucepan, cook the beef, green pepper and onion over medium heat until meat is no longer pink; drain.
2. Stir in the beans, tomatoes, chili powder, cumin and pepper. Bring to a boil. Reduce heat; cover and simmer for 15 minutes or until flavors are blended. Top with cheese.

Nutrition Facts: *1 cup equals 266 calories, 10 g fat (4 g saturated fat), 52 mg cholesterol, 663 mg sodium, 22 g carbohydrate, 7 g fiber, 21 g protein.* **Diabetic Exchanges:** *3 lean meat, 1 starch, 1 vegetable.*

Tex-Mex Beef Barbecues

I took this dish to a potluck recently, and guests loved it! The recipe came from my mom, and it tastes equally good with ground beef.
—LYNDA ZUNIGA CRYSTAL CITY, TEXAS

PREP: 20 MIN. **COOK:** 5 HOURS **MAKES:** 14 SERVINGS

- 1 fresh beef brisket (3½ pounds)
- 1 jar (18 ounces) hickory smoke-flavored barbecue sauce
- ½ cup finely chopped onion
- 1 envelope chili seasoning
- 1 tablespoon Worcestershire sauce
- 1 teaspoon minced garlic
- 1 teaspoon lemon juice
- 14 hamburger buns, split

1. Cut brisket in half; place in a 5-qt. slow cooker.
2. In a small bowl, combine the barbecue sauce, onion, chili seasoning, Worcestershire sauce, garlic and lemon juice. Pour over beef. Cover and cook on high for 5-6 hours or until meat is tender.
3. Remove beef; cool slightly. Shred and return to the slow cooker; heat through. Serve on buns.
Editor's Note: *This is a fresh beef brisket, not corned beef.*

Nutrition Facts: *1 sandwich equals 294 calories, 7 g fat (2 g saturated fat), 47 mg cholesterol, 732 mg sodium, 28 g carbohydrate, 2 g fiber, 28 g protein.* **Diabetic Exchanges:** *3 lean meat, 2 starch.*

Hearty Breaded Fish Sandwiches

Fishing for a burger alternative? Consider it caught. A hint of cayenne is cooled by a creamy yogurt and mayo sauce that will put your local drive-thru to shame.

—TASTE OF HOME TEST KITCHEN

PREP/TOTAL TIME: 30 MIN. **MAKES:** 4 SERVINGS

- ½ cup dry bread crumbs
- ½ teaspoon garlic powder
- ½ teaspoon cayenne pepper
- ½ teaspoon dried parsley flakes
- 4 cod fillets (6 ounces each)
- 4 whole wheat hamburger buns, split
- ¼ cup plain yogurt
- ¼ cup fat-free mayonnaise
- 2 teaspoons lemon juice
- 2 teaspoons sweet pickle relish
- ¼ teaspoon dried minced onion
- 4 lettuce leaves
- 4 slices tomato
- 4 slices sweet onion

1. In a shallow bowl, combine the bread crumbs, garlic powder, cayenne and parsley. Coat fillets with bread crumb mixture.

2. Moisten a paper towel with cooking oil; using long-handled tongs, lightly coat the grill rack. Grill cod, covered, over medium heat or broil 4 in. from the heat for 4-5 minutes on each side or until fish flakes easily with a fork. Grill buns over medium heat for 30-60 seconds or until toasted.

3. Meanwhile, in a small bowl, combine the yogurt, mayonnaise, lemon juice, relish and minced onion; spread over bun bottoms. Top with cod, lettuce, tomato and onion; replace bun tops.

Nutrition Facts: *1 sandwich equals 292 calories, 4 g fat (1 g saturated fat), 68 mg cholesterol, 483 mg sodium, 32 g carbohydrate, 4 g fiber, 32 g protein.* **Diabetic Exchanges:** *5 lean meat, 2 starch.*

Chunky Sausage Lentil Soup

Lentils are an inexpensive but nutritious power food, and these days, a hot, filling and flavorful family meal at a great price is a real comfort. My husband just loves this soup, and it freezes well.

—DLEE SCAR E. HANOVER, NEW JERSEY

PREP: 30 MIN. **COOK:** 40 MIN. **MAKES:** 10 SERVINGS (3½ QUARTS)

- 8 cups water
- 1 package (16 ounces) dried lentils, rinsed
- 1 package (19½ ounces) Italian turkey sausage links, casings removed and crumbled
- 2 medium onions, chopped
- 2 celery ribs, chopped
- 2 medium carrots, cut into ¼-inch slices
- 6 garlic cloves, minced
- 3 cans (14½ ounces each) reduced-sodium beef broth
- 1 can (28 ounces) crushed tomatoes
- 1 medium red potato, diced
- 1½ teaspoons dried thyme
- 1½ teaspoons coarsely ground pepper
  Salad croutons, optional

1. In a large saucepan, bring water and lentils to a boil. Reduce heat; cover and simmer for 18-22 minutes or until lentils are tender. Drain. In a Dutch oven, cook the sausage, onions, celery and carrots over medium heat until meat is no longer pink and vegetables are tender; drain. Add garlic; cook 2 minutes longer.

2. Stir in the broth, tomatoes, potato, thyme and pepper. Bring to a boil. Reduce heat; simmer, uncovered, for 15-20 minutes or until potato is tender. Stir in lentils; heat through. Serve with croutons if desired.

Nutrition Facts: *1⅓ cups (calculated without croutons) equals 314 calories, 6 g fat (1 g saturated fat), 36 mg cholesterol, 681 mg sodium, 43 g carbohydrate, 17 g fiber, 24 g protein.* **Diabetic Exchanges:** *3 lean meat, 2 starch, 2 vegetable.*

Butternut Squash and Roasted Pepper Soup F M

PREP: 30 MIN. **COOK:** 40 MIN.
MAKES: 9 SERVINGS (2¼ QUARTS)

- 2 large sweet red peppers
- 1 medium onion, coarsely chopped
- 1 tablespoon canola oil
- 2 garlic cloves, minced
- 1 medium butternut squash (3 to 3½ pounds), peeled and cubed
- 6 cups vegetable stock
- 1½ teaspoons curry powder
- ½ teaspoon salt
- ¼ teaspoon ground cinnamon
- ¼ teaspoon pepper
  Minced fresh cilantro, optional

1. Cut peppers in half; remove seeds. Broil peppers 4 in. from the heat until skins blister, about 5 minutes. Immediately place peppers in a small bowl; cover and let stand for 20 minutes. Peel off and discard charred skin. Chop peppers.

2. In a large saucepan coated with cooking spray, saute onion in oil for 3 minutes. Add garlic; cook 1 minute longer. Add squash; cook for 3 minutes. Stir in the stock, curry powder, salt, cinnamon, pepper and red peppers. Bring to a boil. Reduce heat; cover and simmer for 20-25 minutes or until squash is tender.

3. Cool slightly. In a blender, process 7 cups soup in batches until smooth. Return all to pan and heat through. Garnish with cilantro if desired.

Nutrition Facts: *1 cup equals 86 calories, 2 g fat (trace saturated fat), 0 cholesterol, 467 mg sodium, 18 g carbohydrate, 5 g fiber, 2 g protein.*

This sweet and savory soup is special to me because it has the heartwarming feeling of home with just enough zip to keep the flavors interesting.
—STACEY PETERSON NEW HAVEN, CONNECTICUT

top tip

Freeze It!

Freeze soup for a quick lunch: Line single-serving freezer-safe bowls with plastic wrap, allowing wrap to hang over edge of bowls. Fill with soup and freeze. Bring the extra plastic wrap over the top of frozen soup, remove soup from bowls, and store in freezer bags. When needed, remove the plastic and reheat in microwave-safe bowl.

Rachel with a Twist

PREP/TOTAL TIME: 30 MIN. **MAKES:** 6 SERVINGS

- ½ cup fat-free mayonnaise
- 1 tablespoon sweet pickle relish
- 1 tablespoon chili sauce
- ½ teaspoon lemon juice
- ⅛ teaspoon white pepper
- 12 ounces cuban bread or French bread, halved lengthwise
- 6 ounces thinly sliced deli turkey
- 6 slices reduced-fat Swiss cheese
- 1 cup sauerkraut, rinsed and well drained
- 1 tablespoon olive oil

1. In a small bowl, combine the first five ingredients; spread over bread bottom. Layer with turkey, cheese and sauerkraut. Replace top. Cut into six slices.

2. In a large skillet over medium heat, toast sandwiches in oil for 4-5 minutes on each side or until cheese is melted, pressing firmly with a large spatula.

Nutrition Facts: *1 slice equals 299 calories, 8 g fat (3 g saturated fat), 22 mg cholesterol, 1,029 mg sodium, 39 g carbohydrate, 2 g fiber, 19 g protein.* **Diabetic Exchanges:** *2½ starch, 2 lean meat, ½ fat.*

> ❝A Reuben sandwich made with lower-fat turkey instead of corned beef is referred to as a "Rachel," and this scrumptious version just may become your new favorite!❞

—**JOY HARRIS** TAMPA, FLORIDA

Asian Beef Sliders

My family loves orange chicken, but we don't eat it often because of the high sodium, fat and calories. These sliders remind us of our favorite takeout—but they're so much healthier.

—**MINDIE HILTON** SUSANVILLE, CALIFORNIA

PREP/TOTAL TIME: 30 MIN. **MAKES:** 4 SERVINGS

- ½ cup orange marmalade, divided
- 2 teaspoons Thai chili sauce, divided
- 1 pound lean ground beef (90% lean)
- 2 slices reduced-fat Swiss cheese, quartered
- 8 slices whole wheat bread, toasted

1. In a large bowl, combine ¼ cup marmalade and 1 teaspoon chili sauce. Crumble beef over mixture and mix well. Shape into eight patties. Moisten a paper towel with cooking oil; using long-handled tongs, lightly coat the grill rack.

2. Grill burgers, covered, over medium heat or broil 4 in. from the heat for 4-5 minutes on each side or until a thermometer reads 160° and juices run clear. Top with cheese; grill 1-2 minutes longer or until cheese is melted.

3. Meanwhile, with a 2-in. round biscuit cutter, cut 16 circles from toasts. In a small microwave-safe bowl, combine remaining marmalade and chili sauce. Microwave for 20 seconds or until heated through.

4. Place burgers on toasts; top with marmalade mixture and remaining toasts.

Nutrition Facts: *2 sliders equals 372 calories, 12 g fat (5 g saturated fat), 76 mg cholesterol, 245 mg sodium, 38 g carbohydrate, 2 g fiber, 29 g protein.* **Diabetic Exchanges:** *4 lean meat, 2½ starch.*

Italian Sausage Kale Soup C

My mom dehydrates the last pick of tomatoes from her garden each fall, and they're perfect for quick soups like this one. If I don't have time to prepare dry beans, canned beans work just as well.

—LORI TERRY CHICAGO, ILLINOIS

PREP: 15 MIN. **COOK:** 20 MIN. **MAKES:** 8 SERVINGS (2 QUARTS)

- 1½ pounds Italian turkey sausage links, casings removed
- 1 medium onion, chopped
- 8 cups chopped fresh kale
- 2 garlic cloves, minced
- ¼ teaspoon crushed red pepper flakes, optional
- ½ cup white wine or chicken stock
- 1 carton (26 ounces) chicken stock
- 1 can (15 ounces) white kidney or cannellini beans, rinsed and drained
- 1 can (14½ ounces) no-salt-added diced tomatoes
- ½ cup sun-dried tomatoes (not packed in oil), chopped
- ¼ teaspoon pepper

1. Crumble sausage into a Dutch oven; add onion. Cook and stir over medium heat until meat is no longer pink. Drain, reserving ¼ cup drippings; set sausage aside. Saute kale in reserved drippings until wilted. Add garlic and, if desired, pepper flakes; cook for 1 minute. Add wine; cook 2 minutes longer.

2. Stir in the stock, beans, diced tomatoes, dried tomatoes, pepper and sausage mixture. Bring to a boil. Reduce heat; cover and simmer for 15-20 minutes or until kale is tender.

Nutrition Facts: *1 cup equals 217 calories, 8 g fat (2 g saturated fat), 51 mg cholesterol, 868 mg sodium, 15 g carbohydrate, 4 g fiber, 18 g protein.*

Heirloom Tomato Soup C M

PREP: 30 MIN. **COOK:** 20 MIN. **MAKES:** 20 SERVINGS (5 QUARTS)

- 1 large sweet onion, halved and thinly sliced
- ¼ cup extra-virgin olive oil
- 6 garlic cloves, minced
- 12 medium heirloom tomatoes, quartered (about 8 pounds)
- 1 large carrot, chopped
- 1 cup fresh corn
- ¼ cup loosely packed basil leaves
- 2 teaspoons sea salt
- 5½ cups reduced-sodium chicken broth
- ⅓ cup heavy whipping cream

1. In a stockpot, saute onion in oil until tender. Add garlic; cook 1 minute longer. Add the tomatoes, carrot, corn, basil and salt. Stir in broth. Bring to a boil. Reduce heat; cover and simmer for 15-20 minutes or until tomatoes are softened, stirring occasionally. Cool slightly.

2. In a food processor, process soup in batches until smooth. Return all to pan and heat through. Ladle into bowls; drizzle each with ¾ teaspoon cream.

Nutrition Facts: *1 cup equals 73 calories, 4 g fat (1 g saturated fat), 5 mg cholesterol, 356 mg sodium, 7 g carbohydrate, 2 g fiber, 2 g protein.* **Diabetic Exchanges:** *1 vegetable, 1 fat.*

"Throughout the late summer months, I make this soup about once a week. Even my son, who normally doesn't like tomatoes, loves my creation."

—KIMBERLY DANEK PINKSON SAN ANSELMO, CALIFORNIA

Sunday Herbed Pot Roast Soup

I used leftover pot roast to make a change-of-pace dinner, and when I served it to my family for dinner, everyone ate it up. I didn't get "What is this?" once.

—**DEONNA WEIGHT** KEARNS, UTAH

PREP: 20 MIN. **COOK:** 35 MIN. **MAKES:** 6 SERVINGS

- 1 **small onion, diced**
- 1 **tablespoon olive oil**
- 3 **medium potatoes, cubed**
- 2 **large carrots, chopped**
- ½ **pound sliced fresh mushrooms**
- 3 **cans (14½ ounces each) reduced-sodium beef broth**
- 4 **teaspoons balsamic vinegar**
- 1 **tablespoon dried parsley flakes**
- ½ **teaspoon garlic powder**
- ½ **teaspoon dried thyme**
- ½ **teaspoon dried rosemary, crushed**
- ¼ **teaspoon pepper**
- ⅛ **teaspoon salt**
- 1½ **cups cubed cooked pot roast**

1. In a large saucepan, saute onion in oil for 2 minutes. Add potatoes and carrots; cook 2 minutes longer. Add mushrooms; cook for 2-3 minutes or until onion is tender.

2. Stir in the broth, vinegar and seasonings. Bring to a boil. Reduce heat; cover and simmer for 13-18 minutes or until potatoes are tender. Stir in beef; heat through.

Nutrition Facts: *1⅓ cups equals 192 calories, 6 g fat (1 g saturated fat), 23 mg cholesterol, 618 mg sodium, 25 g carbohydrate, 3 g fiber, 10 g protein.* **Diabetic Exchanges:** *1 starch, 1 lean meat, 1 vegetable, ½ fat.*

Turkey Meatball Gyros

My whole family loves these, and I appreciate how fast and easy they are. The meatballs can be made the night before or prepared in a big batch to freeze and use as needed.

—**JENNIFER CODUTO** KENT, OHIO

PREP/TOTAL TIME: 30 MIN. **MAKES:** 4 SERVINGS

- ½ **cup seasoned bread crumbs**
- 1 **egg**
- 1 **teaspoon garlic powder**
- ½ **teaspoon salt**
- ¼ **teaspoon pepper**
- 1 **pound lean ground turkey**
- ¾ **cup (6 ounces) reduced-fat plain yogurt**
- ½ **cup finely chopped peeled cucumber**
- 2 **tablespoons finely chopped onion**
- 1½ **teaspoons lemon juice**
- 8 **whole wheat pita pocket halves**
- 2 **cups shredded lettuce**
- 1 **cup chopped tomatoes**

1. In a large bowl, combine the bread crumbs, egg and seasonings. Crumble turkey over mixture and mix well. Shape into 16 balls.

2. Place meatballs on a rack coated with cooking spray in a shallow baking pan. Bake, uncovered, at 400° for 15-20 minutes or until no longer pink.

3. Meanwhile, in a small bowl, combine the yogurt, cucumber, onion and lemon juice. Line pitas with lettuce and tomatoes; add meatballs and drizzle with yogurt sauce.

Nutrition Facts: *2 filled pita pocket halves equals 439 calories, 14 g fat (4 g saturated fat), 145 mg cholesterol, 975 mg sodium, 48 g carbohydrate, 6 g fiber, 32 g protein.*

Turkey Burgers with Mango Salsa

Here's a cookout recipe that will have everyone talking. The secret is mixing a creamy, spreadable cheese into the turkey patties. It gives them a rich taste without overpowering the burger.

—**NANCEE MELIN** TUCSON, ARIZONA

PREP/TOTAL TIME: 30 MIN. **MAKES:** 6 SERVINGS

- ½ **cup dry bread crumbs**
- ⅓ **cup reduced-fat garlic-herb spreadable cheese**
- 2 **green onions, chopped**
- 4½ **teaspoons lemon juice**
- 1½ **teaspoons grated lemon peel**
- 1 **teaspoon minced fresh thyme or ¼ teaspoon dried thyme**
- ½ **teaspoon salt**
- ½ **teaspoon pepper**
- 1½ **pounds lean ground turkey**
- 6 **whole wheat hamburger buns, split**
- ¾ **cup mango salsa**

1. In a large bowl, combine the first eight ingredients. Crumble turkey over mixture and mix well. Shape into six patties.

2. Moisten a paper towel with cooking oil; using long-handled tongs, lightly coat the grill rack. Grill burgers, covered, over medium heat or broil 4 in. from the heat for 4-6 minutes on each side or until a thermometer reads 165° and juices run clear.

3. Grill buns, uncovered, for 1-2 minutes or until toasted. Place burgers on bun bottoms. Top with salsa. Replace bun tops.

Nutrition Facts: *1 burger equals 359 calories, 14 g fat (4 g saturated fat), 98 mg cholesterol, 825 mg sodium, 31 g carbohydrate, 4 g fiber, 26 g protein.* **Diabetic Exchanges:** *3 lean meat, 2 starch.*

Italian Beef Tortellini Stew

This is my first completely original recipe—and it turned out to be awesome! It's a hefty, rich stew full of colorful veggies, tender beef, a splash of red wine and simply wonderful flavors.

—**TAMMY MUNYON** WICHITA, KANSAS

PREP: 25 MIN. **COOK:** 1¾ HOURS
MAKES: 6 SERVINGS (2¼ QUARTS)

- ⅓ **cup all-purpose flour**
- 1 **teaspoon pepper, divided**
- 1 **pound beef stew meat, cut into 1-inch cubes**
- 3 **tablespoons olive oil, divided**
- 2 **medium zucchini, cut into ½-inch pieces**
- 1 **large onion, chopped**
- 2 **celery ribs, sliced**
- 3 **small carrots, sliced**
- 3 **garlic cloves, minced**
- 1½ **teaspoons each dried oregano, basil and marjoram**
- ½ **cup dry red wine or reduced-sodium beef broth**
- 1 **can (28 ounces) crushed tomatoes**
- 3 **cups reduced-sodium beef broth**
- 1 **teaspoon sugar**
- 1 **package (9 ounces) refrigerated cheese tortellini**
- 1 **package (6 ounces) fresh baby spinach**

1. In a large resealable plastic bag, combine flour and ½ teaspoon pepper. Add beef, a few pieces at a time, and shake to coat.

2. In a Dutch oven, brown beef in 2 tablespoon oil; drain. Remove and set aside. In the same pan, saute the zucchini, onion, celery and carrots in remaining oil until tender. Add the garlic, oregano, basil and marjoram; cook 1 minute longer.

3. Add wine, stirring to loosen browned bits from pan. Return beef to pan; add the tomatoes, broth, sugar and remaining pepper. Bring to a boil. Reduce heat; cover and simmer for 1½ hours or until beef is tender. Add tortellini and spinach. Return to a boil. Cook, uncovered, for 7-9 minutes or until tortellini are tender.

Nutrition Facts: *1½ cups equals 416 calories, 16 g fat (5 g saturated fat), 68 mg cholesterol, 642 mg sodium, 43 g carbohydrate, 7 g fiber, 26 g protein.* **Diabetic Exchanges:** *3 starch, 2 lean meat, 1½ fat.*

My three boys love this recipe. I even send it in their school lunches! Occasionally I add ham or garnish with chopped bacon pieces for a meatier option.
—**AMY SAMUEL** NORTH POLE, ALASKA

Creamy Spinach & Potato Soup

PREP: 25 MIN. **COOK:** 20 MIN.
MAKES: 9 SERVINGS

- 6 **cups cubed peeled potatoes**
- 2 **medium leeks (white portion only), chopped**
- 2 **tablespoons canola oil**
- ½ **cup all-purpose flour**
- 1 **teaspoon sodium-free chicken bouillon granules**
- 3 **cups reduced-sodium chicken broth**
- 1 **can (12 ounces) reduced-fat evaporated milk**
- 1 **package (9 ounces) fresh spinach, chopped**
- ½ **teaspoon salt**
- ¼ **teaspoon pepper**
- ½ **cup shredded cheddar cheese**

1. Place potatoes in a large saucepan and cover with water. Bring to a boil. Reduce heat; cover and cook for 10-12 minutes or until tender. Drain. Mash 2 cups potatoes; set aside.

2. In a Dutch oven, saute leeks in oil until tender. Whisk the flour, bouillon granules and broth until smooth. Gradually stir into pan. Add milk. Bring to a boil; cook and stir for 2 minutes or until thickened.

3. Stir in mashed potatoes. Add spinach, salt, pepper and remaining potatoes; cook just until spinach is wilted. Sprinkle with cheese.

Nutrition Facts: *1 cup equals 224 calories, 6 g fat (2 g saturated fat), 10 mg cholesterol, 433 mg sodium, 35 g carbohydrate, 3 g fiber, 9 g protein.*

Did you know?

Many people who don't like onions prefer the taste of leeks— even though they're in the same family. Leeks have a milder flavor, making them a pleasant addition to soups, casseroles and egg dishes. They're also an excellent source of immune-supportive vitamin A and anti-inflammatory vitamin K.

Apple-Beef Panini

Horseradish sauce imparts an exciting twist to beef sandwiches, and the apple adds a refreshing crunch. I don't have a panini press, so my countertop grill serves as a great substitute.
—**DONNA MARIE RYAN** TOPSFIELD, MASSACHUSETTS

PREP/TOTAL TIME: 10 MIN. **MAKES:** 2 SERVINGS

- 4 slices multigrain bread
- 2 slices reduced-fat cheddar cheese
- 2 teaspoons horseradish sauce
- ½ medium apple, thinly sliced
- 4 ounces sliced deli roast beef
  Cooking spray

1. Layer two bread slices with cheese, horseradish sauce, apple and beef. Top with remaining bread. Spritz outsides of sandwiches with cooking spray.
2. Cook on a panini maker or indoor grill for 3-4 minutes or until bread is browned and cheese is melted.
Nutrition Facts: *1 sandwich equals 317 calories, 12 g fat (3 g saturated fat), 49 mg cholesterol, 742 mg sodium, 31 g carbohydrate, 4 g fiber, 23 g protein.* **Diabetic Exchanges:** *3 lean meat, 2 starch, ½ fat.*

Refreshing Gazpacho **C**

When fresh garden tomatoes are available, I make this soup. The recipe looks like a lot of ingredients, but most of them are common pantry items.
—**AMY GURGANUS** PLYMOUTH, NORTH CAROLINA

PREP: 25 MIN. + CHILLING **MAKES:** 12 SERVINGS (3 QUARTS)

- 4 medium tomatoes, seeded and chopped
- 4½ cups tomato juice
- 2 celery ribs, finely chopped
- 1 medium cucumber, peeled and chopped
- 1 medium red onion, finely chopped
- 1 medium sweet red pepper, chopped
- 1 medium green pepper, chopped
- ¼ cup minced fresh cilantro
- ¼ cup cider vinegar
- 2 tablespoons lime juice
- 2 tablespoons olive oil
- 2 teaspoons sugar
- 1 garlic clove, minced
- 1 teaspoon Worcestershire sauce
- ½ teaspoon salt
- ¼ teaspoon pepper
- 2 medium ripe avocados, peeled and cubed

In a large bowl, combine the first 16 ingredients. Cover and refrigerate for at least 4 hours. Serve with avocados.
Nutrition Facts: *1 cup equals 111 calories, 7 g fat (1 g saturated fat), 0 cholesterol, 360 mg sodium, 12 g carbohydrate, 4 g fiber, 2 g protein.* **Diabetic Exchanges:** *1 starch, 1 fat.*

Chunky Pepper Potato Soup 🇫

Here is our favorite vegetable soup recipe. I got it from a friend and made some changes to lighten it up a bit. It is quick, colorful and satisfying—and you would never know it's low-fat!

—**DENISE MAYER** MODESTO, CALIFORNIA

PREP: 20 MIN. **COOK:** 35 MIN. **MAKES:** 8 SERVINGS (2 QUARTS)

- ½ cup chopped onion
- 4 medium potatoes, cubed
- 1 medium green pepper, chopped
- 1 medium sweet red pepper, chopped
- 1 medium sweet yellow pepper, chopped
- 2 cups reduced-sodium chicken broth or vegetable broth
- 3 cups 1% milk, divided
- ¼ cup cornstarch
- 1 teaspoon salt
- ¼ teaspoon pepper
- ⅛ teaspoon cayenne pepper

1. In a large saucepan coated with cooking spray, cook onion until tender. Stir in the potatoes, peppers and broth. Bring to a boil. Reduce heat; cover and simmer for 10-15 minutes or until potatoes are tender.

2. Stir in 2½ cups milk. Combine cornstarch and remaining milk until smooth. Gradually stir into soup. Bring to a boil; cook and stir for 2 minutes or until thickened. Stir in the salt, pepper and cayenne.

Nutrition Facts: *1 cup equals 158 calories, 1 g fat (1 g saturated fat), 4 mg cholesterol, 504 mg sodium, 31 g carbohydrate, 3 g fiber, 7 g protein.* **Diabetic Exchanges:** *2 starch, 1 vegetable.*

Chicken Salad Party Sandwiches

My famous chicken salad arrives at the party chilled in a plastic container. When it's time to set out the food, I stir in the pecans and assemble the sandwiches. They're great for buffet-style potlucks.

—**TRISHA KRUSE** EAGLE, IDAHO

PREP/TOTAL TIME: 20 MIN. **MAKES:** 15 SERVINGS

- 4 cups cubed cooked chicken breast
- 1½ cups dried cranberries
- 2 celery ribs, finely chopped
- 2 green onions, thinly sliced
- ¼ cup chopped sweet pickles
- 1 cup fat-free mayonnaise
- ½ teaspoon curry powder
- ¼ teaspoon coarsely ground pepper
- ½ cup chopped pecans, toasted
- 15 whole wheat dinner rolls
  Torn leaf lettuce
  Frilled toothpicks, optional

1. In a large bowl, combine the first five ingredients. In a small bowl, combine the mayonnaise, curry and pepper. Add to chicken mixture; toss to coat. Chill until serving.

2. Stir pecans into chicken salad. Serve on rolls lined with lettuce. Secure with toothpicks if desired.

Nutrition Facts: *1 sandwich equals 235 calories, 6 g fat (1 g saturated fat), 30 mg cholesterol, 361 mg sodium, 33 g carbohydrate, 4 g fiber, 14 g protein.*

"For a casual springtime meal with a twist, boil up some eggs and dinner will be done presto. I call this an Italian picnic delight!"

—**TENLEY HARALDSON** FORT ATKINSON, WISCONSIN

Pesto Egg Salad Sandwiches

PREP/TOTAL TIME: 10 MIN.
MAKES: 4 SERVINGS

- ½ cup fat-free mayonnaise
- ¼ cup finely chopped red onion
- 4 teaspoons prepared pesto
- ¼ teaspoon salt
- ⅛ teaspoon pepper
- 4 hard-cooked eggs, chopped
- 3 hard-cooked egg whites, chopped
- 8 slices whole wheat bread, toasted
- 8 spinach leaves

In a small bowl, combine the first five ingredients. Gently stir in eggs and egg whites. Spread over four toast slices; top with spinach and remaining toast.

Nutrition Facts: *1 sandwich equals 285 calories, 11 g fat (3 g saturated fat), 217 mg cholesterol, 811 mg sodium, 30 g carbohydrate, 5 g fiber, 18 g protein.* **Diabetic Exchanges:** *2 medium-fat meat, 1½ starch.*

Turkey Florentine Sandwiches

Upgrade a lunchtime classic to a dinnertime feast with a few fancy yet simple tweaks.

—KAREL REYNOLDS
RUTHERFORDTON, NORTH CAROLINA

PREP/TOTAL TIME: 20 MIN.
MAKES: 2 SERVINGS

- ½ cup sliced fresh mushrooms
- 2 teaspoons olive oil
- 1 cup fresh baby spinach
- 2 garlic cloves, minced
- 4 ounces sliced deli turkey breast
- 2 slices part-skim mozzarella cheese
- 4 slices whole wheat bread
  Cooking spray

1. In a small nonstick skillet, saute mushrooms in oil until tender. Add spinach and garlic; cook 1 minute longer.
2. Layer the spinach mixture, turkey and cheese on two bread slices; top with remaining bread. Spritz outsides of sandwiches with cooking spray. Cook on a panini maker or indoor grill for 4-5 minutes or until bread is browned and cheese is melted.

Nutrition Facts: *1 sandwich equals 346 calories, 14 g fat (5 g saturated fat), 35 mg cholesterol, 937 mg sodium, 27 g carbohydrate, 4 g fiber, 27 g protein.* **Diabetic Exchanges:** *3 lean meat, 2 starch, 1 fat.*

Makeover Carl's Chicken Noodle Soup

I like lots of vegetables in my soup, and you can use whatever you have on hand for this one. Simmering bone-in chicken adds robust flavor to my lower-sodium version of a classic.
—CARL BATES PLEASANTON, CALIFORNIA

PREP: 40 MIN. **COOK:** 1 HOUR 40 MIN. **MAKES:** 10 SERVINGS (3¾ QUARTS)

- 1 pound bone-in chicken breast halves
- 12 cups water
- 3 bay leaves
- ½ teaspoon pepper
- 1 medium onion, chopped
- 2 teaspoons olive oil
- 6 garlic cloves, minced
- 3 celery ribs, sliced
- 1½ cups fresh green beans, cut into 1-inch pieces
- 3 medium carrots, sliced
- 2 tablespoons dried parsley flakes
- 4 teaspoons Italian seasoning
- 2 tablespoons reduced-sodium chicken base
- 3½ cups uncooked egg noodles
- 1 cup frozen corn, thawed
- 2 cups frozen okra, thawed and sliced

1. Place the chicken, water, bay leaves and pepper in a large stockpot. Bring to a boil. Reduce heat; cover and simmer for 1 hour or until chicken is tender.
2. Remove chicken from broth; set aside to cool. Strain broth, discarding bay leaves. Skim fat from broth. When cool enough to handle, remove chicken from bones and cut into ½-inch pieces; discard bones.
3. In a large stockpot coated with cooking spray, saute onion in oil until tender. Add garlic; cook 1 minute longer. Add the celery, beans, carrots, parsley and Italian seasoning. Stir in broth and chicken base. Bring to a boil. Reduce heat; cover and simmer for 20 minutes or until vegetables are crisp-tender.
4. Stir in noodles and corn. Return to a boil; cook, uncovered, for 3 minutes. Add okra; cook 4-6 minutes longer or until noodles and okra are tender. Stir in chicken; heat through.

Nutrition Facts: *1½ cups equals 149 calories, 3 g fat (1 g saturated fat), 29 mg cholesterol, 345 mg sodium, 21 g carbohydrate, 3 g fiber, 11 g protein.* **Diabetic Exchanges:** *1 starch, 1 lean meat, 1 vegetable.*

Coleslaw Chicken Wraps ⓜ

This portable specialty is perfect for outdoor dining in the summertime. We like the fun, fresh spin on regular coleslaw showcasing pineapple and toasted almonds.

—BARB AGNEW MAHNOMEN, MINNESOTA

PREP: 15 MIN. + MARINATING **GRILL:** 15 MIN. **MAKES:** 8 SERVINGS

- 1 bottle (16 ounces) reduced-fat poppy seed salad dressing, divided
- 2 pounds boneless skinless chicken breasts
- 1 can (20 ounces) unsweetened pineapple tidbits, drained
- 1 package (14 ounces) coleslaw mix
- 1 medium sweet red pepper, finely chopped
- 8 whole wheat tortillas (8 inches)
- ½ cup sliced almonds, toasted

1. Place 1 cup dressing in a large resealable plastic bag. Add the chicken; seal bag and turn to coat. Refrigerate for 1 hour.
2. Drain and discard marinade. Moisten a paper towel with cooking oil; using long-handled tongs, lightly coat the grill rack.
3. Grill chicken, covered, over medium heat or broil 4 in. from the heat for 6-8 minutes on each side or until a thermometer reads 170°. Let stand 5 minutes before slicing.
4. Meanwhile, in a large bowl, combine the pineapple, coleslaw mix, red pepper and remaining dressing; toss to coat. Divide among tortillas; top with chicken and sprinkle with almonds. Roll up tightly; secure with toothpicks.

Nutrition Facts: *1 wrap equals 407 calories, 11 g fat (1 g saturated fat), 63 mg cholesterol, 628 mg sodium, 46 g carbohydrate, 5 g fiber, 29 g protein.* **Diabetic Exchanges:** *3 lean meat, 2½ starch, 1 fat, ½ fruit.*

Salsa Fish Sandwiches

These spicy and crispy breaded fish fillets are delicious on their own, but when topped with a tangy salsa mixture, they take on a whole new flavor profile.

—HEALTHY COOKING TEST KITCHEN

PREP/TOTAL TIME: 30 MIN. **MAKES:** 4 SERVINGS

- ½ cup dry bread crumbs
- ½ teaspoon garlic powder
- ½ teaspoon cayenne pepper
- ½ teaspoon dried parsley flakes

- 4 cod fillets (6 ounces each)
- 4 whole wheat hamburger buns, split
- ¼ cup fat-free mayonnaise
- ¼ cup salsa
- 4 slices tomato
- ¼ cup minced fresh cilantro

1. In a shallow bowl, combine the bread crumbs, garlic powder, cayenne and parsley. Coat fillets with bread crumb mixture.
2. Moisten a paper towel with cooking oil; using long-handled tongs, lightly coat the grill rack. Grill cod, covered, over medium heat or broil 4 in. from the heat for 4-5 minutes on each side or until fish flakes easily with a fork. Grill buns over medium heat for 30-60 seconds or until toasted.
3. Meanwhile, in a small bowl, combine mayonnaise and salsa; spread over bun bottoms. Top with cod, tomato and cilantro; replace bun tops.

Nutrition Facts: *1 sandwich equals 277 calories, 4 g fat (1 g saturated fat), 66 mg cholesterol, 512 mg sodium, 29 g carbohydrate, 4 g fiber, 31 g protein.* **Diabetic Exchanges:** *5 lean meat, 2 starch.*

Waldorf Turkey Pitas

Living in New York City means not having a lot of time to prepare meals. This idea is quick, easy and healthy, making it perfect for my lifestyle.

—KEVIN SOBOTKA STATEN ISLAND, NEW YORK

PREP/TOTAL TIME: 15 MIN. **MAKES:** 4 SERVINGS

- 2 cups cubed cooked turkey breast
- 2 celery ribs, finely chopped
- 1 medium tart apple, diced
- 1 cup seedless red grapes, halved
- ½ cup fat-free mayonnaise
- 2 ounces fresh mozzarella cheese, diced
- 8 whole wheat pita pocket halves
- 2 cups fresh baby spinach

In a large bowl, combine the first six ingredients. Line pita halves with spinach; fill with turkey mixture.

Nutrition Facts: *2 filled pita halves equals 363 calories, 7 g fat (3 g saturated fat), 75 mg cholesterol, 626 mg sodium, 48 g carbohydrate, 7 g fiber, 30 g protein.*

> I really love African flavors, but you don't encounter them much in America. Here the combination of native African ingredients, all of which are readily accessible to Americans, transports you to a new culinary place.
> —**MICHAEL COHEN** LOS ANGELES, CALIFORNIA

West African Chicken Stew

PREP: 40 MIN. **COOK:** 15 MIN.
MAKES: 8 SERVINGS (2½ QUARTS)

- 1 pound boneless skinless chicken breasts, cut into 1-inch cubes
- ½ teaspoon salt
- ¼ teaspoon pepper
- 3 teaspoons canola oil, divided
- 1 medium onion, thinly sliced
- 6 garlic cloves, minced
- 2 tablespoons minced fresh gingerroot
- 2 cans (15½ ounces each) black-eyed peas, rinsed and drained
- 1 can (28 ounces) crushed tomatoes
- 1 large sweet potato, peeled and cut into 1-inch cubes
- 1 cup reduced-sodium chicken broth
- ¼ cup creamy peanut butter
- ¼ teaspoon cayenne pepper
- 1½ teaspoons minced fresh thyme or ½ teaspoon dried thyme, divided
    Hot cooked brown rice, optional

1. Sprinkle chicken with salt and pepper. In a Dutch oven, cook chicken over medium heat in 2 teaspoons oil for 4-6 minutes or until no longer pink; remove and keep warm. In the same pan, saute onion in remaining oil until tender. Add garlic and ginger; cook 1 minute longer.

2. Stir in the peas, tomatoes, sweet potato, broth, peanut butter, cayenne and 1¼ teaspoons thyme. Bring to a boil. Reduce heat; cover and simmer for 15-20 minutes or until potato is tender. Add chicken; heat through. Serve with rice if desired. Sprinkle with remaining thyme.

Nutrition Facts: *1¼ cups (calculated without rice) equals 275 calories, 7 g fat (1 g saturated fat), 31 mg cholesterol, 636 mg sodium, 32 g carbohydrate, 6 g fiber, 22 g protein.* **Diabetic Exchanges:** *3 lean meat, 2 vegetable, 1 starch, 1 fat.*

Did you know?

A West African dish typically served for Kwanzaa, peanut stew has a base of peanuts, tomatoes and vegetables, and is usually served over rice. Peanuts are sometimes referred to as "groundnuts" in other versions of this dish.

Cilantro-Lime Chicken Sandwiches

Summer's ultimate sandwich offers a yin and yang of special flavors and casual presentation. The creamy spread and heart-healthy avocado will light up your taste buds. Everyone I've shared the recipe with prepares it over and over again.

—DEBBIE SPECKMEYER LAKEWOOD, CALIFORNIA

PREP: 25 MIN. + MARINATING **GRILL:** 15 MIN. **MAKES:** 8 SERVINGS

- ½ cup canola oil
- ¼ cup lime juice
- 4 teaspoons ground cumin
- 8 boneless skinless chicken breast halves (6 ounces each)
- 1 cup fat-free spreadable cream cheese
- ⅓ cup minced fresh cilantro
- ¼ cup chopped red onion
- ⅛ teaspoon salt
- ⅛ teaspoon pepper
- 8 whole wheat hamburger buns, split
- 2 medium tomatoes, sliced
- 1 medium ripe avocado, peeled and thinly sliced

1. In a large resealable plastic bag, combine oil, lime juice and cumin. Add the chicken; seal bag and turn to coat. Refrigerate for at least 1 hour. In a small bowl, combine the cream cheese, cilantro, onion, salt and pepper; chill until serving.

2. Drain and discard marinade. Grill chicken, covered, over medium heat or broil 4 in. from the heat for 6-8 minutes on each side or until a thermometer reads 170°.

3. Spread cream cheese mixture onto buns. Layer with tomatoes, chicken and avocado; replace bun tops.

Nutrition Facts: *1 sandwich equals 476 calories, 21 g fat (3 g saturated fat), 99 mg cholesterol, 530 mg sodium, 29 g carbohydrate, 6 g fiber, 44 g protein.* **Diabetic Exchanges:** *5 lean meat, 2 starch, 2 fat.*

Makeover Chicken Enchilada Soup

Even though they have many other delicious dishes on the menu, I always find myself ordering Chicken Enchilada Soup from Chili's! I decided to try my hand at a healthier version at home.

—TRACI CAMPBELL SAGINAW, TEXAS

PREP: 30 MIN. **COOK:** 25 MIN. **MAKES:** 6 SERVINGS

- 2 corn tortillas (6 inches)
- ½ teaspoon canola oil
- ½ teaspoon chili powder
- ⅛ teaspoon salt
- ⅛ teaspoon cayenne pepper

SOUP

- 1 medium onion, chopped
- 1 tablespoon canola oil
- 1 garlic clove, minced
- 5 cups water, divided
- 2 teaspoons reduced-sodium chicken base
- 1 teaspoon chili powder
- ½ teaspoon ground cumin
- ¼ teaspoon ground coriander
- ⅛ teaspoon cayenne pepper
- ⅓ cup masa harina
- 8 ounces reduced-fat process cheese (Velveeta), cubed
- 2 cups cubed cooked chicken breast
- ¾ cup pico de gallo
- 6 tablespoons shredded Colby-Monterey Jack cheese

1. Cut each tortilla lengthwise into thirds; cut each widthwise into ¼-in. strips. Place strips and oil in a resealable plastic bag; shake to coat. Combine chili powder, salt and cayenne. Add to bag; shake to coat.

2. Arrange tortilla strips on a baking sheet coated with cooking spray. Bake at 400° for 6-8 minutes or until crisp, stirring once. Remove to paper towels to cool; set aside.

3. Meanwhile, in a Dutch oven, saute onion in oil until tender. Add garlic; cook 1 minute longer. Stir in 4 cups water, chicken base, chili powder, cumin, coriander and cayenne. Whisk masa harina and remaining water until smooth; stir into pan. Bring to a boil; cook and stir for 2 minutes or until slightly thickened.

4. Reduce heat. Stir in process cheese until melted. Add chicken; heat through. Ladle into bowls. Top with pico de gallo, shredded cheese and tortilla strips.

Nutrition Facts: *1 cup equals 266 calories, 11 g fat (4 g saturated fat), 56 mg cholesterol, 866 mg sodium, 19 g carbohydrate, 2 g fiber, 24 g protein.*

Veggie Meatball Soup for 3

It's a snap to put together this hearty soup before I leave for work. I just add cooked pasta when I get home, and I have a few minutes to relax before supper is ready.

—**CHARLA TINNEY** TYRONE, OKLAHOMA

PREP: 10 MIN.   **COOK:** 4 HOURS   **MAKES:** 3 CUPS

- 1½ cups reduced-sodium beef broth
- 1 cup frozen mixed vegetables, thawed
- ¾ cup canned stewed tomatoes
- 9 frozen fully cooked homestyle meatballs (½ ounce each), thawed
- 2 bay leaves
- ⅛ teaspoon pepper
- ½ cup uncooked spiral pasta

In a 1½-qt. slow cooker, combine the first six ingredients. Cover and cook on low for 4-5 hours or until heated through. Stir in pasta; cover and cook 20-30 minutes longer or until pasta is tender. Discard bay leaves.

Nutrition Facts: *1 cup equals 250 calories, 11 g fat (5 g saturated fat), 35 mg cholesterol, 671 mg sodium, 26 g carbohydrate, 5 g fiber, 11 g protein.* **Diabetic Exchanges:** *1½ starch, 1½ fat, 1 lean meat, 1 vegetable.*

Chicken Caesar Pitas

Hand-held and picnic friendly, these chicken-stuffed pockets pack a double dose of whole grains from brown rice and whole wheat pitas. The chicken can be made up to 2 days in advance for a fast-fix lunch.

—**TASTE OF HOME TEST KITCHEN**

PREP: 20 MIN. + CHILLING   **GRILL:** 10 MIN.   **MAKES:** 4 SERVINGS

- ¾ teaspoon dried oregano
- ½ teaspoon dried basil
- ¼ teaspoon onion powder
- ¼ teaspoon paprika
- ⅛ teaspoon dried mint
- 1 pound boneless skinless chicken breasts
- 2 cups torn romaine
- 1 cup ready-to-serve brown rice
- ½ cup reduced-fat Caesar vinaigrette
- 8 whole wheat pita pocket halves

1. In a spice grinder or with a mortar and pestle, combine the first five ingredients; grind until mixture becomes fine. Rub over chicken. Moisten a paper towel with cooking oil; using long-handled tongs, lightly coat the grill rack.

2. Grill chicken, covered, over medium heat or broil 4 in. from the heat for 4-5 minutes on each side or until a thermometer reads 170°. When cool enough to handle, cut into ½-in. strips. Refrigerate until chilled.

3. In a large bowl, combine the chicken, romaine and rice. Drizzle with vinaigrette; toss to coat. Serve in pitas.

Nutrition Facts: *2 filled pita halves equals 398 calories, 10 g fat (2 g saturated fat), 65 mg cholesterol, 919 mg sodium, 44 g carbohydrate, 5 g fiber, 31 g protein.* **Diabetic Exchanges:** *3 starch, 3 lean meat, 1 fat.*

- ¼ cup hummus
- 1 whole wheat tortilla (8 inches), room temperature
- ½ cup fresh baby spinach
- ⅓ cup shredded cooked chicken breast
- 2 carrot sticks
- 2 pieces julienned sweet red pepper

Spread hummus over tortilla. Layer with spinach and chicken. Arrange carrot and red pepper down the center of tortilla. Roll up tightly. Cut into slices.

Nutrition Facts: *1 wrap equals 324 calories, 10 g fat (1 g saturated fat), 36 mg cholesterol, 441 mg sodium, 35 g carbohydrate, 7 g fiber, 23 g protein.* **Diabetic Exchanges:** *3 lean meat, 2 starch, 1 vegetable, 1 fat.*

Turkey Sloppy Joes for a Crowd

I found this recipe in my mother's recipe box. Sometimes I serve it over vegetables such as corn or green beans, but it's equally delicious on a bun.

—JULIE CLEMES ADRIAN, MICHIGAN

PREP: 25 MIN. **COOK:** 40 MIN. **MAKES:** 16 SERVINGS

- 3 pounds lean ground turkey
- 3 medium green peppers, chopped
- 3 medium onions, finely chopped
- 2¼ cups ketchup
- ¾ cup water
- 3 tablespoons white vinegar
- 3 tablespoons spicy brown mustard
- 1 jalapeno pepper, seeded and chopped
- ½ teaspoon pepper
- 16 whole wheat hamburger buns, split

1. In a Dutch oven coated with cooking spray, cook the turkey, green peppers and onions over medium heat until meat is no longer pink and vegetables are tender; drain.

2. Stir in the ketchup, water, vinegar, mustard, jalapeno and pepper. Bring to a boil. Reduce heat; cover and simmer for 20-30 minutes, stirring occasionally. Serve on buns.

Editor's Note: *Wear disposable gloves when cutting hot peppers; the oils can burn skin. Avoid touching your face.*

Nutrition Facts: *1 sandwich equals 293 calories, 9 g fat (2 g saturated fat), 67 mg cholesterol, 751 mg sodium, 35 g carbohydrate, 4 g fiber, 19 g protein.* **Diabetic Exchanges:** *2 starch, 2 lean meat.*

Potato-Beef Barley Soup

Hash browns are an unexpected and flavorful twist in this vegetable barley soup. I toss in a can of corn or red and yellow peppers for added color.

—KENDRA MCKENZIE FREDERICKTOWN, OHIO

PREP: 10 MIN. **COOK:** 30 MIN. **MAKES:** 12 SERVINGS (4 QUARTS)

- 1½ pounds lean ground beef (90% lean)
- 1 large green pepper, chopped
- 7 cups water
- 1 package (32 ounces) frozen cubed hash brown potatoes
- 1 can (28 ounces) crushed tomatoes, undrained
- 2 tablespoons reduced-sodium soy sauce
- 2½ teaspoons garlic powder
- 2½ teaspoons dried thyme
- 1½ teaspoons salt
- ½ teaspoon pepper
- 1 package (16 ounces) frozen cut green beans
- ½ cup quick-cooking barley

1. In a Dutch oven coated with cooking spray, cook beef and green pepper over medium heat until meat is no longer pink; drain. Stir in the water, potatoes, tomatoes, soy sauce, garlic powder, thyme, salt and pepper. Bring to a boil. Reduce heat; cover and simmer for 10-15 minutes or until potatoes are tender.

2. Return to a boil; stir in beans and barley. Reduce heat; cover and simmer for 10-12 minutes or until beans and barley are tender. Remove from the heat; let stand for 5 minutes.

Nutrition Facts: *1⅓ cups equals 217 calories, 5 g fat (2 g saturated fat), 35 mg cholesterol, 568 mg sodium, 27 g carbohydrate, 5 g fiber, 16 g protein.* **Diabetic Exchanges:** *2 lean meat, 1 starch, 1 vegetable.*

Lunch Box Chicken Wrap

This lunchbox-friendly wrap is a tasty way to turn leftover chicken into something delicious, and it gets kids to eat more veggies. Using colorful, thin strips of vegetables adds visual interest when the wrap is cut into slices. Suddenly spinach is too pretty to refuse.

—HEALTHY COOKING TEST KITCHEN

PREP/TOTAL TIME: 10 MIN. **MAKES:** 1 SERVING

Mexican Chicken Soup with Cilantro Dumplings

I just had to share this recipe because my whole family thought it was absolutely delicious! It's a filling and comforting twist on traditional chicken soup. Don't be afraid of the jalapeno—the heat factor is pretty mild.

—JENNY DUBINSKY INWOOD, WEST VIRGINIA

PREP: 20 MIN. **COOK:** 40 MIN.
MAKES: 6 SERVINGS (2¼ QUARTS PLUS 12 DUMPLINGS)

- 1 **pound boneless skinless chicken breasts, cut into 1-inch cubes**
- 2 **teaspoons olive oil, divided**
- 1 **medium onion, chopped**
- 1 **tablespoon chili powder**
- 5 **cups reduced-sodium chicken broth**
- 1 **can (15½ ounces) petite diced tomatoes, undrained**
- 1 **can (15 ounces) black beans, rinsed and drained**
- 2 **cups frozen corn**
- 1 **jalapeno pepper, seeded and minced**
- 1 **cup reduced-fat biscuit/baking mix**
- ¼ **cup minced fresh cilantro**
- ¼ **teaspoon ground cumin**
- ⅓ **cup fat-free milk**

1. In a Dutch oven, saute chicken in 1 teaspoon oil until no longer pink. Remove and keep warm.

2. In the same pan, saute onion and chili powder in remaining oil until onion is tender. Add the broth, tomatoes, beans, corn and jalapeno. Bring to a boil. Reduce heat; cover and simmer for 20 minutes. Stir in reserved chicken.

3. In a small bowl, combine the biscuit mix, cilantro and cumin. Stir in milk just until moistened. Drop by tablespoonfuls onto simmering soup. Cover and simmer for 15 minutes or until a toothpick inserted in a dumpling comes out clean (do not lift the cover while simmering).

Editor's Note: *Wear disposable gloves when cutting hot peppers; the oils can burn skin. Avoid touching your face.*

Nutrition Facts: *1½ cups soup with 2 dumplings equals 321 calories, 5 g fat (1 g saturated fat), 42 mg cholesterol, 992 mg sodium, 44 g carbohydrate, 7 g fiber, 26 g protein.* **Diabetic Exchanges:** *3 starch, 2 lean meat, 1 vegetable.*

Couscous Meatball Soup

Looking for something new to try with the ground beef you have in the freezer? I make this quick and healthy meatball soup and serve it with crusty bread. It's even better than chili on a cold day.

—JONATHAN PACE SAN FRANCISCO, CALIFORNIA

PREP: 25 MIN. **COOK:** 40 MIN.
MAKES: 10 SERVINGS (2½ QUARTS)

- 1 **pound lean ground beef (90% lean)**
- 2 **teaspoons dried basil**
- 2 **teaspoons dried oregano**
- ½ **teaspoon salt**
- 1 **large onion, finely chopped**
- 2 **teaspoons canola oil**
- 8 **cups chopped collard greens**
- 8 **cups chopped fresh kale**
- 2 **cartons (32 ounces each) vegetable stock**
- 1 **tablespoon white wine vinegar**
- ½ **teaspoon crushed red pepper flakes**
- ¼ **teaspoon pepper**
- 1 **package (8.8 ounces) Israeli couscous**

1. In a small bowl, combine the beef, basil, oregano and salt. Shape into ½-in. balls. In a large nonstick skillet coated with cooking spray, brown meatballs; drain. Remove meatballs and set aside.

2. In the same skillet, brown onion in oil. Add greens and kale; cook 6-7 minutes longer or until wilted.

3. In a Dutch oven, combine the greens mixture, meatballs, stock, vinegar, pepper flakes and pepper. Bring to a boil. Reduce heat; cover and simmer for 10 minutes. Return to a boil. Stir in couscous. Reduce heat; cover and simmer for 10-15 minutes or until couscous is tender, stirring once.

Nutrition Facts: *1 cup equals 202 calories, 5 g fat (2 g saturated fat), 28 mg cholesterol, 583 mg sodium, 26 g carbohydrate, 2 g fiber, 13 g protein.* **Diabetic Exchanges:** *1½ starch, 1 lean meat, 1 vegetable.*

75

71

73

Side Dishes

"If you're looking for a shift from the traditional green bean casserole for your holiday feast, try this recipe. Its pretty red and green colors make it perfect for a Christmas dinner."

CHRISTINE BERGMAN SUWANEE, GEORGIA
about her recipe, Zesty Garlic Green Beans, on page 72

Smoky Corn Salad 🄵🄼

My zesty, colorful corn salad is an excellent way to perk up any meal. The seasonings add a bold Southwestern flavor that brings folks back for seconds.
—**SHARON DELANEY-CHRONIS** SOUTH MILWAUKEE, WISCONSIN

PREP/TOTAL TIME: 20 MIN. **MAKES:** 6 SERVINGS

- 4 cups fresh or frozen corn, thawed
- 2 tablespoons lime juice
- ½ teaspoon salt
- ¼ teaspoon ground chipotle pepper
- 2 large sweet red peppers, chopped
- ½ cup minced fresh cilantro

1. In a large heavy skillet coated with cooking spray, saute corn until lightly browned. Transfer to a serving bowl.
2. Stir in the lime juice, salt and chipotle pepper. Cool for 5 minutes. Stir in red peppers and cilantro.
Nutrition Facts: *¾ cup equals 105 calories, 1 g fat (trace saturated fat), 0 cholesterol, 216 mg sodium, 23 g carbohydrate, 4 g fiber, 4 g protein.* **Diabetic Exchange:** *1½ starch.*

Chinese-Style Zucchini 🄲🄼

A quick side, this fresh-tasting dish is great alongside salmon. The toasted sesame seeds really bring out the flavor.
—**MARIE RIZZIO** INTERLOCHEN, MICHIGAN

PREP/TOTAL TIME: 20 MIN. **MAKES:** 4 SERVINGS

- 1 pound medium zucchini, thinly sliced
- 4 teaspoons olive oil
- 2 garlic cloves, minced
- 2 tablespoons reduced-sodium soy sauce
- ½ teaspoon sesame seeds, toasted

In a large nonstick skillet, saute zucchini in oil until tender. Add garlic; cook 1 minute longer. Stir in soy sauce; sprinkle with sesame seeds.

Nutrition Facts: *½ cup equals 67 calories, 5 g fat (1 g saturated fat), 0 cholesterol, 316 mg sodium, 5 g carbohydrate, 1 g fiber, 2 g protein.* **Diabetic Exchanges:** *1 vegetable, 1 fat.*

Sweet Zucchini Relish 🄵🄼

Classic relish is made with cucumbers, but this sweet and tangy topper is packed with zucchini, peppers and onions. I serve it with burgers, sandwiches and in any recipes that normally call for pickle relish.
—**JYL BASINGER** CAVE CITY, ARKANSAS

PREP: 1 HOUR + CHILLING **PROCESS:** 15 MIN. **MAKES:** 5 PINTS

- 10 cups shredded zucchini (about 3½ pounds)
- 4 large onions, chopped
- 2 medium green peppers, chopped
- 2 medium sweet red peppers, chopped
- ⅓ cup canning salt
- 2½ cups sugar
- 2½ cups cider vinegar
- 4 teaspoons cornstarch
- 1 teaspoon ground turmeric
- 1 teaspoon curry powder
- 1 teaspoon celery seed
- ½ teaspoon pepper

1. In a large container, combine the zucchini, onions, peppers and salt. Cover and refrigerate overnight. Drain; rinse and drain again.
2. In a stockpot, combine the sugar, vinegar, cornstarch and seasonings; bring to a boil. Add zucchini mixture; return to a boil. Reduce heat; simmer, uncovered, for 12-15 minutes or until slightly thickened. Remove from the heat.
3. Carefully ladle hot mixture into hot 1-pint jars, leaving ½-in. headspace. Remove air bubbles; wipe rims and adjust lids. Process for 15 minutes in a boiling-water canner. Refrigerate remaining relish for up to 1 week.

Editor's Note: *The processing time listed is for altitudes of 1,000 feet or less. For altitudes up to 3,000 feet, add 5 minutes; 6,000 feet, add 10 minutes; 8,000 feet, add 15 minutes; 10,000 feet, add 20 minutes.*

Nutrition Facts: *¼ cup equals 67 calories, trace fat (trace saturated fat), 0 cholesterol, 288 mg sodium, 16 g carbohydrate, 1 g fiber, 1 g protein.*

Easy Colcannon

This tasty and traditional Irish recipe for buttery potatoes and cabbage is good any time of year.

—**PAM KENNEDY** LUBBOCK, TEXAS

PREP/TOTAL TIME: 30 MIN. **MAKES:** 8 SERVINGS

- 1½ **pounds medium red potatoes, cut into 1-inch cubes**
- 7½ **cups chopped cabbage**
- 8 **green onions, chopped**
- 1 **cup fat-free milk**
- ⅓ **cup reduced-fat butter**
- ¾ **teaspoon salt**
- ¼ **teaspoon pepper**

1. Place potatoes in a Dutch oven; cover with water. Bring to a boil. Cover and cook over medium heat for 12-15 minutes or until potatoes are almost tender, adding the cabbage during the last 5 minutes of cooking.
2. Meanwhile, in a small saucepan, combine green onions and milk. Bring to a boil. Reduce heat; simmer, uncovered, for 5-6 minutes or until onions are soft.
3. Drain potato mixture. Mash with milk mixture, butter, salt and pepper.
Nutrition Facts: *¾ cup equals 131 calories, 4 g fat (2 g saturated fat), 11 mg cholesterol, 320 mg sodium, 22 g carbohydrate, 4 g fiber, 4 g protein.* **Diabetic Exchanges:** *1 starch, 1 vegetable, 1 fat.*

Reduced-Sugar Tangy Barbecue Sauce F C

BBQ sauce is a delicious staple to have on hand during the summer grilling season. A homemade alternative to bottled sauce, this low-sugar version can be brushed on chicken, ribs, pork or even turkey.

—**LYNN SAWYER** TWO RIVERS, WISCONSIN

PREP: 15 MIN. **COOK:** 50 MIN. **MAKES:** 2½ CUPS

- 1 **large onion, finely chopped**
- 1 **tablespoon canola oil**
- 1½ **cups reduced-sugar ketchup**
- 1 **cup cider vinegar**
- ¾ **cup water**
- ¾ **cup sugar-free maple-flavored syrup**
- 4½ **teaspoons Worcestershire sauce**
   Sugar substitute equivalent to 1 tablespoon sugar
- 2 **teaspoons reduced-sodium beef bouillon granules**
- ¼ **teaspoon pepper**
- ¼ **teaspoon hot pepper sauce**

In a large nonstick saucepan, saute onion in oil until tender. Stir in the remaining ingredients. Bring to a boil. Reduce heat; simmer, uncovered, for 45-50 minutes or until sauce is thickened and reduced to 2½ cups.
Editor's Note: *This recipe was tested with Splenda no-calorie sweetener.*

Nutrition Facts: *2 tablespoons equals 25 calories, 1 g fat (trace saturated fat), trace cholesterol, 263 mg sodium, 4 g carbohydrate, trace fiber, trace protein.* **Diabetic Exchange:** *Free food.*

Cajun Summer Vegetables F S C M

Put your garden-fresh summertime veggies to good use with a colorful side dish that gets a little heat from Cajun seasoning. It pairs well with any entree and is quick and easy to prepare.

—**NANCY DENTLER** GREENSBORO, NORTH CAROLINA

PREP/TOTAL TIME: 25 MIN. **MAKES:** 6 SERVINGS

- 2 **medium yellow summer squash, sliced**
- 2 **medium zucchini, sliced**
- 1¾ **cups sliced fresh mushrooms**
- ½ **medium onion, sliced and separated into rings**
- ½ **medium red onion, sliced and separated into rings**
- 1 **cup cherry tomatoes**
- ¼ **cup sliced fresh carrots**
- 1 **teaspoon Cajun seasoning**

Place vegetables in a grill wok or basket. Grill, uncovered, over medium heat for 8-12 minutes or until tender, stirring frequently. Transfer to a large bowl. Sprinkle with Cajun seasoning; toss to coat.
Editor's Note: *If you do not have a grill wok or basket, use a disposable foil pan. Poke holes in the bottom of the pan with a meat fork to allow liquid to drain.*

Nutrition Facts: *⅔ cup equals 42 calories, trace fat (trace saturated fat), 0 cholesterol, 105 mg sodium, 9 g carbohydrate, 3 g fiber, 3 g protein.* **Diabetic Exchange:** *1 vegetable.*

Asparagus and Mushrooms in Lemon-Thyme Butter C M

Out of thyme? No worries, the beauty of this dish is its versatility. Simply use another herb of choice instead.
—**SARAH REID** OSHAWA, ONTARIO

PREP/TOTAL TIME: 20 MIN.
MAKES: 4 SERVINGS

- 1 **pound fresh asparagus, trimmed and cut into 1-inch pieces**
- ½ **pound sliced fresh mushrooms**
- 1 **tablespoon butter**
- 1 **teaspoon olive oil**
- 1½ **teaspoons minced fresh thyme or ½ teaspoon dried thyme**
- 1 **teaspoon grated lemon peel**
- ½ **teaspoon salt**
- ½ **teaspoon lemon juice**
- ¼ **teaspoon pepper**

In a large skillet, saute asparagus and mushrooms in butter and oil until tender. Stir in remaining ingredients.

Nutrition Facts: *1 cup equals 64 calories, 4 g fat (2 g saturated fat), 8 mg cholesterol, 324 mg sodium, 5 g carbohydrate, 2 g fiber, 3 g protein.*
Diabetic Exchanges: *1 vegetable, 1 fat.*

Rosemary-Thyme Potatoes M

I love making potato dishes to serve alongside my favorite entrees. Everyone will fall in love with these tender spuds that are perfectly seasoned with rosemary and thyme.
—**CATHY BRANDNER** PIERRE, SOUTH DAKOTA

PREP/TOTAL TIME: 25 MIN.
MAKES: 5 SERVINGS

- 4 **medium red potatoes, cut into ½-inch cubes**
- 3 **tablespoons water**
- 5 **teaspoons butter, melted**
- 1 **garlic clove, minced**
- ½ **teaspoon salt**
- ½ **teaspoon dried thyme**
- ½ **teaspoon dried rosemary, crushed**
- ¼ **teaspoon pepper**

1. Place potatoes and water in a 1½-qt. microwave-safe dish. Cover and microwave on high for 8 minutes or until tender. Drain.
2. Combine the remaining ingredients. Pour over potatoes; toss to coat. Cover and cook 1-2 minutes longer or until flavors are blended, stirring once.

Editor's Note: *This recipe was tested in a 1,100-watt microwave.*

Nutrition Facts: *¾ cup equals 170 calories, 4 g fat (2 g saturated fat), 10 mg cholesterol, 273 mg sodium, 31 g carbohydrate, 3 g fiber, 4 g protein.* **Diabetic Exchanges:** *2 starch, 1 fat.*

Garlic Corn on the Cob S M

Every summer we look forward to fresh corn on the cob. I make it extra special by jazzing it up with garlic.

—**HEATHER CARROLL** COLORADO SPRINGS, COLORADO

PREP/TOTAL TIME: 15 MIN. **MAKES:** 4 SERVINGS

- 4 **garlic cloves, minced**
- 4 **teaspoons olive oil**
- 4 **medium ears sweet corn, husks removed**
- 1 **teaspoon sugar**

1. In a small bowl, combine garlic and oil; brush over corn. Sprinkle with sugar. Place each on a double thickness of heavy-duty foil (about 14 in. x 12. in.). Fold foil over corn and seal tightly.

2. Grill corn, covered, over medium heat for 10-15 minutes or until tender, turning occasionally. Open foil carefully to allow steam to escape.

Nutrition Facts: *1 ear of corn equals 126 calories, 6 g fat (1 g saturated fat), 0 cholesterol, 14 mg sodium, 19 g carbohydrate, 2 g fiber, 3 g protein.* **Diabetic Exchanges:** *1 starch, 1 fat.*

Cranberry Pomegranate Relish F S M

This tart relish combines a powerhouse of nutrients—cranberries and pomegranate. It captures the flavor of the holiday season and adds a beautiful ruby-red color to any meal.

—**ARLENE RAKOCZY** GILBERT, ARIZONA

PREP: 25 MIN. + CHILLING **MAKES:** 1½ CUPS

- 2 **cups fresh or frozen cranberries**
- ½ **cup sugar**
- ½ **cup water**
- 1 **cup pomegranate seeds**

- ¼ **teaspoon ground cinnamon**
- ⅛ **teaspoon pumpkin pie spice**

1. In a small saucepan, combine the cranberries, sugar and water. Cook over medium heat until berries pop, about 15 minutes.

2. Remove from the heat; stir in remaining ingredients. Transfer to a small bowl. Refrigerate until chilled.

Nutrition Facts: *¼ cup equals 94 calories, trace fat (trace saturated fat), 0 cholesterol, 1 mg sodium, 24 g carbohydrate, 2 g fiber, trace protein.*

Cashew Green Beans and Mushrooms C M

PREP/TOTAL TIME: 20 MIN. **MAKES:** 4 SERVINGS

- ½ **pound fresh green beans, trimmed and cut into 1½-inch pieces**
- ½ **pound sliced fresh mushrooms**
- 1 **tablespoon olive oil**
- ¼ **cup unsalted cashews, coarsely chopped**
- ¼ **teaspoon salt**

In a large skillet, saute beans and mushrooms in oil until tender. Stir in cashews and salt.

Nutrition Facts: *¾ cup equals 109 calories, 8 g fat (1 g saturated fat), 0 cholesterol, 154 mg sodium, 9 g carbohydrate, 3 g fiber, 4 g protein.* **Diabetic Exchanges:** *1½ fat, 1 vegetable.*

❝Savory and earthy, this simple green bean side dish couldn't be easier to prepare, and the cashews make it extra special.❞

—**RHODA KNIPPELBERG** VANCOUVER, BRITISH COLUMBIA

Asparagus with Horseradish Dip ⓒ

This is a great hot weather menu item. Serve asparagus on a decorative platter with lemon wedges on the side for garnish. A great flavor variation is to use chopped garlic in place of the horseradish.

—MILDRED LYNN CARUSO BRIGHTON, TENNESSEE

PREP/TOTAL TIME: 15 MIN. **MAKES:** 16 SERVINGS

- 32 **fresh asparagus spears (about 2 pounds), trimmed**
- 1 **cup reduced-fat mayonnaise**
- ¼ **cup grated Parmesan cheese**
- 1 **tablespoon prepared horseradish**
- ½ **teaspoon Worcestershire sauce**

1. Place asparagus in a steamer basket; place in a large saucepan over 1 in. of water. Bring to a boil; cover and steam for 2-4 minutes or until crisp-tender. Drain and immediately place in ice water. Drain and pat dry.

2. In a small bowl, combine the remaining ingredients. Serve with asparagus.

Nutrition Facts: *2 asparagus spears with 1 tablespoon dip equals 63 calories, 5 g fat (1 g saturated fat), 6 mg cholesterol, 146 mg sodium, 3 g carbohydrate, trace fiber, 1 g protein.* **Diabetic Exchange:** *1 fat.*

Potato Basil Scramble Ⓜ

At our house, we argue over who gets the leftovers of this popular dish. I grow my own herbs, so I toss in fresh basil, but dried works just as well. We love this for dinner with fruit salad and English muffins. It also makes a hearty breakfast for the weekend.

—TERRI ZOBEL RALEIGH, NORTH CAROLINA

PREP/TOTAL TIME: 30 MIN. **MAKES:** 4 S ERVINGS

- 2 **cups cubed potatoes**
- ½ **cup chopped onion**
- ½ **chopped green pepper**
- 1 **tablespoon vegetable oil**
- 2 **cups egg substitute**
- 2 **tablespoons minced fresh basil**
- ½ **teaspoon salt**
- ⅛ **teaspoon cayenne pepper**

1. Place potatoes in a microwave-safe bowl; add 1 in. of water. Cover and microwave on high for 7 minutes; drain.

2. In a large nonstick skillet coated with cooking spray, saute the onion, green pepper and potatoes in oil until tender. Add the egg substitute, basil, salt and pepper. Cook and stir over medium heat until eggs are completely set.

Editor's Note: *This recipe was tested in a 1,100-watt microwave.*

Nutrition Facts: *1 serving (1 cup) equals 163 calories, 4 g fat (0.55 g saturated fat), 0 cholesterol, 549 mg sodium, 19 g carbohydrate, 2 g fiber, 14 g protein.* **Diabetic Exchanges:** *2 lean meat, 1 starch.*

Spinach Pantry Soufflé ⓒⓂ

PREP: 35 MIN. **BAKE:** 30 MIN. **MAKES:** 6 SERVINGS

- 6 **egg whites**
- 2 **tablespoons grated Parmesan cheese**
- 1 **can (10¾ ounces) reduced-fat reduced-sodium condensed cream of mushroom soup, undiluted**
- 1 **cup (4 ounces) shredded reduced-fat Mexican cheese blend**
- 1 **teaspoon ground mustard**
- 1 **package (10 ounces) frozen chopped spinach, thawed and squeezed dry**
- 2 **egg yolks, beaten**

1. Let egg whites stand at room temperature for 30 minutes. Coat a 2-qt. soufflé dish with cooking spray and lightly sprinkle with Parmesan cheese; set aside.

2. In a small saucepan, combine the soup, cheese blend and mustard; cook and stir over medium heat for 5 minutes or until cheese is melted. Transfer to a large bowl; stir in spinach. Stir a small amount of soup mixture into egg yolks; return all to the bowl, stirring constantly.

3. In a small bowl with clean beaters, beat egg whites until stiff peaks form. With a spatula, stir a fourth of the egg whites into spinach mixture until no white streaks remain. Fold in remaining egg whites until combined. Transfer to prepared dish.

4. Bake at 375° for 30-35 minutes or until the top is puffed and center appears set. Serve immediately.

Nutrition Facts: *1 serving equals 140 calories, 8 g fat (3 g saturated fat), 90 mg cholesterol, 453 mg sodium, 7 g carbohydrate, 1 g fiber, 12 g protein.* **Diabetic Exchanges:** *2 medium-fat meat, ½ starch.*

 top tip You can cover and refrigerate an unbaked soufflé for up to 2 hours before baking, but it won't rise as much. It's also important not to let any yolk spill into the egg whites during preparation or the whites won't achieve full volume.

—HEALTHY COOKING TEST KITCHEN

"We have always loved soufflés, but I got tired of slaving over the white sauce. One day I substituted condensed soup for the white sauce, and we all thought it was great. When we started watching our fat intake, I switched to the reduced-fat, reduced-sodium soup, reduced-fat cheese and just two egg yolks."

—DIANE CONRAD NORTH BEND, OREGON

Makeover Garden Side Dish

Who could resist serving tender veggies smothered in cheese on a bed of fluffy rice—and with an hour to spare?

—JANE DAVIS MARION, INDIANA

PREP: 20 MIN.   **COOK:** 20 MIN.   **MAKES:** 12 SERVINGS

2⅓ cups reduced-sodium chicken broth
2 cups chopped onions, divided
3 tablespoons reduced-sodium soy sauce
1 tablespoon butter
½ teaspoon dried thyme
3 cups instant brown rice
4 cups fresh cauliflowerets
4 cups fresh broccoli florets
2 medium sweet red peppers, julienned
2 tablespoons olive oil
2 garlic cloves, minced
½ cup salted cashews
1 cup (4 ounces) shredded cheddar cheese

1. In a Dutch oven, combine the broth, 1 cup onion, soy sauce, butter and thyme. Bring to a boil; stir in rice. Reduce heat; cover and simmer for 5 minutes or until liquid is absorbed. Remove from the heat. Let stand for 5 minutes.

2. Meanwhile, in large skillet or another Dutch oven, saute cauliflower, broccoli, peppers and remaining onion in oil until crisp-tender. Add garlic; cook 1 minute longer. Spoon over rice.

3. Sprinkle with cashews and cheese. Cover and let stand until cheese is melted.

Nutrition Facts: *¾ cup equals 224 calories, 10 g fat (4 g saturated fat), 13 mg cholesterol, 391 mg sodium, 26 g carbohydrate, 4 g fiber, 8 g protein.*

Herbed Butternut Squash F M

This is just one of many ways we prepare butternut squash—it's a winter staple in our house.

—JENN TIDWELL FAIR OAKS, CALIFORNIA

PREP/TOTAL TIME: 25 MIN.   **MAKES:** 6 SERVINGS

1 medium butternut squash (about 3 pounds), peeled and cut into ½-inch slices
1 tablespoon olive oil
1½ teaspoons dried oregano
1 teaspoon dried thyme
½ teaspoon salt
¼ teaspoon pepper

Place all ingredients in a large bowl; toss to coat. Grill, covered, over medium heat or broil 4 in. from the heat for 6-8 minutes on each side or until tender.

Nutrition Facts: *1 serving equals 108 calories, 2 g fat (trace saturated fat), 0 cholesterol, 205 mg sodium, 23 g carbohydrate, 7 g fiber, 2 g protein.* **Diabetic Exchanges:** *1 starch, ½ fat.*

? Did you know?

Before refrigerators were around, varieties of squash harvested in fall were known as winter vegetables because they could last until December. That's why we call butternut squash, along with acorn squash and others, "winter squash." They should be stored, unwashed, in a cool, dry, well-ventilated area for up to 4 weeks.

Veggie-Topped Polenta Slices

When there wasn't a lot of food in my kitchen one day, so I created this—and the results were amazing! My boyfriend loved my "cabinet creation," and we even serve these as appetizers.

—JENN TIDWELL FAIR OAKS, CALIFORNIA

PREP: 20 MIN. **COOK:** 20 MIN. **MAKES:** 4 SERVINGS

- 1 tube (1 pound) polenta, cut into 12 slices
- 2 tablespoons olive oil, divided
- 1 medium zucchini, chopped
- 2 shallots, minced
- 2 garlic cloves, minced
- 3 tablespoons reduced-sodium chicken broth
- ½ teaspoon pepper
- ⅛ teaspoon salt
- 4 plum tomatoes, seeded and chopped
- 2 tablespoons minced fresh basil or 2 teaspoons dried basil
- 1 tablespoon minced fresh parsley
- ½ cup shredded part-skim mozzarella cheese

1. In a large nonstick skillet, cook polenta in 1 tablespoon oil over medium heat for 9-11 minutes on each side or until golden brown.

2. Meanwhile, in another large skillet, saute zucchini in remaining oil until tender. Add shallots and garlic; cook 1 minute longer. Add the broth, pepper and salt. Bring to a boil; cook until liquid is almost evaporated.

3. Stir in the tomatoes, basil and parsley; heat through. Serve with polenta; sprinkle with cheese.

Nutrition Facts: *3 polenta slices with 1 cup vegetable mixture equals 222 calories, 9 g fat (2 g saturated fat), 8 mg cholesterol, 558 mg sodium, 28 g carbohydrate, 2 g fiber, 7 g protein.* **Diabetic Exchanges:** *1½ starch, 1½ fat, 1 vegetable.*

Blue Cheese Soufflé **C** **M**

Lightened up to fewer than 100 calories per serving and packed with protein, this rich and flavorful soufflé is a great side for beef.

—SARAH VASQUES MILFORD, NEW HAMPSHIRE

PREP: 25 MIN. **BAKE:** 25 MIN. **MAKES:** 8 SERVINGS

- 5 egg whites
- 6 tablespoons grated Parmesan cheese, divided
- 3 tablespoons all-purpose flour
- ½ teaspoon salt
- ¼ teaspoon pepper
  Dash ground nutmeg
  Dash cayenne pepper
- 1 cup fat-free milk
- ⅓ cup crumbled blue cheese
- 4 egg yolks
- ⅛ teaspoon cream of tartar

1. Let egg whites stand at room temperature for 30 minutes. Coat a 2-qt. soufflé dish with cooking spray and lightly sprinkle with 2 tablespoons Parmesan cheese; set aside.

2. In a small saucepan, combine flour and spices. Gradually whisk in milk. Bring to a boil, stirring constantly. Cook and stir 1 minute longer or until thickened. Reduce heat. Stir in blue cheese and remaining Parmesan cheese. Remove from the heat; transfer to a large bowl.

3. Stir a small amount of hot mixture into egg yolks; return all to the bowl, stirring constantly. Allow to cool slightly.

4. In another large bowl with clean beaters, beat egg whites and cream of tartar until stiff peaks form. With a spatula, stir a fourth of the egg whites into cheese mixture until no white streaks remain. Fold in remaining egg whites until combined.

5. Transfer to prepared dish. Bake at 350° for 25-30 minutes or until the top is puffed and center appears set. Serve immediately.

Nutrition Facts: *1 serving equals 95 calories, 5 g fat (3 g saturated fat), 111 mg cholesterol, 335 mg sodium, 5 g carbohydrate, trace fiber, 8 g protein.* **Diabetic Exchanges:** *1 medium-fat meat, ½ fat.*

Zesty Garlic Green Beans F S C M

If you're looking for a shift from the traditional green bean casserole for your holiday feast, try this recipe. Its pretty red and green colors make it perfect for a Christmas dinner.
—CHRISTINE BERGMAN SUWANEE, GEORGIA

PREP/TOTAL TIME: 25 MIN. **MAKES:** 10 SERVINGS

- ½ cup oil-packed sun-dried tomatoes
- 1 cup sliced sweet onion
- 3 garlic cloves, minced
- 1½ teaspoons lemon-pepper seasoning
- 2 packages (16 ounces each) frozen French-style green beans

1. Drain tomatoes, reserving 2 tablespoons oil. In a Dutch oven, saute onion in reserved oil for 8-10 minutes or until tender.
2. Add the tomatoes, garlic and lemon-pepper; cook and stir for 2 minutes. Add frozen green beans and stir to coat. Cover and cook for 8 minutes or just until heated through, stirring occasionally.
3. Uncover and cook 2-3 minutes longer or until liquid is almost evaporated.
Nutrition Facts: ⅔ cup equals 76 calories, 3 g fat (trace saturated fat), 0 cholesterol, 85 mg sodium, 9 g carbohydrate, 3 g fiber, 2 g protein. **Diabetic Exchanges:** 1 vegetable, 1 fat.

Carrot Brown Rice Pilaf M

This versatile and colorful dish complements a variety of meats and vegetarian entrees. To give it a fun, crunchy texture and additional flavor and protein, stir in 2 cups of bean sprouts just before serving.
—PAULETTE CROSS LOWVILLE, NEW YORK

PREP: 15 MIN. **COOK:** 45 MIN. **MAKES:** 4 SERVINGS

- 1 large onion, finely chopped
- 2 medium carrots, shredded
- 1 tablespoon butter
- 1 cup uncooked brown rice
- 2½ cups vegetable stock
- 1 tablespoon dried parsley flakes
- ¼ teaspoon salt
- ⅛ teaspoon pepper

1. In a large saucepan, saute onion and carrots in butter until tender. Add rice; cook and stir for 3-4 minutes or until rice is lightly browned.
2. Stir in the stock, parsley, salt and pepper. Bring to a boil. Reduce heat; cover and simmer for 40-45 minutes or until rice is tender. Fluff with a fork.
Nutrition Facts: ¾ cup equals 231 calories, 4 g fat (2 g saturated fat), 8 mg cholesterol, 551 mg sodium, 44 g carbohydrate, 3 g fiber, 4 g protein.

Grilled Zucchini with Onions C M

Wondering what to do with all of your garden zucchini? Tired of the same old bread and cupcakes? My grilled recipe is a great change of pace with the added bonus of being healthy.
—ALIA SHUTTLEWORTH AUBURN, CALIFORNIA

PREP/TOTAL TIME: 20 MIN. **MAKES:** 4 SERVINGS

- 6 small zucchini, halved lengthwise
- 4 teaspoons olive oil, divided
- 2 green onions, thinly sliced
- 2 tablespoons lemon juice
- ½ teaspoon salt
- ⅛ teaspoon crushed red pepper flakes

1. Drizzle zucchini with 2 teaspoons oil. Grill, covered, over medium heat for 8-10 minutes or until tender, turning once.
2. Place in a large bowl. Add the green onions, lemon juice, salt, pepper flakes and remaining oil; toss to coat.
Nutrition Facts: 3 zucchini halves equals 73 calories, 5 g fat (1 g saturated fat), 0 cholesterol, 314 mg sodium, 7 g carbohydrate, 2 g fiber, 2 g protein. **Diabetic Exchanges:** 1 vegetable, 1 fat.

> My family begs me to make this recipe at Thanksgiving and Christmas. They like it because pumpkin pie spice enhances the flavor of the sweet potatoes. I like the fact that it can be made a day ahead and warmed before serving.
> —SENJA MERRILL SANDY, UTAH

Favorite Mashed Sweet Potatoes F S M

PREP/TOTAL TIME: 20 MIN.
MAKES: 8 SERVINGS

- 6 medium sweet potatoes, peeled and cubed
- 3 tablespoons orange juice
- 2 tablespoons brown sugar
- 2 tablespoons maple syrup
- ¼ teaspoon pumpkin pie spice

Place potatoes in a Dutch oven and cover with water. Bring to a boil. Reduce heat; cover and cook for 10-15 minutes or until tender. Drain. Mash potatoes with remaining ingredients.

Nutrition Facts: ⅔ cup equals 117 calories, trace fat (trace saturated fat), 0 cholesterol, 10 mg sodium, 28 g carbohydrate, 3 g fiber, 1 g protein. **Diabetic Exchange:** 2 starch.

Rosemary Sweet Potato Fries M

A local restaurant got me hooked on sweet potato fries. I started making them at home with different seasonings to match the taste. I'm thrilled with the results!
—JACKIE GREGSTON HALLSVILLE, TEXAS

PREP: 15 MIN. **BAKE:** 30 MIN.
MAKES: 4 SERVINGS

- 3 tablespoons olive oil
- 1 tablespoon minced fresh rosemary
- 1 garlic clove, minced
- 1 teaspoon cornstarch
- ¾ teaspoon salt
- ⅛ teaspoon pepper
- 3 large sweet potatoes, peeled and cut into ¼-inch julienned strips (about 2¼ pounds)

1. In a large resealable plastic bag, combine the first six ingredients. Add sweet potatoes; shake to coat.
2. Arrange in a single layer on two 15-in. x 10-in. x 1-in. baking pans coated with cooking spray. Bake, uncovered, at 425° for 30-35 minutes or until tender and lightly browned, turning occasionally.

Nutrition Facts: 1 serving equals 256 calories, 10 g fat (1 g saturated fat), 0 cholesterol, 459 mg sodium, 39 g carbohydrate, 5 g fiber, 3 g protein.

Heavenly Baked Sweet Potatoes Ⓜ

These luscious baked sweet potatoes taste homey—a bit like pumpkin pie. They also feature fruits and nuts for added nutrition. If you like, toss some mini marshmallows on top to make them extra indulgent.

—CYNTHIA PETERSON ROSWELL, NEW MEXICO

PREP: 30 MIN. **BAKE:** 55 MIN. **MAKES:** 10 SERVINGS

- 1 can (8 ounces) unsweetened pineapple chunks
- ½ cup packed brown sugar
- ¼ cup apple cider or unsweetened apple juice
- ¼ cup maple syrup
- ¼ cup butter, cubed
- ¾ teaspoon ground cinnamon
- ⅛ teaspoon ground cloves
- 3 large sweet potatoes, peeled and cut into ¼-inch slices
- 3 medium apples, peeled and cut into ¼-inch slices
- ¾ teaspoon salt
- ⅓ cup chopped pecans

1. Drain pineapple, reserving juice; set pineapple aside. In a small saucepan, combine the brown sugar, apple cider, maple syrup, butter and reserved pineapple juice. Bring to a boil; cook until liquid is reduced to ¾ cup and syrupy, about 20 minutes. Stir in cinnamon and cloves; set aside and keep warm.

2. Layer half of the potatoes, apples and pineapple in a 13-in. x 9-in. baking dish coated with cooking spray. Repeat layers. Sprinkle with salt. Pour reduced liquid over top. Cover and bake at 400° for 40 minutes or just until tender.

3. Sprinkle with pecans. Bake, uncovered, 13-18 minutes longer or until potatoes and apples are tender.

Nutrition Facts: *1 serving equals 231 calories, 8 g fat (3 g saturated fat), 12 mg cholesterol, 224 mg sodium, 41 g carbohydrate, 4 g fiber, 2 g protein.*

Fruited Goat Cheese Stuffing

My sweet and savory side dish incorporates creamy goat cheese for an unexpected twist on a seasonal favorite. Your guests will be impressed!

—JENNIFER CODUTO KENT, OHIO

PREP: 20 MIN. **BAKE:** 30 MIN. **MAKES:** 10 SERVINGS

- 1 pound whole wheat bread, cubed
- 1 cup chopped dates
- 1 medium onion, chopped
- ¼ cup minced fresh sage
- 1 tablespoon minced fresh rosemary or 1 teaspoon dried rosemary, crushed
- 1 teaspoon minced fresh marjoram or ¼ teaspoon dried marjoram
- 2 tablespoons butter
- 1 cup dried cherries, chopped
- ¼ teaspoon salt
- ¼ teaspoon pepper
- 3 cups reduced-sodium chicken broth
- ¾ cup crumbled goat cheese

1. Place bread cubes in an ungreased 15-in. x 10-in. x 1-in. baking pan. Bake at 350° for 10 minutes or until toasted; set aside to cool. Meanwhile, in a large skillet, saute the dates, onion, sage, rosemary and marjoram in butter until onion is tender. Remove from the heat.

2. Place bread cubes in a large bowl. Stir in the onion mixture, cherries, salt and pepper. Add broth; toss to coat. Sprinkle with cheese; toss gently.

3. Transfer to a 13-in. x 9-in. baking dish coated with cooking spray. Bake, uncovered, at 350° for 30-35 minutes or until top is lightly browned.

Nutrition Facts: *¾ cup equals 299 calories, 10 g fat (6 g saturated fat), 29 mg cholesterol, 665 mg sodium, 44 g carbohydrate, 6 g fiber, 10 g protein.*

Honey-Spiced Carrots [M]

These honey-infused carrots are a favorite at our house. You can use your food processor to quickly chop the carrots into matchsticks or purchase them pre-cut at the grocery store.

—**LAURA MCALLISTER** MORGANTON, NORTH CAROLINA

PREP/TOTAL TIME: 20 MIN. **MAKES:** 4 SERVINGS

- 8 large carrots, julienned
- ½ teaspoon salt
- ½ teaspoon ground cinnamon
- ¼ teaspoon ground ginger
- ¼ teaspoon pepper
- 2 tablespoons butter
- 2 tablespoons honey

In a Dutch oven, saute the first five ingredients in butter until carrots are tender. Stir in honey; cook 1 minute longer.

Nutrition Facts: ¾ cup equals 143 calories, 6 g fat (4 g saturated fat), 15 mg cholesterol, 435 mg sodium, 23 g carbohydrate, 4 g fiber, 1 g protein.

Spicy Cran-Apple Sauce [F][S][C][M]

I like to use two different kinds of apples for this and serve it as a condiment or side dish to turkey, pork, fish or chicken. It's also nice as a dessert topping over vanilla ice cream, yogurt or cheesecake.

—**KYE FEASEL** CANAL WINCHESTER, OHIO

PREP: 15 MIN. **COOK:** 20 MIN. **MAKES:** ABOUT 5 CUPS

- 1 can (20 ounces) unsweetened pineapple tidbits, undrained
- 1 package (12 ounces) fresh or frozen cranberries
- 2 medium apples, peeled and cut into ½-inch pieces
- ½ cup sugar
- ¼ cup pitted dried plums, chopped
- 1 teaspoon ground cinnamon
- ¼ teaspoon ground cloves
- ¼ teaspoon ground nutmeg

1. In a large saucepan, combine all ingredients. Cook over medium heat until berries pop and apples are tender, about 20 minutes. Remove from the heat; mash if desired.

2. Transfer to a large bowl; chill until serving.

Nutrition Facts: ¼ cup equals 53 calories, trace fat (trace saturated fat), 0 cholesterol, 3 mg sodium, 14 g carbohydrate, 1 g fiber, trace protein. **Diabetic Exchange:** ½ starch.

Harvest Squash Casserole [M]

This is a healthy recipe flavored with autumn cranberries and pecans. It goes very well with a roasted turkey and makes a colorful side dish.

—**MARY ANN LEE** CLIFTON PARK, NEW YORK

PREP: 35 MIN. **BAKE:** 40 MIN. **MAKES:** 10 SERVINGS

- 1 large butternut squash (about 6 pounds), peeled, seeded and cubed
- 1 large onion, finely chopped
- 1 tablespoon butter
- 2 garlic cloves, minced
- 3 eggs, lightly beaten
- 2 tablespoons sugar
- 2 teaspoons salt
- ½ teaspoon pepper
- 1 cup chopped fresh or frozen cranberries
- ¾ cup chopped pecans

TOPPING

- 2 cups soft whole wheat bread crumbs
- 2 tablespoons butter, melted

1. Place squash in a Dutch oven; cover with water. Bring to a boil. Reduce heat; cover and cook for 15-20 minutes or just until tender. Drain. In a large bowl, mash squash and set aside.

2. In a large nonstick skillet, saute onion in butter until tender. Add garlic; cook 1 minute longer. Add to squash. Stir in the eggs, sugar, salt and pepper. Gently fold in cranberries and pecans. Transfer to a 13-in. x 9-in. baking dish coated with cooking spray.

3. For topping, combine bread crumbs and melted butter; sprinkle over casserole. Bake at 350° for 40-45 minutes or until a knife inserted near the center comes out clean.

Nutrition Facts: ¾ cup equals 273 calories, 12 g fat (3 g saturated fat), 72 mg cholesterol, 593 mg sodium, 39 g carbohydrate, 10 g fiber, 7 g protein.

78

85

82

Good Mornings

"My girlfriend loves pumpkin, so I enjoy making this for her on cool Sunday mornings. I like to freeze homemade pumpkin puree in 1-cup batches because I find the flavor infinitely more satisfying."

CHARLES INSLER SILVER SPRING, MARYLAND
about his recipe, Buttermilk Pumpkin Waffles, on page 86

Fruity Smoothies F S M

Because grapes and blueberries are loaded with antioxidants, this powerful combination can help stop platelet clumping and lower your risk of heart disease. Strawberry or blueberry yogurt also work with the flavors in this smoothie.

—JULIE PUDERBAUGH BERWICK, PENNSYLVANIA

PREP/TOTAL TIME: 10 MIN. **MAKES:** 3 SERVINGS

- 2 tablespoons orange juice
- 2 tablespoons cherry juice blend
- 1 cup fresh strawberries, hulled
- 1 cup seedless red grapes
- ¾ cup (6 ounces) raspberry yogurt
- ½ cup fresh or frozen blueberries
  Red grapes and fresh strawberries, optional

In a blender, combine all ingredients; cover and process for 20-30 seconds or until blended. Pour into chilled glasses; garnish with grapes and strawberries if desired. Serve immediately.

Nutrition Facts: ¾ cup (calculated without garnishes) equals 137 calories, 1 g fat (1 g saturated fat), 3 mg cholesterol, 35 mg sodium, 30 g carbohydrate, 2 g fiber, 3 g protein. **Diabetic Exchanges:** 1 fruit, ½ reduced-fat milk.

Banana Oatmeal Pancakes M

 These pancakes have less sodium per serving than other pancakes made from mixes. Decrease sodium even further by stretching the mix with banana, oats and walnuts. In our house we just sprinkle these with a little confectioners' sugar, because the fruit is so sweet you don't need syrup.

—PATRICIA SWART GALLOWAY, NEW JERSEY

PREP: 10 MIN. **COOK:** 5 MIN./BATCH **MAKES:** 16 PANCAKES

- 2 cups complete whole wheat pancake mix
- 1 large firm banana, finely chopped
- ½ cup old-fashioned oats
- ¼ cup chopped walnuts

Prepare pancake batter according to package directions. Stir in the banana, oats and walnuts. Pour batter by ¼ cupfuls onto a hot griddle coated with cooking spray; turn when bubbles form on top. Cook until the second side is golden brown.

Nutrition Facts: 2 pancakes equals 155 calories, 4 g fat (trace saturated fat), 0 cholesterol, 293 mg sodium, 28 g carbohydrate, 4 g fiber, 7 g protein. **Diabetic Exchange:** 2 starch.

 top tip Instead of using syrup, *Healthy Cooking* Food Editor and Registered Dietitian Peggy Woodward thaws frozen berries to top her pancakes in the morning. The fruit's juice soaks into the pancakes much like syrup and tastes just as sweet while adding a healthy dose of antioxidants to start the day.

Scrambled Egg Pockets M

We used a simple homemade pizza dough to make these protein- and fiber-packed egg pockets, but a store-bought dough works, too. They make a great handheld breakfast on the go or an easy weeknight dinner.
—**HEALTHY COOKING TEST KITCHEN**

PREP: 20 MIN. **BAKE:** 15 MIN. **MAKES:** 4 SERVINGS

- 2 **cups egg substitute, divided**
- ½ **cup shredded part-skim mozzarella cheese**
- ¼ **cup oil-packed sun-dried tomatoes, chopped**
- 1 **tablespoon minced fresh basil or 1 teaspoon dried basil**
- 1 **lb. prepared pizza dough**
- 2 **tablespoons grated Parmesan cheese**

1. Set aside 2 tablespoons egg substitute. In a large nonstick skillet coated with cooking spray, cook and stir remaining egg substitute over medium heat until almost set. Stir in mozzarella cheese, tomatoes and basil. Cook and stir until completely set. Remove from the heat.
2. On a floured surface, roll dough into a 13-in. square. Cut into four squares; transfer to a 15-in. x 10-in. x 1-in. baking pan coated with cooking spray. Spoon egg mixture over half of each square to within ½ in. of edges.
3. Brush edges of dough with 1 tablespoon reserved egg substitute. Fold one corner over filling to the opposite corner, forming a triangle; press edges with a fork to seal. Cut slits in top. Brush with remaining egg substitute; sprinkle with Parmesan cheese. Bake at 400° for 12-15 minutes or until golden brown.

Nutrition Facts: *1 pocket equals 351 calories, 8 g fat (3 g saturated fat), 10 mg cholesterol, 669 mg sodium, 47 g carbohydrate, 8 g fiber, 25 g protein.*

Gluten-Free Baked Oatmeal M

Sometimes I treat myself to a few chocolate chips sprinkled on this fruity, delicious oatmeal. It's also good served with vanilla soy milk.
—**JENNIFER BANYAY** NORTHRIDGEVILLE, OHIO

PREP: 15 MIN. **BAKE:** 30 MIN. **MAKES:** 6 SERVINGS

- ½ **cup raisins**
- 1½ **cups boiling water**
- 2 **cups gluten-free old-fashioned oats**
- ⅓ **cup packed brown sugar**
- 1 **teaspoon pumpkin pie spice**
- ¼ **teaspoon salt**
- 1¼ **cups fat-free milk**
- 1 **medium apple, peeled and finely chopped**
- 2 **tablespoons butter, melted**
- ¼ **cup chopped walnuts**

1. Place raisins in a small bowl. Cover with boiling water; let stand for 5 minutes.
2. Meanwhile, in a large bowl, combine the oats, brown sugar, pie spice and salt. Stir in the milk, apple and butter. Let stand for 5 minutes. Drain raisins; stir into oat mixture.
3. Transfer to an 8-in. square baking dish coated with cooking spray. Sprinkle with walnuts. Bake, uncovered, at 350° for 30-35 minutes or until a knife inserted near the center comes out clean.

Editor's Note: *Read all ingredient labels for possible gluten content prior to use. Ingredient formulas can change, and production facilities vary among brands. If you're concerned that your brand may contain gluten, contact the company.*

Nutrition Facts: *⅔ cup equals 275 calories, 9 g fat (3 g saturated fat), 11 mg cholesterol, 154 mg sodium, 45 g carbohydrate, 4 g fiber, 7 g protein.* **Diabetic Exchanges:** *2 starch, 1 fruit, 1 fat.*

Strawberry Banana Blast F S C M

PREP/TOTAL TIME: 10 MIN.
MAKES: 4 SERVINGS

- 1 **cup orange juice**
- 2 **cups frozen unsweetened strawberries**
- 1 **medium banana, sliced and frozen**
- ¾ **cup (6 ounces) strawberry-banana yogurt**

In a blender, combine all ingredients; cover and process until blended. Pour into chilled glasses; serve immediately.

Nutrition Facts: *1 cup equals 122 calories, 1 g fat (trace saturated fat), 2 mg cholesterol, 24 mg sodium, 28 g carbohydrate, 2 g fiber, 3 g protein.* **Diabetic Exchanges:** *1½ fruit, ½ starch.*

Baked Peach Pancake M

For presentation, I take this right from the oven to the table, fill it with peaches and sour cream and serve it with bacon or ham.

—NANCY WILKINSON
PRINCETON, NEW JERSEY

PREP: 10 MIN. **BAKE:** 25 MIN.
MAKES: 6 SERVINGS

- 2 **cups fresh or frozen sliced peeled peaches**
- 4 **teaspoons sugar**
- 1 **teaspoon lemon juice**
- 3 **eggs**
- ½ **cup all-purpose flour**
- ½ **cup whole milk**
- ½ **teaspoon salt**
- 2 **tablespoons butter**
  Ground nutmeg
  Sour cream, optional

1. In a small bowl, combine peaches, sugar and lemon juice; set aside. In a large bowl, beat eggs until fluffy. Add the flour, milk and salt; beat until smooth.
2. Place butter in a 10-in. ovenproof skillet in a 400° oven for 3-5 minutes or until melted. Immediately pour batter into hot skillet. Bake for 20-25 minutes or until pancake has risen and puffed all over.
3. Fill with peach slices and sprinkle with nutmeg. Serve immediately with sour cream if desired.

Nutrition Facts: *1 piece (calculated without sour cream) equals 157 calories, 7 g fat (4 g saturated fat), 119 mg cholesterol, 277 mg sodium, 18 g carbohydrate, 1 g fiber, 5 g protein.* **Diabetic Exchanges:** *1 medium-fat meat, 1 fat, ½ starch, ½ fruit.*

This thick and creamy smoothie was created for the strawberry lover, but the banana flavor comes through nicely. It's refreshing without being too sweet and makes a fruity mid-morning snack. **—COLLEEN BELBEY** WARWICK, RHODE ISLAND

Makeover Brie and Sausage Brunch Bake

I've made this for holidays, as well as for a weekend at a friend's cabin, and I always get requests for the recipe. It's a convenient make-ahead dish that reheats well and still tastes great the next day.

—BECKY HICKS FOREST LAKE, MINNESOTA

PREP: 30 MIN. + CHILLING **BAKE:** 40 MIN. + STANDING
MAKES: 12 SERVINGS

- 1 **pound lean ground turkey**
- 1 **small onion, chopped**
- 1 **teaspoon fennel seed**
- 1¼ **teaspoons pepper, divided**
- ¼ **teaspoon cayenne pepper**
- ⅛ **teaspoon ground nutmeg**
- 8 **cups cubed day-old sourdough bread**
- ½ **cup chopped roasted sweet red peppers**
- 6 **ounces Brie cheese, rind removed and cubed**
- ½ **cup grated Parmesan cheese**
- 2 **tablespoons minced fresh basil or 2 teaspoons dried basil**
- 2 **cups egg substitute**
- 2 **cups 2% milk**
- 1 **tablespoon Dijon mustard**
- 1 **cup (4 ounces) shredded part-skim mozzarella cheese**
- 3 **green onions, sliced**

1. In a large skillet, cook the turkey, onion, fennel, ¼ teaspoon pepper, cayenne and nutmeg over medium heat until meat is no longer pink; drain.
2. Place bread cubes in a 13-in. x 9-in. baking dish coated with cooking spray. Layer with turkey mixture, red peppers, Brie and Parmesan cheeses and basil. In a large bowl, whisk the egg substitute, milk, mustard and remaining pepper; pour over top. Cover and refrigerate overnight.
3. Remove from the refrigerator 30 minutes before baking. Bake, uncovered, at 350° for 35-40 minutes or until a knife inserted near the center comes out clean.
4. Sprinkle with mozzarella cheese. Bake 4-6 minutes longer or until cheese is melted. Let stand for 10 minutes before cutting. Sprinkle with green onions.

Nutrition Facts: *1 piece equals 260 calories, 11 g fat (5 g saturated fat), 55 mg cholesterol, 545 mg sodium, 18 g carbohydrate, 1 g fiber, 21 g protein.* **Diabetic Exchanges:** *2 lean meat, 1½ fat, 1 starch.*

Turkey Breakfast Sausage **C**

These hearty patties are loaded with flavor but contain a fraction of the sodium and fat found in commercial breakfast sausage links.

—JUDY CULBERTSON DANSVILLE, NEW YORK

PREP/TOTAL TIME: 25 MIN. **MAKES:** 8 SERVINGS

- 1 **pound lean ground turkey**
- ¾ **teaspoon salt**
- ½ **teaspoon rubbed sage**
- ½ **teaspoon pepper**
- ¼ **teaspoon ground ginger**

1. Crumble turkey into a large bowl. Add the salt, sage, pepper and ginger. Shape into eight 2-in. patties.
2. In a nonstick skillet coated with cooking spray, cook patties over medium heat for 6-8 minutes on each side or until a thermometer reads 165° and juices run clear.

Nutrition Facts: *1 patty equals 85 calories, 5 g fat (1 g saturated fat), 45 mg cholesterol, 275 mg sodium, trace carbohydrate, trace fiber, 10 g protein.* **Diabetic Exchanges:** *1 lean meat, ½ fat.*

Onion-Garlic Hash Browns **S C**

I love to top my finished hash browns with a sprinkling of chopped parsley and shredded cheddar cheese.

—CINDI HAYWARD-BOGER ARDMORE, ALABAMA

PREP: 20 MIN. **COOK:** 3 HOURS **MAKES:** 12 SERVINGS

- 1 **large red onion, chopped**
- 1 **small sweet red pepper, chopped**
- 1 **small green pepper, chopped**
- ¼ **cup butter, cubed**
- 1 **tablespoon olive oil**
- 4 **garlic cloves, minced**
- 1 **package (30 ounces) frozen shredded hash brown potatoes**
- ½ **teaspoon salt**
- ½ **teaspoon pepper**
- 3 **drops hot pepper sauce, optional**

1. In a large skillet, saute onion and peppers in butter and oil until crisp-tender. Add garlic; cook 1 minute longer. Stir in the hash browns, salt, pepper and pepper sauce if desired.
2. Transfer to a 5-qt. slow cooker coated with cooking spray. Cover and cook on low for 3-4 hours or until heated through.

Nutrition Facts: *½ cup equals 110 calories, 5 g fat (3 g saturated fat), 10 mg cholesterol, 136 mg sodium, 15 g carbohydrate, 1 g fiber, 2 g protein.* **Diabetic Exchanges:** *1 starch, 1 fat.*

Smoked Salmon Quiche

My son fishes for salmon on the Kenai River in Alaska and smokes much of what he catches. My mother passed this recipe on to me to help me find new ways to cook with salmon. Regular salmon also works in this quiche, but the smoked flavor can't be beat!

—ROSE MARIE CHERVEN ANCHORAGE, ALASKA

PREP: 30 MIN. **BAKE:** 35 MIN. + STANDING **MAKES:** 8 SERVINGS

- 1 sheet refrigerated pie pastry
- 1 cup (4 ounces) shredded reduced-fat Swiss cheese
- 1 tablespoon all-purpose flour
- 3 plum tomatoes, seeded and chopped
- 2 tablespoons finely chopped onion
- 2 teaspoons canola oil
- 3 ounces smoked salmon fillet, flaked (about ½ cup)
- 4 eggs
- 1 cup whole milk
- ¼ teaspoon salt

1. On a lightly floured surface, unroll pastry. Transfer to a 9-in. pie plate. Trim pastry to ½ in. beyond edge of plate; flute edges.
2. In a small bowl, combine cheese and flour. Transfer to pastry.
3. In a large skillet, saute tomatoes and onion in oil just until tender. Remove from heat; stir in salmon. Spoon over cheese mixture.
4. In a small bowl, whisk the eggs, milk and salt. Pour into pastry. Bake at 350° for 35-40 minutes or until a knife inserted near the center comes out clean. Let stand for 15 minutes before cutting.

Nutrition Facts: *1 piece equals 235 calories, 13 g fat (5 g saturated fat), 122 mg cholesterol, 348 mg sodium, 17 g carbohydrate, trace fiber, 12 g protein.* **Diabetic Exchanges:** *2 medium-fat meat, 1 starch.*

Green Eggs and Ham Sandwiches

PREP/TOTAL TIME: 20 MIN.
MAKES: 4 SERVINGS

- 4 eggs
- ¼ cup fat-free milk
- 3 tablespoons prepared pesto
- 4 whole wheat English muffins, split and toasted
- 2 slices deli ham, halved
- 4 slices reduced-fat provolone cheese

1. Heat a 10-in. nonstick skillet coated with cooking spray over medium heat. Whisk the eggs, milk and pesto. Add to skillet (mixture should set immediately at edges).
2. As eggs set, push cooked edges toward the center, letting uncooked portion flow underneath. When the eggs are set and top appears glossy, remove from skillet and cut into quarters.
3. On each English muffin bottom, layer ham, eggs and cheese. Replace tops.

Nutrition Facts: *1 sandwich equals 329 calories, 15 g fat (5 g saturated fat), 230 mg cholesterol, 716 mg sodium, 29 g carbohydrate, 5 g fiber, 22 g protein.*

Chia Orange Yogurt ⑤Ⓜ

Chia seeds deliver a big doses of high-quality fat—they're 34 percent pure omega-3 oils. They also deliver fiber, calcium, phosphorus, magnesium, manganese, copper, iron and zinc. I love this chia yogurt parfait because it tastes like you're eating dessert for breakfast.

—MARION MCNEILL MAYFIELD HTS, OHIO

PREP: 10 MIN. + CHILLING
MAKES: 1 SERVING

- ⅓ cup fat-free milk or almond milk
- ¼ cup old-fashioned oats
- ¼ cup reduced-fat plain Greek yogurt
- 1 tablespoon orange marmalade spreadable fruit
- 1½ teaspoons chia seeds
- ¼ teaspoon vanilla extract
- ⅓ cup orange segments, chopped

In a jar with a tight-fitting lid, combine the milk, oats, yogurt, marmalade, chia seeds and vanilla. Cover and shake to combine. Stir in orange segments. Cover and refrigerate for 8 hours or overnight.

Nutrition Facts: *1 cup equals 245 calories, 5 g fat (1 g saturated fat), 5 mg cholesterol, 59 mg sodium, 39 g carbohydrate, 6 g fiber, 13 g protein.* **Diabetic Exchanges:** *2½ starch, 1 lean meat.*

Makeover Real-Man Quiche

This quiche is one of my husband's favorites, probably because it has bacon. Sometimes I add sliced fresh white or baby portobello mushrooms and saute them with the onions for more "meatiness." The makeover version looks wonderful!

—**RUBY HOCHSTETLER** HOLLAND, MICHIGAN

PREP: 15 MIN. **BAKE:** 35 MIN. + STANDING
MAKES: 2 QUICHES (8 SERVINGS EACH)

- 1 package (14.1 ounces) refrigerated pie pastry
- 8 bacon strips
- 2 large onions, chopped
- 8 egg whites
- 4 eggs
- 3 cups fat-free milk
- 3 cups (12 ounces) shredded part-skim mozzarella cheese
- 1 package (10 ounces) frozen chopped spinach, thawed and squeezed dry
- ½ cup chopped sun-dried tomatoes (not packed in oil)
- 2 tablespoons cornstarch
- 1 teaspoon dried basil
- ½ teaspoon pepper

1. On a lightly floured surface, unroll pastries. Transfer to two 9-in. pie plates. Trim pastry to ½ in. beyond edge of plate; flute edges.

2. In a large nonstick skillet, cook bacon over medium heat until crisp. Remove to paper towels with a slotted spoon; drain and crumble. In the same skillet, saute onions until tender.

3. In a large bowl, whisk the egg whites, egg, milk, cheese, spinach, onions, tomatoes, cornstarch, basil and pepper. Divide between pastries. Sprinkle with bacon.

4. Bake at 375° for 35-40 minutes or until a knife inserted near the center comes out clean. Let stand for 10 minutes before cutting.

Nutrition Facts: *1 piece equals 248 calories, 13 g fat (6 g saturated fat), 75 mg cholesterol, 378 mg sodium, 20 g carbohydrate, 1 g fiber, 13 g protein.*

Overnight Brunch Casserole

I love to cook for company and host brunches frequently. Standing out from most egg bakes, this casserole combines scrambled eggs and a cheese sauce that bake up into a rich and creamy dish.

—**CANDACE HESCH** MOSINEE, WISCONSIN

PREP: 30 MIN. + CHILLING **BAKE:** 40 MIN. + STANDING
MAKES: 12 SERVINGS

- 3 tablespoons butter, divided
- 2 tablespoons all-purpose flour
- ½ teaspoon salt
- ⅛ teaspoon pepper
- 2 cups fat-free milk
- 5 slices reduced-fat process American cheese product, chopped
- 1½ cups sliced fresh mushrooms
- 2 green onions, finely chopped
- 1 cup cubed fully cooked ham
- 2 cups egg substitute
- 4 eggs

TOPPING
- 3 slices whole wheat bread, cubed
- 4 teaspoons butter, melted
- ⅛ teaspoon paprika

1. In a large saucepan, melt 2 tablespoons butter. Stir in the flour, salt and pepper until smooth; gradually add milk. Bring to a boil; cook and stir for 2 minutes or until slightly thickened. Stir in cheese until melted. Remove from the heat.

2. In a large nonstick skillet, saute mushrooms and green onions in remaining butter until tender. Add ham; heat through. Whisk egg substitute and eggs; add to skillet. Cook and stir until almost set. Stir in cheese sauce.

3. Transfer to a 13-in. x 9-in. baking dish coated with cooking spray. Toss bread cubes with butter. Arrange over egg mixture; sprinkle with paprika. Cover and refrigerate overnight.

4. Remove from the refrigerator 30 minutes before baking. Bake, uncovered, at 350° for 40-45 minutes or until a knife inserted near the center comes out clean. Let stand for 10 minutes before cutting.

Nutrition Facts: *1 piece equals 150 calories, 7 g fat (4 g saturated fat), 91 mg cholesterol, 509 mg sodium, 8 g carbohydrate, 1 g fiber, 13 g protein.* **Diabetic Exchanges:** *2 lean meat, 1 fat, ½ starch.*

Apple-Raisin Baked Oatmeal Ⓜ

PREP: 20 MIN. **BAKE:** 35 MIN.
MAKES: 6 SERVINGS

- 3 cups old-fashioned oats
- ½ cup packed brown sugar
- 2 teaspoons baking powder
- 1½ teaspoons ground cinnamon
- ½ teaspoon salt
- ⅛ teaspoon ground nutmeg
- 2 eggs
- 2 cups fat-free milk
- 1 medium apple, chopped
- ⅓ cup raisins
- ⅓ cup chopped walnuts

1. In a large bowl, combine the first six ingredients. Whisk eggs and milk; stir into dry ingredients until blended. Let stand for 5 minutes. Stir in the apple, raisins and walnuts.

2. Transfer to an 8-in. square baking dish coated with cooking spray. Bake, uncovered, at 350° for 35-40 minutes or until edges are lightly browned and a thermometer reads 160°.

Nutrition Facts: *1 piece (calculated without additional milk) equals 349 calories, 9 g fat (1 g saturated fat), 72 mg cholesterol, 397 mg sodium, 60 g carbohydrate, 5 g fiber, 12 g protein.*

Creamy Orange Smoothies Ⓢ Ⓜ

I love this citrus-showcasing combo of orange flavors blended with cream cheese.

—**ROXANNE CHAN** ALBANY, CALiFORNIA

PREP/TOTAL TIME: 15 MIN.
MAKES: 12 SERVINGS (¾ CUP EACH)

- 4 cups orange juice
- 3 containers (6 ounces each) orange creme yogurt
- 3 medium bananas, peeled and cut into chunks
- 2 cans (11 ounces each) mandarin oranges, drained
- 6 ounces reduced-fat cream cheese, cubed

Place half of each ingredient in a blender; cover and process until blended. Transfer to a large pitcher. Repeat, adding second batch to the same pitcher; stir to combine. Serve immediately or chill until serving.

Nutrition Facts: *¾ cup equals 159 calories, 4 g fat (2 g saturated fat), 12 mg cholesterol, 85 mg sodium, 29 g carbohydrate, 1 g fiber, 4 g protein.*

Buttermilk Pumpkin Waffles M

My girlfriend loves pumpkin, so I enjoy making this for her on cool Sunday mornings. I like to freeze homemade pumpkin puree in 1-cup batches because I find the flavor infinitely more satisfying.

—CHARLES INSLER SILVER SPRING, MARYLAND

PREP: 20 MIN. **COOK:** 5 MIN./BATCH **MAKES:** 6 SERVINGS

- ¾ cup all-purpose flour
- ½ cup whole wheat flour
- 2 tablespoons brown sugar
- 1 teaspoon baking powder
- 1 teaspoon ground cinnamon
- ½ teaspoon ground ginger
- ¼ teaspoon baking soda
- ¼ teaspoon salt
- ¼ teaspoon ground cloves
- 2 eggs
- 1¼ cups buttermilk
- ½ cup fresh or canned pumpkin
- 2 tablespoons butter, melted
  Butter and maple syrup, optional

1. In a large bowl, combine the first nine ingredients. In a small bowl, whisk the eggs, buttermilk, pumpkin and butter. Stir into dry ingredients just until moistened.
2. Bake in a preheated waffle iron according to manufacturer's directions until golden brown. Serve with butter and syrup if desired.
Nutrition Facts: *2 waffles (calculated without butter and syrup) equals 194 calories, 6 g fat (3 g saturated fat), 83 mg cholesterol, 325 mg sodium, 28 g carbohydrate, 3 g fiber, 7 g protein.* **Diabetic Exchanges:** *2 starch, 1 fat.*

Lime-Honey Fruit Salad F S M

Nothing is more refreshing to me than a seasonal fruit salad enhanced with this simple lime-honey dressing.

—VICTORIA SHEVLIN CAPE CORAL, FLORIDA

PREP: 20 MIN. + CHILLING **MAKES:** 12 SERVINGS (¾ CUP EACH)

- 1 teaspoon cornstarch
- ¼ cup lime juice
- ¼ cup honey
- ½ teaspoon poppy seeds
- 3 medium Gala or Red Delicious apples, cubed
- 2 medium pears, cubed
- 2 cups seedless red grapes
- 2 cups green grapes

1. In a small microwave-safe bowl, combine cornstarch and lime juice until smooth. Microwave, uncovered, on high for 20 seconds; stir. Cook 15 seconds longer; stir. Stir in honey and poppy seeds.
2. In a large bowl, combine the apples, pears and grapes. Pour dressing over fruit; toss to coat. Cover and refrigerate overnight.
Editor's Note: *This recipe was tested in a 1,100-watt microwave.*
Nutrition Facts: *¾ cup equals 96 calories, trace fat (trace saturated fat), 0 cholesterol, 2 mg sodium, 25 g carbohydrate, 2 g fiber, 1 g protein.* **Diabetic Exchange:** *1½ fruit.*

Sausage and Egg Grits

I always mix my sausage, grits and eggs together so I thought it would be great to make a casserole that did the same. It's loaded with down-home flavor without using any butter!

—JEANNINE QUILLER RALEIGH, NORTH CAROLINA

PREP: 15 MIN. **COOK:** 20 MIN. **MAKES:** 6 SERVINGS

- 4 ounces breakfast turkey sausage links, casings removed
- 1½ cups egg substitute
- 1¼ cups whole milk, divided
- 3 cups water
- ⅛ teaspoon salt
- 1 cup quick-cooking grits
- ¾ cup shredded reduced-fat cheddar cheese, divided
- 2 green onions, chopped
- ⅛ teaspoon pepper

1. Crumble sausage into a large skillet; cook over medium heat until no longer pink. Remove to paper towels with a slotted spoon. Whisk egg substitute and ¼ cup milk; add to same skillet. Cook and stir until set; remove from the heat.
2. Meanwhile, in a Dutch oven, bring water, salt and remaining milk to a boil. Slowly stir in grits. Reduce heat; cook and stir for 5-7 minutes or until thickened.
3. Stir in half of the cheese. Add the sausage, eggs, green onions and pepper; heat through. Serve in bowls; sprinkle with remaining cheese.
Nutrition Facts: *1 cup equals 208 calories, 6 g fat (3 g saturated fat), 25 mg cholesterol, 369 mg sodium, 24 g carbohydrate, 1 g fiber, 16 g protein.* **Diabetic Exchanges:** *2 lean meat, 1½ starch.*

Raisin Nut Oatmeal M

The oats, fruit and spices in this nostalgic meal bake together overnight. There's no better feeling than waking up to a ready-to-eat hot breakfast.

—**VALERIE SAUBER** ADELANTO, CALIFORNIA

PREP: 10 MIN. **COOK:** 7 HOURS **MAKES:** 6 SERVINGS

- 3½ cups fat-free milk
- 1 large apple, peeled and chopped
- ¾ cup steel-cut oats
- ¾ cup raisins
- 3 tablespoons brown sugar
- 4½ teaspoons butter, melted
- ¾ teaspoon ground cinnamon
- ½ teaspoon salt
- ¼ cup chopped pecans

In a 3-qt. slow cooker coated with cooking spray, combine the first eight ingredients. Cover and cook on low for 7-8 hours or until liquid is absorbed. Spoon oatmeal into bowls; sprinkle with pecans.

Editor's Note: *You may substitute 1½ cups quick-cooking oats for the steel-cut oats and increase the fat-free milk to 4½ cups.*

Nutrition Facts: *¾ cup with 2 teaspoons pecans equals 289 calories, 9 g fat (3 g saturated fat), 10 mg cholesterol, 282 mg sodium, 47 g carbohydrate, 4 g fiber, 9 g protein.*

French Toast with Apple Topping M

Why wait in line for Sunday brunch when you can whip up this simple, elegant French toast for two? You can also double this recipe and use pear instead of apple.

—**JANIS SCHARNOTT** FONTANA, WISCONSIN

PREP/TOTAL TIME: 20 MIN. **MAKES:** 2 SERVINGS

- 1 medium apple, peeled and thinly sliced
- 1 tablespoon brown sugar
- ¼ teaspoon ground cinnamon
- 2 tablespoons reduced-fat butter, divided
- 1 egg
- ¼ cup 2% milk
- 1 teaspoon vanilla extract
- 4 slices French bread (½ inch thick)
  Maple syrup, optional

1. In a large skillet, saute the apple, brown sugar and cinnamon in 1 tablespoon butter until apple is tender.
2. In a shallow bowl, whisk the egg, milk and vanilla. Dip both sides of bread in egg mixture.
3. In a large skillet, melt remaining butter over medium heat. Cook bread on both sides until golden brown. Serve with apple mixture and maple syrup if desired.

Editor's Note: *This recipe was tested with Land O'Lakes light stick butter.*

Nutrition Facts: *2 slices with ¼ cup apple mixture (calculated without syrup) equals 219 calories, 10 g fat (5 g saturated fat), 113 mg cholesterol, 279 mg sodium, 29 g carbohydrate, 2 g fiber, 6 g protein.*
Diabetic Exchanges: *1½ starch, 1½ fat, ½ fruit.*

Banana French Toast Bake M

Hamburger buns and bananas come together in this whimsical, make-ahead dish the whole family will love. It's the ultimate breakfast for dinner.

—**NANCY ZIMMERMAN** CAPE MAY COURT HOUSE, NEW JERSEY

PREP: 20 MIN. + CHILLING **BAKE:** 55 MIN. + STANDING
MAKES: 8 SERVINGS

- 6 whole wheat hamburger buns
- 1 package (8 ounces) reduced-fat cream cheese
- 3 medium bananas, sliced
- 6 eggs
- 4 cups fat-free milk
- ¼ cup sugar
- ¼ cup maple syrup
- ½ teaspoon ground cinnamon

1. Cut buns into 1-in. cubes; place half in a 13-in. x 9-in. baking dish coated with cooking spray. Cut cream cheese into ¾-in. cubes; place over buns. Top with the bananas and remaining bun cubes.
2. In a large bowl, beat eggs. Add milk, sugar, syrup and cinnamon; mix well. Pour over bun mixture. Cover and refrigerate for 8 hours or overnight.
3. Remove from the refrigerator 30 minutes before baking. Cover and bake at 350° for 30 minutes. Uncover; bake 25-30 minutes longer or until a knife inserted near the center comes out clean. Let stand for 10 minutes before serving.

Nutrition Facts: *1 serving equals 341 calories, 12 g fat (6 g saturated fat), 181 mg cholesterol, 379 mg sodium, 47 g carbohydrate, 4 g fiber, 15 g protein.*

96

92

94

Ready in 30

❝Tropical and flavorful, this breakfast pizza puts a fun spin on breakfast for dinner. Kids love layering on the toppings, and it's a great way to use leftover ham.❞

HOLLY CIANI TABERG, NEW YORK
about her recipe, Hawaiian Breakfast Pizza, on page 93

Cantaloupe Chicken Salad with Yogurt Chive Dressing

It's hard to find recipes that my four children and husband love. That's why this refreshing combination of melon and chicken is so special to our family.

—ELIZABETH KING DULUTH, MINNESOTA

PREP/TOTAL TIME: 30 MIN. **MAKES:** 5 SERVINGS

- ½ **cup plain yogurt**
- ½ **cup reduced-fat mayonnaise**
- 1 **tablespoon minced chives**
- 1 **tablespoon lime juice**
- ¼ **teaspoon salt**
- 5 **cups cubed cantaloupe**
- 2½ **cups cubed cooked chicken breast**
- 1 **medium cucumber, seeded and chopped**
- 1 **cup green grapes, halved**

In a large bowl, combine the first five ingredients. Add the cantaloupe, chicken, cucumber and grapes; toss gently to combine. Chill until serving.

Nutrition Facts: *2 cups equals 290 calories, 11 g fat (2 g saturated fat), 65 mg cholesterol, 380 mg sodium, 24 g carbohydrate, 2 g fiber, 24 g protein.* **Diabetic Exchanges:** *3 lean meat, 1½ fruit, 1 fat.*

Sesame-Orange Salmon C

We're always looking for new and interesting ways to prepare salmon. Here, an Asian-inspired butter lends ideal flavor for citrus lovers. Using reduced-fat butter saves 40 calories and 4 grams of fat per serving but still adds a generous coating to the salmon.

—HEALTHY COOKING TEST KITCHEN

PREP/TOTAL TIME: 15 MIN. **MAKES:** 2 SERVINGS

- 2 **salmon fillets (4 ounces each)**
- 5 **teaspoons reduced-fat butter, melted**
- 1½ **teaspoons reduced-sodium soy sauce**
- ¾ **teaspoon grated orange peel**
- ½ **teaspoon sesame seeds**

Place salmon skin side down on a broiler pan. Combine butter, soy sauce, orange peel and sesame seeds. Brush one-third of mixture over salmon. Broil 3-4 in. from the heat for 7-9 minutes or until fish flakes easily with a fork, basting occasionally with remaining butter mixture.

Editor's Note: *This recipe was tested with Land O'Lakes light stick butter.*

Nutrition Facts: *1 fillet equals 225 calories, 16 g fat (5 g saturated fat), 69 mg cholesterol, 288 mg sodium, 1 g carbohydrate, trace fiber, 20 g protein.* **Diabetic Exchanges:** *3 lean meat, 1½ fat.*

Sausage Spinach Salad C

A fast way to turn a tangy summer salad into a hearty meal is to add sausage. I use chicken sausage but you can use different varieties and flavors. The mustard dressing is also nice with smoked salmon or chicken.

—DEB WILLIAMS PEORIA, ARIZONA

PREP/TOTAL TIME: 20 MIN. **MAKES:** 2 SERVINGS

- 2 **fully cooked Italian chicken sausage links (3 ounces each), cut into ¼-inch slices**
- ½ **medium onion, halved and sliced**
- 4 **teaspoons olive oil, divided**
- 4 **cups fresh baby spinach**
- 1½ **teaspoons balsamic vinegar**
- 1 **teaspoon stone-ground mustard**

1. In a large nonstick skillet coated with cooking spray, cook sausage and onion in 1 teaspoon oil until sausage is browned.
2. Meanwhile, place spinach in a large bowl. In a small bowl, whisk the vinegar, mustard and remaining oil. Drizzle over spinach; toss to coat. Stir in sausage mixture; serve immediately.

Nutrition Facts: *2½ cups equals 244 calories, 16 g fat (3 g saturated fat), 65 mg cholesterol, 581 mg sodium, 8 g carbohydrate, 2 g fiber, 17 g protein.* **Diabetic Exchanges:** *2 lean meat, 2 vegetable, 2 fat.*

Green Chili Breakfast Burritos

PREP/TOTAL TIME: 25 MIN.
MAKES: 6 SERVINGS

- 6 **eggs**
- 3 **egg whites**
- 1 **jalapeno pepper, seeded and minced**
   Dash cayenne pepper
- 4 **breakfast turkey sausage links, casings removed**
- ¾ **cup shredded reduced-fat Mexican cheese blend**
- 1 **can (4 ounces) chopped green chilies, drained**
- 6 **whole wheat tortillas (8 inches), warmed**
- 6 **tablespoons salsa**

1. In a small bowl, whisk the eggs, egg whites, jalapeno and cayenne; set aside.

2. Crumble sausage into a large skillet; cook over medium heat until no longer pink. Drain. Push sausage to the sides of pan. Pour egg mixture into center of pan. Cook and stir until set. Sprinkle with cheese and chilies. Remove from the heat; cover and let stand until cheese is melted.

3. Place ⅓ cup mixture off center on each tortilla. Fold sides and end over filling and roll up. Top with salsa.

Editor's Note: *Wear disposable gloves when cutting hot peppers; the oils can burn skin. Avoid touching your face.*

Nutrition Facts: *1 burrito with 1 tablespoon salsa equals 290 calories, 12 g fat (3 g saturated fat), 232 mg cholesterol, 586 mg sodium, 25 g carbohydrate, 2 g fiber, 19 g protein.* **Diabetic Exchanges:** *2 medium-fat meat, 1½ starch.*

? Did you know?

The official state question in New Mexico is "Red or Green?" In a restaurant, this refers to the type of chili you want with your meal. If you can't decide, order "Christmas," and you'll be served both.

Better-For-You Buttermilk Pancakes M

PREP: 15 MIN. **COOK:** 10 MIN./BATCH **MAKES:** 16 PANCAKES

- 1 cup all-purpose flour
- 1 cup whole wheat flour
- 2 tablespoons sugar
- 2 teaspoons baking powder
- 1 teaspoon baking soda
- 2 egg whites
- 1 egg
- 2 cups buttermilk
- 2 tablespoons canola oil
  Fresh mixed berries, optional

1. In a large bowl, combine the first five ingredients. Combine the egg whites, egg, buttermilk and oil; stir into dry ingredients just until moistened.

2. Pour batter by ¼ cupfuls onto a hot griddle coated with cooking spray. Turn when bubbles just form on top; cook until second side is golden brown. Serve with berries if desired.

Nutrition Facts: *2 pancakes (calculated without berries) equals 189 calories, 5 g fat (1 g saturated fat), 29 mg cholesterol, 345 mg sodium, 29 g carbohydrate, 2 g fiber, 7 g protein.* **Diabetic Exchanges:** *2 starch, 1 fat.*

> ❝This recipe is perfect for adding whatever fruits you have on hand. My family's favorite is to add frozen blueberries.❞
>
> —JANET SCHUBERT RIB LAKE, WISCONSIN

Asian Pork and Noodle Soup C

This healthy, light soup is quick to make and has authentic flavor from ginger, sesame, soy sauce and green onions. Cantonese bean thread noodles, also called cellophane noodles, are typically soaked in hot water for 10-15 minutes then rinsed and used in soups and stir-fries.

—**JEAN HINES** GOODYEAR, ARIZONA

PREP/TOTAL TIME: 30 MIN. **MAKES:** 6 SERVINGS

- 2 ounces uncooked bean thread noodles
- 2 medium carrots, cut into ¼-inch diagonal slices
- 1 cup coarsely chopped bok choy
- 1 tablespoon sesame oil
- 1 tablespoon minced fresh gingerroot
- 3½ cups reduced-sodium chicken broth
- 1 cup water
- 1 tablespoon reduced-sodium soy sauce
- ¼ teaspoon coarsely ground pepper
- ¾ cup cubed cooked pork tenderloin
- 3 green onions, thinly sliced diagonally

Soak noodles according to package directions. Meanwhile, in a large saucepan, saute carrots and bok choy in oil until tender. Add ginger; cook 1 minute longer. Stir in the broth, water, soy sauce, pepper and noodles. Bring to a boil. Reduce heat; simmer until noodles are tender. Stir in pork and green onions; heat through.

Nutrition Facts: *1 cup equals 116 calories, 4 g fat (1 g saturated fat), 16 mg cholesterol, 476 mg sodium, 13 g carbohydrate, 1 g fiber, 8 g protein.* **Diabetic Exchanges:** *1 starch, 1 lean meat, ½ fat.*

Salmon with Garlic-Rosemary Butter S C

High in omega-3 fatty acids with a rich flavor, salmon is a healthy choice for anyone trying to include more seafood in their diet. A hint of rosemary is the secret to making this dish stand out from the rest.

—**HEALTHY COOKING TEST KITCHEN**

PREP/TOTAL TIME: 15 MIN. **MAKES:** 2 SERVINGS

- 2 salmon fillets (4 ounces each)
- 5 teaspoons reduced-fat butter, melted

1 garlic clove, minced
¾ teaspoon honey
¼ teaspoon dried rosemary, crushed

Place salmon skin side down on a broiler pan. Combine butter, garlic, honey and rosemary. Brush one-third of mixture over salmon. Broil 3-4 in. from the heat for 7-9 minutes or until fish flakes easily with a fork, basting occasionally with remaining butter mixture.

Editor's Note: *This recipe was tested with Land O'Lakes light stick butter.*

Nutrition Facts: *1 fillet equals 229 calories, 15 g fat (5 g saturated fat), 69 mg cholesterol, 136 mg sodium, 4 g carbohydrate, trace fiber, 19 g protein.* **Diabetic Exchanges:** *3 lean meat, 1½ fat.*

Taco Salad Tacos

I was making tacos one night and noticed I was out of spicy taco sauce. Using a combination of spices and fat-free Catalina salad dressing rescued our family taco night.
—**CHERYL PLAINTE** PRUDENVILLE, MICHIGAN

PREP/TOTAL TIME: 30 MIN. **MAKES:** 4 SERVINGS

1 pound extra-lean ground beef (95% lean)
1 medium onion, chopped
1 tablespoon chili powder
1 teaspoon garlic powder
1 teaspoon reduced-sodium beef bouillon granules
1 teaspoon ground cumin
¼ teaspoon salt
SALAD
3 cups torn romaine
1 large tomato, seeded and chopped
1 medium sweet orange pepper, chopped
3 green onions, chopped
8 taco shells, warmed
½ cup fat-free Catalina salad dressing
Shredded reduced-fat Colby-Monterey Jack cheese and reduced-fat sour cream, optional

1. In a large skillet, cook beef and onion over medium heat until meat is no longer pink. Stir in the chili powder, garlic powder, bouillon, cumin and salt; remove from the heat.
2. In a large bowl, combine the romaine, tomato, orange pepper and green onions. Spoon beef mixture into taco shells; top with salad mixture. Drizzle with dressing. Serve with cheese and sour cream if desired.

Nutrition Facts: *2 tacos (caluated without cheese and sour cream) equals 334 calories, 11 g fat (4 g saturated fat), 65 mg cholesterol, 722 mg sodium, 33 g carbohydrate, 6 g fiber, 26 g protein.* **Diabetic Exchanges:** *3 lean meat, 2 vegetable, 1½ starch.*

Soy Shrimp with Rice Noodles

Rice noodles come in a variety of thicknesses, similar to Italian pastas like fettuccine, linguine and vermicelli. Use whichever shape you prefer in this so-easy Asian-inspired dish.
—**HEALTHY COOKING TEST KITCHEN**

PREP/TOTAL TIME: 20 MIN. **MAKES:** 4 SERVINGS

1 package (8.8 ounces) thin rice noodles
1 cup frozen shelled edamame

1 pound uncooked medium shrimp, peeled and deveined
3 tablespoons olive oil, divided
2 garlic cloves, minced
¼ cup reduced-sodium soy sauce
¼ teaspoon pepper

1. Cook rice noodles according to package directions, adding the edamame during the last 4 minutes of cooking.
2. In a large nonstick skillet, saute shrimp in 2 tablespoons oil for 2 minutes. Add garlic; cook 1-2 minutes longer or until shrimp turn pink.
3. Drain noodle mixture; add to skillet. Stir in the soy sauce, pepper and remaining oil; toss to coat.

Nutrition Facts: *1½ cups equals 444 calories, 14 g fat (2 g saturated fat), 138 mg cholesterol, 744 mg sodium, 50 g carbohydrate, 2 g fiber, 27 g protein.* **Diabetic Exchanges:** *3 starch, 3 lean meat, 2 fat.*

Hawaiian Breakfast Pizza

Tropical and flavorful, this breakfast pizza puts a fun spin on breakfast for dinner. Kids love layering on the toppings, and it's a great way to use leftover ham.
—**HOLLY CIANI** TABERG, NEW YORK

PREP/TOTAL TIME: 30 MIN. **MAKES:** 6 SLICES

1 prebaked 12-inch thin whole wheat pizza crust
6 eggs
¼ teaspoon pepper
1 cup cubed fully cooked ham
1 cup unsweetened pineapple tidbits, drained
¾ cup shredded cheddar cheese
1 tablespoon minced fresh parsley
Salsa and reduced-fat sour cream, optional

1. Place crust on an ungreased 12-in. pizza pan; set aside.
2. Whisk eggs and pepper; stir into a large nonstick skillet coated with cooking spray. Cook and stir over medium heat until almost set. Transfer to pizza crust. Top with ham and pineapple. Sprinkle with cheese.
3. Bake at 400° for 9-12 minutes or until the cheese is melted. Sprinkle with parsley. Serve with salsa and sour cream if desired.

Nutrition Facts: *1 slice (calculated without optional ingredients) equals 294 calories, 12 g fat (6 g saturated fat), 240 mg cholesterol, 688 mg sodium, 28 g carbohydrate, 4 g fiber, 20 g protein.*

Feta Chicken Salad C

I grew up eating lots of chicken because my father was the manager at a poultry facility. This is the one dish that never gets boring.

—CHERYL LUNDQUIST
WAKE FOREST, NORTH CAROLINA

PREP: 20 MIN. + CHILLING
MAKES: 4 SERVINGS

- 2 **cups shredded cooked chicken breasts**
- ½ **cup cherry tomatoes, halved**
- ½ **cup finely chopped red onion**
- ½ **cup chopped seedless cucumber**
- ½ **cup chopped sweet yellow pepper**
- 4 **teaspoons lemon juice**
- 4 **teaspoons olive oil**
- ½ **teaspoon Greek seasoning**
- ½ **teaspoon salt**
- ⅛ **teaspoon pepper**
- ¼ **cup crumbled feta cheese**

In a large bowl, combine the first five ingredients. In a small bowl, whisk the lemon juice, oil, Greek seasoning, salt and pepper. Pour over chicken mixture; toss to coat. Refrigerate for at least 1 hour. Just before serving, sprinkle with cheese.

Nutrition Facts: *1 cup equals 198 calories, 9 g fat (2 g saturated fat), 63 mg cholesterol, 540 mg sodium, 5 g carbohydrate, 1 g fiber, 24 g protein.* **Diabetic Exchanges:** *3 lean meat, 1 vegetable, 1 fat.*

Did you know?

Researchers linked getting a relatively high proportion of calories from monounsaturated fats like those in olive oil with lower rates of cognitive decline—especially when these fats are consumed as part of a typical Mediterranean diet rich in vegetables, whole grains, legumes and fish. Your brain needs these good fats to perform well.

Grilled Sesame Orange Tuna Steaks

This recipe was a collaboration between my son and I. He entered this in a contest because he aspires to be a chef someday. These tuna steaks look fancy, but they're easy to make.

—LORNA MCFADDEN PORT ORCHARD, WASHINGTON

PREP/TOTAL TIME: 25 MIN. **MAKES:** 4 SERVINGS

- 1½ **cups instant brown rice**
- 2 **cups fresh sugar snap peas**
- 2 **tablespoons honey**
- 1 **tablespoon butter**
- 1 **snack-size cup (4 ounces) mandarin oranges, drained**
- ¼ **cup unsalted cashews, coarsely chopped**
- 4 **tuna steaks (6 ounces each)**
- 5 **tablespoons sesame ginger marinade, divided**

1. Cook rice according to package directions. In a large skillet, saute peas and honey in butter until crisp-tender. Add oranges and cashews; cook and stir 1 minute longer.
2. Brush tuna with 2 tablespoons marinade. Moisten a paper towel with cooking oil; using long-handled tongs, lightly coat the grill rack. Grill tuna, covered, over high heat or broil 3-4 in. from the heat for 3-4 minutes on each side for medium-rare or until slightly pink in the center.
3. Brush tuna with remaining marinade; serve with rice and snap pea mixture.

Editor's Note: *This recipe won 3rd place in Healthy Cooking's Summer Sizzle Grilling Contest.*

Nutrition Facts: *1 steak with ¾ cup rice and ½ cup snap pea mixture equals 506 calories, 10 g fat (3 g saturated fat), 84 mg cholesterol, 822 mg sodium, 56 g carbohydrate, 4 g fiber, 47 g protein.*

Asian Citrus Salmon C

A light, citrus-infused marinade makes something special of these salmon fillets that are done in no time flat. If you keep fresh gingerroot in the freezer, it's easier to peel and mince.

—RANDI AMADOR DINUBA, CALIFORNIA

PREP: 20 MIN. + MARINATING **BROIL:** 10 MIN. **MAKES:** 4 SERVINGS

- 1 medium orange
- 4 salmon fillets (6 ounces each)
- ½ cup reduced-sodium soy sauce
- ¼ cup sliced red onion
- ¼ cup olive oil
- 2 garlic cloves, minced
- 2 teaspoons minced fresh gingerroot
- ¼ teaspoon salt
- ⅛ teaspoon pepper
- ½ cup slivered almonds, toasted

1. Finely grate ½ teaspoon peel and squeeze juice from orange; place in a large resealable plastic bag. Add the salmon, soy sauce, onion, oil, garlic and ginger; seal bag and turn to coat. Refrigerate for 30 minutes. Drain and discard marinade.
2. Place salmon on a baking sheet. Broil 4-6 in. from the heat for 10-12 minutes or until fish flakes easily with a fork. Sprinkle with salt and pepper; top with almonds.

Nutrition Facts: *1 fillet equals 382 calories, 25 g fat (4 g saturated fat), 85 mg cholesterol, 475 mg sodium, 6 g carbohydrate, 2 g fiber, 32 g protein.* **Diabetic Exchanges:** *4 lean meat, 3 fat.*

Italian Tilapia C

Fresh Italian flavors turn mild-tasting tilapia fillets into a family-pleasing meal. You could also use a sprinkling of Parmesan cheese in place of fresh mozzarella.

—HEALTHY COOKING TEST KITCHEN

PREP/TOTAL TIME: 25 MIN. **MAKES:** 6 SERVINGS

- 6 tilapia fillets (6 ounces each)
- 1 cup diced tomatoes with roasted garlic
- ½ cup julienned roasted sweet red peppers
- ½ cup sliced fresh mushrooms
- ½ cup diced fresh mozzarella cheese
- ½ teaspoon dried basil

Place fillets in a 15-in. x 10-in. x 1-in. baking pan coated with cooking spray. Top with tomatoes, peppers, mushrooms, cheese and basil. Bake at 400° for 15-20 minutes or until fish flakes easily with a fork.

Nutrition Facts: *1 fillet equals 190 calories, 4 g fat (2 g saturated fat), 90 mg cholesterol, 335 mg sodium, 4 g carbohydrate, trace fiber, 34 g protein.* **Diabetic Exchanges:** *5 lean meat, ½ fat.*

Stuffed-Olive Cod F C

Take advantage of the olive bar in your supermarket and put a new twist on cod. This simple high-protein, low-fat entree is a weeknight lifesaver.

—TRIA OLSEN QUEEN CREEK, ARIZONA

PREP/TOTAL TIME: 25 MIN. **MAKES:** 4 SERVINGS

- 4 cod fillets (6 ounces each)
- 1 teaspoon dried oregano
- ¼ teaspoon salt
- 1 medium lemon, thinly sliced
- ⅓ cup garlic-stuffed olives, halved
- 1 shallot, thinly sliced
- 2 tablespoons water
- 2 tablespoons olive juice

1. Sprinkle fillets with oregano and salt. Place in a large nonstick skillet coated with cooking spray; top the fillets with lemon slices.
2. Arrange olives and shallot around fillets; add water and olive juice. Bring to a boil. Reduce heat; cover and steam for 8-10 minutes or until fish flakes easily with a fork.

Nutrition Facts: *1 fillet equals 163 calories, 3 g fat (trace saturated fat), 65 mg cholesterol, 598 mg sodium, 4 g carbohydrate, trace fiber, 27 g protein.* **Diabetic Exchange:** *4 lean meat.*

What's in the Fridge Frittata C

Great for a last-minute breakfast, brunch or lunch, guests rave about the crab and Swiss combination in this frittata. I also like to use sausage and cheddar with asparagus or whatever's in season.

—DEBORAH POSEY VIRGINIA BEACH, VIRGINIA

PREP/TOTAL TIME: 25 MIN. **MAKES:** 4 SERVINGS

- 6 eggs
- ⅓ cup chopped onion
- ⅓ cup chopped sweet red pepper
- ⅓ cup chopped fresh mushrooms
- 1 tablespoon olive oil
- 1 can (6 ounces) lump crabmeat, drained
- ¼ cup shredded Swiss cheese

1. In a small bowl, whisk eggs; set aside. In an 8-in. ovenproof skillet, saute the onion, pepper and mushrooms in oil until tender. Reduce heat; sprinkle with crab. Top with eggs. Cover and cook for 5-7 minutes or until nearly set.
2. Uncover skillet; sprinkle with cheese. Broil 3-4 in. from the heat for 2-3 minutes or until eggs are completely set. Let stand for 5 minutes. Cut into wedges.

Nutrition Facts: *1 wedge equals 215 calories, 13 g fat (4 g saturated fat), 361 mg cholesterol, 265 mg sodium, 3 g carbohydrate, 1 g fiber, 21 g protein.* **Diabetic Exchanges:** *3 lean meat, 1½ fat.*

Easy Curried Shrimp

I like to serve this dish with grapes or green veggies for added color. It's also nice with dried coconut or pineapple instead of apricots.
—**DONA STONE** CLEARWATER, FLORIDA

PREP/TOTAL TIME: 20 MIN.   **MAKES:** 4 SERVINGS

- 1 tablespoon butter
- 2 teaspoons curry powder
- ¾ teaspoon ground cumin
- ¼ teaspoon salt
- ¼ teaspoon garlic powder
- ¼ teaspoon ground coriander
- ¼ teaspoon ground cinnamon
- 1 cup light coconut milk
- 1 pound uncooked large shrimp, peeled and deveined
- ⅓ cup chopped dried apricots
- 2 cups hot cooked brown rice

1. In a large skillet, melt butter. Add the curry, cumin, salt, garlic powder, coriander and cinnamon; cook over medium heat until lightly browned. Stir in coconut milk. Bring to a boil. Reduce heat; simmer, uncovered, for 3-4 minutes or until thickened.
2. Add shrimp; cook and stir for 2-4 minutes or until shrimp turn pink. Stir in apricots; heat through. Serve with rice.

Nutrition Facts: ⅔ cup shrimp with ½ cup rice equals 309 calories, 10 g fat (5 g saturated fat), 145 mg cholesterol, 316 mg sodium, 33 g carbohydrate, 3 g fiber, 21 g protein. **Diabetic Exchanges:** 3 lean meat, 2 starch, 1 fat.

Slaw-Topped Fish Sandwiches

Replacing basic lettuce and tomato toppings with cool and creamy coleslaw makes this spicy breaded fish sandwich a whole meal in one sandwich—and way healthier than what's at the drive-thru.
—**HEALTHY COOKING TEST KITCHEN**

PREP/TOTAL TIME: 30 MIN.   **MAKES:** 4 SERVINGS

- ½ cup dry bread crumbs
- ½ teaspoon garlic powder
- ½ teaspoon cayenne pepper
- ½ teaspoon dried parsley flakes
- 4 cod fillets (6 ounces each)
- 4 whole wheat hamburger buns, split
- ¼ cup plain yogurt
- ¼ cup fat-free mayonnaise

- 2 teaspoons red wine vinegar
- ¼ teaspoon dried minced onion
- 1½ cups coleslaw mix

1. In a shallow bowl, combine the bread crumbs, garlic powder, cayenne and parsley. Coat fillets with bread crumb mixture.
2. Moisten a paper towel with cooking oil; using long-handled tongs, lightly coat the grill rack. Grill cod, covered, over medium heat or broil 4 in. from the heat for 4-5 minutes on each side or until fish flakes easily with a fork. Grill buns over medium heat for 30-60 seconds or until toasted.
3. Meanwhile, in a small bowl, combine yogurt, mayonnaise, vinegar and minced onion; stir in coleslaw mix. Serve cod on buns topped with slaw mixture.

Nutrition Facts: 1 sandwich equals 284 calories, 4 g fat (1 g saturated fat), 68 mg cholesterol, 463 mg sodium, 29 g carbohydrate, 4 g fiber, 32 g protein. **Diabetic Exchanges:** 5 lean meat, 2 starch.

Chicken Parmesan Patty Melts

I came up with this dish to re-create the comforting flavors of a restaurant-style sandwich. Now it's my husband's favorite dinner.
—**DEBORAH BIGGS** OMAHA, NEBRASKA

PREP/TOTAL TIME: 30 MIN.   **MAKES:** 4 SERVINGS

- 5 tablespoons grated Parmesan cheese, divided
- 1 cup marinara sauce, divided
- ¼ teaspoon pepper
- ⅛ teaspoon salt
- 1 pound lean ground chicken
- 2 ounces fresh mozzarella cheese, thinly sliced
- 2 ciabatta rolls, split and toasted

1. In a large bowl, combine 3 tablespoons Parmesan cheese, 2 tablespoons marinara sauce, pepper and salt. Crumble chicken over mixture and mix well. Shape into four patties.
2. Place on a baking sheet coated with cooking spray. Broil 4 in. from the heat for 4-6 minutes on each side or until a thermometer reads 165° and juices run clear.
3. Top with remaining marinara, mozzarella and remaining Parmesan. Broil 1-2 minutes longer or until cheeses are melted. Top each roll half with a patty.

Nutrition Facts: 1 sandwich equals 420 calories, 13 g fat (5 g saturated fat), 98 mg cholesterol, 658 mg sodium, 43 g carbohydrate, 3 g fiber, 34 g protein. **Diabetic Exchanges:** 4 lean meat, 2½ starch, 1 fat.

Southwest Flank Steak S C

A perfectly balanced rub imparts the infused flavor of an hours-long marinade without the waiting time. Leftovers are great for topping Caesar salads.

—KENNY FISHER LANCASTER, OHIO

PREP/TOTAL TIME: 25 MIN. **MAKES:** 6 SERVINGS

- 3 **tablespoons packed brown sugar**
- 3 **tablespoons chili powder**
- 4½ **teaspoons ground cumin**
- 1 **tablespoon garlic powder**
- 1 **tablespoon cider vinegar**
- 1½ **teaspoons Worcestershire sauce**
- ½ **teaspoon cayenne pepper**
- 1 **beef flank steak (1½ pounds)**

1. In a small bowl, combine the first seven ingredients; rub over steak.

2. Moisten a paper towel with cooking oil; using long-handled tongs, lightly coat the grill rack. Grill steak, covered, over medium heat or broil 4 in. from the heat for 6-8 minutes on each side or until thermometer reaches desired doneness (for medium-rare, a thermometer should read 145°; medium, 160°; well-done, 170°).

3. Let steak stand for 5 minutes. To serve, thinly slice across the grain.

Nutrition Facts: *3 ounces cooked beef equals 219 calories, 9 g fat (4 g saturated fat), 54 mg cholesterol, 127 mg sodium, 11 g carbohydrate, 2 g fiber, 23 g protein.* **Diabetic Exchanges:** *3 lean meat, 1 starch.*

Snappy Chicken Stir-Fry

Don't just reheat leftover chicken, stir-fry it up with some frozen vegetables for a super-speedy weeknight meal. We don't call this recipe "snappy" for nothing!

—HEALTHY COOKING TEST KITCHEN

PREP/TOTAL TIME: 30 MIN **MAKES:** 4 SERVINGS

- 3 **tablespoons cornstarch**
- 1½ **cups reduced-sodium chicken broth**
- 3 **tablespoons reduced-sodium soy sauce**
- ¾ **teaspoon garlic powder**
- ¾ **teaspoon ground ginger**
- ¼ **teaspoon crushed red pepper flakes**
- 1 **package (16 ounces) frozen sugar snap stir-fry vegetable blend**
- 1 **tablespoon sesame or canola oil**
- 2 **cups cubed cooked chicken breast**
- 2 **cups hot cooked brown rice**
- ¼ **cup sliced almonds, toasted**

1. In a small bowl, combine the cornstarch, broth, soy sauce, garlic powder, ginger and pepper flakes; set aside.

2. In a large skillet or wok, stir-fry vegetable blend in oil for 5-7 minutes or until vegetables are tender.

3. Stir cornstarch mixture and add to the pan. Bring to a boil; cook and stir for 2 minutes or until thickened. Add chicken; heat through. Serve with rice; sprinkle with almonds.

Nutrition Facts: *1 cup chicken mixture with ½ cup rice and 1 tablespoon almonds equals 365 calories, 9 g fat (1 g saturated fat), 54 mg cholesterol, 753 mg sodium, 39 g carbohydrate, 5 g fiber, 27 g protein.* **Diabetic Exchanges:** *3 lean meat, 2½ starch, 1 fat.*

Beef and Blue Cheese Penne with Pesto

Unique and simple to prepare, my steak and cheese dish is filled with bold flavors. Best of all, it takes just 30 minutes to set this meal on the table.

—**FRANCES PIETSCH** FLOWER MOUND, TEXAS

PREP/TOTAL TIME: 30 MIN. **MAKES:** 4 SERVINGS

- 2 **cups uncooked whole wheat penne pasta**
- 2 **beef tenderloin steaks (6 ounces each)**
- ¼ **teaspoon salt**
- ¼ **teaspoon pepper**
- 6 **cups fresh baby spinach, chopped**
- 2 **cups grape tomatoes, halved**
- 5 **tablespoons prepared pesto**
- ¼ **cup chopped walnuts**
- ¼ **cup crumbled Gorgonzola cheese**

1. Cook pasta according to package directions.

2. Meanwhile, sprinkle steaks with salt and pepper. Grill steaks, covered, over medium heat or broil 4 in. from the heat for 5-7 minutes on each side or until meat reaches desired doneness (for medium-rare, a thermometer should read 145°; medium, 160°; well-done, 170°).

3. Drain pasta and transfer to a large bowl. Add the spinach, tomatoes, pesto and walnuts; toss to coat. Thinly slice steaks. Divide pasta mixture among four serving plates. Top with beef; sprinkle with cheese.

Nutrition Facts: *1 serving equals 532 calories, 22 g fat (6 g saturated fat), 50 mg cholesterol, 434 mg sodium, 49 g carbohydrate, 9 g fiber, 35 g protein.*

Microwaved Parmesan Chicken C

This has been a family staple ever since a friend gave me the recipe years ago. It's too good and fast not to share.

—**MICHAEL HERMAN** CARNEY, MICHIGAN

PREP/TOTAL TIME: 10 MIN. **MAKES:** 2 SERVINGS

- 2 **boneless skinless chicken breast halves (4 ounces each)**
- 4 **teaspoons reduced-sodium soy sauce**
- ¼ **teaspoon garlic powder**
- ⅛ **teaspoon pepper**
- ¼ **cup grated Parmesan cheese**
- 1 **teaspoon butter**

Place chicken in a microwave-safe dish. Top with soy sauce, garlic powder and pepper. Sprinkle with cheese and dot with butter. Cover and cook on high for 4-5 minutes or until a thermometer reads 170°.

Nutrition Facts: *1 chicken breast half equals 190 calories, 7 g fat (4 g saturated fat), 76 mg cholesterol, 624 mg sodium, 1 g carbohydrate, trace fiber, 27 g protein.* **Diabetic Exchanges:** *3 lean meat, 1 fat.*

? Did you know?

Diets rich in spinach have proven to be beneficial in helping patients recover motor skills like walking following a stroke or neurological damage. Aim to make it one of your daily seven to ten servings of fruit and vegetables.

102

109

104

Beef Entrees

66 This recipe is healthy yet satisfying, quick yet delicious. I can have a hearty meal on the table in under 30 minutes, and one that my children will gobble up! If you aren't fond of kale, stir in baby spinach or chopped broccoli instead. 99

KIM VAN DUNK CALDWELL, NEW JERSEY
about her recipe, Hearty Vegetable Beef Ragout, on page 105

Light Mexican Casserole

A must-try dinner: Here's a healthy layered casserole using whole wheat tortillas, lean beef and more veggies than traditional recipes.

—HEALTHY COOKING TEST KITCHEN

PREP: 30 MIN. **BAKE:** 25 MIN. **MAKES:** 6 SERVINGS

- 1 **pound extra-lean ground beef (95% lean)**
- 1 **medium onion, chopped**
- 1 **medium green pepper, chopped**
- ¾ **cup water**
- 1 **tablespoon all-purpose flour**
- 1 **tablespoon hot chili powder**
- 1 **teaspoon garlic powder**
- ½ **teaspoon ground cumin**
- ½ **teaspoon ground coriander**
- ¼ **teaspoon salt**
- 1 **can (16 ounces) refried beans**
- ½ **cup salsa**
- 4 **whole wheat tortillas (8 inches)**
- 1 **cup frozen corn**
- ¾ **cup shredded sharp cheddar cheese**
  Shredded lettuce and chopped tomatoes, optional

1. In a large nonstick skillet, cook the beef, onion and green pepper over medium heat until meat is no longer pink. Stir in the water, flour, chili powder, garlic powder, cumin, coriander and salt. Bring to a boil. Reduce heat; simmer, uncovered, for 5-6 minutes or until thickened.

2. In a small bowl, combine beans and salsa. Place two tortillas in a round 2½-qt. baking dish coated with cooking spray. Layer with half of the beef mixture, bean mixture and corn; repeat layers. Top with cheese.

3. Bake, uncovered, at 350° for 25-30 minutes or until heated through and cheese is melted. Let stand for 5 minutes before cutting. Serve with lettuce and tomatoes if desired.

Nutrition Facts: *1 piece (calculated without lettuce and tomatoes) equals 367 calories, 11 g fat (5 g saturated fat), 64 mg cholesterol, 657 mg sodium, 39 g carbohydrate, 8 g fiber, 26 g protein.* **Diabetic Exchanges:** *3 lean meat, 2½ starch, 1 vegetable, ½ fat.*

Java Roast Beef C

Coffee adds richness to the gravy, which is perfect for sopping up with crusty bread or draping over mashed potatoes.

—CHARLA SACKMANN ORANGE CITY, IOWA

PREP: 10 MIN. **COOK:** 8 HOURS **MAKES:** 12 SERVINGS

- 5 **garlic cloves, minced**
- 1½ **teaspoons salt**
- ¾ **teaspoon pepper**
- 1 **boneless beef chuck roast (3 to 3½ pounds)**
- 1½ **cups strong brewed coffee**
- 2 **tablespoons cornstarch**
- ¼ **cup cold water**

Combine the garlic, salt and pepper; rub over beef. Transfer to a 4-qt. slow cooker. Pour coffee around meat. Cover and cook on low for 8-10 hours or until meat is tender. Remove meat to a serving platter; keep warm. Skim fat from cooking juices; transfer to a small saucepan. Bring to a boil. Combine cornstarch and water until smooth; gradually stir into the pan. Bring to a boil; cook and stir for 2 minutes or until thickened. Serve with meat.

Nutrition Facts: *3 ounces cooked beef with 2½ tablespoons gravy equals 199 calories, 11 g fat (4 g saturated fat), 74 mg cholesterol, 342 mg sodium, 2 g carbohydrate, trace fiber, 22 g protein.* **Diabetic Exchange:** *3 lean meat.*

I had ground beef and veggies on hand so I came up with this pizza-flavored casserole. I never expected my family to love it so much. It's a good way to sneak in some extra veggies for the kids.

—JENNIFER WISE SELINSGROVE, PENNSYLVANIA

Penne Beef Bake

PREP: 35 MIN. **BAKE:** 25 MIN.
MAKES: 8 SERVINGS

- 1 package (12 ounces) whole wheat penne pasta
- 1 pound lean ground beef (90% lean)
- 2 medium zucchini, finely chopped
- 1 large green pepper, finely chopped
- 1 small onion, finely chopped
- 1 jar (24 ounces) meatless spaghetti sauce
- 1½ cups reduced-fat Alfredo sauce
- 1 cup (4 ounces) shredded part-skim mozzarella cheese, divided
- ¼ teaspoon garlic powder

1. Cook penne according to package directions. Meanwhile, in a Dutch oven, cook the beef, zucchini, pepper and onion over medium heat until meat is no longer pink; drain. Stir in the spaghetti sauce, Alfredo sauce, ½ cup mozzarella cheese and garlic powder. Drain penne; stir into meat mixture.

2. Transfer to a 13-in. x 9-in. baking dish coated with cooking spray. Cover and bake at 375° for 20 minutes. Sprinkle with remaining mozzarella cheese. Bake, uncovered, 3-5 minutes longer or until cheese is melted.

Nutrition Facts: *1⅓ cups equals 395 calories, 12 g fat (6 g saturated fat), 62 mg cholesterol, 805 mg sodium, 45 g carbohydrate, 7 g fiber, 25 g protein.*
Diabetic Exchanges: *3 starch, 2 lean meat, 1 fat.*

Store-Bought Sauce

When shopping for spaghetti sauce, compare labels to find the lowest in sodium and sugar. Aim for less than 375 mg sodium and 6 g sugar per serving.

Tender Salsa Beef

This is my Mexican-style twist on comfort food. To keep it kid-friendly, use mild salsa.

—**STACIE STAMPER** NORTH WILKESBORO, NORTH CAROLINA

PREP: 15 MIN. **COOK:** 8 HOURS **MAKES:** 8 SERVINGS

- 1½ **pounds beef stew meat, cut into ¾-inch cubes**
- 2 **cups salsa**
- 1 **tablespoon brown sugar**
- 1 **tablespoon reduced-sodium soy sauce**
- 1 **garlic clove, minced**
- 4 **cups hot cooked brown rice**

In a 3-qt. slow cooker, combine the beef, salsa, brown sugar, soy sauce and garlic. Cover and cook on low for 8-10 hours or until meat is tender. Using a slotted spoon, serve beef with rice.

Nutrition Facts: ½ cup beef mixture with ½ cup rice equals 259 calories, 7 g fat (2 g saturated fat), 53 mg cholesterol, 356 mg sodium, 28 g carbohydrate, 2 g fiber, 19 g protein. **Diabetic Exchanges:** 2 starch, 2 lean meat.

Keep it lean. According to federal guidelines, 29 cuts of beef qualify as lean. Among them are sirloin, flank steak, tenderloin, T-bone and 95% lean ground beef. Look for the words "loin" or "round" when selecting meat, and trim excess visible fat before cooking.

Italian Burritos

No beans about it: Nothing but beef, cheese, garlic and sauce is stuffed inside these baked burritos. My family is very picky, so I came up with these to satisfy everyone.

—**DONNA HOLTER** CENTENNIAL, COLORADO

PREP: 20 MIN. **BAKE:** 20 MIN. **MAKES:** 8 SERVINGS

- 1 **pound lean ground beef (90% lean)**
- 1 **cup marinara sauce**
- ½ **cup shredded part-skim mozzarella cheese**
- ¼ **cup grated Parmesan cheese**
- ¼ **teaspoon garlic powder**
- 8 **whole wheat tortillas (8 inches), warmed**

1. In large skillet, cook beef over medium heat until no longer pink; drain. Stir in the marinara, cheeses and garlic powder.
2. Spoon ⅓ cup filling off center on each tortilla. Fold sides and ends over filling and roll up. Place on a baking sheet coated with cooking spray.
3. Bake at 375° for 18-20 minutes or until heated through and bottoms are lightly browned.

Nutrition Facts: 1 burrito equals 275 calories, 10 g fat (3 g saturated fat), 42 mg cholesterol, 326 mg sodium, 26 g carbohydrate, 3 g fiber, 18 g protein. **Diabetic Exchanges:** 2 starch, 2 lean meat.

Flank Steak Crostini F S C

Perfect for holidays or as a Sunday football snack, my flank steak crostini is a friend and family favorite.

—**DONNA EVARO** CASPER, WYOMING

PREP: 25 MIN. **GRILL:** 15 MIN. **MAKES:** 3 DOZEN

- 1 **beef flank steak (1½ pounds)**
- ½ **teaspoon salt**
- ½ **teaspoon pepper**
- 3 **tablespoons olive oil**
- 3 **garlic cloves, minced**
- 1 **teaspoon dried basil**
- 1 **French bread baguette (10½ ounces), cut into 36 slices**
- ½ **cup finely chopped fresh portobello mushrooms**
- ¼ **cup shredded part-skim mozzarella cheese**
- 2 **tablespoons grated Parmesan cheese**
- 1 **tablespoon minced chives**

1. Sprinkle beef with salt and pepper. Grill beef, covered, over medium heat or broil 4 in. from the heat for 6-8 minutes on each side or until a meat reaches desired doneness (for medium-rare, a thermometer should read 145°; medium, 160°; well-done, 170°). Let stand for 5 minutes. Thinly slice across the grain.

2. Meanwhile, in a small bowl, combine the oil, garlic and basil; brush over baguette slices. Place on baking sheets. Bake at 400° for 5 minutes. Top with mushrooms and mozzarella cheese. Bake 2-3 minutes longer or until cheese is melted.

3. Top with sliced steak, Parmesan cheese and chives. Serve immediately.

Nutrition Facts: *1 crostini equals 63 calories, 3 g fat (1 g saturated fat), 10 mg cholesterol, 105 mg sodium, 5 g carbohydrate, trace fiber, 5 g protein.*

Hearty Vegetable Beef Ragout

This recipe is healthy yet satisfying, quick yet delicious. I can have a hearty meal on the table in under 30 minutes, and one that my children will gobble up! If you aren't fond of kale, stir in baby spinach or chopped broccoli instead.

—**KIM VAN DUNK** CALDWELL, NEW JERSEY

PREP/TOTAL TIME: 30 MIN. **MAKES:** 8 SERVINGS

- 4 **cups uncooked whole wheat spiral pasta**
- 1 **pound lean ground beef (90% lean)**
- 1 **large onion, chopped**
- 3 **garlic cloves, minced**
- 2 **cans (14½ ounces each) Italian diced tomatoes, undrained**
- 1 **jar (24 ounces) meatless spaghetti sauce**
- 2 **cups finely chopped fresh kale**
- 1 **package (9 ounces) frozen peas, thawed**
- ¾ **teaspoon garlic powder**
- ¼ **teaspoon pepper**
  Grated Parmesan cheese, optional

1. Cook pasta according to package directions. Meanwhile, in a Dutch oven, cook the beef, onion and garlic over medium heat until meat is no longer pink; drain.

2. Stir in the tomatoes, spaghetti sauce, kale, peas, garlic powder and pepper. Bring to a boil. Reduce heat; simmer, uncovered, for 8-10 minutes or until kale is tender. Drain pasta; stir into sauce. Serve with cheese if desired.

Nutrition Facts: *1½ cups (calculated without cheese) equals 302 calories, 5 g fat (2 g saturated fat), 35 mg cholesterol, 837 mg sodium, 43 g carbohydrate, 7 g fiber, 20 g protein.* **Diabetic Exchanges:** *2 starch, 2 lean meat, 2 vegetable.*

Chocolate-Chipotle Sirloin Steak C

Looking to do something a little different with grilled sirloin? Add smoky heat and chocolaty, rich color with this easy five-ingredient rub.

—HEALTHY COOKING TEST KITCHEN

PREP: 10 MIN.+ CHILLING
GRILL: 20 MIN.
MAKES: 4 SERVINGS

- 3 tablespoons baking cocoa
- 2 tablespoons chopped chipotle peppers in adobo sauce
- 4 teaspoons Worcestershire sauce
- 2 teaspoons brown sugar
- ½ teaspoon salt
- 1½ pounds beef top sirloin steak

1. Place the first five ingredients in a blender; cover and process until blended. Rub over beef. Cover and refrigerate for at least 2 hours.
2. Grill beef, covered, over medium heat or broil 4 in. from the heat for 8-10 minutes on each side or until meat reaches desired doneness (for medium-rare, a thermometer should read 145°; medium, 160°; well-done, 170°).

Nutrition Facts: *5 ounces cooked beef equals 246 calories, 7 g fat (3 g saturated fat), 69 mg cholesterol, 477 mg sodium, 6 g carbohydrate, 1 g fiber, 37 g protein.*
Diabetic Exchange: *5 lean meat.*

Feta Stuffed Peppers

One of my favorite meals when I was younger was a recipe my mother made called Quick Chili Rice Casserole. I put a Greek spin on it and stuffed it in a pepper. It works great paired with a garden salad and fresh bread.

—SACHA MORGAN WOODSTOCK, GEORGIA

PREP: 35 MIN. **BAKE:** 30 MIN. **MAKES:** 3 SERVINGS

- 3 large green peppers
- ½ pound lean ground beef (90% lean)
- 1 small onion, chopped
- 1 can (14½ ounces) diced tomatoes, undrained
- 2 cups chopped fresh spinach
- ¾ cup uncooked whole wheat orzo pasta
- 2 tablespoons minced fresh oregano or 2 teaspoons dried oregano
- ¼ teaspoon salt
- ¼ teaspoon pepper
- 6 tablespoons crumbled feta cheese

1. Cut peppers in half lengthwise and remove seeds. In a Dutch oven, cook peppers in boiling water for 3-5 minutes. Drain and rinse in cold water; invert onto paper towels.
2. In a large skillet, cook beef and onion over medium heat until meat is no longer pink. Stir in the tomatoes, spinach, orzo, oregano, salt and pepper. Bring to a boil. Reduce heat; cover and simmer for 5-7 minutes or until orzo is tender.
3. Spoon into peppers. Place in an 11-in. x 7-in. baking dish coated with cooking spray. Cover and bake at 350° for 30-35 minutes or until peppers are tender.
4. Sprinkle with cheese; bake 5 minutes longer or until cheese is softened.

Nutrition Facts: *2 stuffed pepper halves equals 369 calories, 10 g fat (4 g saturated fat), 55 mg cholesterol, 567 mg sodium, 46 g carbohydrate, 13 g fiber, 26 g protein.* **Diabetic Exchanges:** *3 starch, 2 lean meat, ½ fat.*

top tip | Rub It In

Rubs are combinations of herbs and spices that are rubbed onto meat, fish or poultry to add a flavor boost. For a savory rub, combine 1 tablespoon each dried marjoram and basil, 2 teaspoons each dried thyme and rosemary, crushed, and ¾ teaspoon dried oregano. Store in an airtight container. Rub over steaks just before grilling.

—DONNA BROCKETT
KINGFISHER, OKLAHOMA

Zippy Sirloin Steak 🄲

The spicy coating on this steak packs a lot of punch, and it's such an easy rub to put together. Leftovers make an impressive steak salad for lunch.

—**LISA FINNEGAN** FORKED RIVER, NEW JERSEY

PREP: 15 MIN. + MARINATING **GRILL:** 20 MIN. **MAKES:** 6 SERVINGS

> 1 tablespoon paprika
> 2 teaspoons pepper
> 1½ teaspoons kosher salt
> 1½ teaspoons brown sugar
> 1½ teaspoons ground cumin
> 1½ teaspoons chili powder
> 1 teaspoon sugar
> ¼ teaspoon cayenne pepper
> 1 beef sirloin tip steak (1½ pounds)

1. In a small bowl, combine the first eight ingredients. Rub over both sides of beef. Cover and refrigerate for 2 hours.

2. Moisten a paper towel with cooking oil; using long-handled tongs, lightly coat the grill rack. Grill beef, covered, over medium heat or broil 4 in. from the heat for 8-10 minutes on each side or until meat reaches desired doneness (for medium-rare, a thermometer should read 145°; medium, 160°; well-done, 170°). Let stand for 5 minutes before slicing.

Nutrition Facts: *3 ounces cooked beef equals 160 calories, 6 g fat (2 g saturated fat), 73 mg cholesterol, 512 mg sodium, 3 g carbohydrate, 1 g fiber, 23 g protein.* **Diabetic Exchange:** *3 lean meat.*

Sassy Pot Roast 🄲

 We lost this recipe for several years, so it's even more special to us now that we found it again. I love walking into my home after a long day at the office and smelling this lovely pot roast. The lemon juice and vinegar make the meat really tender.

—**SUSAN BURKETT** MONROEVILLE, PENNSYLVANIA

PREP: 15 MIN. **COOK:** 8 HOURS **MAKES:** 8 SERVINGS

> 1 boneless beef chuck roast (2 pounds)
> ½ teaspoon salt
> ½ teaspoon pepper
> 2 teaspoons olive oil
> 1 large onion, chopped
> 1 can (8 ounces) tomato sauce
> ¼ cup water
> ¼ cup lemon juice
> ¼ cup cider vinegar
> ¼ cup ketchup
> 2 tablespoons brown sugar
> 1 tablespoon Worcestershire sauce
> ½ teaspoon ground mustard
> ½ teaspoon paprika

1. Sprinkle beef with salt and pepper. In a large skillet, brown beef in oil on all sides; drain.

2. Transfer to a 4-qt. slow cooker. Sprinkle with onion. Combine the remaining ingredients. Pour over meat. Cover and cook on low for 8-10 hours or until meat is tender. Skim fat. If desired, thicken pan juices.

Nutrition Facts: *3 ounces cooked beef equals 243 calories, 12 g fat (4 g saturated fat), 74 mg cholesterol, 443 mg sodium, 10 g carbohydrate, 1 g fiber, 23 g protein.* **Diabetic Exchange:** *3 lean meat.*

Makeover Husband's Dinner Delight

My husband, Steve, loves beef, and he especially loves casseroles. He likes to eat the leftovers with tortilla chips. It's like a whole new dish the second time around.

—**SHERRI COX** LUCASVILLE, OHIO

PREP: 35 MIN. **BAKE:** 25 MIN. **MAKES:** 8 SERVINGS

8 ounces uncooked whole wheat egg noodles
1½ pounds extra-lean ground beef (95% lean)
1 medium onion, chopped
1 medium green pepper, chopped
1 garlic clove, minced
3 cans (8 ounces each) tomato sauce
1 tablespoon sugar
⅛ teaspoon salt
⅛ teaspoon pepper
1½ cups (12 ounces) 2% cottage cheese
4 ounces reduced-fat cream cheese
¼ cup reduced-fat sour cream
3 green onions, chopped
½ cup shredded sharp cheddar cheese

1. Cook noodles according to package directions. Meanwhile, in a Dutch oven, cook beef, onion, green pepper and garlic over medium heat until meat is no longer pink and vegetables are tender; drain.

2. Stir in the tomato sauce, sugar, salt and pepper. Drain noodles; stir into sauce. Pour half the beef mixture into a 13-in. x 9-in. baking dish coated with cooking spray.

3. In a small bowl, combine the cottage cheese, cream cheese, sour cream and green onions. Spread over beef mixture. Top with remaining beef mixture.

4. Cover and bake at 350° for 20 minutes. Uncover; sprinkle with cheddar cheese. Bake 5-10 minutes longer or until cheese is melted.

Nutrition Facts: *1¼ cups equals 343 calories, 11 g fat (6 g saturated fat), 74 mg cholesterol, 737 mg sodium, 33 g carbohydrate, 5 g fiber, 31 g protein.* **Diabetic Exchanges:** *3 lean meat, 2 starch, 1 fat.*

Taco Pizza Grande

My family loves this pizza. To save time during preparation, I usually brown the beef while the pizza dough is rising. Then just put it into the refrigerator until the rest of the recipe is ready to assemble.

—**MARLA ALEXANDER** BELOIT, WISCONSIN

PREP: 25 MIN. + RISING **BAKE:** 30 MIN. **MAKES:** 6 SERVINGS

1½ teaspoons active dry yeast
¾ cup warm water (110° to 115°)
1 tablespoon sugar
1 teaspoon salt
1¾ to 2¼ cups all-purpose flour
½ pound lean ground beef (90% lean)
2 teaspoons taco seasoning
¼ cup water
¾ cup fat-free refried beans
1 teaspoon olive oil
¾ cup chopped tomatoes
¼ cup chopped onion
¼ cup sliced ripe olives
1½ cups (6 ounces) shredded reduced-fat cheddar cheese

1. In a large bowl, dissolve yeast in warm water. Add the sugar, salt and 1 cup flour; beat until smooth. Stir in enough remaining flour to form a soft dough. Turn onto a lightly floured surface; knead until smooth and elastic, about 6-8 minutes. Place in a bowl coated with cooking spray, turning once to coat the top. Cover and let rise in a warm place for 20 minutes.

2. Meanwhile, in a small skillet, cook beef over medium heat until no longer pink; drain. Add taco seasoning and water; bring to a boil. Stir in refried beans; heat through.

3. Punch dough down; roll into a 13-in. circle. Transfer to a 12-in. pizza pan coated with cooking spray; build up edges slightly. Cover and let rest for 10 minutes. Dot with oil. Spread beef mixture over dough. Bake at 350° for 25 minutes or until crust is lightly browned. Sprinkle with tomatoes, onion, olives and cheese. Bake 5-10 minutes longer or until cheese is melted.

Nutrition Facts: *1 slice equals 336 calories, 11 g fat (5 g saturated fat), 39 mg cholesterol, 864 mg sodium, 40 g carbohydrate, 3 g fiber, 21 g protein.*

Mini Mediterranean Pizzas

PREP: 30 MIN. **BAKE:** 5 MIN.
MAKES: 4 SERVINGS

- 8 ounces lean ground beef (90% lean)
- ¼ cup finely chopped onion
- 2 garlic cloves, minced
- 1 can (8 ounces) tomato sauce
- 1 teaspoon minced fresh rosemary or ¼ teaspoon dried rosemary, crushed
- 2 whole wheat pita breads (6 inches), cut in half horizontally
- 1 medium tomato, seeded and chopped
- ½ cup fresh baby spinach, thinly sliced
- 12 Greek pitted olives, thinly sliced
- ½ cup shredded part-skim mozzarella cheese
- ¼ cup crumbled feta cheese

1. In a large nonstick skillet coated with cooking spray, cook the beef, onion and garlic over medium heat for 5-6 minutes or until meat is no longer pink; drain. Stir in tomato sauce and rosemary; bring to a boil. Reduce heat; simmer, uncovered, for 6-9 minutes or until thickened.

2. Place pita halves, cut side up, on a baking sheet. Top with meat mixture, tomato, spinach and olives. Sprinkle with cheeses. Bake at 400° for 4-6 minutes or until cheeses are melted.

Nutrition Facts: *1 pizza equals 287 calories, 12 g fat (5 g saturated fat), 47 mg cholesterol, 783 mg sodium, 25 g carbohydrate, 4 g fiber, 21 g protein.*
Diabetic Exchanges: *2 lean meat, 1½ starch, 1 fat.*

I was on a mini-pizza kick and had served up Mexican and Italian versions. I experimented with a Mediterranean variation and these were born.
—**JENNY DUBINSKY** INWOOD, WEST VIRGINIA

Did you know?

Olives, in addition to being a healthy source of monounsaturated fat (healthier for the heart than saturated fat), contain antioxidants called polyphenols. Research suggests polyphenols help reduce inflammation in the blood vessels and help improve cholesterol and triglyceride levels.

Steak San Marino

As a busy pastor's wife and mother of three, my day runs smoother when I serve this delicious, inexpensive dish. The steak is so tender and flavorful, my kids gobble it up and my husband asks for seconds.

—**LAEL GRIESS** HULL, IOWA

PREP: 15 MIN. **COOK:** 7 HOURS **MAKES:** 6 SERVINGS

- ¼ cup all-purpose flour
- ½ teaspoon salt
- ½ teaspoon pepper
- 1 beef top round steak (1½ pounds), cut into six pieces
- 2 large carrots, sliced
- 1 celery rib, sliced
- 1 can (8 ounces) tomato sauce
- 2 garlic cloves, minced
- 1 bay leaf
- 1 teaspoon Italian seasoning
- ½ teaspoon Worcestershire sauce
- 3 cups hot cooked brown rice

1. In a large resealable plastic bag, combine the flour, salt and pepper. Add beef, a few pieces at a time, and shake to coat. Transfer to a 4-qt. slow cooker.

2. In a small bowl, combine the carrots, celery, tomato sauce, garlic, bay leaf, Italian seasoning and Worcestershire sauce. Pour over beef. Cover and cook on low for 7-9 hours or until beef is tender. Discard bay leaf. Serve with rice.

Nutrition Facts: *3 ounces cooked beef with ½ cup rice and ⅓ cup sauce equals 286 calories, 5 g fat (1 g saturated fat), 64 mg cholesterol, 368 mg sodium, 30 g carbohydrate, 3 g fiber, 29 g protein.* **Diabetic Exchanges:** *3 lean meat, 2 starch.*

Saucy Beef and Cabbage Dinner

Using cabbage is a great way to bulk up a meal without adding extra fat and calories. The cabbage in this dish is tender but still has a nice crunch.

—**MARCIA DOYLE** POMPANO, FLORIDA

PREP: 15 MIN. **COOK:** 25 MIN. **MAKES:** 8 SERVINGS

- 1 pound lean ground beef (90% lean)
- 1 large onion, chopped
- 1 cup sliced fresh mushrooms
- 1 medium head cabbage, chopped
- 1 can (46 ounces) reduced-sodium tomato juice
- 1 cup instant brown rice
- 1 can (6 ounces) tomato paste
- ¼ cup packed brown sugar
- 2 tablespoons lemon juice
- 1 teaspoon dried thyme
- 1 teaspoon dried parsley flakes
- ½ teaspoon pepper

1. In a Dutch oven, cook the beef, onion and mushrooms over medium heat until meat is no longer pink; drain.

2. Add the remaining ingredients. Bring to a boil. Reduce heat; cover and simmer for 15-20 minutes or until cabbage and rice are tender.

Nutrition Facts: *1⅓ cups equals 253 calories, 5 g fat (2 g saturated fat), 35 mg cholesterol, 170 mg sodium, 36 g carbohydrate, 5 g fiber, 17 g protein.* **Diabetic Exchanges:** *2 lean meat, 2 vegetable, 1½ starch.*

Bourbon Steak Portobellos C

I love this grilled dish—especially when I add fresh jalapenos to the pretty pepper medley.

—**KATHY VANDERBURG** NICEVILLE, FLORIDA

PREP: 30 MIN. + MARINATING   **GRILL:** 25 MIN.   **MAKES:** 4 SERVINGS

- ¼ cup reduced-sodium soy sauce
- ¼ cup bourbon
- 2 tablespoons dark brown sugar
- 1 beef top sirloin steak (¾ inch thick and 1 pound)
- 4 large portobello mushrooms
- ½ large sweet red pepper, cut into strips
- ½ large sweet yellow pepper, cut into strips
- ½ large sweet onion, halved and sliced
- 1 tablespoon olive oil
- ½ teaspoon salt, divided
- ½ teaspoon pepper, divided
- ¾ cup shredded part-skim mozzarella cheese

1. In a small bowl, combine the soy sauce, bourbon and brown sugar; stir until sugar is dissolved. Pour ⅓ cup into a large resealable plastic bag; add steak. Seal bag and refrigerate for 1 hour.

2. Remove and discard stems and gills from mushrooms. Place mushrooms in a shallow dish; brush both sides with remaining marinade; cover and let stand at room temperature for 1 hour.

3. In a small bowl, combine the peppers, onion, oil and ¼ teaspoon each salt and pepper; toss to coat. Spread in a single layer on a grilling grid; place on a grill rack. Grill, covered, over medium heat for 5-8 minutes or until crisp-tender. Cover and keep warm.

4. Sprinkle steak with remaining salt and pepper. Grill steak, covered, over medium heat for 8-10 minutes on each side or until a thermometer reads 145° for medium-rare, 160° for medium and 170° for well-done.

5. Meanwhile, grill mushrooms, covered, over medium heat for 6-8 minutes or until tender, turning once. Spoon pepper mixture into mushrooms. Cut steak into slices; arrange over pepper mixture. Sprinkle with cheese. Grill, covered, for 3-4 minutes or until cheese is melted.

Nutrition Facts: *1 serving equals 301 calories, 12 g fat (4 g saturated fat), 58 mg cholesterol, 637 mg sodium, 13 g carbohydrate, 2 g fiber, 32 g protein.* **Diabetic Exchanges:** *4 lean meat, 2 vegetable, 1 fat.*

Sweet and Sour Brisket

Here's one dinner that never gets old. It's tender and juicy with a great sweet and sour twist. We'd eat it every night if we could!

—**JOLIE ALBERTAZZIE** MORENO VALLEY, CALIFORNIA

PREP: 15 MIN.   **COOK:** 8 HOURS   **MAKES:** 10 SERVINGS

- 1 can (28 ounces) crushed tomatoes
- 1 medium onion, halved and thinly sliced
- ½ cup raisins
- ¼ cup packed brown sugar
- 2 tablespoons lemon juice
- 3 garlic cloves, minced
- 1 fresh beef brisket (3 pounds)
- ½ teaspoon salt
- ¼ teaspoon pepper

1. In a small bowl, combine the tomatoes, onion, raisins, brown sugar, lemon juice and garlic. Pour half into a 4- or 5-qt. slow cooker coated with cooking spray. Sprinkle meat with salt and pepper. Transfer to slow cooker. Top with remaining tomato mixture. Cover and cook on low for 8-10 hours or until meat is tender.

2. Remove brisket to a serving platter and keep warm. Skim fat from cooking juices. Thinly slice meat across the grain. Serve with tomato mixture.

Editor's Note: *This is a fresh beef brisket, not corned beef.*

Nutrition Facts: *4 ounces cooked beef with ⅓ cup sauce equals 248 calories, 6 g fat (2 g saturated fat), 58 mg cholesterol, 272 mg sodium, 19 g carbohydrate, 2 g fiber, 30 g protein.* **Diabetic Exchanges:** *4 lean meat, 1 starch.*

Makeover Easy Beef-Stuffed Shells

I like to make this ahead of time and bake it the next day for an easy, comforting meal. The pesto is the best part; it makes a surprising filling for the cheesy shells.

—**BLAIR LONERGAN** ROCHELLE, VIRGINIA

PREP: 45 MIN. + CHILLING **BAKE:** 45 MIN. **MAKES:** 10 SERVINGS

- 20 uncooked jumbo pasta shells
- 1 pound lean ground beef (90% lean)
- 1 large onion, chopped
- 1 medium green pepper, chopped
- 1¼ cups reduced-fat ricotta cheese
- 1½ cups (6 ounces) shredded reduced-fat Italian cheese blend, divided
- ¼ cup grated Parmesan cheese
- ¼ cup prepared pesto
- 1 egg, lightly beaten
- 1 can (14½ ounces) Italian diced tomatoes, undrained
- 1 can (8 ounces) no-salt-added tomato sauce
- 1 teaspoon Italian seasoning

1. Cook pasta according to package directions to al dente; drain and rinse in cold water. In a large skillet, cook the beef, onion and green pepper over medium heat until meat is no longer pink; drain. In a large bowl, combine the ricotta cheese, 1 cup Italian cheese blend, Parmesan cheese, pesto, egg and half of the beef mixture.

2. In a small bowl, combine the tomatoes, tomato sauce and Italian seasoning. Spread ¾ cup into a 13-in x 9-in. baking dish coated with cooking spray. Spoon cheese mixture into pasta shells; place in baking dish. Combine remaining beef mixture and tomato mixture; spoon over shells. Sprinkle with remaining cheese. Cover and refrigerate overnight.

3. Remove from the refrigerator 30 minutes before baking. Cover and bake at 350° for 40 minutes. Uncover; bake 5-10 minutes longer or until cheese is melted.

Nutrition Facts: *2 stuffed shells equals 295 calories, 12 g fat (5 g saturated fat), 70 mg cholesterol, 436 mg sodium, 23 g carbohydrate, 2 g fiber, 22 g protein.* **Diabetic Exchanges:** *3 lean meat, 1½ starch, 1 fat.*

Makeover Easy-Does-It Spaghetti

The beauty of this entree is that it comes together all in one pot, with a simple homemade sauce. Allspice adds a little interest to this recipe, but you can also use Italian seasoning instead.

—**CAROL BENZEL-SCHMIDT** STANWOOD, WASHINGTON

PREP: 10 MIN. **COOK:** 25 MIN. **MAKES:** 4 SERVINGS

- 1 pound lean ground beef (90% lean)
- 1¾ cups sliced fresh mushrooms
- 3 cups tomato juice
- 1 can (14½ ounces) no-salt-added diced tomatoes, drained
- 1 can (8 ounces) no-salt-added tomato sauce
- 1 tablespoon dried minced onion
- ½ teaspoon salt
- ½ teaspoon garlic powder
- ½ teaspoon ground mustard
- ¼ teaspoon pepper
- ⅛ teaspoon ground allspice
- ⅛ teaspoon ground mace, optional
- 6 ounces uncooked multigrain spaghetti, broken into pieces
  Shaved Parmesan cheese, optional

1. In a Dutch oven, cook beef and mushrooms over medium heat until meat is no longer pink; drain. Add the tomato juice, tomatoes, tomato sauce, onion, salt, garlic powder, mustard, pepper, allspice and mace if desired.

2. Bring to a boil. Stir in spaghetti. Cover and simmer for 12-15 minutes or until spaghetti is tender. Garnish with cheese if desired.

Nutrition Facts: *1½ cups (calculated without cheese) equals 414 calories, 10 g fat (4 g saturated fat), 71 mg cholesterol, 925 mg sodium, 48 g carbohydrate, 6 g fiber, 33 g protein.* **Diabetic Exchanges:** *3 starch, 3 lean meat.*

119

122

118

Chicken Favorites

“My Cuban mother-in-law makes the best Arroz Con Pollo, but it's very time-consuming. This is my quick weeknight version of the dish she makes.”

JACQUELINE CORREA LANDING, NEW JERSEY
about her recipe, Chicken & Rice Skillet, on page 118

Greek Chicken and Artichokes

PREP/TOTAL TIME: 30 MIN. **MAKES:** 4 SERVINGS

- ¾ pound boneless skinless chicken breasts, cubed
- 1¼ teaspoons Greek seasoning
- 1 tablespoon olive oil
- 1 cup sliced fresh mushrooms
- 1 can (14½ ounces) no-salt-added diced tomatoes, undrained
- 1 can (14 ounces) water-packed artichoke hearts, rinsed, drained and quartered
- 2 cups cooked brown rice
- ¼ cup crumbled feta cheese

1. Sprinkle chicken with Greek seasoning. In a large skillet, brown chicken in oil. Add mushrooms; cook 2 minutes longer. Drain.

2. Stir in tomatoes and artichokes. Bring to a boil. Reduce heat; cover and simmer for 8-12 minutes or until chicken is cooked through. Serve with rice; sprinkle with cheese.

Nutrition Facts: *1 cup chicken mixture with ½ cup rice and 1 tablespoon cheese equals 309 calories, 7 g fat (2 g saturated fat), 51 mg cholesterol, 704 mg sodium, 34 g carbohydrate, 4 g fiber, 25 g protein.* **Diabetic Exchanges:** *3 lean meat, 2 vegetable, 1½ starch, 1 fat.*

> "I'm a huge fan of wild rice and wild rice mixes. Try it in place of brown rice to add a nutty flavor to this dish."
>
> —CAITLIN CHANEY TAMPA, FLORIDA

Apricot-Glazed Chicken Kabobs

I have made this recipe for my family for years and it's still everyone's favorite. I like to serve it with rice on the side.

—AMY CHELLINO SHOREWOOD, ILLINOIS

PREP: 20 MIN. + MARINATING **GRILL:** 10 MIN.
MAKES: 4 SERVINGS

- ½ cup apricot spreadable fruit
- 3 tablespoons reduced-sodium soy sauce
- 1 tablespoon lemon juice
- 1 tablespoon honey
- 2 teaspoons Chinese five-spice powder
- ¼ teaspoon crushed red pepper flakes
- 1½ pounds boneless skinless chicken breasts, cut into 1-inch cubes
- 1 medium red onion, cut into 1-inch pieces
- 1 medium zucchini, cut into 1-inch pieces
- 1 medium yellow summer squash, cut into 1-inch pieces

1. In a small bowl, combine the first six ingredients. Pour ½ cup marinade into a large resealable plastic bag. Add the chicken; seal bag and turn to coat. Refrigerate for at least 8 hours or overnight. Cover and refrigerate remaining marinade.

2. Drain and discard marinade. On four metal or soaked wooden skewers, alternately thread the chicken, onion, zucchini and summer squash. Moisten a paper towel with cooking oil; using long-handled tongs, lightly coat the grill rack.

3. Grill kabobs, covered, over medium heat or broil 4 in. from the heat for 10-15 minutes or until juices run clear, turning and basting occasionally with reserved marinade.

Nutrition Facts: *1 kabob equals 268 calories, 4 g fat (1 g saturated fat), 94 mg cholesterol, 341 mg sodium, 20 g carbohydrate, 2 g fiber, 36 g protein.* **Diabetic Exchanges:** *5 lean meat, 1 starch, 1 vegetable.*

My husband knows he's in for a treat when I begin rolling my enchiladas. This is his favorite dish, and the makeover version is yummy! We think it's a home run. —RYNNETTA GARNER DALLAS, TEXAS

Makeover Sour Cream Chicken Enchiladas

PREP: 30 MIN. **BAKE:** 15 MIN.
MAKES: 12 SERVINGS

- 4 **cups cubed cooked chicken breast**
- 1 **tablespoon chili powder**
- 1 **teaspoon garlic salt**
- 1 **teaspoon ground cumin**
- 12 **flour tortillas (8 inches), warmed**

SAUCE

- 2 **tablespoons all-purpose flour**
- 1½ **cups reduced-sodium chicken broth**
- 1½ **cups (12 ounces) reduced-fat sour cream**
- 1 **cup (4 ounces) shredded Monterey Jack cheese**
- 1 **cup (4 ounces) shredded Mexican cheese blend**
  Chopped tomatoes, optional

1. In a large bowl, combine the chicken, chili powder, garlic salt and cumin. Place ⅓ cup chicken mixture down the center of each tortilla. Roll up and place seam side down in two 13-in. x 9-in. baking dishes coated with cooking spray

2. In a large saucepan, whisk flour and broth until smooth. Bring to a boil; cook and stir for 2 minutes. Reduce heat; stir in sour cream and Monterey Jack cheese until melted. Pour sauce over enchiladas; sprinkle with Mexican cheese blend.

3. Bake, uncovered, at 350° for 15-20 minutes or until bubbly. Top with tomatoes if desired.

Nutrition Facts: *1 enchilada (calculated without tomatoes) equals 338 calories, 13 g fat (6 g saturated fat), 63 mg cholesterol, 645 mg sodium, 29 g carbohydrate, trace fiber, 25 g protein.* **Diabetic Exchanges:** *3 lean meat, 2 starch, 1 fat.*

? Did you know?

A classic white sauce starts by combining equal parts butter and flour before adding liquid. Because this recipe contains no butter, the flour is combined with broth in step 2 until smooth.

Chipotle-Lime Chicken Thighs

After plates are scraped clean, this stellar meal keeps on giving. Use the chicken bones to make your own stock, and freeze the remaining chipotle peppers and sauce for a smoky Sunday chili.

—NANCY BROWN DAHINDA, ILLINOIS

PREP: 15 MIN. + CHILLING **GRILL:** 20 MIN. **MAKES:** 4 SERVINGS

- 2 garlic cloves, peeled
- ¾ teaspoon salt
- 1 tablespoon lime juice
- 1 tablespoon minced chipotle pepper in adobo sauce
- 2 teaspoons adobo sauce
- 1 teaspoon chili powder
- 4 bone-in chicken thighs (about 1½ pounds)

1. Place garlic on a cutting board; sprinkle with salt. Using the flat side of a knife, mash garlic. Continue to mash until it reaches a paste consistency; transfer to a small bowl.
2. Stir in the lime juice, pepper, adobo sauce and chili powder. Gently loosen skin from chicken thighs; rub garlic mixture under skin. Cover and refrigerate overnight.
3. Moisten a paper towel with cooking oil; using long-handled tongs, lightly coat the grill rack. Grill chicken, covered, over medium-low heat for 20-25 minutes or until a thermometer reads 180°, turning once. Remove and discard skin before serving.

Nutrition Facts: *1 chicken thigh equals 209 calories, 11 g fat (3 g saturated fat), 87 mg cholesterol, 596 mg sodium, 2 g carbohydrate, trace fiber, 25 g protein.* **Diabetic Exchange:** *3 lean meat.*

Chicken & Rice Skillet

My Cuban mother-in-law makes the best Arroz Con Pollo, but it's very time-consuming. This is my quick weeknight version of the dish she makes.

—JACQUELINE CORREA LANDING, NEW JERSEY

PREP: 10 MIN. **COOK:** 25 MIN. **MAKES:** 4 SERVINGS

- 1 medium onion, chopped
- 2 teaspoons olive oil
- 1 cup uncooked long grain rice
- 2 garlic cloves, minced
- 1 can (14½ ounces) reduced-sodium chicken broth
- 1 can (14 ounces) diced tomatoes and green chilies, undrained
- 3 tablespoons water
- ½ teaspoon ground cumin
- ½ teaspoon dried oregano
- 2 cups cubed cooked chicken breast
- 1 cup frozen peas

1. In a large nonstick skillet coated with cooking spray, saute onion in oil until tender.
2. Add rice and garlic; cook and stir for 3-4 minutes or until rice is lightly browned. Add the broth, tomatoes, water, cumin and oregano. Bring to a boil. Reduce heat; cover and simmer for 15-20 minutes or until rice is tender. Add chicken and peas; heat through.

Nutrition Facts: *1½ cups equals 364 calories, 5 g fat (1 g saturated fat), 54 mg cholesterol, 783 mg sodium, 50 g carbohydrate, 4 g fiber, 28 g protein.*

Chicken Soba Noodle Toss

This is one of my favorite meals for busy weeknights. You can prep all the ingredients the day before and then put the dish together just before dinner.
—**ELIZABETH BROWN** LOWELL, MASSACHUSETTS

PREP/TOTAL TIME: 30 MIN. **MAKES:** 4 SERVINGS

- 2 teaspoons cornstarch
- ½ cup reduced-sodium chicken broth
- 2 tablespoons brown sugar
- 3 garlic cloves, minced
- 1 tablespoon butter, melted
- 1 tablespoon reduced-sodium soy sauce
- 1 tablespoon hoisin sauce
- 2 teaspoons minced fresh gingerroot
- 2 teaspoons rice vinegar
- ¼ teaspoon pepper
- 6 ounces uncooked Japanese soba noodles
- ¾ pound chicken tenderloins, cubed
- 4 teaspoons canola oil, divided
- 3 cups fresh broccoli stir-fry blend
- ¼ cup chopped unsalted cashews

1. In a small bowl, combine the first 10 ingredients until blended; set aside.
2. Cook noodles according to package directions. Meanwhile, in a large skillet or wok, stir-fry chicken in 2 teaspoons oil until no longer pink. Remove and keep warm.
3. Stir-fry broccoli blend in remaining oil for 4-6 minutes or until vegetables are crisp-tender.
4. Stir cornstarch mixture and add to the pan. Bring to a boil; cook and stir for 2 minutes or until thickened. Drain noodles; add to pan. Add chicken; heat through. Sprinkle with cashews.

Nutrition Facts: *1½ cups equals 417 calories, 12 g fat (3 g saturated fat), 58 mg cholesterol, 715 mg sodium, 52 g carbohydrate, 2 g fiber, 30 g protein.*

Moist Lemon Herb Chicken ⒞

I wanted a healthy, flavorful chicken recipe that was fast, easy and a real crowd-pleaser. I got lucky and hit the jackpot with this one!
—**KALI WRASPIR** OLYMPIA, WASHINGTON

PREP/TOTAL TIME: 25 MIN. **MAKES:** 4 SERVINGS

- 4 boneless skinless chicken breast halves (6 ounces each)
- ½ teaspoon salt
- ¼ teaspoon pepper
- 1 tablespoon olive oil
- 1 tablespoon herbes de Provence
- 2 teaspoons grated lemon peel
- 3 tablespoons lemon juice

1. Sprinkle chicken with salt and pepper. In a large ovenproof skillet coated with cooking spray, brown chicken in oil. Sprinkle herbes de Provence and lemon peel over chicken; add lemon juice to pan.
2. Bake, uncovered, at 375° for 12-15 minutes or until a thermometer reads 170°.

Editor's Note: *Look for herbes de Provence in the spice aisle.*

Nutrition Facts: *1 chicken breast half equals 220 calories, 7 g fat (2 g saturated fat), 94 mg cholesterol, 378 mg sodium, 2 g carbohydrate, 1 g fiber, 35 g protein.* **Diabetic Exchanges:** *5 lean meat, ½ fat.*

Grilled Lemon-Rosemary Chicken S C

Broiled or grilled, this simple chicken recipe has been a star in my recipe box for years. Try it with your favorite herbs.

—REBECCA SODERGREN CENTERVILLE, OHIO

PREP: 10 MIN. + MARINATING **GRILL:** 15 MIN. **MAKES:** 6 SERVINGS

- ¼ cup lemon juice
- 3 tablespoons honey
- 2 teaspoons canola oil
- 1 teaspoon dried rosemary, crushed
- ½ teaspoon salt
- ⅛ teaspoon pepper
- 6 boneless skinless chicken breast halves (6 ounces each)

1. In a large resealable plastic bag, combine the first six ingredients. Add the chicken; seal bag and turn to coat. Refrigerate for 2 hours.
2. Drain and discard marinade. Moisten a paper towel with cooking oil; using long-handled tongs, lightly coat the grill rack. Grill chicken, covered, over medium heat or broil 4 in. from the heat for 6-8 minutes on each side or until a thermometer reads 170°.
Nutrition Facts: *1 chicken breast half equals 187 calories, 4 g fat (1 g saturated fat), 94 mg cholesterol, 102 mg sodium, 1 g carbohydrate, trace fiber, 34 g protein.* **Diabetic Exchange:** *5 lean meat.*

Tuscan Chicken and Beans F

Rosemary and beans work together to make this a nice, rustic Italian meal.
—MARIE RIZZIO INTERLOCHEN, MICHIGAN

PREP/TOTAL TIME: 30 MIN. **MAKES:** 4 SERVINGS

- 1 pound boneless skinless chicken breasts, cut into ¾-inch pieces
- 2 teaspoons minced fresh rosemary or ½ teaspoon dried rosemary
- ¼ teaspoon salt
- ¼ teaspoon coarsely ground pepper
- 1 cup reduced-sodium chicken broth
- 2 tablespoons sun-dried tomatoes (not packed in oil), chopped
- 1 can (15½ ounces) white kidney or cannellini beans, rinsed and drained

1. In a small bowl, combine the chicken, rosemary, salt and pepper. In a large nonstick skillet coated with cooking spray, cook chicken over medium heat until browned.
2. Stir in broth and tomatoes. Bring to a boil. Reduce heat; simmer, uncovered, for 3-5 minutes or until chicken juices run clear. Add beans; heat through.
Nutrition Facts: *1 cup equals 216 calories, 3 g fat (1 g saturated fat), 63 mg cholesterol, 517 mg sodium, 17 g carbohydrate, 4 g fiber, 28 g protein.* **Diabetic Exchanges:** *3 lean meat, 1 starch.*

Makeover Stuffed Chicken Breasts with Mushroom Sauce

This was my great-grandmother's recipe. I have another version made with mushroom soup, which cuts down on prep time, but sometimes you just can't take shortcuts! Try serving it with egg noodles and steamed veggies.

—JULIE STACK PEWAUKEE, WISCONSIN

PREP: 35 MIN. **BAKE:** 45 MIN.
MAKES: 4 SERVINGS

- 4 boneless skinless chicken breast halves (6 ounces each)
- 1 small onion, chopped
- ¼ cup chopped green pepper
- ½ teaspoon canola oil
- ¾ cup seasoned bread crumbs
- ¼ cup water
- ½ teaspoon poultry seasoning
- ¼ cup all-purpose flour
- ¾ teaspoon paprika
- ¼ teaspoon salt
- ¼ teaspoon pepper
  Cooking spray

MUSHROOM SAUCE
- ½ pound sliced fresh mushrooms
- ¼ cup finely chopped onion
- 2½ teaspoons canola oil
- 1 tablespoon all-purpose flour
- ½ cup 2% milk
- ½ cup reduced-fat sour cream
- ¼ teaspoon salt
- ⅛ teaspoon pepper

1. Flatten chicken to ½-in. thickness. For stuffing, in a small nonstick skillet coated with cooking spray, saute onion and green pepper in oil until tender. Transfer to a small bowl. Stir in the bread crumbs, water and poultry seasoning.
2. Place ¼ cup stuffing over each chicken breast. Roll up from a short side and secure with toothpicks. In a shallow bowl, combine the flour, paprika, salt and pepper. Coat chicken in flour mixture.
3. Place seam side down in an 11-in. x 7-in. baking dish coated with cooking spray. Spritz chicken with cooking spray. Bake, uncovered, at 350° for 45-50 minutes or until a thermometer reads 170°. Discard toothpicks.
4. Meanwhile, in a large skillet, saute mushrooms and onion in oil until tender. Whisk flour and milk; add to pan. Bring to a boil; cook and stir for 1 minute or until thickened. Remove from the heat; stir in the sour cream, salt and pepper. Serve with chicken.
Nutrition Facts: *1 stuffed chicken breast half with about ⅓ cup sauce equals 401 calories, 13 g fat (3 g saturated fat), 106 mg cholesterol, 627 mg sodium, 27 g carbohydrate, 2 g fiber, 43 g protein.*
Diabetic Exchanges: *5 lean meat, 1 starch, 1 vegetable, 1 fat.*

We love Hoppin' John, so I developed this new (and faster) version. I like to mix my chopped green onions in with the hot cooked rice before serving. —**DEBRA KEIL** OWASSO, OKLAHOMA

Healthy Hoppin' John

PREP: 15 MIN. **COOK:** 35 MIIN.
MAKES: 6 SERVINGS

- 1 **large onion, chopped**
- 1 **cup fresh baby carrots, halved lengthwise**
- 2 **celery ribs with leaves, chopped**
- 1 **tablespoon olive oil**
- 1 **package (12 ounces) fully cooked spicy chicken sausage links, cut into ½-inch slices**
- 2 **garlic cloves, minced**
- 2 **cans (15½ ounces each) black-eyed peas, rinsed and drained**
- 2 **cups chicken stock**
- 1 **bay leaf**
- ½ **teaspoon dried thyme**
- ¼ **teaspoon pepper**
- ⅛ **teaspoon cayenne pepper**
- 1 **tablespoon cider vinegar**
- 3 **cups cooked brown rice**
- 2 **green onions, chopped**
- 1 **green onion, thinly sliced**

1. In a large nonstick skillet, saute the onion, carrots and celery in oil for 3 minutes. Add sausage; cook 3 minutes longer. Add garlic; cook 2 minutes longer.
2. Stir in the peas, stock, bay leaf, thyme, pepper and cayenne. Bring to a boil. Reduce heat; cover and simmer for 15 minutes. Stir in vinegar. Simmer, uncovered, 5-10 minutes longer or until carrots are tender.
3. Discard bay leaf. Combine rice and chopped green onions; divide among six bowls. Top with sausage mixture. Sprinkle with sliced green onion.

Nutrition Facts: *1 serving equals 352 calories, 8 g fat (2 g saturated fat), 43 mg cholesterol, 817 mg sodium, 48 g carbohydrate, 7 g fiber, 22 g protein.*

? **Did you know?**
Symbolizing coins, black-eyed peas are thought to bring prosperity as well as luck in the New Year. Legend has it that their popularity in the South dates back to the Civil War, when Vicksburg, Mississippi, was under siege and many of its citizens survived on this humble food.
—**HEALTHY COOKING TEST KITCHEN**

Skillet Chicken Burritos

PREP/TOTAL TIME: 30 MIN.
MAKES: 8 SERVINGS

- 1 cup (8 ounces) reduced-fat sour cream
- ¼ cup chopped fresh cilantro
- 2 tablespoons chopped pickled jalapeno slices
- 2 teaspoons chopped onion
- 2 teaspoons Dijon mustard
- 1 teaspoon grated lime peel

BURRITOS

- 2 cups cubed cooked chicken breast
- 1 can (15 ounces) black beans, rinsed and drained
- 1 can (11 ounces) Mexicorn, drained
- 1 cup (4 ounces) shredded reduced-fat cheddar cheese
- ¼ teaspoon salt
- 8 whole wheat tortillas (8 inches), warmed
  Cooking spray
  Salsa, optional

1. In a small bowl, combine the first six ingredients. In a large bowl, combine the chicken, beans, corn, cheese, salt and ½ cup sour cream mixture. Spoon ½ cup chicken mixture on each tortilla. Fold sides and ends over filling and roll up. Spritz both sides with cooking spray.

2. In a large nonstick skillet or griddle coated with cooking spray, cook burritos in batches over medium heat for 3-4 minutes on each side or until golden brown. Serve with remaining sour cream mixture and salsa if desired.

Nutrition Facts: *1 burrito with 1 tablespoon sour cream mixture (calculated without salsa) equals 349 calories, 10 g fat (4 g saturated fat), 46 mg cholesterol, 770 mg sodium, 40 g carbohydrate, 5 g fiber, 23 g protein.* **Diabetic Exchanges:** *3 lean meat, 2½ starch.*

Burritos are my "go-to" when I'm hurrying to make dinner. Preparing them in the skillet saves time and gives the hand-held treats a crispy outside and gooey interior.
—**SCARLETT ELROD** NEWNAN, GEORGIA

Tortilla Warm-Up

To prevent tortillas from tearing when you roll them up for chicken burritos, simply warm them slightly in a nonstick skillet before filling. Warm tortillas are more pliable.

—**CONNIE D.** SPRINGFIELD, MISSOURI

Creamy Chicken Boxty

PREP: 30 MIN. + STANDING
COOK: 10 MIN./BATCH **MAKES:** 4 SERVINGS

- 1 medium potato, peeled and grated
- 1½ cups fat-free milk
- 1 cup all-purpose flour
- ¾ cup mashed potato (made with fat-free milk)
- ¼ teaspoon salt
- ¼ teaspoon pepper

FILLING

- 2 bacon strips, chopped
- 2 cups sliced fresh mushrooms
- 1 medium leek (white portion only), chopped
- ¼ cup half-and-half cream
- 2 tablespoons all-purpose flour
- ¾ cup fat-free milk
- 2 cups cubed cooked chicken breast
- ¼ teaspoon salt
- ¼ teaspoon pepper

1. Place grated potato in a colander to drain; squeeze to remove excess liquid. Pat dry. In a large bowl, combine the grated potato, milk, flour, mashed potato, salt and pepper. Let stand for 20 minutes.

2. Meanwhile, in a large nonstick skillet, cook bacon over medium heat until crisp. Add mushrooms and leek; cook until tender. Gradually add cream. Whisk together flour and milk; add to pan. Bring to a boil. Cook and stir for 2 minutes or until thickened. Stir in the chicken, salt and pepper; heat through. Remove from the heat and keep warm.

3. Coat another large nonstick skillet with cooking spray; heat over medium heat. Pour ¾ cup batter into center of skillet; lift and tilt pan to coat bottom evenly. Cook until top appears dry; turn and cook 2-3 minutes longer. Remove and keep warm. Repeat with remaining batter, coating skillet with cooking spray as needed.

4. Spoon filling onto pancakes.

Nutrition Facts: *1 boxty equals 434 calories, 9 g fat (3 g saturated fat), 72 mg cholesterol, 515 mg sodium, 52 g carbohydrate, 3 g fiber, 33 g protein.*

"A creamy chicken filling flavored with bacon and leeks, wrapped in tender potato pancakes, this hearty recipe is light but filling and fabulous."

—HEALTHY COOKING TEST KITCHEN

Hearty Paella

I had paella for the first time in Spain. And it was so good, I've been on the quest to re-create the rich flavors of that dish ever since. We love the shrimp, chicken, spices and olives in this easy make-at-home version.

—LIBBY WALP CHICAGO, ILLINOIS

PREP: 25 MIN. **COOK:** 30 MIN. **MAKES:** 6 SERVINGS

- 1¼ pounds boneless skinless chicken breasts, cut into 1-inch cubes
- 1 tablespoon olive oil
- 1 cup uncooked long grain rice
- 1 medium onion, chopped
- 2 garlic cloves, minced
- 2¼ cups reduced-sodium chicken broth
- 1 can (14½ ounces) diced tomatoes, undrained
- 1 teaspoon dried oregano
- ½ teaspoon paprika
- ¼ teaspoon salt
- ¼ teaspoon pepper
- ⅛ teaspoon saffron threads
- ⅛ teaspoon ground turmeric
- 1 pound uncooked medium shrimp, peeled and deveined
- ¾ cup frozen peas
- 12 pimiento-stuffed olives
- 1 medium lemon, cut into six wedges

1. In a large skillet over medium heat, cook chicken in oil until no longer pink. Remove and keep warm. Add rice and onion to the pan; cook until rice is lightly browned and onion is tender, stirring frequently. Add garlic; cook 1 minute longer.

2. Stir in the broth, tomatoes, oregano, paprika, salt, pepper, saffron and turmeric. Bring to a boil. Reduce heat to low; cover and cook for 10 minutes.

3. Add the shrimp, peas and olives. Cover and cook 10 minutes longer or until rice is tender, shrimp turn pink and liquid is absorbed. Add chicken; heat through. Serve with lemon wedges.

Nutrition Facts: *1⅓ cups equals 367 calories, 8 g fat (1 g saturated fat), 144 mg cholesterol, 778 mg sodium, 36 g carbohydrate, 3 g fiber, 37 g protein.* **Diabetic Exchanges:** *5 lean meat, 2 starch, 1 vegetable, 1 fat.*

Chicken Tacos with Avocado Salsa

I make these to accommodate various food allergies in our family. Served with a simple green salad, it's a meal my family enjoys together.
—**CHRISTINE SCHENHER** EXETER, CALIFORNIA

PREP/TOTAL TIME: 30 MIN. **MAKES:** 4 SERVINGS

- 1 **pound boneless skinless chicken breasts, cut into ½-inch strips**
- ⅓ **cup water**
- 1 **tablespoon chili powder**
- 1 **teaspoon sugar**
- 1 **teaspoon onion powder**
- 1 **teaspoon paprika**
- 1 **teaspoon ground cumin**
- 1 **teaspoon dried oregano**
- ½ **teaspoon salt**
- ½ **teaspoon garlic powder**
- 1 **medium ripe avocado, peeled and cubed**
- 1 **cup fresh or frozen corn**
- 1 **cup cherry tomatoes, quartered**
- 2 **teaspoons lime juice**
- 8 **taco shells, warmed**

1. In a large nonstick skillet coated with cooking spray, brown chicken. Add the water, chili powder, sugar, onion powder, paprika, cumin, oregano, salt and garlic powder. Cook over medium heat for 5-6 minutes or until chicken is no longer pink, stirring occasionally.

2. Meanwhile, in a small bowl, gently combine the avocado, corn, tomatoes and lime juice. Spoon chicken mixture into taco shells; top with avocado salsa.

Nutrition Facts: *2 tacos equals 354 calories, 15 g fat (3 g saturated fat), 63 mg cholesterol, 474 mg sodium, 30 g carbohydrate, 6 g fiber, 27 g protein.* **Diabetic Exchanges:** *3 lean meat, 2 starch, 1 fat.*

Chicken Bow Tie Alfredo

Bow ties are back in style and back on your heart-healthy menu. Because real Parmigiano-Reggiano cheese has an intense flavor, you can get away with using less, making it ideal for lending gusto to lighter meals.
—**HEALTHY COOKING TEST KITCHEN**

PREP: 20 MIN. **COOK:** 20 MIN. **MAKES:** 6 SERVINGS

- 4 **cups uncooked multigrain bow tie pasta**
- ½ **pound sliced fresh mushrooms**
- 1 **medium onion, chopped**
- 2 **teaspoons olive oil**
- 2 **garlic cloves, minced**
- ½ **cup white wine or reduced-sodium chicken broth**
- 4 **ounces fat-free cream cheese, cubed**
- 2 **tablespoons cornstarch**
- 2 **cups whole milk**
- 2 **cups cubed cooked chicken breast**
- ½ **cup grated Parmigiano-Reggiano cheese**
- 2 **tablespoons minced fresh basil or 2 teaspoons dried basil**
- ¼ **teaspoon pepper**
- ⅛ **teaspoon salt**
  Additional grated Parmigiano-Reggiano cheese, optional

1. Cook pasta according to package directions. Meanwhile, in a large nonstick skillet coated with cooking spray, saute mushrooms and onion in oil until tender. Add the garlic; cook 1 minute longer. Stir in wine. Bring to a boil; cook for 2 minutes. Stir in cream cheese until melted.

2. Combine cornstarch and milk until smooth; stir into skillet. Bring to a boil; cook and stir for 2 minutes or until thickened. Add the chicken, cheese, basil, pepper and salt; cook and stir until cheese is melted.

3. Drain pasta; add to chicken mixture. Heat through. Sprinkle with additional cheese if desired.

Nutrition Facts: *1¼ cups (calculated without additional cheese) equals 430 calories, 10 g fat (3 g saturated fat), 51 mg cholesterol, 345 mg sodium, 50 g carbohydrate, 5 g fiber, 33 g protein.*

Chicken in Tomato-Basil Cream Sauce

This recipe was inspired by all our fresh garden tomatoes and herbs. In summer, I grill the chicken with some Italian seasonings and a bit of garlic powder, but on rainy days or in winter, I cook it on the stovetop.

—RACHEL KOWASIC VALRICO, FLORIDA

PREP: 20 MIN. **COOK:** 30 MIN. **MAKES:** 4 SERVINGS

- 1 **pound boneless skinless chicken breasts, cut into ½-inch cubes**
- 3 **teaspoons butter, divided**
- 8 **plum tomatoes, seeded and chopped**
- 1 **small onion, finely chopped**
- 1 **garlic clove, minced**
- ½ **cup reduced-sodium chicken broth**
- 1 **cup uncooked whole wheat orzo pasta**
- 1 **cup evaporated milk**
- ½ **cup loosely packed basil leaves, julienned**
- ¾ **teaspoon salt**
- ¼ **teaspoon pepper**
- ¼ **cup crumbled feta cheese**

1. In a large nonstick skillet coated with cooking spray, cook chicken in 2 teaspoons butter until no longer pink. Remove and keep warm. In the same skillet, saute tomatoes and onion in remaining butter until onion is softened. Add garlic; cook 1 minute longer.

2. Stir in broth. Bring to a boil; add orzo. Reduce heat. Cover and simmer for 10-12 minutes or until orzo is tender. Stir in the chicken, milk, basil, salt and pepper; heat through (do not boil). Sprinkle with cheese just before serving.

Nutrition Facts: *1½ cups equals 417 calories, 12 g fat (6 g saturated fat), 94 mg cholesterol, 723 mg sodium, 41 g carbohydrate, 9 g fiber, 35 g protein.* **Diabetic Exchanges:** *3 lean meat, 2 starch, 1 vegetable, ½ whole milk, ½ fat.*

Barbecued Chicken-Stuffed Potatoes

This tasty dish combines some of my favorite things—the toppings for supreme nachos, tender chicken and the warm comfort of a baked potato.

—ELLEN FINGER LANCASTER, PENNSYLVANIA

PREP/TOTAL TIME: 30 MIN. **MAKES:** 8 SERVINGS

- 4 **large potatoes**
  Cooking spray
- 1 **teaspoon garlic salt with parsley**
- 1½ **cups cubed cooked chicken breast**
- ⅔ **cup barbecue sauce**
- 1 **can (16 ounces) chili beans, undrained**
- 1 **can (2¼ ounces) sliced ripe olives, drained**
- 2 **green onions, sliced**
- 1½ **cups (6 ounces) shredded reduced-fat Colby-Monterey Jack cheese**
- 2 **plum tomatoes, chopped**
- ½ **cup reduced-fat sour cream**

1. Scrub and pierce potatoes. Coat with cooking spray and rub with garlic salt with parsley; place on a microwave-safe plate. Microwave, uncovered, on high for 18-22 minutes or until tender, turning once.

2. Cut each potato in half lengthwise. Scoop out the pulp, leaving ½-in. shells. Discard pulp or save for another use.

3. In a large bowl, combine chicken and barbecue sauce. Spoon into potato shells. Top with beans, olives and green onions; sprinkle with cheese. Place on a baking sheet. Bake, uncovered, at 375° for 10-12 minutes or until heated through. Serve with tomatoes and sour cream.

Editor's Note: *This recipe was tested in a 1,100-watt microwave.*

Nutrition Facts: *1 stuffed potato half equals 237 calories, 8 g fat (4 g saturated fat), 36 mg cholesterol, 737 mg sodium, 25 g carbohydrate, 5 g fiber, 19 g protein.* **Diabetic Exchanges:** *2 lean meat, 1½ starch, ½ fat.*

Enchilada Chicken C

PREP: 15 MIN. **BAKE:** 20 MIN.
MAKES: 4 SERVINGS

- 4 **boneless skinless chicken breast halves (6 ounces each)**
- 2 **teaspoons salt-free Southwest chipotle seasoning blend**
- 1 **tablespoon olive oil**
- ¼ **cup enchilada sauce**
- ½ **cup shredded sharp cheddar cheese**
- 2 **tablespoons minced fresh cilantro**

Sprinkle the chicken with seasoning blend. In an ovenproof skillet, brown chicken in oil. Top with enchilada sauce, cheese and cilantro. Bake at 350° for 18-20 minutes or until a thermometer reads 170°.

Nutrition Facts: *1 chicken breast half equals 265 calories, 11 g fat (5 g saturated fat), 109 mg cholesterol, 252 mg sodium, 2 g carbohydrate, trace fiber, 38 g protein.*
Diabetic Exchanges: *5 lean meat, 1 fat.*

Makeover Mediterranean Chicken & Beans

Not only does this cooking method make really juicy chicken thighs, it saves you time scrubbing an extra pan.

—**MARIE RIZZIO** INTERLOCHEN, MICHIGAN

PREP: 25 MIN. **COOK:** 20 MIN.
MAKES: 6 SERVINGS

- 2 **tablespoons all-purpose flour**
- 1 **teaspoon garlic salt**
- 1 **teaspoon dried rosemary, crushed**
- ½ **teaspoon pepper**
- 6 **bone-in chicken thighs (about 2¼ pounds), skin removed**
- 2 **tablespoons olive oil**
- 1 **can (15 ounces) white kidney or cannellini beans, rinsed and drained**
- 1 **can (14½ ounces) diced tomatoes, undrained**
- 6 **slices provolone cheese**

1. In a large resealable plastic bag, combine the flour, garlic salt, rosemary and pepper. Add chicken, a few pieces at a time, and shake to coat.
2. In a large skillet, brown chicken in oil. Stir in beans and tomatoes; bring to a boil. Reduce heat. Cover and simmer for 20-25 minutes or until chicken juices run clear. Remove from the heat. Top with cheese. Cover and let stand for 5 minutes or until cheese is melted.
Nutrition Facts: *1 serving equals 378 calories, 20 g fat (7 g saturated fat), 102 mg cholesterol, 690 mg sodium, 15 g carbohydrate, 4 g fiber, 33 g protein.*

Margherita Chicken C

Fresh basil gets all the respect in this super supper—even forks will stand at attention when it hits the table.

—**JUDY ARMSTRONG** PRAIRIEVILLE, LOUISIANA

PREP: 25 MIN. + MARINATING **GRILL:** 10 MIN. **MAKES:** 4 SERVINGS

- 4 **boneless skinless chicken breast halves (6 ounces each)**
- ½ **cup reduced-fat balsamic vinaigrette**
- 3 **garlic cloves, minced**
- ½ **teaspoon salt**
- ¼ **teaspoon pepper**
- ¼ **cup marinara sauce**
- 16 **fresh basil leaves**
- 2 **plum tomatoes, thinly sliced lengthwise**
- 1 **cup frozen artichoke hearts, thawed and chopped**
- 3 **green onions, chopped**
- ¼ **cup shredded part-skim mozzarella cheese**

1. Flatten chicken to ½-in. thickness. In a large resealable plastic bag, combine vinaigrette and garlic. Add the chicken; seal bag and turn to coat. Refrigerate for 30 minutes. Drain and discard marinade. Sprinkle chicken with salt and pepper.
2. Moisten a paper towel with cooking oil; using long-handled tongs, lightly coat the grill rack. Grill chicken, covered, over medium heat or broil 4 in. from the heat for 5 minutes. Turn; carefully top with marinara, basil, tomatoes, artichokes, onions and cheese. Cover and cook 5-6 minutes longer or until chicken is no longer pink and cheese is melted.
Nutrition Facts: *1 chicken breast half equals 273 calories, 8 g fat (2 g saturated fat), 98 mg cholesterol, 606 mg sodium, 10 g carbohydrate, 3 g fiber, 38 g protein.*
Diabetic Exchanges: *5 lean meat, 1 vegetable, ½ fat.*

"We enjoy Southwestern flavors, and this six-ingredient recipe never gets boring. The chicken sizzles in the skillet before getting baked and comes out tender and juicy every time."

—**NANCY SOUSLEY** LAFAYETTE, INDIANA

130

132

136

Turkey Specialties

*"*I came up with this simple dish as a way to use up leftover turkey from holiday dinners. It's become a family tradition to enjoy it the day after Thanksgiving and Christmas.*"*

KARI JOHNSTON MARWAYNE, ALBERTA
about her recipe, Turkey Fettuccine Skillet, on page 140

Italian Mushroom Meat Loaf **C**

PREP: 30 MIN. **BAKE:** 1 HOUR **MAKES:** 8 SERVINGS

- 1 **egg, lightly beaten**
- ¼ **pound medium fresh mushrooms, chopped**
- ½ **cup old-fashioned oats**
- ½ **cup chopped red onion**
- ¼ **cup ground flaxseed**
- ½ **teaspoon pepper**
- 1 **package (19½ ounces) Italian turkey sausage links, casings removed and crumbled**
- 1 **pound lean ground beef (90% lean)**
- 1 **cup marinara or meatless spaghetti sauce**

1. In a large bowl, combine the egg, mushrooms, oats, onion, flax and pepper. Crumble turkey and beef over mixture and mix well.

2. Shape into a 10-in. x 4-in. loaf. Place in a 13-in. x 9-in. baking dish coated with cooking spray. Bake, uncovered, at 350° for 50 minutes; drain. Top with marinara sauce. Bake 10-15 minutes longer or until no pink remains and a thermometer reads 165°.

Nutrition Facts: *1 slice equals 261 calories, 14 g fat (3 g saturated fat), 103 mg cholesterol, 509 mg sodium, 10 g carbohydrate, 2 g fiber, 25 g protein.* **Diabetic Exchanges:** *3 lean meat, ½ starch.*

> ❝Healthful oats and flaxseed amp up the nutrition in this tasty Italian meat loaf.❞
>
> —**KYLIE WERNING** CANDLER, NORTH CAROLINA

Sweet and Sour Turkey Meatballs

I'm always looking for recipes that are big on taste but quick and easy to prepare with little clean up. This one has it all. It's my son's favorite recipe, and he requests it whenever he comes home to visit. I often double the recipe so that we have leftovers for the next day's lunches.

—**MICHELE ORTHNER** EDMONTON, ALBERTA

PREP: 50 MIN. **COOK:** 25 MIN. **MAKES:** 6 SERVINGS

- 1 **large onion, chopped**
- 2 **large carrots, chopped**
- 1 **medium green pepper, chopped**
- 1 **tablespoon olive oil**
- 1 **can (15 ounces) tomato sauce**
- 1 **can (14½ ounces) reduced-sodium chicken broth**
- 1 **can (8 ounces) unsweetened crushed pineapple, undrained**
- ¼ **cup packed brown sugar**
- ¼ **cup white vinegar**
- ¼ **cup ketchup**
- 1 **egg, beaten**
- ¼ **cup fat-free milk**
- 1 **slice white bread, torn into small pieces**
- ½ **cup shredded zucchini**
- ½ **teaspoon salt**
- ½ **teaspoon garlic powder**
- ½ **teaspoon pepper**
- 1 **pound lean ground turkey**
- 2 **cups uncooked instant brown rice**

1. In a Dutch oven coated with cooking spray, saute the onion, carrots and green pepper in oil until tender. Add the tomato sauce, broth, pineapple, brown sugar, vinegar and ketchup. Bring to a boil. Reduce heat; simmer, uncovered, for 10 minutes.

2. Meanwhile, in a large bowl, combine the egg, milk, bread, zucchini, salt, garlic powder and pepper. Crumble turkey over mixture and mix well. Shape into 2-in. balls. Carefully add to tomato mixture. Cover and simmer for 15-20 minutes or until meatballs are no longer pink.

3. Add rice. Bring to a boil. Reduce heat; cover and simmer for 5 minutes or until liquid is absorbed. Let stand for 5 minutes. Fluff with a fork.

Nutrition Facts: *1 cup equals 389 calories, 11 g fat (2 g saturated fat), 95 mg cholesterol, 991 mg sodium, 53 g carbohydrate, 4 g fiber, 21 g protein.*

Taco Pita Pizzas

Friday nights are pizza night at our house. Our lighter version of the taco pizza at a place in town is our favorite!
—**JOANNE WILTZ** SANTEE, CALIFORNIA

PREP/TOTAL TIME: 25 MIN. **MAKES:** 4 SERVINGS

- 1 **pound lean ground turkey**
- ⅓ **cup finely chopped onion**
- 1 **can (4 ounces) chopped green chilies, drained**
- 4 **whole wheat pita breads (6 inches)**
- 1 **cup salsa**
- 1 **cup (4 ounces) shredded reduced-fat Mexican cheese blend**
- 1 **cup shredded lettuce**
- 1 **medium tomato, seeded and chopped**

1. In a large skillet, cook turkey and onion over medium heat until meat is no longer pink; drain. Stir in chilies. Place pitas on an ungreased baking sheet.

2. Spread 2 tablespoons salsa over each pita. Top with turkey mixture; sprinkle with cheese. Bake at 400° for 5-10 minutes or until cheese is melted. Serve with lettuce, tomato and remaining salsa.

Nutrition Facts: *1 pizza equals 459 calories, 17 g fat (6 g saturated fat), 110 mg cholesterol, 1,006 mg sodium, 45 g carbohydrate, 6 g fiber, 35 g protein.* **Diabetic Exchanges:** *4 lean meat, 2 starch, 2 vegetable, 1 fat.*

Swiss Turkey Stromboli

Similar to a calzone, stromboli is a type of turnover stuffed with various cheeses, meats and veggies—usually baked inside a pizza dough. Use this simple recipe to experiment with your favorite flavor combinations.
—**HEALTHY COOKING TEST KITCHEN**

PREP: 25 MIN. **BAKE:** 15 MIN. + STANDING **MAKES:** 4 SERVINGS

- 3 **cups sliced fresh mushrooms**
- 1 **medium onion, chopped**
- 1 **tablespoon canola oil**
- 2 **tablespoons spicy brown mustard**
- 1 **lb. prepared pizza dough**
- 3 **slices reduced-fat Swiss cheese**
- 6 **ounces sliced deli turkey**
- 1 **egg white**
- 1 **teaspoon water**

1. In a large nonstick skillet, saute mushrooms and onion in oil until tender. Stir in mustard; set aside.

2. On a floured surface, roll dough into a 15-in. x 10-in. rectangle. Layer the cheese, mushroom mixture and turkey lengthwise over half of dough to within ½ in. of edges. Fold dough over filling; pinch seams to seal and tuck ends under. Transfer to a baking sheet coated with cooking spray.

3. Combine egg white and water; brush over dough. Cut slits in top. Bake at 400° for 12-15 minutes or until golden brown. Let stand for 10 minutes before cutting.

Nutrition Facts: *1 slice equals 385 calories, 12 g fat (2 g saturated fat), 23 mg cholesterol, 804 mg sodium, 50 g carbohydrate, 8 g fiber, 23 g protein.*

Savory Turkey Potpies

Who would ever suspect that a traditional potpie could be on the lighter side? My comforting entree promises to warm you up on winter's chilliest nights—without adding inches to your waistline!

—JUDY WILSON SUN CITY WEST, ARIZONA

PREP: 25 MIN. **BAKE:** 20 MIN. **MAKES:** 8 SERVINGS

- 1 small onion, chopped
- ¼ cup all-purpose flour
- 3 cups chicken stock
- 3 cups cubed cooked turkey breast
- 1 package (16 ounces) frozen peas and carrots
- 2 medium red potatoes, cooked and cubed
- 3 tablespoons minced fresh parsley
- 1 tablespoon minced fresh thyme
- ¼ teaspoon pepper
- 1 sheet refrigerated pie pastry
  Additional fresh parsley or thyme leaves, optional
- 1 egg
- 1 teaspoon water
- ½ teaspoon kosher salt

1. In a Dutch oven coated with cooking spray, saute onion until tender. In a small bowl, whisk flour and stock until smooth; gradually stir into Dutch oven. Bring to a boil; cook and stir for 2 minutes or until thickened. Remove from the heat. Add the turkey, peas and carrots, potatoes, parsley, thyme and pepper; stir gently.

2. Divide turkey mixture among eight 10-oz. ramekins. On a lightly floured surface, unroll pastry. Cut out eight 3-in. circles. Gently press parsley into pastries if desired. Place over turkey mixture. Beat egg and water; brush over tops. Sprinkle with salt.

3. Place ramekins on a baking sheet. Bake at 425° for 20-25 minutes or until crusts are golden brown.

Nutrition Facts: *1 potpie equals 279 calories, 9 g fat (3 g saturated fat), 77 mg cholesterol, 495 mg sodium, 28 g carbohydrate, 3 g fiber, 22 g protein.* **Diabetic Exchanges:** *2 starch, 2 lean meat, ½ fat.*

Mediterranean Turkey Potpies

Your clan will love these wonderful, stick-to-the-ribs potpies featuring a unique flavor twist. I always use the leftovers from our big holiday turkey to prepare this recipe. I think my family enjoys the potpies more than the original feast!

—MARIE RIZZIO INTERLOCHEN, MICHIGAN

PREP: 30 MIN. **BAKE:** 20 MIN. **MAKES:** 6 SERVINGS

- 2 medium onions, thinly sliced
- 2 teaspoons olive oil
- 3 garlic cloves, minced
- 3 tablespoons all-purpose flour
- 1¼ cups reduced-sodium chicken broth
- 1 can (14½ ounces) no-salt-added diced tomatoes, undrained
- 2½ cups cubed cooked turkey breast
- 1 can (14 ounces) water-packed artichoke hearts, rinsed, drained and sliced
- ½ cup pitted ripe olives, halved
- ¼ cup sliced pepperoncini
- 1 tablespoon minced fresh oregano or 1 teaspoon dried oregano
- ¼ teaspoon pepper

CRUST
- 1 loaf (1 pound) frozen pizza dough, thawed
- 1 egg white
- 1 teaspoon minced fresh oregano or ¼ teaspoon dried oregano

1. In a Dutch oven, saute onions in oil until tender. Add garlic; cook 2 minutes longer. In a small bowl, whisk flour and broth until smooth; gradually stir into onion mixture. Stir in tomatoes. Bring to a boil; cook and stir for 2 minutes or until thickened.

2. Remove from the heat. Add the turkey, artichokes, olives, pepperoncini, oregano and pepper; stir gently. Divide turkey mixture among six 10-oz. ramekins.

3. Roll out 2 ounces dough to fit each ramekin (reserve remaining dough for another use). Cut slits in dough; place over filling. Press to seal edges. Combine egg white and oregano; brush over dough.

4. Place ramekins on a baking sheet. Bake at 425° for 18-22 minutes or until crusts are golden brown.

Nutrition Facts: *1 potpie equals 326 calories, 4 g fat (1 g saturated fat), 50 mg cholesterol, 699 mg sodium, 43 g carbohydrate, 3 g fiber, 26 g protein.* **Diabetic Exchanges:** *2 starch, 2 lean meat, 2 vegetable, ½ fat.*

Spicy Turkey Quesadillas

A bit of spice livens up cranberries and turkey while fat-free cream cheese rounds out the bold flavors in this easy appetizer.

—HEALTHY COOKING TEST KITCHEN

PREP/TOTAL TIME: 25 MIN. **MAKES:** 2 SERVINGS

- 3 ounces fat-free cream cheese
- ¼ cup chopped fresh or frozen cranberries, thawed
- 1 tablespoon chopped green chilies
- 1½ teaspoons honey
- 1 teaspoon Louisiana-style hot sauce
- 4 flour tortillas (6 inches)
- 1 cup diced cooked turkey breast

1. In a small bowl, beat cream cheese until smooth. Stir in the cranberries, chilies, honey and hot sauce until blended. Spread over one side of each tortilla. Place turkey on two tortillas; top with remaining tortillas.

2. Cook in a large nonstick skillet over medium heat for 2-3 minutes on each side or until lightly browned. Cut into wedges.

Nutrition Facts: *1 quesadilla equals 343 calories, 7 g fat (1 g saturated fat), 64 mg cholesterol, 751 mg sodium, 35 g carbohydrate, 1 g fiber, 33 g protein.* **Diabetic Exchanges:** *3 lean meat, 2 starch.*

Savory Turkey Potpies

Mediterranean Turkey Potpies

Garlic-Ginger Turkey Tenderloins 🅵🅲

PREP/TOTAL TIME: 30 MIN.
MAKES: 4 SERVINGS

- 1 **package (20 ounces) turkey breast tenderloins**
- 3 **tablespoons brown sugar, divided**
- 8 **teaspoons reduced-sodium soy sauce, divided**
- 2 **tablespoons minced fresh gingerroot**
- 6 **garlic cloves, minced**
- ½ **teaspoon pepper**
- 1 **tablespoon cornstarch**
- 1 **cup reduced-sodium chicken broth**

1. Place turkey in a shallow 3-qt. baking dish coated with cooking spray. In a small bowl, combine 2 tablespoons brown sugar, 6 teaspoons soy sauce, ginger, garlic and pepper. Set half aside; sprinkle remaining mixture over turkey.
2. Bake, uncovered, at 375° for 25-30 minutes or until a thermometer reads 170°. Let stand for 5 minutes before slicing.
3. Meanwhile, in a small saucepan, combine the cornstarch and broth until smooth. Stir in reserved soy sauce mixture and remaining brown sugar and soy sauce. Bring to a boil; cook and stir for 2 minutes or until thickened. Serve with turkey.

Nutrition Facts: *4 ounces cooked turkey equals 212 calories, 2 g fat (1 g saturated fat), 69 mg cholesterol, 639 mg sodium, 14 g carbohydrate, trace fiber, 35 g protein.*
Diabetic Exchanges: *4 lean meat, 1 starch.*

This good-for-you Asian entree can be on your family's plates quicker than Chinese takeout...and for a lot less money! It has a ginger, brown sugar and soy sauce that infuses the turkey tenderloins with spice as they bake.
—HEALTHY COOKING TEST KITCHEN

Did you know?

A comforting way to relieve the chills and congestions of a cold is to make ginger tea. Simmer one or two slices of fresh gingerroot in water for 10 minutes. Add a pinch of cinnamon if desired for extra flavor.

Mediterranean One-Dish Meal

I came up with this recipe one night when I was improvising with what I had on hand. I love to make simple, healthful, one-dish meals with lots of vegetables. Feta and Greek olives give this one a depth of flavor people seem to love!

—**DONNA JESSER** EVERETT, WASHINGTON

PREP: 15 MIN. **COOK:** 25 MIN. **MAKES:** 4 SERVINGS

- ¾ pound Italian turkey sausage links, cut into 1-inch pieces
- 1 medium onion, chopped
- 2 garlic cloves, minced
- 1 can (14½ ounces) no-salt-added diced tomatoes, undrained
- ¼ cup Greek olives
- 1 teaspoon dried oregano
- ½ cup quinoa, rinsed
- 3 cups fresh baby spinach
- ½ cup crumbled feta cheese

1. In a large nonstick skillet coated with cooking spray, cook sausage and onion over medium heat until sausage is browned and onion is tender. Add garlic; cook 1 minute longer. Stir in the tomatoes, olives and oregano; bring to a boil.

2. Stir in quinoa. Top with spinach. Reduce heat; cover and simmer for 12-15 minutes or until liquid is absorbed and spinach is tender. Remove from the heat; fluff with a fork. Sprinkle with cheese.

Editor's Note: *Look for quinoa in the cereal, rice or organic food aisle.*

Nutrition Facts: *1 cup equals 307 calories, 14 g fat (3 g saturated fat), 58 mg cholesterol, 845 mg sodium, 26 g carbohydrate, 5 g fiber, 21 g protein.* **Diabetic Exchanges:** *2 lean meat, 2 vegetable, 1 starch, 1 fat.*

French Onion Turkey Shepherd's Pie

In this healthier version of a traditional recipe, I punch up the flavor of turkey with caramelized onions and brandy, cut saturated fat with heart-healthy canola oil, and save a few calories for a sprinkling of gooey cheese. Serve with a side of lemony green beans to round out the meal.

—**JENNIFER BECKMAN** FALLS CHURCH, VIRGINIA

PREP: 40 MIN. **BAKE:** 30 MIN. **MAKES:** 4 SERVINGS

- 1 pound medium potatoes, peeled and cubed
- 2 large onions, peeled, halved and thinly sliced
- ½ teaspoon salt, divided
- 1 tablespoon canola oil
- 2¼ cups reduced-sodium beef broth, divided
- ¼ teaspoon pepper
- 1 pound extra-lean ground turkey
- 2 tablespoons all-purpose flour
- 2 tablespoons brandy or additional reduced-sodium beef broth
- 1 tablespoon stone-ground mustard
- 1 tablespoon Worcestershire sauce
- 1 cup frozen peas
- ⅓ cup shredded Gruyere or Swiss cheese

1. Place potatoes in a large saucepan and cover with water. Bring to a boil. Reduce heat; cover and cook for 10-15 minutes or until tender.

2. Meanwhile, in a large skillet, saute onions and ¼ teaspoon salt in oil until softened. Reduce the heat to medium-low; cook, stirring occasionally, for 30 minutes or until deep golden brown.

3. Drain potatoes. Mash with ¼ cup broth and pepper; set aside and keep warm.

4. In a nonstick skillet, cook turkey over medium heat until no longer pink; drain. Add the flour, brandy, mustard, Worcestershire sauce and remaining broth and salt. Cook and stir for 5-7 minutes or until thickened. Stir in peas and onion mixture.

5. Transfer to a 1½-qt. baking dish coated with cooking spray; spread with potato mixture. Bake, covered, at 375° for 20 minutes. Sprinkle with cheese. Bake, uncovered, 10-15 minutes longer or until golden brown.

Nutrition Facts: *1¼ cups equals 360 calories, 9 g fat (2 g saturated fat), 58 mg cholesterol, 803 mg sodium, 32 g carbohydrate, 4 g fiber, 37 g protein.* **Diabetic Exchanges:** *4 lean meat, 1½ starch, 1 vegetable, 1 fat.*

Sausage Pasta with Vegetables

PREP/TOTAL TIME: 25 MIN. **MAKES:** 4 SERVINGS

- 2 **cups uncooked whole wheat penne pasta**
- 1 **pound Italian turkey sausage links, casings removed**
- 1¾ **cups sliced fresh mushrooms**
- 1 **can (14½ ounces) fire-roasted diced tomatoes with garlic, undrained**
- 1 **package (6 ounces) fresh baby spinach**
- ¼ **cup shredded part-skim mozzarella cheese**

1. Cook penne according to package directions.
2. Meanwhile, in a Dutch oven, cook sausage and mushrooms over medium heat until meat is no longer pink; drain. Stir in tomatoes; bring to a boil. Add spinach; cook and stir until spinach is wilted.
3. Drain pasta; stir into turkey mixture. Sprinkle with cheese; remove from the heat. Cover and let stand until the cheese is melted.
Nutrition Facts: *1½ cups equals 445 calories, 13 g fat (3 g saturated fat), 72 mg cholesterol, 1,020 mg sodium, 51 g carbohydrate, 8 g fiber, 32 g protein.*

> ❝I made this tempting pasta for my pastor and his family. They loved it so much we nicknamed it "Jason's Pasta." It's a sneaky way to get kids and adults alike to eat more veggies.❞

—SUZIE FOUTTY MANSFIELD, OHIO

Spice-Rubbed Turkey 🅲

A neighbor served this turkey several years ago. My family was impressed, and they now request I make them the "lemon-filled one" ever since!

—SUSAN GREISHAW ARCHER, FLORIDA

PREP: 20 MIN. **BAKE:** 3½ HOURS + STANDING
MAKES: 28 SERVINGS

- 6 **teaspoons salt**
- 1¼ **teaspoons cayenne pepper**
- 1 **teaspoon pepper**
- ½ **teaspoon garlic powder**
- ½ **teaspoon chili powder**
- 1 **turkey (14 pounds)**
- 2 **tablespoons olive oil**
- 5 **small lemons**
- 2 **medium onions, cut into wedges**

1. In a small bowl combine the first five ingredients. With fingers, carefully loosen skin from the turkey; rub half the spice mixture under the skin.
2. Brush turkey with oil. Rub remaining spice mixture over turkey. Place lemons inside the neck and body cavity. Tuck wings under turkey; tie drumsticks together.
3. Arrange onions in a shallow roasting pan coated with cooking spray. Place turkey, breast side up, over onions.
4. Bake, uncovered, at 325° for 3½ to 4 hours or until a thermometer inserted in thigh reads 180°, basting occasionally with pan drippings. Cover loosely with foil if turkey browns too quickly. Cover and let stand for 20 minutes before carving.
5. Remove lemons from cavity. When cool enough to handle, halve the lemons and squeeze the juice over turkey if desired. Discard onions.
Nutrition Facts: *4 ounces cooked turkey (calculated without skin) equals 208 calories, 7 g fat (2 g saturated fat), 86 mg cholesterol, 586 mg sodium, 2 g carbohydrate, trace fiber, 33 g protein.* **Diabetic Exchange:** *4 lean meat.*

Pizza Pasta

I use Parmesan and mozzarella cheeses and toss in some of my favorite pizza toppings. Kids love it, and best of all, it only takes 10 minutes to prepare.

—KERRIE DEVAY NEW ORLEANS, LOUISIANA

PREP: 10 MIN. **BAKE:** 65 MIN. **MAKES:** 6 SERVINGS

- 4 **cups uncooked multigrain bow tie pasta**
- 2 **cans (14½ ounces each) fire-roasted diced tomatoes, undrained**
- ¾ **cup water**
- 12 **slices turkey pepperoni, quartered**
- 1 **tablespoon prepared pesto**
- ¼ **teaspoon pepper**
- ¾ **cup shredded Italian cheese blend**

1. In a large bowl, combine the pasta, tomatoes, water, pepperoni, pesto and pepper. Transfer to an 11-in. x 7-in. x 2-in. baking dish coated with cooking spray.
2. Cover and bake at 350° for 45 minutes. Stir; cover and bake 15 minutes longer or until pasta is tender. Top with cheese. Bake, uncovered, for 4-6 minutes or until cheese is melted.

Nutrition Facts: *1¼ cups equals 318 calories, 7 g fat (2 g saturated fat), 15 mg cholesterol, 584 mg sodium, 47 g carbohydrate, 5 g fiber, 16 g protein.* **Diabetic Exchanges:** *2½ starch, 1 medium-fat meat, 1 vegetable.*

Turkey Enchilada Stack

As a child, my husband was one of the pickiest kids around, but my mother-in-law could always get him to dig in to this enchilada dish. So I knew it was a winner!

—ASHLEY WOLF ALABASTER, ALABAMA

PREP/TOTAL TIME: 20 MIN. **MAKES:** 4 SERVINGS

- 1 pound lean ground turkey
- 2 cans (8 ounces each) no-salt-added tomato sauce
- 3 teaspoons dried minced onion
- ½ teaspoon garlic powder
- ½ teaspoon pepper
- ¼ teaspoon salt
- 4 whole wheat tortillas (8 inches)
- ⅔ cup shredded reduced-fat cheddar cheese
  Optional toppings: shredded lettuce, chopped tomatoes and reduced-fat sour cream

1. In a large skillet, cook turkey over medium heat until meat is no longer pink; drain. Stir in the tomato sauce, minced onion, garlic powder, pepper and salt; heat through.

2. In a 2½-qt. round microwave-safe dish coated with cooking spray, layer one tortilla, about ¾ cup meat mixture and a scant 3 tablespoons cheese. Repeat layers three times. Cover and cook on high for 4-5 minutes or until cheese is melted. Let stand for 5 minutes before cutting. Serve with toppings if desired.

Editor's Note: *This recipe was tested in a 1,100-watt microwave.*

Nutrition Facts: *1 piece (calculated without optional ingredients) equals 404 calories, 16 g fat (5 g saturated fat), 103 mg cholesterol, 582 mg sodium, 31 g carbohydrate, 3 g fiber, 29 g protein.* **Diabetic Exchanges:** *4 lean meat, 2 starch, 1 fat.*

Southwest Turkey Bulgur Dinner

In the past few years, I've been trying to incorporate more whole grains in our dinners. Bulgur is one of my favorite grains to work with because of its quick cooking time. Besides being high in fiber and rich in minerals, it has a mild, nutty flavor that my kids enjoy.

—MARIA VASSEUR VALENCIA, CALIFORNIA

PREP: 15 MIN. **COOK:** 30 MIN. **MAKES:** 4 SERVINGS

- 8 ounces lean ground turkey
- 1 small onion, chopped
- 1 garlic clove, minced
- 1 can (16 ounces) kidney beans, rinsed and drained
- 1 can (14½ ounces) diced tomatoes with mild green chilies
- 1½ cups water
- ½ cup frozen corn
- 1 tablespoon chili powder
- 1 teaspoon ground cumin
- ¼ teaspoon pepper
- ⅛ teaspoon salt
- 1 cup bulgur

TOPPING

- ½ cup fat-free plain Greek yogurt
- 1 tablespoon finely chopped green onion
- 1 tablespoon minced fresh cilantro

1. In a large nonstick skillet coated with cooking spray, cook turkey and onion over medium heat until meat is no longer pink. Add garlic; cook 1 minute longer.

2. Stir in the beans, tomatoes, water, corn, chili powder, cumin, pepper and salt. Bring to a boil. Stir in bulgur. Reduce heat; cover and simmer for 13-18 minutes or until bulgur is tender.

3. Remove from the heat; let stand 5 minutes. Fluff with a fork. Meanwhile, in a small bowl, combine the yogurt, green onion and cilantro. Serve with turkey mixture.

Nutrition Facts: *1¼ cups with 2 tablespoons topping equals 387 calories, 6 g fat (1 g saturated fat), 45 mg cholesterol, 628 mg sodium, 59 g carbohydrate, 14 g fiber, 27 g protein.*

Barbecued Turkey on Buns

I feel good serving these luscious sandwiches that make the most of unsweetened pineapple juice. Folks never guess they're made with ground turkey.

—**CHRISTA NORWALK** LA VALLE, WISCONSIN

PREP: 10 MIN. **COOK:** 35 MIN. **MAKES:** 6 SERVINGS

- 1 **pound lean ground turkey**
- ½ **cup chopped onion**
- ½ **cup chopped green pepper**
- 1 **can (6 ounces) tomato paste**
- 1 **can (6 ounces) unsweetened pineapple juice**
- ¼ **cup water**
- 2 **teaspoons Dijon mustard**
- ½ **teaspoon garlic powder**
- ½ **teaspoon salt**
- ⅛ **teaspoon pepper**
- 6 **whole wheat hamburger buns, split and toasted**

1. In a large saucepan coated with cooking spray, cook the turkey, onion and green pepper over medium heat until meat is no longer pink; drain.

2. Stir in the tomato paste, pineapple juice, water, mustard, garlic powder, salt and pepper. Bring to a boil. Reduce heat; simmer, uncovered, for 20-30 minutes or until sauce is thickened. Spoon ⅓ cup onto each bun.

Nutrition Facts: *1 sandwich equals 280 calories, 8 g fat (2 g saturated fat), 60 mg cholesterol, 538 mg sodium, 34 g carbohydrate, 6 g fiber, 18 g protein.* **Diabetic Exchanges:** *2 starch, 2 lean meat, 1 vegetable.*

Autumn Turkey Tenderloins

PREP/TOTAL TIME: 30 MIN. **MAKES:** 5 SERVINGS

- 1¼ **pounds turkey breast tenderloins**
- 1 **tablespoon butter**
- 1 **cup unsweetened apple juice**
- 1 **medium apple, sliced**
- 1 **tablespoon brown sugar**
- 2 **teaspoons chicken bouillon granules**
- ¼ **teaspoon ground cinnamon**
- ¼ **teaspoon ground nutmeg**
- 1 **tablespoon cornstarch**
- 2 **tablespoons cold water**
- ½ **cup chopped walnuts, toasted**

1. In a large skillet, brown turkey in butter. Add the apple juice, apple, brown sugar, bouillon, cinnamon and nutmeg. Bring to a boil. Reduce heat; cover and simmer for 10-12 minutes or until a thermometer reads 170°.

2. Using a slotted spoon, remove turkey and apple slices to a serving platter; keep warm.

3. Combine cornstarch and water until smooth; stir into pan juices. Bring to a boil; cook and stir for 2 minutes or until thickened. Spoon over turkey and apple. Sprinkle with walnuts.

Nutrition Facts: *1 serving equals 274 calories, 11 g fat (2 g saturated fat), 62 mg cholesterol, 423 mg sodium, 16 g carbohydrate, 2 g fiber, 30 g protein.* **Diabetic Exchanges:** *4 lean meat, 2 fat, 1 fruit.*

❝This out-of-the-ordinary meal is perfect for cool nights with family, friends or company. With cinnamon and brown sugar, it's slightly sweet, and the walnuts add a wonderful toasty and nutty crunch.❞

—**BRENDA LION** WARREN, PENNSYLVANIA

Turkey Pecan Enchiladas

PREP: 25 MIN. **BAKE:** 45 MIN.
MAKES: 12 SERVINGS

- 1 medium onion, chopped
- 4 ounces reduced-fat cream cheese
- 1 tablespoon water
- 1 teaspoon ground cumin
- ¼ teaspoon pepper
- ⅛ teaspoon salt
- 4 cups cubed cooked turkey breast
- ¼ cup chopped pecans, toasted
- 12 flour tortillas (6 inches), warmed
- 1 can (10¾ ounces) reduced-fat reduced-sodium condensed cream of chicken soup, undiluted
- 1 cup (8 ounces) reduced-fat sour cream
- 1 cup fat-free milk
- 2 tablespoons canned chopped green chilies
- ½ cup shredded reduced-fat cheddar cheese
- 2 tablespoons minced fresh cilantro

1. In a small nonstick skillet coated with cooking spray, cook and stir onion over medium heat until tender. Set aside.
2. In a large bowl, beat the cream cheese, water, cumin, pepper and salt until smooth. Stir in the onion, turkey and pecans.
3. Spoon ⅓ cup turkey mixture down the center of each tortilla. Roll up and place seam side down in a 13-in. x 9-in. baking dish coated with cooking spray. Combine the soup, sour cream, milk and chilies; pour over enchiladas.
4. Cover and bake at 350° for 40 minutes. Uncover; sprinkle with cheese. Bake 5 minutes longer or until heated through and cheese is melted. Sprinkle with cilantro.

Nutrition Facts: *1 enchilada equals 263 calories, 10 g fat (4 g saturated fat), 59 mg cholesterol, 472 mg sodium, 20 g carbohydrate, 1 g fiber, 22 g protein.*
Diabetic Exchanges: *2 lean meat, 1½ starch, ½ fat.*

Turkey Cutlets with Cool Pepper Sauce **C**

Crisp breading surrounds tender turkey cutlets in this refreshing recipe. Topped with a sour-cream sauce that features lively jalapeno and lemon, it has just the right kick!

—**JEANNIE KLUGH** LANCASTER, PENNSYLVANIA

PREP/TOTAL TIME: 25 MIN. **MAKES:** 4 SERVINGS (½ CUP SAUCE)

- 3 tablespoons reduced-fat sour cream
- 2 tablespoons reduced-fat mayonnaise
- 2 tablespoons minced seeded jalapeno pepper
- 2 teaspoons lemon juice
- ¼ teaspoon grated lemon peel
- ⅛ teaspoon plus ¼ teaspoon pepper, divided
- ½ cup seasoned bread crumbs
- 2 tablespoons grated Parmesan cheese
- 1 tablespoon minced fresh parsley
- 1 garlic clove, minced
- 1 package (17.6 ounces) turkey breast cutlets
- 1 tablespoon olive oil
  Lemon wedges and sliced jalapeno peppers, optional

1. For sauce, in a small bowl, combine the sour cream, mayonnaise, jalapeno, lemon juice and peel and ⅛ teaspoon pepper; set aside.

2. In a large resealable plastic bag, combine the bread crumbs, Parmesan cheese, parsley, garlic and remaining pepper. Add turkey, a few pieces at a time, and shake to coat.

3. In a large nonstick skillet, cook turkey in oil in batches over medium heat for 1-2 minutes on each side or until no longer pink. Serve with sauce. Garnish with lemon wedges and jalapenos if desired.

Editor's Note: *Wear disposable gloves when cutting hot peppers; the oils can burn skin. Avoid touching your face.*

Nutrition Facts: *4 ounces cooked turkey with 2 tablespoons sauce equals 242 calories, 9 g fat (2 g saturated fat), 78 mg cholesterol, 296 mg sodium, 9 g carbohydrate, 1 g fiber, 31 g protein.* **Diabetic Exchanges:** *4 lean meat, 1½ fat, ½ starch.*

Turkey Fettuccine Skillet

I came up with this simple dish as a way to use up leftover turkey from holiday dinners. It's become a family tradition to enjoy it the day after Thanksgiving and Christmas.

—**KARI JOHNSTON** MARWAYNE, ALBERTA

PREP: 10 MIN. **COOK:** 30 MIN. **MAKES:** 6 SERVINGS

- 8 ounces uncooked fettuccine
- ½ cup chopped onion
- ½ cup chopped celery
- 4 garlic cloves, minced
- 1 teaspoon canola oil
- 1 cup sliced fresh mushrooms
- 2 cups fat-free milk
- 1 teaspoon salt-free seasoning blend
- ¼ teaspoon salt
- 2 tablespoons cornstarch
- ½ cup fat-free half-and-half
- ⅓ cup grated Parmesan cheese
- 3 cups cubed cooked turkey breast
- ¾ cup shredded part-skim mozzarella cheese

1. Cook fettuccine according to package directions. Meanwhile, in a large ovenproof skillet coated with cooking spray, saute the onion, celery and garlic in oil for 3 minutes. Add mushrooms; cook and stir until vegetables are tender. Stir in the milk, seasoning blend and salt. Bring to a boil.

2. Combine cornstarch and half-and-half until smooth; stir into skillet. Cook and stir for 2 minutes or until thickened and bubbly. Stir in Parmesan cheese just until melted.

3. Stir in turkey. Drain fettuccine; add to turkey mixture. Heat through. Sprinkle with mozzarella cheese. Broil 4-6 in. from the heat for 2-3 minutes or until cheese is melted.

Nutrition Facts: *1 cup equals 361 calories, 7 g fat (3 g saturated fat), 76 mg cholesterol, 343 mg sodium, 38 g carbohydrate, 2 g fiber, 34 g protein.* **Diabetic Exchanges:** *4 lean meat, 2½ starch, ½ fat.*

Open-Faced Meatball Sandwiches

My husband and I love meatball subs, so I tried to come up with a slimmed-down version that's easy to make after a long day. The meatballs freeze well for a soothing batch another night, too!

—**KAREN BARTHEL** NORTH CANTON, OHIO

PREP: 30 MIN. **COOK:** 10 MIN. **MAKES:** 8 SERVINGS

- ¼ cup egg substitute
- ½ cup soft bread crumbs
- ¼ cup finely chopped onion
- 2 garlic cloves, minced
- ½ teaspoon onion powder
- ½ teaspoon dried oregano
- ½ teaspoon dried basil
- ¼ teaspoon pepper
  Dash salt
- 1¼ pounds lean ground turkey
- 2 cups garden-style pasta sauce
- 4 hoagie buns, split
- 2 tablespoons shredded part-skim mozzarella cheese
  Shredded Parmesan cheese, optional

1. In a large bowl, combine the first nine ingredients. Crumble turkey over mixture and mix well. Shape into 40 meatballs, 1 in. each. In a large skillet coated with cooking spray, brown meatballs in batches; drain.
2. Place meatballs in a large saucepan. Add the pasta sauce; bring to a boil. Reduce heat; cover and simmer for 10-15 minutes or until meat is no longer pink.
3. Spoon meatballs and sauce onto bun halves; sprinkle with mozzarella cheese and Parmesan cheese if desired.

Nutrition Facts: *1 meatball sandwich equals 275 calories, 10 g fat (3 g saturated fat), 60 mg cholesterol, 542 mg sodium, 28 g carbohydrate, 3 g fiber, 19 g protein.* **Diabetic Exchanges:** *2 lean meat, 1½ starch, 1 vegetable, ½ fat.*

Italian-Style Cabbage Rolls

Here's a great way to get your family to eat their veggies. Not only is this one of my gang's favorite dinners, but my son loves to help me roll the turkey filling into the cabbage leaves.

—**ERIKA NIEHOFF** EVELETH, MINNESOTA

PREP: 45 MIN. **BAKE:** 50 MIN. **MAKES:** 5 SERVINGS

- ⅓ cup uncooked brown rice
- 1 medium head cabbage
- ½ cup shredded carrot
- ¼ cup finely chopped onion
- ¼ cup egg substitute
- 1 can (10¾ ounces) reduced-sodium condensed tomato soup, undiluted, divided
- 1 can (10¾ ounces) reduced-fat reduced-sodium condensed vegetable beef soup, undiluted, divided
- 2 tablespoons Italian seasoning, divided
- ¼ teaspoon cayenne pepper
- ¼ teaspoon pepper
- 1 pound lean ground turkey

1. Cook rice according to package directions. Meanwhile, cook cabbage in boiling water just until leaves fall off head. Set aside 10 large leaves for rolls. (Refrigerate remaining cabbage for another use.) Cut out the thick vein from the bottom of each reserved leaf, making a V-shaped cut.
2. In a large bowl, combine the carrot, onion, egg substitute, 2 tablespoons tomato soup, 2 tablespoons vegetable soup, 1 tablespoon Italian seasoning, cayenne, pepper and rice. Crumble turkey over mixture and mix well. Place about ⅓ cupful on each cabbage leaf. Overlap cut ends of leaf; fold in sides, beginning from the cut end. Roll up completely to enclose filling.
3. Place rolls seam side down in an 11-in. x 7-in. baking dish coated with cooking spray. Combine the remaining soups; pour over cabbage rolls. Sprinkle with remaining Italian seasoning. Cover and bake at 350° for 50-60 minutes or until cabbage is tender and a thermometer reads 165°.

Nutrition Facts: *2 cabbage rolls equals 293 calories, 10 g fat (3 g saturated fat), 74 mg cholesterol, 582 mg sodium, 29 g carbohydrate, 4 g fiber, 22 g protein.* **Diabetic Exchanges:** *3 lean meat, 1½ starch, 1 vegetable.*

Southwestern Stuffed Turkey Breast **C**

PREP: 40 MIN.
BAKE: 1¼ HOURS + STANDING
MAKES: 8 SERVINGS

- ⅓ cup sun-dried tomatoes (not packed in oil)
- ⅔ cup boiling water
- 1½ teaspoons dried oregano
- 1 teaspoon salt
- ¾ teaspoon ground cumin
- ½ teaspoon ground coriander
- ¼ teaspoon crushed red pepper flakes
- 1 small onion, chopped
- 1 small green pepper, diced
- 1 garlic clove, minced
- 1 tablespoon olive oil
- 1 cup frozen corn, thawed
- ½ cup dry bread crumbs
- 1½ teaspoons grated lime peel
- 1 boneless skinless turkey breast half (2 pounds)

1. Place tomatoes in a small bowl; cover with boiling water. Cover and let stand for 5 minutes. Drain, reserving 3 tablespoons liquid; set aside. Meanwhile, combine seasonings in a small bowl.

2. In a large skillet, saute the tomatoes, onion, green pepper and garlic in oil until tender. Stir in corn and 2 teaspoons seasonings; remove from the heat. Stir in bread crumbs and reserved tomato liquid. Add lime peel to remaining seasonings; set side.

3. Cover turkey with plastic wrap. Flatten to ½-in. thickness; remove plastic. Sprinkle turkey with half of lime-seasoning mixture; spread vegetable mixture to within 1 in. of edges. Roll up jelly-roll style, starting with a short side; tie with kitchen string. Sprinkle with remaining lime-seasoning mixture. Place on a rack in a shallow roasting pan; cover loosely with foil.

4. Bake at 350° for 1 hour. Uncover; bake 15-30 minutes longer or until a thermometer reads 170°, basting occasionally with pan drippings. Let stand for 15 minutes before slicing.

Nutrition Facts: *1 slice equals 200 calories, 3 g fat (1 g saturated fat), 70 mg cholesterol, 458 mg sodium, 12 g carbohydrate, 2 g fiber, 30 g protein.* **Diabetic Exchanges:** *3 lean meat, 1 starch.*

This luscious turkey breast is a sure hit with family and friends around the holidays. The moist stuffing gives it a hint of Southwestern flair.
—**BERNICE JANOWSKI** STEVENS POINT, WISCONSIN

Turkey Mole Tacos

In contrast to traditional tacos, these taste complete as-is, without need for further garnishes or sauces. I've also made this using bite-sized pieces of chicken thighs and increasing the cooking time accordingly.

—HELEN GLAZIER SEATTLE, WASHINGTON

PREP: 25 MIN. **COOK:** 20 MIN. **MAKES:** 6 SERVINGS

- 1¼ pounds lean ground turkey
- 1 celery rib, chopped
- 4 green onions, chopped
- 2 garlic cloves, minced
- 1 can (14½ ounces) diced tomatoes, undrained
- 1 jar (7 ounces) roasted sweet red peppers, drained and chopped
- 2 ounces 53% cacao dark baking chocolate, chopped
- 4 teaspoons chili powder
- 1 teaspoon ground cumin
- ½ teaspoon salt
- ¼ teaspoon ground cinnamon
- ¼ cup lightly salted mixed nuts, coarsely chopped
- 12 corn tortillas (6 inches), warmed

1. In a large nonstick skillet coated with cooking spray, cook the turkey, celery, green onions and garlic over medium heat until meat is no longer pink and vegetables are tender; drain.

2. Stir in the tomatoes, red peppers, chocolate, chili powder, cumin, salt and cinnamon. Bring to a boil. Reduce heat; cover and simmer for 10 minutes, stirring occasionally.

3. Remove from the heat; stir in nuts. Place about ⅓ cup filling on each tortilla.

Nutrition Facts: *2 tacos equals 369 calories, 15 g fat (5 g saturated fat), 75 mg cholesterol, 612 mg sodium, 37 g carbohydrate, 6 g fiber, 22 g protein.* **Diabetic Exchanges:** *3 lean meat, 2 starch, 1 vegetable, 1 fat.*

Turkey Stroganoff with Spaghetti Squash

My twin sister and I came up with this entree after we both successfully lost weight but still wanted to indulge in comfort food. Spaghetti squash is a fantastic gluten-free alternative to pasta, and we use it in many recipes.

—COURTNEY VARELA ALISO VIEJO, CALIFORNIA

PREP: 25 MIN. **COOK:** 15 MIN. **MAKES:** 6 SERVINGS

- 1 medium spaghetti squash (about 4 pounds)
- 1 pound lean ground turkey
- 2 cups sliced fresh mushrooms
- 1 medium onion, chopped
- 2 garlic cloves, minced
- ½ cup white wine or beef stock
- 3 tablespoons cornstarch
- 2 cups beef stock
- 2 tablespoons Worcestershire sauce
- 1 tablespoon Montreal steak seasoning
- 1 teaspoon minced fresh thyme or ¼ teaspoon dried thyme
- ¼ cup half-and-half cream
  Grated Parmesan cheese and minced fresh parsley, optional

1. Cut squash in half lengthwise; discard seeds. Place squash cut side down on a microwave-safe plate. Microwave, uncovered, on high for 15-18 minutes or until tender.

2. Meanwhile, in a large nonstick skillet, cook the turkey, mushrooms and onion over medium heat until turkey is no longer pink; drain. Add garlic; cook 1 minute longer. Stir in wine.

3. Combine cornstarch and stock until smooth. Add to pan. Stir in the Worcestershire sauce, steak seasoning and thyme. Bring to a boil; cook and stir for 2 minutes or until thickened. Reduce heat. Stir in cream; heat through.

4. When squash is cool enough to handle, use a fork to separate strands. Serve with turkey mixture. Sprinkle with cheese and parsley if desired.

Nutrition Facts: *¾ cup stroganoff with ⅔ cup squash (calculated without cheese) equals 246 calories, 9 g fat (3 g saturated fat), 65 mg cholesterol, 677 mg sodium, 25 g carbohydrate, 4 g fiber, 17 g protein.* **Diabetic Exchanges:** *2 lean meat, 1½ starch.*

148

155

161

Pork,
Ham & More

"I don't remember where I found this recipe, but it has become one of my favorite entrees to serve company. I usually prepare it with a side of roasted vegetables."

KATHY KANTRUD FENTON, MICHIGAN
about her recipe, Spiced Pork Medallions with Bourbon Sauce, on page 151

California Club Pizza

You can use your favorite store-bought pizza dough or make your own for this West Coast-inspired pie. Our food editor and registered dietitian, Peggy Woodward, came up with this BLT-like combination for her family's pizza night.
—HEALTHY COOKING TEST KITCHEN

PREP: 25 MIN. **BAKE:** 10 MIN.
MAKES: 4 SERVINGS

- 1 tablespoon cornmeal
- 1 pound prepared pizza dough
- ½ cup shredded reduced-fat Mexican cheese blend
- 3 bacon strips, cooked and crumbled
- 3 cups shredded romaine
- ¼ cup fat-free mayonnaise
- 1 tablespoon lime juice
- 3 teaspoons minced fresh cilantro, divided
- 1 cup alfalfa sprouts
- 1 medium tomato, thinly sliced
- ½ medium ripe avocado, peeled and cut into 8 slices

1. Coat a 12-in. pizza pan with cooking spray; sprinkle with cornmeal. On a floured surface, roll dough into a 13-in. circle. Transfer to prepared pan; build up edges slightly. Sprinkle with cheese and bacon. Bake at 450° for 10-12 minutes or until crust is lightly browned.
2. Meanwhile, place romaine in a large bowl. In a small bowl, combine the mayonnaise, lime juice and 2 teaspoons cilantro. Pour over romaine; toss to coat. Arrange over warm pizza. Top with sprouts, tomato, avocado and remaining cilantro. Serve immediately.
Nutrition Facts: *2 slices equals 372 calories, 14 g fat (3 g saturated fat), 18 mg cholesterol, 634 mg sodium, 53 g carbohydrate, 11 g fiber, 16 g protein.*

Creamy Ham Penne

Mixing spreadable cheese with whole wheat pasta, broccoli and fat-free milk for a main dish is a healthier use of this convenience product than simply spreading it on crackers.
—BARBARA PLETZKE HERNDON, VIRGINIA

PREP/TOTAL TIME: 30 MIN. **MAKES:** 4 SERVINGS

- 2 cups uncooked whole wheat penne pasta
- 2 cups fresh broccoli florets
- 1 cup fat-free milk
- 1 package (6½ ounces) reduced-fat garlic-herb spreadable cheese
- 1 cup cubed fully cooked ham
- ¼ teaspoon pepper

In a large saucepan, cook penne according to package directions, adding broccoli during the last 5 minutes of cooking; drain. Remove and set aside. In the same pan, combine milk and spreadable cheese. Cook and stir over medium heat for 3-5 minutes or until cheese is melted. Add the ham, pepper and penne mixture; heat through.
Nutrition Facts: *1¼ cups equals 371 calories, 8 g fat (5 g saturated fat), 47 mg cholesterol, 672 mg sodium, 49 g carbohydrate, 7 g fiber, 25 g protein.*

top tip Dip In

Fans of dip will love this trick: Combine equal parts salsa and fat-free peppercorn ranch salad dressing as a dunking sauce for the crust of California Club Pizza.
—HEALTHY COOKING TEST KITCHEN

Tender Pork Chops with Mango Salsa **S**

To save time, I make the salsa and season the pork in the morning so it's ready to throw on the grill later. For a spicier topping, I toss minced jalapenos into the salsa.

—ANDREA RIVERA WESTBURY, NEW YORK

PREP: 15 MIN. + MARINATING **GRILL:** 10 MIN.
MAKES: 4 SERVINGS

- 3 **tablespoons cider vinegar**
- 1 **tablespoon salt-free steak grilling blend**
- 1 **tablespoon olive oil**
- 4 **bone-in pork loin chops (7 ounces each)**

SALSA
- 2 **medium mangoes, peeled and chopped**
- 1 **cup chopped sweet onion**
- 1 **jalapeno pepper, seeded and finely chopped**
- 1 **tablespoon lemon juice**
- 2 **teaspoons honey**

1. In a large resealable plastic bag, combine the vinegar, grilling blend and oil. Add the pork; seal bag and turn to coat. Refrigerate for at least 2 hours.
2. Drain and discard marinade. Grill chops, covered, over medium heat or broil 4-5 in. from the heat for 4-5 minutes on each side or until a thermometer reads 145°. Let stand for 5 minutes before serving.
3. Meanwhile, in a small bowl, combine the salsa ingredients. Serve with chops.

Editor's Note: *Wear disposable gloves when cutting hot peppers; the oils can burn skin. Avoid touching your face.*

Nutrition Facts: *1 pork chop with ¾ cup salsa equals 330 calories, 12 g fat (4 g saturated fat), 86 mg cholesterol, 67 mg sodium, 25 g carbohydrate, 3 g fiber, 31 g protein.* **Diabetic Exchanges:** *4 lean meat, 1 fruit, ½ starch, ½ fat.*

Skillet Apple Pork Chops **C**

With fresh sage and apple, this dish is tasty, easy and done in a flash. I keep a jar with three cloves of garlic covered in olive oil and use that instead of garlic butter. The garlic oil is delicious for salads also.

—LORRAINE CALAND SHUNIAH, ONTARIO

PREP/TOTAL TIME: 30 MIN. **MAKES:** 4 SERVINGS

- 4 **boneless pork loin chops (4 ounces each)**
- 1 **medium apple, peeled and sliced**
- 1 **tablespoon canola oil**
- ½ **cup unsweetened apple juice**
- 1 **tablespoon Dijon mustard**
- 1 **garlic clove, minced**
- 1 **teaspoon rubbed sage**
- ¼ **teaspoon salt**
- ⅛ **teaspoon crushed red pepper flakes**

1. In a large skillet, cook pork chops and apple in oil over medium heat for 8-10 minutes or until a thermometer inserted in pork reads 145°. Remove and keep warm. Add remaining ingredients to pan.
2. Bring to a boil; cook until liquid is reduced by half. Serve with chops and apple.

Nutrition Facts: *1 serving equals 218 calories, 10 g fat (3 g saturated fat), 55 mg cholesterol, 270 mg sodium, 9 g carbohydrate, 1 g fiber, 22 g protein.* **Diabetic Exchanges:** *3 lean meat, 1 fat, ½ fruit.*

Asian Pork Stir-Fry

Working two jobs leaves little time for me to grocery shop, so I cook with whatever veggies and leftover meat I have on hand.
—**DEBORAH SHEAHEN** HICKORY, NORTH CAROLINA

PREP/TOTAL TIME: 30 MIN. **MAKES:** 4 SERVINGS

- 2 **tablespoons cornstarch**
- ½ **cup water**
- ½ **cup reduced-sodium chicken broth**
- 2 **garlic cloves, minced**
- 2 **teaspoons minced fresh gingerroot**
- 1 **pound pork tenderloin, cut into ½-inch pieces**
- 2 **tablespoons sesame or canola oil, divided**
- 1½ **cups sliced fresh mushrooms**
- 1 **cup bean sprouts**
- 1 **cup sliced bok choy**
- 1 **cup fresh snow peas**
- 1 **small sweet red pepper, cut into ¾-inch pieces**
- 2 **tablespoons reduced-sodium soy sauce**
- 2 **cups hot cooked brown rice**

1. In a small bowl, combine cornstarch and water until smooth. Stir in the broth, garlic and ginger; set aside.
2. In a large skillet or wok, stir-fry pork in 1 tablespoon oil until no longer pink. Remove and keep warm.
3. Stir-fry the mushrooms, bean sprouts, bok choy, peas, pepper and soy sauce in remaining oil for 4-5 minutes or until vegetables are crisp-tender.
4. Stir cornstarch mixture and add to the pan. Bring to a boil; cook and stir for 1 minute or until thickened. Add pork; heat through. Serve with rice.

Nutrition Facts: *1 cup stir-fry with ½ cup rice equals 386 calories, 12 g fat (3 g saturated fat), 63 mg cholesterol, 565 mg sodium, 38 g carbohydrate, 6 g fiber, 32 g protein.* **Diabetic Exchanges:** *3 lean meat, 2 vegetable, 1½ starch, 1½ fat.*

Tomato-Topped Italian Pork Chops 🄲

Busy night ahead of you? Time to bring out the slow cooker! You're only seven ingredients away from a saucy, delicious meal. This zesty pork dinner is ready for you when you walk through the door after a long, hard day at work. Simply add a veggie and supper is all set to enjoy!

—**KRYSTLE CHASSE** RADIUM HOT SPRINGS, BRITISH COLUMBIA

PREP: 25 MIN. **COOK:** 8 HOURS **MAKES:** 6 SERVINGS

- 6 **bone-in pork loin chops (7 ounces each)**
- 1 **tablespoon canola oil**
- 1 **small onion, chopped**
- ½ **cup chopped carrot**
- 1 **can (14½ ounces) diced tomatoes, drained**
- ¼ **cup reduced-fat balsamic vinaigrette**
- 2 **teaspoons dried oregano**

1. In a large skillet, brown chops in oil in batches. Transfer to a 4- or 5-qt. slow cooker coated with cooking spray. Saute onion and carrot in drippings until tender. Stir in the tomatoes, vinaigrette and oregano; pour over chops.
2. Cover and cook on low for 8-10 hours or until meat is tender.

Nutrition Facts: *1 pork chop equals 267 calories, 12 g fat (3 g saturated fat), 86 mg cholesterol, 234 mg sodium, 7 g carbohydrate, 2 g fiber, 31 g protein.* **Diabetic Exchanges:** *4 lean meat, 1 vegetable, 1 fat.*

Southwestern Pineapple Pork Chops C

PREP/TOTAL TIME: 30 MIN.   **MAKES:** 4 SERVINGS

- 4   boneless pork loin chops (5 ounces each)
- ½   teaspoon garlic pepper blend
- 1   tablespoon canola oil
- 1   can (8 ounces) unsweetened crushed pineapple, undrained
- 1   cup medium salsa
     Minced fresh cilantro

Sprinkle pork chops with pepper blend. In a large skillet, brown chops in oil. Remove and keep warm. In the same skillet, combine pineapple and salsa. Bring to a boil. Return chops to the pan. Reduce heat; cover and simmer for 15-20 minutes or until tender. Sprinkle with cilantro.

Nutrition Facts: *1 pork chop with ⅓ cup sauce equals 274 calories, 12 g fat (3 g saturated fat), 68 mg cholesterol, 315 mg sodium, 13 g carbohydrate, trace fiber, 27 g protein.* **Diabetic Exchanges:** *4 lean meat, 1 fat, ½ fruit.*

66 My husband and I love visiting the Southwest. After a recent trip, I wanted to come up with some dishes that had a Southwestern flair. This is one of our fast and healthy go-to recipes. 99

—**LISA VARNER** EL PASO, TEXAS

Lamb Stew

My grandmother used to make this stew as a special Sunday meal and a memorable treat from Ireland. If you like your stew thick and rich, you've got to try this.

—**VICKIE DESOURDY** WASHINGTON, NORTH CAROLINA

PREP: 40 MIN.   **BAKE:** 1½ HOURS
MAKES: 8 SERVINGS (2½ QUARTS)

- 2   pounds lamb stew meat, cut into 1-inch cubes
- 1   tablespoon butter
- 1   tablespoon olive oil
- 1   pound carrots, sliced
- 2   medium onions, thinly sliced
- 2   garlic cloves, minced
- 1½   cups reduced-sodium chicken broth
- 1   bottle (12 ounces) Guinness stout or additional reduced-sodium chicken broth
- 6   medium red potatoes, peeled and cut into 1-inch cubes
- 4   bay leaves
- 2   fresh thyme sprigs
- 2   fresh rosemary sprigs
- 2   teaspoons salt
- 1½   teaspoons pepper
- ¼   cup heavy whipping cream

1. In an ovenproof Dutch oven, brown lamb in butter and oil in batches. Remove and keep warm. In the same pan, saute carrots and onions in drippings until crisp-tender. Add garlic; cook 1 minute longer. Gradually add broth and beer. Stir in the lamb, potatoes, bay leaves, thyme, rosemary, salt and pepper.
2. Cover and bake at 325° for 1½ to 2 hours or until meat and vegetables are tender, stirring every 30 minutes. Discard bay leaves, thyme and rosemary. Stir in cream; heat through.

Nutrition Facts: *1¼ cups equals 311 calories, 12 g fat (5 g saturated fat), 88 mg cholesterol, 829 mg sodium, 23 g carbohydrate, 4 g fiber, 26 g protein.* **Diabetic Exchanges:** *3 lean meat, 2 vegetable, 1 starch, 1 fat.*

> I don't remember where I found this recipe, but it has become one of my favorite entrees to serve company. I usually prepare it with a side of roasted vegetables.
>
> —**KATHY KANTRUD** FENTON, MICHIGAN

Spiced Pork Medallions with Bourbon Sauce **C**

PREP/TOTAL TIME: 25 MIN.
MAKES: 4 SERVINGS

- ½ cup bourbon or reduced-sodium chicken broth
- ¼ cup packed dark brown sugar
- 3 tablespoons white vinegar
- 3 tablespoons reduced-sodium soy sauce
- 2 garlic cloves, minced
- ½ teaspoon pepper
- ½ teaspoon chili powder
- ¼ teaspoon ground cinnamon
- ⅛ teaspoon salt
- ⅛ teaspoon ground allspice
- 1 pork tenderloin (1 pound), cut into 12 slices

1. In a small saucepan, combine the bourbon, brown sugar, vinegar, soy sauce, garlic and pepper. Bring to a boil; cook until liquid is reduced to about ½ cup, stirring occasionally.

2. Meanwhile, combine the chili powder, cinnamon, salt and allspice; rub over pork slices.

3. In a large skillet coated with cooking spray, cook pork over medium heat for 2-4 minutes on each side or until tender. Serve with sauce.

Nutrition Facts: *3 ounces pork with 2 tablespoons sauce equals 221 calories, 4 g fat (1 g saturated fat), 63 mg cholesterol, 581 mg sodium, 15 g carbohydrate, trace fiber, 23 g protein.* **Diabetic Exchanges:** *3 lean meat, 1 starch.*

Tenderloin to the Rescue

Keep pork tenderloin in the freezer for last-minute meals since it thaws and cooks quickly. Thaw tenderloin using the "defrost" cycle of your microwave according to the manufacturer's directions. Cut pork tenderloin while partially frozen into thin, even slices, and cut those slices into strips. Use in place of beef or chicken in your favorite stir-fry or fajita recipes.

Italian Pork and Potato Casserole

This recipe has been enjoyed by three generations of my family. My mother concocted it years ago using a few items she said were handy at the time. The aroma from these ingredients brings back fond memories of home.

—THERESA KREYCHE TUSTIN, CALIFORNIA

PREP: 10 MIN. **BAKE:** 45 MIN.
MAKES: 6 SERVINGS

- 6 **cups sliced red potatoes**
- 3 **tablespoons water**
- 1 **garlic clove, minced**
- ½ **teaspoon salt**
- ⅛ **teaspoon pepper**
- 6 **boneless pork loin chops (6 ounces each)**
- 1 **jar (24 ounces) marinara sauce**
- ¼ **cup shredded Parmesan cheese**

1. Place potatoes and water in a microwave-safe dish. Cover and microwave on high for 5 minutes or just until tender; drain.
2. Place potatoes in a 13-in. x 9-in. baking dish coated with cooking spray. Sprinkle with garlic, salt and pepper. Top with pork chops and marinara sauce. Cover and bake at 350° for 40-45 minutes or until a thermometer reads 145° and potatoes are tender.
3. Sprinkle with cheese. Bake, uncovered, 3-5 minutes longer or until cheese is melted.
Nutrition Facts: *1 pork chop with 1 cup potatoes and ½ cup sauce equals 412 calories, 11 g fat (4 g saturated fat), 84 mg cholesterol, 506 mg sodium, 38 g carbohydrate, 4 g fiber, 39 g protein.*
Diabetic Exchanges: *5 lean meat, 2½ starch.*

Dijon Pork Medallions C

My husband likes anything with Dijon, so these quick-fix pork medallions are one of his favorites.

—JOYCE MOYNIHAN LAKEVILLE, MINNESOTA

PREP/TOTAL TIME: 20 MIN. **MAKES:** 4 SERVINGS

- 1 **pork tenderloin (1 pound)**
- 1½ **teaspoons lemon-pepper seasoning**
- 2 **tablespoons butter**
- 2 **tablespoons lemon juice**
- 1 **tablespoon Worcestershire sauce**
- 1 **teaspoon Dijon mustard**
- 1 **tablespoon minced fresh parsley**

1. Cut pork into eight slices; flatten to 1-in. thickness. Sprinkle with lemon-pepper. In a large nonstick skillet, cook pork in butter over medium heat for 3-4 minutes on each side or until tender. Remove and keep warm.
2. Stir the lemon juice, Worcestershire sauce and mustard into skillet; heat through. Serve with pork; sprinkle with parsley.
Nutrition Facts: *2 pork slices with about 2 teaspoons sauce equals 189 calories, 10 g fat (5 g saturated fat), 78 mg cholesterol, 330 mg sodium, 2 g carbohydrate, trace fiber, 23 g protein.*
Diabetic Exchanges: *3 lean meat, 1 fat.*

Did you know?

Due to breeding and feeding changes over the last 20 years, the fat content of pork has been reduced to make it a leaner product. Some of the leanest cuts of pork are boneless loin roasts or chops, boneless sirloin roasts or chops and bone-in pork loin chops. Ounce for ounce, pork tenderloin is almost as lean as boneless skinless chicken breast.

Light Ham Tetrazzini

If you're bringing this slow-cooked tetrazzini to a potluck, add the cooked spaghetti to the crock just before heading to the gathering. Insulated carrying cases keep the food hot and make this dish easy to transport.

—**SUSAN BLAIR** STERLING, MICHIGAN

PREP: 15 MIN. **COOK:** 4 HOURS
MAKES: 10 SERVINGS

- 2 cans (10¾ ounces each) reduced-fat reduced-sodium condensed cream of mushroom soup, undiluted
- 2 cups sliced fresh mushrooms
- 2 cups cubed fully cooked ham
- 1 cup fat-free evaporated milk
- ¼ cup white wine or water
- 2 teaspoons prepared horseradish
- 1 package (14½ ounces) uncooked multigrain spaghetti
- 1 cup shredded Parmesan cheese

1. In a 5-qt. slow cooker, combine the soup, mushrooms, ham, milk, wine and horseradish. Cover and cook on low for 4 hours.

2. Cook spaghetti according to package directions; drain. Add spaghetti and cheese to slow cooker; toss to coat.

Nutrition Facts: *1 cup equals 279 calories, 5 g fat (2 g saturated fat), 26 mg cholesterol, 734 mg sodium, 37 g carbohydrate, 4 g fiber, 20 g protein.* **Diabetic Exchanges:** *2½ starch, 1 lean meat, ½ fat.*

Rosemary Pork Loin C

I started growing rosemary in my garden after I discovered this pork recipe. My husband and I think it's restaurant-quality, and we look forward to making it after work.

—**JUDY LEARNED** BOYERTOWN, PENNSYLVANIA

PREP: 15 MIN. + STANDING **GRILL:** 20 MIN. **MAKES:** 4 SERVINGS

- 1 garlic clove, minced
- ¾ teaspoon salt
- 1 tablespoon olive oil
- 2 teaspoons minced fresh rosemary
- ¼ teaspoon pepper
- 1 pork tenderloin (1 pound)

1. Place garlic on a cutting board; sprinkle with salt. Using the flat side of a knife, mash garlic. Continue to mash until it reaches a paste consistency. Transfer to a small bowl.

2. Stir in the oil, rosemary and pepper; brush over pork. Let stand for 20 minutes.

3. Moisten a paper towel with cooking oil; using long-handled tongs, lightly coat the grill rack. Grill pork, covered, over medium heat or broil 4 in. from the heat for 9-11 minutes on each side or until a thermometer reads 145°. Let stand for 5 minutes before slicing.

Nutrition Facts: *3 ounces cooked pork equals 163 calories, 7 g fat (2 g saturated fat), 63 mg cholesterol, 488 mg sodium, trace carbohydrate, trace fiber, 23 g protein.*
Diabetic Exchanges: *3 lean meat, ½ fat.*

Did you know?

Rosemary, oregano, lemon balm and other herbs contain rosmarinic oil in their leaves. According to a Japanese study, rosmarinic acid, an extract of the oil, has an anti-inflammatory effect that helps reduce the symptoms of seasonal allergies.

Apricot Pork Tenderloin

Fresh rosemary-scented pork tenderloin and sweet potatoes bake together in this easy one-dish meal. You can serve leftover pork over your favorite rice for dinner the next night.

—**JUDY ARMSTRONG** PRAIRIEVILLE, LOUISIANA

PREP: 10 MIN. **COOK:** 25 MIN.
MAKES: 2 SERVINGS PLUS LEFTOVERS

- 1 pork tenderloin (1 pound)
- ¼ teaspoon salt, divided
- ¼ teaspoon pepper
- ¼ cup apricot preserves
- 2½ teaspoons minced fresh rosemary, divided
- 1 teaspoon prepared horseradish
- 1 garlic clove, minced
- 1 large sweet potato, peeled and thinly sliced
- 1 tablespoon olive oil

1. Sprinkle pork with ⅛ teaspoon salt and pepper. Place in a 13-in. x 9-in. baking dish coated with cooking spray. In a small bowl, whisk the preserves, 2 teaspoons rosemary, horseradish and garlic; brush over pork.

2. In a another small bowl, combine the potato, olive oil and remaining rosemary; place around tenderloin. Sprinkle potato with remaining salt.

3. Bake at 375° for 25-30 minutes or until a thermometer inserted in pork reads 145°. Let pork stand for 5 minutes. Slice half of the pork and serve with potato. Save remaining pork for Pork with Spanish Rice or for another use.

Nutrition Facts: *3 ounces cooked pork with ¾ cup potato equals 350 calories, 11 g fat (2 g saturated fat), 63 mg cholesterol, 213 mg sodium, 39 g carbohydrate, 3 g fiber, 25 g protein.*

Groundnut Stew C

PREP/TOTAL TIME: 30 MIN. **MAKES:** 7 SERVINGS

- 6 ounces lamb stew meat, cut into ½-inch pieces
- 6 ounces pork stew meat, cut into ½-inch pieces
- 2 tablespoons peanut oil
- 1 large onion, cut into wedges
- 1 large green pepper, cut into wedges
- 1 cup chopped tomatoes
- 4 cups cubed eggplant
- 2 cups water
- ½ cup fresh or frozen sliced okra
- ½ cup creamy peanut butter
- 1 teaspoon salt
- ½ teaspoon pepper
  Hot cooked rice

1. In a large skillet, brown meat in oil; set aside. In a food processor, combine the onion, green pepper and tomatoes; cover and process until blended.

2. In a large saucepan, combine the eggplant, water, okra and onion mixture. Bring to a boil. Reduce heat; cook, uncovered, for 7-9 minutes or until vegetables are tender.

3. Stir in the peanut butter, salt, pepper and browned meat. Cook, uncovered, for 10 minutes or until heated through. Serve with rice.

Nutrition Facts: *1 cup (prepared with lean beef stew meat and reduced-fat peanut butter; calculated without rice) equals 230 calories, 13 g fat (3 g saturated fat), 31 mg cholesterol, 470 mg sodium, 14 g carbohydrate, 4 g fiber, 16 g protein.* **Diabetic Exchanges:** *2 lean meat, 1 starch, 1 fat.*

❝My Aunt Linda was a missionary in Africa for more than 40 years. She gave me the recipe for this thick, stew-like dish with chunks of lamb, pork, eggplant, okra and a hint of peanut butter.❞

—**HEATHER EWALD** BOTHELL, WASHINGTON

Pork Tenderloin with Cranberry-Pear Chutney

Cranberries and pears go great with pork, and the brilliant color of the chutney just radiates festivity.

—AMANDA REED NASHVILLE, TENNESSEE

PREP: 45 MIN. + MARINATING **BAKE:** 25 MIN.
MAKES: 4 SERVINGS (1 CUP CHUTNEY)

 3 green onions, chopped
 2 tablespoons lemon juice
 2 tablespoons olive oil
 1 tablespoon honey
 2 teaspoons grated lemon peel
 1 garlic clove, minced
 1 teaspoon salt
 1 teaspoon minced fresh sage or ¼ teaspoon dried sage leaves
 1 teaspoon minced fresh rosemary or ¼ teaspoon dried rosemary, crushed
 1 teaspoon pepper
 1 pound pork tenderloin
CHUTNEY
 1 cup fresh or frozen cranberries, thawed
 1 cup chopped peeled ripe pear
 ½ cup sugar
 ¼ cup water
 2 tablespoons minced fresh mint or 2 teaspoons dried mint

1. In a large resealable plastic bag, combine the first 10 ingredients. Add the pork; seal bag and turn to coat. Refrigerate for at least 8 hours or overnight.
2. For chutney, in a large saucepan, combine all ingredients. Bring to a boil. Reduce heat; cover and simmer for 20 minutes. Uncover; simmer 20-25 minutes longer or until desired consistency, stirring occasionally. Cool to room temperature.
3. Meanwhile, drain and discard marinade. Place pork on a rack in a shallow roasting pan. Bake at 425° for 25-30 minutes or until a thermometer reads 145°. Let stand for 5 minutes before slicing. Serve with chutney.

Nutrition Facts: *3 ounces cooked pork with ¼ cup chutney equals 306 calories, 7 g fat (2 g saturated fat), 63 mg cholesterol, 342 mg sodium, 38 g carbohydrate, 3 g fiber, 23 g protein.*
Diabetic Exchanges: *3 lean meat, 1 starch, 1 fruit, ½ fat.*

Spicy Lamb Curry

This is a fantastic curry that I've tweaked over the years using a blend of aromatic spices. Fenugreek seeds can be found in specialty spice stores and are common in Middle Eastern curries and chutneys, but you can leave them out of this recipe.

—JANIS KRACHT WINDSOR, NEW YORK

PREP: 25 MIN. + MARINATING **COOK:** 1 HOUR
MAKES: 6 SERVINGS

 3 tablespoons ground cumin
 2 tablespoons ground ginger
 1 tablespoon ground coriander
 1 tablespoon ground fenugreek, optional
 4 garlic cloves, minced
 1 teaspoon ground cloves
 ½ teaspoon ground cinnamon
 2 pounds lamb stew meat, cut into ¾-inch pieces
 1 tablespoon olive oil
 2 large onions, chopped
 ½ cup water
 2 tablespoons paprika
 2 tablespoons tomato paste
 1 teaspoon salt
 1 teaspoon ground mustard
 1 teaspoon chili powder
 1 cup (8 ounces) plain yogurt
 3 cups hot cooked brown rice
   Optional toppings: cubed fresh pineapple, flaked coconut and toasted sliced almonds

1. In a large resealable plastic bag, combine the first seven ingredients. Add the lamb; seal bag and turn to coat. Refrigerate for 8 hours or overnight.
2. In a Dutch oven, brown meat in oil in batches; remove and keep warm. In the same pan, cook onions in drippings until tender. Add the water, paprika, tomato paste, salt, mustard and chili powder.
3. Return lamb to pan. Bring to a boil. Reduce heat; cover and simmer for 1 to 1½ hours or until meat is tender. Remove from the heat; stir in yogurt. Serve with rice. Top with pineapple, coconut and almonds if desired.

Editor's Note: *Fenugreek is available from Penzeys Spices. Call 800-741-7787 or visit penzeys.com.*

Nutrition Facts: *¾ cup curry with ½ cup rice (calculated without optional toppings) equals 419 calories, 14 g fat (4 g saturated fat), 104 mg cholesterol, 534 mg sodium, 36 g carbohydrate, 6 g fiber, 37 g protein.* **Diabetic Exchanges:** *4 lean meat, 2 starch, 1 vegetable, 1 fat.*

Caribbean-Spiced Pork Tenderloin with Peach Salsa ☐

PREP: 15 MIN. **GRILL:** 20 MIN.
MAKES: 4 SERVINGS (1⅓ CUPS SALSA)

- ¾ cup chopped peeled fresh peaches
- 1 small sweet red pepper, chopped
- 1 jalapeno pepper, seeded and chopped
- 2 tablespoons finely chopped red onion
- 2 tablespoons minced fresh cilantro
- 1 tablespoon lime juice
- 1 garlic clove, minced
- ⅛ teaspoon salt
- ⅛ teaspoon pepper
- 2 tablespoons olive oil
- 1 tablespoon brown sugar
- 1 tablespoon Caribbean jerk seasoning
- 1 teaspoon dried thyme
- 1 teaspoon dried rosemary, crushed
- ½ teaspoon seasoned salt
- 1 pork tenderloin (1 pound)

1. In a small bowl, combine the first nine ingredients; set aside. In another small bowl, combine the oil, brown sugar, jerk seasoning, thyme, rosemary and seasoned salt. Rub over pork.

2. Grill, covered, over medium heat for 9-11 minutes on each side or until a thermometer reads 145°. Let stand for 5 minutes before slicing. Serve with salsa.

Editor's Note: *Wear disposable gloves when cutting hot peppers; the oils can burn skin. Avoid touching your face.*

Nutrition Facts: *3 ounces cooked pork with ⅓ cup salsa equals 229 calories, 11 g fat (2 g saturated fat), 63 mg cholesterol, 522 mg sodium, 9 g carbohydrate, 1 g fiber, 23 g protein.* **Diabetic Exchanges:** *3 lean meat, 1½ fat, ½ starch.*

I love this recipe because of the depth of flavors and burst of colors. Plus, it's quick and easy for me to make and is a summertime grilling favorite when peaches are in season.
—**HOLLY BAUER** WEST BEND, WISCONSIN

Secret Ingredient Saucy Chops 🄲

Coffee, steak sauce, molasses and chocolate combine with garlic and thyme to drape these juicy chops in a thick, savory sauce.

—TASTE OF HOME TEST KITCHEN

PREP/TOTAL TIME: 30 MIN. **MAKES:** 4 SERVINGS

- 4 **bone-in pork loin chops (7 ounces each)**
- ½ **teaspoon salt**
- ½ **teaspoon pepper**
- 1 **tablespoon canola oil**
- ¾ **cup strong brewed coffee**
- 2 **tablespoons steak sauce**
- 1 **tablespoon molasses**
- ¼ **teaspoon garlic powder**
- ¼ **teaspoon dried thyme**
- 1 **ounce semisweet chocolate, chopped**

1. Sprinkle pork chops with salt and pepper. In a large nonstick skillet, cook chops in oil over medium heat for 4-6 minutes on each side or until a thermometer reads 160°. Remove and keep warm.

2. Add the coffee, steak sauce, molasses, garlic powder and thyme to the pan. Bring to a boil; cook until liquid is reduced by half. Whisk in chocolate until melted. Return pork chops to pan; heat through.

Nutrition Facts: *1 pork chop equals 295 calories, 14 g fat (5 g saturated fat), 86 mg cholesterol, 500 mg sodium, 10 g carbohydrate, 1 g fiber, 31 g protein.* **Diabetic Exchanges:** *4 lean meat, 1 fat, ½ starch.*

Pork with Spanish Rice

This is my solution for having leftover pork; it's perfect for two people. We sometimes eat it on a corn tortilla or with a salad.

—REBECCA HODGES HUNTSVILLE, ALABAMA

PREP: 5 MIN. **COOK:** 50 MIN. **MAKES:** 2 SERVINGS

- ½ **cup uncooked brown rice**
- 2 **teaspoons canola oil**
- ¾ **cup reduced-sodium chicken broth**
- ½ **cup water**
- ½ **cup diced tomatoes and green chilies**
- 1½ **cups cubed cooked Apricot Pork Tenderloin**

In a small saucepan, saute rice in oil until lightly browned. Add the broth, water and tomatoes. Bring to a boil. Reduce heat; cover and simmer for 40-45 minutes or until rice is tender. Add pork; heat through.

Editor's Note: *This recipe was tested with the Apricot Pork Tenderloin on p. 156.*

Nutrition Facts: *1¾ cups equals 408 calories, 10 g fat (2 g saturated fat), 63 mg cholesterol, 659 mg sodium, 51 g carbohydrate, 2 g fiber, 28 g protein.*

? Did you know?

Chocolate has earthy notes that can work as well with savory foods as with desserts. Even a small amount of chocolate can punch up the flavor of smoky ingredients like chipotle pepper, chili powder and paprika. It can also temper and complement the heat of cayenne and jalapeno peppers or enhance the flavors of such warm spices as cinnamon, nutmeg and cloves. In salads, you can use a moderately sweet chocolate to offset the tang of vinegar and tomatoes while adding richness and depth of flavor.

Glazed Lamb Chops C

With a flavorful two-ingredient sauce to marinate these lamb chops, they're so much easier than you think! I like to serve them with wild rice and green beans.

—**MITZI SENTIFF** ANNAPOLIS, MARYLAND

PREP/TOTAL TIME: 25 MIN.   **MAKES:** 4 SERVINGS

⅓   **cup thawed orange juice concentrate**
⅓   **cup barbecue sauce**
4   **lamb loin chops (1 inch thick and about 6 ounces each)**

1. In a small saucepan, combine the orange juice concentrate and barbecue sauce. Cook and stir over medium heat for 3-4 minutes or until heated through; set aside ⅓ cup for serving. Spread remaining sauce over both sides of lamb chops. Place on a broiler pan.
2. Broil 4-6 in. from the heat for 4-9 minutes on each side or until meat reaches desired doneness (for medium-rare, a thermometer should read 145°; medium, 160°; well-done, 170°). Serve with reserved sauce.

Nutrition Facts: *1 lamb chop with about 4 teaspoons sauce equals 209 calories, 7 g fat (3 g saturated fat), 68 mg cholesterol, 251 mg sodium, 12 g carbohydrate, trace fiber, 22 g protein.*

Chili Pork Tenderloin C

This lean dinner takes the tough out of pork and puts the tender back in tenderloin. It's a weeknight favorite for my family.

—**RENEE BARFIELD** THOMASTON, GEORGIA

PREP: 10 MIN.   **BAKE:** 25 MIN.   **MAKES:** 3 SERVINGS

1   **tablespoon lime juice**
1   **teaspoon chili powder**
1   **teaspoon reduced-sodium soy sauce**
½   **teaspoon sugar**
½   **teaspoon salt**
¼   **teaspoon pepper**
1   **pork tenderloin (1 pound)**
1   **tablespoon canola oil**

1. In a small bowl, combine the first six ingredients; brush over pork. In a large ovenproof skillet, brown pork in oil on all sides.
2. Bake at 375° for 25-30 minutes or until a thermometer reads 145°. Let stand for 5 minutes before slicing.

Nutrition Facts: *4 ounces cooked pork equals 224 calories, 10 g fat (2 g saturated fat), 84 mg cholesterol, 529 mg sodium, 2 g carbohydrate, trace fiber, 30 g protein.* **Diabetic Exchanges:** *4 lean meat, 1 fat.*

Slow-Cooked Pork Tacos

Sometimes I'll substitute Bibb lettuce leaves for the tortillas to make crunchy lettuce wraps, and I find that leftovers are perfect for burritos.

—**KATHLEEN WOLF** NAPERVILLE, ILLINOIS

PREP: 20 MIN.   **COOK:** 4 HOURS   **MAKES:** 10 TACOS

- 1   boneless pork sirloin roast (2 pounds), cut into 1-inch pieces
- 1½ cups salsa verde
- 1   medium sweet red pepper, chopped
- 1   medium onion, chopped
- ¼   cup chopped dried apricots
- 2   tablespoons lime juice
- 2   garlic cloves, minced
- 1   teaspoon ground cumin
- ½   teaspoon salt
- ¼   teaspoon white pepper
     Dash hot pepper sauce
- 10 flour tortillas (8 inches), warmed
     Reduced-fat sour cream, thinly sliced green onions, cubed avocado, shredded reduced-fat cheddar cheese and chopped tomato, optional

1. In a 3-qt. slow cooker, combine the first 11 ingredients. Cover and cook on high for 4-5 hours or until meat is tender.

2. Shred pork with two forks. Place about ½ cup pork mixture down the center of each tortilla. Serve with toppings if desired.

Nutrition Facts: *1 taco (calculated without optional toppings) equals 301 calories, 8 g fat (2 g saturated fat), 54 mg cholesterol, 616 mg sodium, 32 g carbohydrate, 1 g fiber, 24 g protein.*
Diabetic Exchanges: *3 lean meat, 2 starch.*

Hoisin Pork Wraps

I found this recipe while at the dentist's office and altered it to make it my own. It's a fun dish to serve as a buffet item because the guests can make their own wraps. Even my grandchildren like it.

—**LINDA WOO** DERBY, KANSAS

PREP: 25 MIN.   **COOK:** 7 HOURS   **MAKES:** 15 SERVINGS

- 1   boneless whole pork loin roast (3 pounds)
- 1   cup hoisin sauce, divided
- 1   tablespoon minced fresh gingerroot
- 6   cups shredded red cabbage
- 1½ cups shredded carrots
- ¼   cup thinly sliced green onions
- 3   tablespoons rice vinegar
- 4½ teaspoons sugar
- 15 flour tortillas (8 inches), warmed

1. Cut roast in half. Combine ⅓ cup hoisin sauce and ginger; rub over pork. Transfer to a 3-qt. slow cooker. Cover and cook on low for 7-8 hours or until pork is tender.

2. Meanwhile, in a large bowl, combine the cabbage, carrots, onions, vinegar and sugar. Chill until serving.

3. Shred meat with two forks and return to the slow cooker; heat through. Place 2 teaspoons remaining hoisin sauce down the center of each tortilla; top with ⅓ cup shredded pork and ⅓ cup coleslaw. Roll up.

Nutrition Facts: *1 serving equals 314 calories, 8 g fat (2 g saturated fat), 46 mg cholesterol, 564 mg sodium, 37 g carbohydrate, 1 g fiber, 23 g protein.* **Diabetic Exchanges:** *2½ starch, 2 lean meat.*

164

165

166

Fish & Seafood

❝If you're looking for a dish that's fast and healthy, this one has it all. Round it out with steamed sugar snap peas for a simple weeknight meal.❞

JENNIE RICHARDS RIVERTON, UTAH
about her recipe, Salmon with Lemon-Dill Butter, on page 173

Add garlic, cook 1 minute longer or until vegetables are crisp-tender. Add eggs; cook and stir until set.

3. Drain the noodles; add to shrimp mixture. Stir vinegar mixture and add to the skillet. Bring to a boil. Add shrimp, bean sprouts and green onions; heat through. Sprinkle with cilantro and peanuts.

Nutrition Facts: *1 cup equals 352 calories, 10 g fat (2 g saturated fat), 208 mg cholesterol, 955 mg sodium, 38 g carbohydrate, 4 g fiber, 28 g protein.* **Diabetic Exchanges:** *3 lean meat, 2 starch, 1 vegetable, 1 fat.*

Baked Tilapia F C

I like to serve this dish with lemon and tartar sauce and fresh veggies on the side. Using plain bread crumbs instead of seasoned crumbs lets you control the amount of salt and seasonings you use.

—BRANDI CASTILLO SANTA MARIA, CALIFORNIA

PREP/TOTAL TIME: 20 MIN.   **MAKES:** 4 SERVINGS

- ¾ **cup soft bread crumbs**
- ⅓ **cup grated Parmesan cheese**
- 1 **teaspoon garlic salt**
- 1 **teaspoon dried oregano**
- 4 **tilapia fillets (5 ounces each)**

1. In a shallow bowl, combine the bread crumbs, cheese, garlic salt and oregano. Coat fillets in crumb mixture. Place on a baking sheet coated with cooking spray.

2. Bake at 425° for 8-12 minutes or until fish flakes easily with a fork.

Nutrition Facts: *1 fillet equals 143 calories, 2 g fat (1 g saturated fat), 72 mg cholesterol, 356 mg sodium, 2 g carbohydrate, trace fiber, 28 g protein.* **Diabetic Exchange:** *4 lean meat.*

Colorful Shrimp Pad Thai

Bright, fresh veggie flavors, a splash of tart lime juice, the crunch of peanuts and a hint of heat make my healthy and beautiful shrimp stir-fry a real standout!

—HEALTHY COOKING TEST KITCHEN

PREP: 30 MIN.   **COOK:** 15 MIN.   **MAKES:** 6 SERVINGS

- 6 **ounces uncooked thick rice noodles**
- ¼ **cup rice vinegar**
- 3 **tablespoons reduced-sodium soy sauce**
- 2 **tablespoons sugar**
- 2 **tablespoons fish sauce or additional reduced-sodium soy sauce**
- 1 **tablespoon lime juice**
- 2 **teaspoons Thai chili sauce**
- 1 **teaspoon sesame oil**
- ¼ **teaspoon crushed red pepper flakes**

STIR-FRY

- 1½ **pounds uncooked medium shrimp, peeled and deveined**
- 3 **teaspoons sesame oil, divided**
- 2 **cups fresh snow peas**
- 2 **medium carrots, grated**
- 2 **garlic cloves, minced**
- 2 **eggs, lightly beaten**
- 2 **cups bean sprouts**
- 2 **green onions, chopped**
- ¼ **cup minced fresh cilantro**
- ¼ **cup unsalted dry roasted peanuts, chopped**

1. Cook noodles according to package directions. Meanwhile, in a small bowl, combine the vinegar, soy sauce, sugar, fish sauce, lime juice, chili sauce, oil and pepper flakes until blended; set aside.

2. In a large nonstick skillet or wok, stir-fry shrimp in 2 teaspoons oil until shrimp turn pink; remove and keep warm. Stir-fry snow peas and carrots in remaining oil for 1-2 minutes.

Broiled Salmon with Mediterranean Lentils

I used to weight-train to keep myself in shape for my work as a volunteer firefighter, and I often prepared this dish. It's loaded with fiber, protein and antioxidants. Now that I'm a stay-at-home mom, I make it to give me energy to chase the kids.

—DAWN E. BRYANT THEDFORD, NEBRASKA

PREP: 15 MIN. **COOK:** 55 MIN. **MAKES:** 4 SERVINGS

- 1 small carrot, julienned
- ¼ cup chopped onion
- 1 tablespoon olive oil
- ½ cup dried lentils, rinsed
- ½ cup dried green split peas
- 2 garlic cloves, minced
- 2 teaspoons capers, drained
- 2½ cups water
- ½ teaspoon salt
- ½ teaspoon pepper
- 2 tablespoons lemon juice

SALMON

- 4 salmon fillets (4 ounces each)
  Butter-flavored cooking spray
- ¼ teaspoon salt
- ⅛ teaspoon pepper

1. In a small saucepan, saute carrot and onion in oil until tender. Add the lentils, peas, garlic and capers; cook and stir 3 minutes longer.

2. Add the water, salt and pepper. Bring to a boil. Reduce heat; cover and simmer for 45-50 minutes or until tender. Stir in lemon juice.

3. Spritz fillets with butter-flavored spray; sprinkle with salt and pepper. Broil 4-6 in. from the heat for 7-9 minutes or until fish flakes easily with a fork. Serve with lentil mixture.

Nutrition Facts: *1 salmon fillet with ½ cup lentils equals 422 calories, 16 g fat (3 g saturated fat), 67 mg cholesterol, 568 mg sodium, 33 g carbohydrate, 14 g fiber, 35 g protein.*

Grilled Greek Fish C

Living in Tampa, we eat a lot of fresh fish, mostly grouper, mahi-mahi and tilapia—all sweet white fish that work well with this marinade.

—JUDY BATSON TAMPA, FLORIDA

PREP: 15 MIN. + MARINATING **GRILL:** 10 MIN.
MAKES: 4 SERVINGS

- ⅓ cup lemon juice
- 3 tablespoons olive oil
- 2 tablespoons minced fresh oregano
- 2 tablespoons minced fresh mint
- 1 garlic clove, minced
- ½ teaspoon grated lemon peel
- ½ teaspoon Greek seasoning
- 4 tilapia fillets (6 ounces each)

1. In a large resealable plastic bag, combine the first seven ingredients. Add the tilapia; seal bag and turn to coat. Refrigerate for 30 minutes. Drain and discard marinade.

2. Moisten a paper towel with cooking oil; using long-handled tongs, lightly coat the grill rack. Grill tilapia, covered, over medium heat or broil 4 in. from the heat for 4-5 minutes on each side or until fish flakes easily with a fork.

Nutrition Facts: *1 fillet equals 223 calories, 10 g fat (2 g saturated fat), 83 mg cholesterol, 162 mg sodium, 2 g carbohydrate, trace fiber, 32 g protein.* **Diabetic Exchanges:** *5 lean meat, 1½ fat.*

Shrimp Tortellini Pasta Toss

Hearty and comforting cheese tortellini can be part of a healthy diet, especially when bulked up with shrimp and whatever vegetables you have on hand.

—HEALTHY COOKING TEST KITCHEN

PREP/TOTAL TIME: 20 MIN. **MAKES:** 4 SERVINGS

- 1 package (9 ounces) refrigerated cheese tortellini
- 1 cup frozen peas
- 1 pound uncooked medium shrimp, peeled and deveined
- 3 tablespoons olive oil, divided
- 2 garlic cloves, minced
- ¼ teaspoon salt
- ¼ teaspoon dried thyme
- ¼ teaspoon pepper

1. Cook tortellini according to package directions, adding the peas during the last 5 minutes of cooking.

2. In a large nonstick skillet, saute shrimp in 2 tablespoons oil for 2 minutes. Add garlic; cook 1-2 minutes longer or until shrimp turn pink.

3. Drain tortellini mixture; add to skillet. Stir in the salt, thyme, pepper and remaining oil; toss to coat.

Nutrition Facts: *1¼ cups equals 413 calories, 17 g fat (4 g saturated fat), 165 mg cholesterol, 559 mg sodium, 36 g carbohydrate, 3 g fiber, 29 g protein.* **Diabetic Exchanges:** *4 lean meat, 2 starch, 2 fat.*

Orange Salmon with Sauteed Spinach

I love orange marmalade and wanted a lighter version of orange salmon without heavy spice rubs or brown sugar. What a rewarding outcome this was.

—JANET CAICO HILLSBOROUGH, NORTH CAROLINA

PREP/TOTAL TIME: 30 MIN. **MAKES:** 4 SERVINGS

    4 salmon fillets (4 ounces each)
    ¼ teaspoon plus ⅛ teaspoon pepper, divided
    ¼ teaspoon salt, divided
    ½ cup orange marmalade spreadable fruit
    2 tablespoons half-and-half cream
    2 tablespoons reduced-sodium soy sauce
    1 tablespoon minced fresh gingerroot
  4½ teaspoons plus 1 tablespoon reduced-fat butter, divided
    2 garlic cloves, minced
    1 tablespoon olive oil
    1 package (6 ounces) fresh baby spinach

1. Sprinkle salmon with ¼ teaspoon pepper and ⅛ teaspoon salt; set aside.
2. In a small saucepan, combine the marmalade, cream, soy sauce, ginger and 4½ teaspoons butter. Bring to a boil. Reduce heat; simmer, uncovered, until slightly thickened, about 5 minutes; set aside.
3. Moisten a paper towel with cooking oil; using long-handled tongs, lightly coat the grill rack. Place salmon skin side down on grill rack. Grill, covered, over medium heat or broil 4 in. from the heat for 10-12 minutes or until fish flakes easily with a fork.
4. In a large skillet, saute garlic in oil and remaining butter for 1 minute. Add spinach and remaining salt and pepper; cook for 4-5 minutes or until spinach is wilted. Divide spinach among four plates; top each with salmon. Drizzle with marmalade sauce.
Nutrition Facts: *1 fillet with ¼ cup spinach mixture and 2 tablespoons sauce equals 346 calories, 19 g fat (5 g saturated fat), 70 mg cholesterol, 604 mg sodium, 24 g carbohydrate, 1 g fiber, 21 g protein.* **Diabetic Exchanges:** *3 lean meat, 2 fat, 1½ starch, 1 vegetable.*

California Shrimp Tacos with Corn Salsa

PREP/TOTAL TIME: 25 MIN.
MAKES: 4 SERVINGS

    1 can (11 ounces) Mexicorn, drained
    ¾ cup chopped seeded tomatoes
    ½ cup black beans, rinsed and drained
    ¼ cup minced fresh cilantro
    3 garlic cloves, minced
    ¼ teaspoon pepper
    ½ cup guacamole
    3 tablespoons reduced-fat ranch salad dressing
   16 uncooked large shrimp, peeled and deveined
    3 teaspoons chili powder
    ½ teaspoon Cajun seasoning
    8 taco shells, warmed

1. In a small bowl, combine the first six ingredients. In another small bowl, combine guacamole and salad dressing.
2. In a large bowl, toss shrimp with chili powder and Cajun seasoning. In a large nonstick skillet coated with cooking spray, saute shrimp until pink, about 5 minutes.
3. Place two shrimp in each taco shell. Top with ⅓ cup corn salsa; drizzle with 1 tablespoon guacamole mixture.
Nutrition Facts: *2 tacos equals 342 calories, 14 g fat (3 g saturated fat), 83 mg cholesterol, 1,007 mg sodium, 40 g carbohydrate, 7 g fiber, 17 g protein.*
Diabetic Exchanges: *2½ starch, 2 lean meat, 1½ fat.*

Did you know?

Iron plays an important role in immunity, energy and temperature regulation, and it comes in two forms: heme iron (from animal foods) and non-heme iron (from plant foods). Vitamin C helps increase the absorption of non-heme iron, so serve your Orange Salmon with Spinach with a few slices of orange on the side. Eating a heme iron food (such as salmon) with a non-heme one also boosts iron absorption.

66After trying fish tacos, I fell in love.
I wanted to re-create them at home
and thought *Why not use shrimp?* It's
an affordable, healthy way to feed my
seafood-loving family.99

—**KAYLA PETERS** CECILIA, KENTUCKY

Salmon Spinach Salad

The great thing about this salad is being able to do variations. If you don't have goat cheese, try feta.

—STEPHANIE MATTHEWS TEMPE, ARIZONA

PREP: 25 MIN. **GRILL:** 10 MIN. **MAKES:** 4 SERVINGS

- 4 **salmon fillets (4 ounces each)**
- 6 **tablespoons thawed orange juice concentrate, divided**
- ½ **teaspoon salt, divided**
- ½ **teaspoon paprika**
- ¼ **teaspoon pepper**
- 5 **cups fresh baby spinach**
- 1 **medium navel orange, peeled and cut into ½-inch pieces**
- 2 **green onions, thinly sliced**
- ¼ **cup chopped walnuts, toasted**
- 4½ **teaspoons balsamic vinegar**
- 1 **tablespoon olive oil**
- 1 **garlic clove, minced**
- ¼ **cup crumbled goat cheese**

1. Brush salmon with 4 tablespoons orange juice concentrate. Sprinkle with ¼ teaspoon salt, paprika and pepper. Moisten a paper towel with cooking oil; using long-handled tongs, lightly coat the grill rack. Grill salmon, covered, over medium heat or broil 4 in. from the heat for 8-10 minutes or until fish flakes easily with a fork.

2. Meanwhile, in a large bowl, combine the spinach, orange, green onions and walnuts. In a small bowl, whisk the vinegar, oil, garlic, remaining orange juice concentrate and salt. Drizzle over salad; toss to coat.

3. Divide among plates; sprinkle with cheese. Top with salmon.

Nutrition Facts: *1 serving equals 350 calories, 21 g fat (4 g saturated fat), 66 mg cholesterol, 420 mg sodium, 19 g carbohydrate, 3 g fiber, 24 g protein.* **Diabetic Exchanges:** *3 lean meat, 2½ fat, 1 starch.*

Cilantro-Basil Grilled Shrimp Ⓒ

With plenty of cilantro and basil in my garden and a bottle of tequila in the pantry, I knew just what to do to these shrimp. The crushed red pepper really gives them an extra kick!

—TAMI PENUNURI LEAUGE CITY, TEXAS

PREP: 15 MIN. + MARINATING **GRILL:** 5 MIN. **MAKES:** 4 SERVINGS

- 3 **tablespoons orange juice**
- 3 **tablespoons olive oil**
- 2 **tablespoons minced fresh cilantro**
- 2 **tablespoons minced fresh basil**
- 2 **tablespoons tequila**
- ¾ **teaspoon salt**
- ½ **teaspoon crushed red pepper flakes**
- ¼ **teaspoon pepper**
- 1 **pound uncooked large shrimp, peeled and deveined**

1. In a large resealable plastic bag, combine the first eight ingredients. Add the shrimp; seal bag and turn to coat. Refrigerate for 30 minutes.

2. Drain and discard marinade. Thread shrimp onto four metal or soaked wooden skewers. Moisten a paper towel with cooking oil; using long-handled tongs, lightly coat the grill rack.

3. Grill shrimp, covered, over medium heat or broil 4 in. from the heat for 5-8 minutes or until shrimp turn pink, turning once.

Nutrition Facts: *3 ounces cooked shrimp equals 124 calories, 4 g fat (1 g saturated fat), 138 mg cholesterol, 245 mg sodium, 1 g carbohydrate, trace fiber, 18 g protein.* **Diabetic Exchanges:** *3 lean meat, ½ fat.*

Mediterranean Tilapia Ⓒ

I recently became a fan of tilapia because of its mild taste; it's also low in calories and fat. Plus, I like how easy it is to top with my favorite ingredients.

—**ROBIN BRENNEMAN** HILLIARD, OHIO

PREP/TOTAL TIME: 25 MIN. **MAKES:** 6 SERVINGS

- 6 tilapia fillets (6 ounces each)
- 1 cup canned Italian diced tomatoes
- ½ cup water-packed artichoke hearts, chopped
- ½ cup sliced ripe olives
- ½ cup crumbled feta cheese

1. Place fillets in a 15-in. x 10-in. x 1-in. baking pan coated with cooking spray. Top with tomatoes, artichoke, olives and cheese. Bake at 400° for 15-20 minutes or until fish flakes easily with a fork.

Nutrition Facts: *1 fillet equals 197 calories, 4 g fat (2 g saturated fat), 88 mg cholesterol, 446 mg sodium, 5 g carbohydrate, 1 g fiber, 34 g protein.* **Diabetic Exchanges:** *5 lean meat, ½ fat.*

Shrimp Asparagus Fettuccine

Fettuccine lovers rejoice. This is a quick and healthy way to enjoy your favorite pasta. You could also use leftover chicken instead of shrimp in this versatile weeknight dinner.

—**TASTE OF HOME TEST KITCHEN**

PREP/TOTAL TIME: 20 MIN. **MAKES:** 4 SERVINGS

- 1 package (9 ounces) refrigerated fettuccine
- 1 cup cut fresh asparagus (1-inch pieces)
- 1 pound uncooked medium shrimp, peeled and deveined
- 3 tablespoons olive oil, divided
- 2 garlic cloves, minced
- ¾ teaspoon dried basil
- ¼ teaspoon salt
- ¼ teaspoon pepper

1. Bring 4 quarts water to a boil. Add fettuccine and asparagus. Boil for 2-3 minutes or until pasta is tender.

2. In a large nonstick skillet, saute shrimp in 2 tablespoons oil for 2 minutes. Add garlic; cook 1-2 minutes longer or until shrimp turn pink.

3. Drain fettuccine mixture; add to skillet. Stir in the basil, salt, pepper and remaining oil; toss to coat.

Nutrition Facts: *1½ cups equals 394 calories, 17 g fat (4 g saturated fat), 165 mg cholesterol, 519 mg sodium, 32 g carbohydrate, 2 g fiber, 28 g protein.* **Diabetic Exchanges:** *3 lean meat, 2½ starch, 2 fat.*

Garlic-Ginger Salmon Packets Ⓒ

With minimal effort and mess, this tender salmon fillet has the makings of a dinnertime staple. Citrus, garlic and ginger bring out the best in this low calorie entree.

—**LISA FINNEGAN** FORKED RIVER, NEW JERSEY

PREP: 20 MIN. **GRILL:** 15 MIN. **MAKES:** 4 SERVINGS

- 4 salmon fillets (6 ounces each)
- 1 tablespoon minced fresh gingerroot
- 1 tablespoon minced fresh cilantro
- 2 garlic cloves, minced
- 2 teaspoons grated lemon peel
- 2 teaspoons grated orange peel
- 1½ teaspoons grated lime peel
- 2 tablespoons rice vinegar
- 2 tablespoons reduced-sodium soy sauce
- ¼ teaspoon pepper

1. Place each salmon fillet on a double thickness of heavy-duty foil (about 12 in. square). Combine the ginger, cilantro, garlic and peels; spoon over salmon.

2. In a small bowl, combine the vinegar, soy sauce and pepper; drizzle over salmon. Fold foil around fish and seal tightly.

3. Grill, covered, over medium heat for 15-20 minutes or until fish flakes easily with a fork. Open foil carefully to allow steam to escape.

Nutrition Facts: *1 fillet equals 279 calories, 16 g fat (3 g saturated fat), 85 mg cholesterol, 389 mg sodium, 3 g carbohydrate, trace fiber, 29 g protein.* **Diabetic Exchanges:** *5 lean meat, 1 fat.*

Salmon with Honey Pecan Sauce

PREP/TOTAL TIME: 30 MIN.
MAKES: 4 SERVINGS

- 4 salmon fillets (4 ounces each)
- ½ teaspoon seasoned salt
- ¼ teaspoon pepper
- ¼ cup finely chopped pecans, toasted
- ¼ cup honey
- 3 tablespoons reduced-fat butter

1. Place salmon skin side down on a broiler pan; sprinkle with seasoned salt and pepper. Broil 3-4 in. from the heat for 7-9 minutes or until fish flakes easily with a fork.

2. Meanwhile, in a small saucepan, cook the pecans, honey and butter over medium heat for 8-10 minutes or until bubbly. Serve with salmon.

Editor's Note: *This recipe was tested with Land O'Lakes light stick butter.*

Nutrition Facts: *1 fillet with 2 tablespoons sauce equals 330 calories, 20 g fat (5 g saturated fat), 68 mg cholesterol, 319 mg sodium, 19 g carbohydrate, 1 g fiber, 20 g protein.* **Diabetic Exchanges:** *3 lean meat, 2½ fat, 1 starch.*

Southwest Tilapia 🄲

Tilapia's mild, neutral taste takes on a creamy Southwestern flavor in this no-fail recipe. Cod and halibut also work well in this dish.

—HEALTHY COOKING TEST KITCHEN

PREP/TOTAL TIME: 25 MIN.
MAKES: 6 SERVINGS

- 6 tilapia fillets (6 ounces each)
- 1 cup diced tomatoes with mild green chilies
- ½ cup frozen corn, thawed
- ½ cup cubed avocado
- ½ cup cubed cheddar cheese
- ½ teaspoon dried cilantro flakes

1. Place fillets in a 15-in. x 10-in. x 1-in. baking pan coated with cooking spray. Top with tomatoes, corn, avocado, cheese and cilantro. Bake at 400° for 15-20 minutes or until fish flakes easily with a fork.

Nutrition Facts: *1 fillet equals 230 calories, 7 g fat (3 g saturated fat), 94 mg cholesterol, 290 mg sodium, 7 g carbohydrate, 2 g fiber, 35 g protein.* **Diabetic Exchanges:** *5 lean meat, 1 fat.*

I love the explosion of sweet and buttery flavors in every bite of this dish. In summer, sauteed zucchini makes the perfect side dish. —ALICE STANKO WARREN, MICHIGAN

Hearty Shrimp Risotto

Super creamy and packed with shrimp, this impressive Italian meal is special enough to serve company. Laced with the warm flavors of white wine, goat cheese and fresh spinach, it's scrumptious, comforting and quick to make.
—**LYDIA BECKER** PARKVILLE, MISSOURI

PREP: 15 MIN. **COOK:** 35 MIN. **MAKES:** 4 SERVINGS

- 4 **cups reduced-sodium chicken broth**
- 1 **small onion, finely chopped**
- 1 **tablespoon olive oil**
- 1 **cup uncooked arborio rice**
- 1 **fresh thyme sprig**
- 1 **bay leaf**
- ¼ **teaspoon pepper**
- ¾ **cup white wine or additional reduced-sodium chicken broth**
- 1 **pound uncooked medium shrimp, peeled and deveined**
- 2 **cups chopped fresh spinach**
- 4 **ounces fresh goat cheese, crumbled**

1. In a small saucepan, heat broth and keep warm. In a large nonstick skillet coated with cooking spray, saute onion in oil until tender. Add the rice, thyme, bay leaf and pepper; cook and stir for 2-3 minutes. Reduce heat; stir in wine. Cook and stir until all of the liquid is absorbed.

2. Add heated broth, ½ cup at a time, stirring constantly. Allow the liquid to absorb between additions. Cook just until risotto is creamy and rice is almost tender. (Cooking time is about 20 minutes.) Add the shrimp and spinach; cook until shrimp turn pink and spinach is wilted.

3. Stir in cheese. Discard thyme and bay leaf. Serve immediately.

Nutrition Facts: *1¼ cups equals 405 calories, 9 g fat (3 g saturated fat), 157 mg cholesterol, 832 mg sodium, 45 g carbohydrate, 1 g fiber, 28 g protein.* **Diabetic Exchanges:** *3 lean meat, 2½ starch, 1 fat.*

Tuna-Stuffed Baked Potatoes

Using canned tuna keeps this dish right in a target budget. A dollop of pickle relish on top brings out that classic tuna salad flavor.
—**KAREN SEGER** HOUSTON, OHIO

PREP: 25 MIN. **BAKE:** 25 MIN. **MAKES:** 4 SERVINGS

- 4 **medium baking potatoes**
- 1 **cup (8 ounces) fat-free cottage cheese**
- 1 **can (5 ounces) albacore white tuna in water, drained and flaked**
- 1 **celery rib, chopped**
- 1 **medium onion, finely chopped**
- ½ **cup shredded cheddar cheese, divided**
- ¼ **teaspoon paprika**
- ¼ **teaspoon salt**
- ¼ **teaspoon pepper**

1. Scrub and pierce potatoes; place on a microwave-safe plate. Microwave, uncovered, on high for 15-20 minutes or until tender, turning once.

2. When cool enough to handle, cut each potato in half lengthwise. Scoop out the pulp, leaving thin shells.

3. In a small bowl, mash the pulp. Add the cottage cheese, tuna, celery, onion, ¼ cup cheese, paprika, salt and pepper. Spoon into potato shells. Place on a baking sheet. Bake, uncovered, at 350° for 18-22 minutes or until heated through. Sprinkle with remaining cheese. Bake 5 minutes longer or until cheese is melted.

Editor's Note: *This recipe was tested in a 1,100-watt microwave.*

Nutrition Facts: *2 stuffed potato halves equals 321 calories, 5 g fat (3 g saturated fat), 32 mg cholesterol, 603 mg sodium, 46 g carbohydrate, 4 g fiber, 23 g protein.* **Diabetic Exchanges:** *3 starch, 2 lean meat.*

Grilled Shrimp with Lemon Vinaigrette C

I keep my marinades heart-healthy by choosing monounsaturated oils such as olive oil, and I use lower-calorie spice- or citrus-based marinades, sauces and rubs to add flavor.

—AMBER MASSEY FORT WORTH, TEXAS

PREP: 10 MIN. + MARINATING **GRILL:** 5 MIN. **MAKES:** 4 SERVINGS

- ¼ cup lemon juice
- 3 tablespoons coarsely chopped fresh parsley
- 1 tablespoon finely grated lemon peel
- 1 tablespoon olive oil
- 2 garlic cloves, minced
- 2 teaspoons Dijon mustard
- ½ teaspoon salt
- ¼ teaspoon pepper
- 1¼ pounds uncooked large shrimp, peeled and deveined

1. In a large bowl, whisk the first eight ingredients; add shrimp. Cover and refrigerate for 30 minutes.

2. Drain and discard marinade. Thread shrimp onto metal or soaked wooden skewers. Moisten a paper towel with cooking oil; using long-handled tongs, lightly coat the grill rack. Grill shrimp, covered, over medium heat for 5-8 minutes or until shrimp turn pink, turning once.

Nutrition Facts: *3 ounces cooked shrimp equals 140 calories, 4 g fat (1 g saturated fat), 172 mg cholesterol, 346 mg sodium, 2 g carbohydrate, trace fiber, 23 g protein.* **Diabetic Exchange:** *3 lean meat.*

Mediterranean Cod C

On the rare occasion that my teacher friend and I get to sit on the deck and enjoy a summer lunch, this is what we always have. We each take a bundle and eat them right out of the parchment.

—MELISSA CHILTON HARLOWTON, MONTANA

PREP: 25 MIN. **BAKE:** 15 MIN. **MAKES:** 4 SERVINGS

- 4 cups shredded cabbage
- 1 large sweet onion, thinly sliced
- 4 garlic cloves, minced
- 4 cod fillets (6 ounces each)
- ¼ cup pitted Greek olives, chopped
- ½ cup crumbled feta cheese
- ¼ teaspoon salt
- ¼ teaspoon pepper
- 4 teaspoons olive oil

1. Cut parchment paper or heavy-duty foil into four 18-in. x 12-in. pieces; place 1 cup cabbage on each. Top with onion, garlic, cod, olives, cheese, salt and pepper; drizzle with oil.

2. Fold parchment paper over fish. Bring edges of paper together on all sides and crimp to seal, forming a large packet. Repeat with remaining ingredients. Place on baking sheets.

3. Bake at 450° for 12-15 minutes or until fish flakes easily with a fork. Open packets carefully to allow steam to escape.

Nutrition Facts: *1 packet equals 270 calories, 10 g fat (3 g saturated fat), 72 mg cholesterol, 532 mg sodium, 12 g carbohydrate, 3 g fiber, 31 g protein.* **Diabetic Exchanges:** *5 lean meat, 2 vegetable, 2 fat.*

Thai Shrimp Pasta

I came up with this recipe when my son was home from the Navy. He loves Thai food and I wanted to make something special but simple. There wasn't a noodle left in the bowl!

—**JANA RIPPEE** CASA GRANDE, ARIZONA

PREP/TOTAL TIME: 30 MIN. **MAKES:** 4 SERVINGS

- 8 **ounces thin flat rice noodles**
- 3 **teaspoons curry powder**
- 1 **can (13.66 ounces) light coconut milk**
- 1 **pound uncooked medium shrimp, peeled and deveined**
- ¼ **teaspoon salt**
- ¼ **teaspoon pepper**
- ½ **cup minced fresh cilantro**
    Lime wedges, optional

1. Soak noodles according to package directions. Meanwhile, in a large dry skillet over medium heat, toast curry powder until aromatic, about 1-2 minutes. Stir in the coconut milk, shrimp, salt and pepper. Bring to a boil. Reduce heat; simmer, uncovered, for 5-6 minutes or until shrimp turn pink.

2. Drain noodles; add to pan. Stir in cilantro; heat through. Serve with lime wedges if desired.

Nutrition Facts: *1 cup equals 361 calories, 9 g fat (5 g saturated fat), 138 mg cholesterol, 284 mg sodium, 44 g carbohydrate, 2 g fiber, 22 g protein.* **Diabetic Exchanges:** *3 lean meat, 2½ starch, 1 fat.*

Salmon with Lemon-Dill Butter S C

If you're looking for a dish that's fast and healthy, this one has it all. Round it out with steamed sugar snap peas for a simple weeknight meal.

—**JENNIE RICHARDS** RIVERTON, UTAH

PREP/TOTAL TIME: 15 MIN. **MAKES:** 2 SERVINGS

- 2 **salmon fillets (4 ounces each)**
- 5 **teaspoons reduced-fat butter, melted**
- ¾ **teaspoon lemon juice**
- ½ **teaspoon grated lemon peel**
- ½ **teaspoon snipped fresh dill**

Place salmon skin side down on a broiler pan. Combine the butter, lemon juice, lemon peel and dill. Brush one-third of mixture over salmon. Broil 3-4 in. from the heat for 7-9 minutes or until fish flakes easily with a fork, basting occasionally with remaining butter mixture.

Editor's Note: *This recipe was tested with Land O'Lakes light stick butter.*

Nutrition Facts: *1 fillet equals 219 calories, 15 g fat (5 g saturated fat), 69 mg cholesterol, 136 mg sodium, 1 g carbohydrate, trace fiber, 19 g protein.* **Diabetic Exchanges:** *3 lean meat, 1½ fat.*

Garlic Shrimp and Rice

My son's favorite food is shrimp, so I'm always looking for quick and simple ways to make it. You can use garlic salt instead of minced garlic cloves and salt.

—**JULIE TRANI** CHESAPEAKE, VIRGINIA

PREP/TOTAL TIME: 20 MIN. **MAKES:** 4 SERVINGS

- 1 **cup instant brown rice**
- 1 **pound uncooked medium shrimp, peeled and deveined**
- 2 **garlic cloves, minced**
- ¾ **teaspoon salt**
- 3 **tablespoons reduced-fat butter**
- 2 **tablespoons olive oil**
- 1 **package (6 ounces) fresh baby spinach**

1. Cook rice according to package directions. Meanwhile, in a large skillet, cook the shrimp, garlic and salt in butter and oil for 1 minute. Add spinach. Cover and cook until shrimp turn pink and spinach is wilted. Stir in rice.

Editor's Note: *This recipe was tested with Land O'Lakes light stick butter.*

Nutrition Facts: *1 cup equals 290 calories, 14 g fat (4 g saturated fat), 149 mg cholesterol, 687 mg sodium, 21 g carbohydrate, 2 g fiber, 22 g protein.* **Diabetic Exchanges:** *3 lean meat, 2-½ fat, 1 starch.*

California Sushi Rolls F S C

Even if raw fish isn't your thing, you'll join the rolls of sushi lovers with this fabulous version. It makes a great presentation on party trays!

—**HEALTHY COOKING TEST KITCHEN**

PREP: 1 HOUR + STANDING **MAKES:** 64 PIECES

- 2 **cups sushi rice, rinsed and drained**
- 2 **cups water**
- ¼ **cup rice vinegar**
- 2 **tablespoons sugar**
- ½ **teaspoon salt**
- 2 **tablespoons sesame seeds, toasted**
- 2 **tablespoons sesame seeds**
   Bamboo sushi mat
- 8 **nori sheets**
- 1 **small cucumber, seeded and julienned**
- 3 **ounces imitation crabmeat, julienned**
- 1 **medium ripe avocado, peeled and julienned**
   Reduced-sodium soy sauce, prepared wasabi and pickled ginger slices, optional

1. In a large saucepan, combine rice and water; let stand for 30 minutes. Bring to a boil. Reduce heat to low; cover and simmer for 15-20 minutes or until water is absorbed and rice is tender. Remove from the heat. Let stand, covered, for 10 minutes.

2. Meanwhile, in small bowl, combine the vinegar, sugar and salt, stirring until sugar is dissolved.

3. Transfer rice to a large shallow bowl; drizzle with vinegar mixture. With a wooden paddle or spoon, stir rice with a slicing motion to cool slightly. Cover with a damp cloth to keep moist. (Rice mixture may be made up to 6 hours ahead and stored at room temperature, covered with a damp towel. Do not refrigerate.)

4. Sprinkle sesame seeds onto a plate; set aside. Place sushi mat on a work surface so mat rolls away from you; line with plastic wrap. Place ¾ cup rice on plastic. With moistened fingers, press rice into an 8-in. square. Top with one nori sheet.

5. Arrange a small amount of cucumber, crab and avocado about 1½ in. from bottom edge of nori sheet. Lifting bottom edge of the bamboo mat, roll up the rice mixture jelly-roll style, being sure to lift plastic from rice. Roll bamboo mat over sushi roll, pressing firmly, to make a more compact roll. When the roll is complete, tighten the roll to make more compact.

6. Remove mat; roll sushi rolls in sesame seeds. Cover with plastic wrap. Repeat with remaining ingredients to make eight rolls. Cut each into eight pieces. Serve with soy sauce, wasabi and ginger slices if desired.

Editor's Note: *Look for nori sheets in the international foods section.*

Nutrition Facts: *1 piece (calculated without optional ingredients) equals 35 calories, 1 g fat (trace saturated fat), trace cholesterol, 30 mg sodium, 6 g carbohydrate, 1 g fiber, 1 g protein.* **Diabetic Exchange:** *½ starch.*

Lime and chili add a kick that really makes this recipe pop. The grilled peppers are a great way to get my family to eat veggies.

—**LIBBY WALP** CHICAGO, ILLINOIS

Chili-Lime Shrimp Kabobs F S C

PREP: 10 MIN. + MARINATING
GRILL: 10 MIN.
MAKES: 12 KABOBS

- 2 **tablespoons lime juice**
- 2 **tablespoons olive oil**
- 4½ **teaspoons white wine vinegar**
- 2 **garlic cloves, crushed**
- 1 **teaspoon chili powder**
- ¼ **teaspoon salt**
- ¼ **teaspoon pepper**
- 24 **uncooked medium shrimp, peeled and deveined**
- 1 **large sweet red pepper, cut into 24 pieces**

1. In a large resealable plastic bag, combine the first seven ingredients. Add the shrimp; seal bag and turn to coat. Refrigerate for 1 hour. Drain and discard marinade.

2. On each of 12 metal or soaked wooden skewers, alternately thread two shrimp and two red pepper pieces. Grill kabobs, covered, over medium heat or broil 4 in. from the heat for 5-8 minutes or until shrimp turn pink, turning once.

Nutrition Facts: *1 kabob equals 32 calories, 1 g fat (trace saturated fat), 31 mg cholesterol, 46 mg sodium, 1 g carbohydrate, trace fiber, 4 g protein.* **Diabetic Exchange:** *1 lean meat.*

Shrimp Selection

When buying fresh shrimp, avoid those that have a yellow color to their meat or black spots or rings on the shells (unless they are Tiger shrimp) or meat. Keep in mind that most fresh shrimp that is sold has actually been previously frozen and thawed.

—**HEALTHY COOKING TEST KITCHEN**

178

182

183

Meatless Mains

"Tangy from balsamic and mellowed with chocolate, this light vinaigrette stays well-blended and also would be great over berries or watermelon."

HEALTHY COOKING TEST KITCHEN
about the Spinach Pear Salad with Chocolate Vinaigrette on page 184

Greek Pizzas Ⓜ

PREP/TOTAL TIME: 30 MIN. **MAKES:** 4 SERVINGS

- 4 pita breads (6 inches)
- 1 cup reduced-fat ricotta cheese
- ½ teaspoon garlic powder
- 1 package (10 ounces) frozen chopped spinach, thawed and squeezed dry
- 3 medium tomatoes, sliced
- ¾ cup crumbled feta cheese
- ¾ teaspoon dried basil

1. Place pita breads on a baking sheet. Combine ricotta cheese and garlic powder; spread over pitas. Top with spinach, tomatoes, feta cheese and basil.

2. Bake at 400° for 12-15 minutes or until bread is lightly browned.

Nutrition Facts: *1 pizza equals 320 calories, 7 g fat (4 g saturated fat), 26 mg cholesterol, 642 mg sodium, 46 g carbohydrate, 6 g fiber, 17 g protein.* **Diabetic Exchanges:** *2 starch, 2 vegetable, 1 lean meat, 1 fat.*

❝Customizable pita pizzas are a great way to please the whole family for lunch or dinner. Try using different vegetables and cheese blends to change things up. Sliced zucchini works well instead of tomato.❞

—**DORIS ALLERS** PORTAGE, MICHIGAN

Spaghetti Squash with Balsamic Vegetables and Toasted Pine Nuts Ⓜ

The veggies can be prepped while the squash is cooking in the microwave, so I can have a satisfying and healthy meal on the table in 30 minutes.

—**DEANNA MCDONALD** KALAMAZOO, MICHIGAN

PREP: 20 MIN. **COOK:** 15 MIN. **MAKES:** 6 SERVINGS

- 1 medium spaghetti squash (about 4 pounds)
- 1 cup chopped carrots
- 1 small red onion, halved and sliced
- 1 tablespoon olive oil
- 4 garlic cloves, minced
- 1 can (15½ ounces) great northern beans, rinsed and drained
- 1 can (14½ ounces) diced tomatoes, drained
- 1 can (14 ounces) water-packed artichoke hearts, rinsed, drained and halved
- 1 medium zucchini, chopped
- 3 tablespoons balsamic vinegar
- 2 teaspoons minced fresh thyme or ½ teaspoon dried thyme
- ¼ teaspoon salt
- ¼ teaspoon pepper
- ½ cup pine nuts, toasted

1. Cut squash in half lengthwise; discard seeds. Place squash cut side down on a microwave-safe plate. Microwave, uncovered, on high for 15-18 minutes or until tender.

2. Meanwhile, in a large nonstick skillet, saute carrots and onion in oil until tender. Add garlic; cook 1 minute longer. Stir in the beans, tomatoes, artichokes, zucchini, vinegar, thyme, salt and pepper. Cook and stir over medium heat for 8-10 minutes or until heated through.

3. When squash is cool enough to handle, use a fork to separate strands. Serve with bean mixture. Sprinkle with nuts.

Nutrition Facts: *¾ cup bean mixture with ⅔ cup squash and 4 teaspoons nuts equals 275 calories, 10 g fat (1 g saturated fat), 0 cholesterol, 510 mg sodium, 41 g carbohydrate, 10 g fiber, 11 g protein.* **Diabetic Exchanges:** *2½ starch, 1½ fat, 1 lean meat.*

You don't need a fancy pasta maker for this homemade treat. Try your hand at fresh pasta with this easy-to-work-with dough. The spinach gives it a nice color without overpowering the flavor. —HEALTHY COOKING TEST KITCHEN

Homemade Pasta M

PREP: 30 MIN. + STANDING
COOK: 10 MIN./BATCH
MAKES: 8 SERVINGS

- 1 package (10 ounces) frozen chopped spinach, thawed and squeezed dry
- ¼ cup packed fresh parsley sprigs
- 3½ to 4 cups all-purpose flour
- ½ teaspoon salt
- 4 eggs
- 3 tablespoons water
- 1 tablespoon olive oil
  Marinara sauce

1. Place spinach and parsley in a food processor; cover and process until finely chopped. Add 3½ cups flour and salt; process until blended. Add the eggs, water and oil. Process for 15-20 seconds or until dough forms a ball.
2. Turn onto a floured surface; knead for 8-10 minutes or until smooth and elastic, adding remaining flour if necessary. Cover and let rest for 30 minutes. Divide into fourths.
3. On a floured surface, roll each portion to 1/16-in. thickness. Dust top of dough with flour to prevent sticking; cut into ¼-in. slices. Separate the slices; allow noodles to dry on kitchen towels for at least 1 hour before cooking.
4. To cook, fill a Dutch oven three-fourths full with water. Bring to a boil. Add noodles in batches; cook, uncovered, for 8-10 minutes or until tender. Drain. Serve with sauce.

Nutrition Facts: *1 cup (calculated without sauce) equals 259 calories, 5 g fat (1 g saturated fat), 106 mg cholesterol, 211 mg sodium, 43 g carbohydrate, 3 g fiber, 10 g protein.*

Fresh Parsley

To keep fresh parsley in the refrigerator for several weeks, wash the entire bunch in warm water, shake off all excess moisture, wrap in paper towel and seal in a plastic bag. If you need longer storage time, remove the paper towel and place the sealed bag in the freezer. Then simply break off and crumble the amount of parsley you need for soups, stews and other cooked dishes.

Zucchini Burgers M

The patties for this omelet-like veggie burger hold together well while cooking and are hearty enough to serve bunless. I like to make them in summer with fresh-picked zucchini.

—KIMBERLY DANEK PINKSON
SAN ANSELMO, CALIFORNIA

PREP: 20 MIN.
COOK: 5 MIN./BATCH **MAKES:** 4 SERVINGS

- 2 cups shredded zucchini
- 1 medium onion, finely chopped
- ½ cup dry bread crumbs
- 2 eggs, lightly beaten
- ⅛ teaspoon salt
  Dash cayenne pepper
- 3 hard-cooked egg whites, chopped
- 2 tablespoons canola oil
- 4 whole wheat hamburger buns, split
- 4 lettuce leaves
- 4 slices tomato
- 4 slices onion

1. In a sieve or colander, drain zucchini, squeezing to remove excess liquid. Pat dry. In a small bowl, combine the zucchini, onion, bread crumbs, eggs, salt and cayenne. Gently stir in cooked egg whites.
2. Heat 1 tablespoon oil in a large nonstick skillet over medium-low heat. Drop batter by scant ⅔ cupfuls into oil; press lightly to flatten. Fry in batches until golden brown on both sides, using remaining oil as needed.
3. Serve on buns with lettuce, tomato and onion.

Nutrition Facts: *1 burger equals 314 calories, 12 g fat (2 g saturated fat), 106 mg cholesterol, 467 mg sodium, 40 g carbohydrate, 6 g fiber, 13 g protein.*
Diabetic Exchanges: *2 starch, 1½ fat, 1 lean meat, 1 vegetable.*

Vegetarian Chili Ole! F M

This hearty chili can be made ahead by mixing the ingredients in a bowl the night before and storing them in the fridge overnight. In the morning, I toss them in my slow cooker so when I get home I have a spicy meal ready to go.
—MARJORIE AU HONOLULU, HAWAII

PREP: 35 MIN. **COOK:** 6 HOURS **MAKES:** 7 SERVINGS

- 1 can (16 ounces) kidney beans, rinsed and drained
- 1 can (15 ounces) black beans, rinsed and drained
- 1 can (14½ ounces) diced tomatoes, undrained
- 1½ cups frozen corn
- 1 large onion, chopped
- 1 medium zucchini, chopped
- 1 medium sweet red pepper, chopped
- 1 can (4 ounces) chopped green chilies
- 1 ounce Mexican chocolate, chopped
- 1 cup water
- 1 can (6 ounces) tomato paste
- 1 tablespoon cornmeal
- 1 tablespoon chili powder
- ½ teaspoon salt
- ½ teaspoon dried oregano
- ½ teaspoon ground cumin
- ¼ teaspoon hot pepper sauce, optional
  Optional toppings: diced tomatoes, chopped green onions and queso fresco

1. In a 4-qt. slow cooker, combine the first nine ingredients. Combine the water, tomato paste, cornmeal, chili powder, salt, oregano, cumin and pepper sauce if desired until smooth; stir into slow cooker. Cover and cook on low for 6-8 hours or until vegetables are tender.
2. Serve with toppings of your choice.

Nutrition Facts: *1 cup (calculated without optional ingredients) equals 216 calories, 1 g fat (trace saturated fat), 0 cholesterol, 559 mg sodium, 43 g carbohydrate, 10 g fiber, 11 g protein.*
Diabetic Exchanges: *2½ starch, 1 lean meat.*

Did you know?

One cup of black beans offers 15 grams of fiber. Add beans to four dishes a week and you could cut your risk of heart disease by 22 percent, according to researchers at Tulane University.

Mediterranean Pasta Caesar Toss ⓜ

Get creative using convenience items with a fresh take on ravioli. Try this lightened-up pasta toss for an alfresco dinner, or double it for a family picnic.

—**LIBBY WALP** CHICAGO, ILLINOIS

PREP/TOTAL TIME: 30 MIN. **MAKES:** 4 SERVINGS

- 1 **package (9 ounces) refrigerated cheese ravioli**
- 1 **cup frozen cut green beans, thawed**
- 1 **cup cherry tomatoes, halved**
- ¾ **teaspoon coarsely ground pepper**
- ⅓ **cup reduced-fat creamy Caesar salad dressing**
- 3 **tablespoons shredded Parmesan cheese**

1. In a large saucepan, cook ravioli according to package directions, adding the green beans during the last 3 minutes of cooking. Drain.

2. In a serving bowl, combine the ravioli mixture, tomatoes and pepper. Add dressing; toss to coat. Sprinkle with cheese.

Nutrition Facts: *1 cup equals 264 calories, 10 g fat (4 g saturated fat), 28 mg cholesterol, 649 mg sodium, 31 g carbohydrate, 3 g fiber, 12 g protein.* **Diabetic Exchanges:** *1½ starch, 1 lean meat, 1 vegetable, 1 fat.*

Black Bean and Corn Tacos ⓜ

We eat meatless meals a few times a week, so I replaced the beef with nutty brown rice to bulk up these tacos. I also like to swap in quinoa.

—**KRISTIN RIMKUS** SNOHOMISH, WASHINGTON

PREP/TOTAL TIME: 30 MIN. **MAKES:** 4 SERVINGS

- 1 **medium onion, finely chopped**
- 1 **medium green pepper, finely chopped**
- 1 **small sweet red pepper, finely chopped**
- 1 **can (15 ounces) black beans, rinsed and drained**
- 2 **large tomatoes, seeded and chopped**
- 2 **cups shredded cabbage**
- 1 **cup fresh or frozen corn**
- 2 **tablespoons reduced-sodium taco seasoning**
- 2 **tablespoons lime juice**
- 2 **garlic cloves, minced**
- 1 **cup ready-to-serve brown rice**
- 8 **taco shells, warmed**
- ½ **cup shredded reduced-fat Mexican cheese blend**
- ½ **cup reduced-fat sour cream**

1. In a large nonstick skillet coated with cooking spray, saute onion and peppers until crisp-tender. Add the beans, tomatoes, cabbage, corn, taco seasoning, lime juice and garlic. Cook and stir over medium heat for 8-10 minutes or until vegetables are tender. Stir in rice; heat through.

2. Spoon bean mixture into taco shells. Top with cheese and sour cream.

Nutrition Facts: *2 tacos equals 423 calories, 12 g fat (4 g saturated fat), 20 mg cholesterol, 682 mg sodium, 64 g carbohydrate, 10 g fiber, 17 g protein.*

Quinoa Tabouleh M

When my mom and sister developed several food allergies, we had to modify many recipes. I substituted quinoa for couscous in this tabouleh. Now we make it all the time!
—**JENNIFER KLANN** CORBETT, OREGON

PREP: 35 MIN. + CHILLING **MAKES:** 8 SERVINGS

- 2 **cups water**
- 1 **cup quinoa, rinsed**
- 1 **can (15 ounces) black beans, rinsed and drained**
- 1 **small cucumber, peeled and chopped**
- 1 **small sweet red pepper, chopped**
- ⅓ **cup minced fresh parsley**
- ¼ **cup lemon juice**
- 2 **tablespoons olive oil**
- ½ **teaspoon salt**
- ½ **teaspoon pepper**

1. In a large saucepan, bring water to a boil. Add quinoa. Reduce heat; cover and simmer for 12-15 minutes or until liquid is absorbed. Remove from the heat; fluff with a fork. Transfer to a bowl; cool completely.

2. Add the beans, cucumber, red pepper and parsley. In a small bowl, whisk the remaining ingredients; drizzle over salad and toss to coat. Refrigerate until chilled.

Editor's Note: *Look for quinoa in the cereal, rice or organic food aisle.*

Nutrition Facts: *¾ cup equals 159 calories, 5 g fat (1 g saturated fat), 0 cholesterol, 255 mg sodium, 24 g carbohydrate, 4 g fiber, 6 g protein.* **Diabetic Exchanges:** *1½ starch, 1 fat.*

Hearty Asian Lettuce Salad M

It may sound nutty, but this vegetarian version of your favorite restaurant salad packs in 13 grams of protein and is bursting with juicy flavor.
—**HEALTHY COOKING TEST KITCHEN**

PREP/TOTAL TIME: 20 MIN. **MAKES:** 2 SERVINGS

- 1 **cup ready-to-serve brown rice**
- 1 **cup frozen shelled edamame**
- 3 **cups spring mix salad greens**
- ¼ **cup reduced-fat sesame ginger salad dressing**
- 1 **medium navel orange, peeled and sectioned**
- 4 **radishes, sliced**
- 2 **tablespoons sliced almonds, toasted**

1. Prepare rice and edamame according to package directions.

2. In a large bowl, combine the salad greens, rice and edamame. Drizzle with salad dressing and toss to coat. Divide salad mixture between two plates; top with orange segments, radishes and almonds.

Nutrition Facts: *1 serving equals 329 calories, 10 g fat (1 g saturated fat), 0 cholesterol, 430 mg sodium, 44 g carbohydrate, 7 g fiber, 13 g protein.* **Diabetic Exchanges:** *3 starch, 1½ fat.*

Spinach Pear Salad with Chocolate Vinaigrette

PREP/TOTAL TIME: 15 MIN.
MAKES: 4 SERVINGS

- 1 ounce milk chocolate, chopped
- 3 tablespoons balsamic vinegar
- 3 tablespoons canola oil
- 1 teaspoon honey
- ¼ teaspoon salt
- ⅛ teaspoon pepper
- 1 package (6 ounces) fresh baby spinach
- 1 large pear, sliced
- 3 tablespoons dried cranberries
- 2 tablespoons sliced almonds, toasted

1. In a microwave, melt chocolate; stir until smooth. Whisk in the vinegar, oil, honey, salt and pepper; set aside.
2. Divide spinach among four salad plates. Top with pear, cranberries and almonds. Drizzle with dressing.

Nutrition Facts: *1 serving equals 215 calories, 14 g fat (2 g saturated fat), 1 mg cholesterol, 185 mg sodium, 23 g carbohydrate, 3 g fiber, 3 g protein.*
Diabetic Exchanges: *2 fat, 1 starch, 1 vegetable.*

Meatless Lentil Soup

This has been my husband's favorite soup our whole 30-year married life. He enjoys taking a thermos of it to work during the winter. It's delicious served with warm biscuits and butter.

—JANET CHASE BERRIEN SPRINGS, MICHIGAN

PREP: 15 MIN.   **COOK:** 35 MIN.
MAKES: 8 SERVINGS (3 QUARTS)

- 2 large carrots, halved and sliced
- 2 celery ribs, sliced
- 1 medium onion, chopped
- 10 cups water
- 1 package (16 ounces) dried lentils, rinsed
- 4 small red potatoes, diced
- 2 bay leaves
- 2 teaspoons salt
- 1 teaspoon pepper

1. In a large nonstick saucepan coated with cooking spray, cook the carrots, celery and onion over medium heat for 5 minutes.
2. Stir in the water, lentils, potatoes, bay leaves, salt and pepper. Bring to a boil. Reduce heat; cover and simmer for 30-35 minutes or until lentils are tender. Discard bay leaves.

Nutrition Facts: *1½ cups equals 245 calories, 1 g fat (trace saturated fat), 0 cholesterol, 617 mg sodium, 44 g carbohydrate, 19 g fiber, 16 g protein.*

Tangy from balsamic and mellowed with chocolate, this light vinaigrette stays well-blended and also would be great over berries or watermelon. **—HEALTHY COOKING TEST KITCHEN**

Grilled Portobello Burgers

Tastes like a bistro-style grilled cheese, but eats like a hearty burger—meet the new cheese-bello.

—MARY HAAS HEWITT, NEW JERSEY

PREP/TOTAL TIME: 25 MIN. **MAKES:** 4 SERVINGS

- 4 large portobello mushrooms (4 to 4½ inches), stems removed
- 6 tablespoons reduced-fat balsamic vinaigrette, divided
- 4 slices red onion
- 1 cup roasted sweet red peppers, drained
- 4 slices fresh mozzarella cheese
- 4 kaiser rolls, split
- ¼ cup fat-free mayonnaise

1. Brush mushrooms with 4 tablespoons vinaigrette. Grill mushrooms and onion, covered, over medium heat for 3-4 minutes on each side or until tender. Top mushrooms with red peppers, onion and cheese. Grill, covered, 2-3 minutes longer or until cheese is melted. Grill rolls, uncovered, for 1-2 minutes or until toasted.

2. Spread roll bottoms with mayonnaise and drizzle with remaining vinaigrette. Top with mushrooms; replace roll tops.

Nutrition Facts: *1 burger equals 354 calories, 12 g fat (4 g saturated fat), 17 mg cholesterol, 979 mg sodium, 42 g carbohydrate, 3 g fiber, 15 g protein.* **Diabetic Exchanges:** *2 starch, 1 medium-fat meat, 1 vegetable, 1 fat.*

top tip **Asparagus Tips**

To clean asparagus, soak in cold water, then cut or snap off the tough whitish portion. Store bundled stalks upright in a bowl filled with 1 inch of water in the refrigerator, or wrap the cut ends in damp paper towels, then cover with plastic wrap and refrigerate.

—HEALTHY COOKING TEST KITCHEN

Asian Vegetable Pasta

A little peanut butter and a sprinkling of peanuts give this dish plenty of flavor. While red pepper flakes offer a little kick, brown sugar balances it out with a hint of sweetness.

—MITZI SENTIFF ANNAPOLIS, MARYLAND

PREP/TOTAL TIME: 20 MIN. **MAKES:** 5 SERVINGS

- 4 quarts water
- 1 pound fresh asparagus, trimmed and cut into 1-inch pieces
- 8 ounces uncooked angel hair pasta
- ¾ cup julienned carrots
- ⅓ cup reduced-fat creamy peanut butter
- 3 tablespoons rice vinegar
- 3 tablespoons reduced-sodium soy sauce
- 2 tablespoons brown sugar
- ½ teaspoon crushed red pepper flakes
- ¼ cup unsalted peanuts, chopped

1. In a Dutch oven, bring the water to a boil. Add asparagus and pasta; cook for 3 minutes. Stir in carrots; cook for 1 minute or until pasta is tender. Drain and keep warm.

2. In a small saucepan, combine the peanut butter, vinegar, soy sauce, brown sugar and pepper flakes. Bring to a boil over medium heat, stirring constantly. Pour over pasta mixture; toss to coat. Sprinkle with peanuts.

Nutrition Facts: *1 cup equals 358 calories, 10 g fat (2 g saturated fat), 0 cholesterol, 472 mg sodium, 54 g carbohydrate, 5 g fiber, 15 g protein.*

Veggie-Stuffed Eggplant F M

For years, I cooked for my late husband and our five children. Now it's just me and my great-grandson. This hearty and nutritious dish is one we both enjoy.
—RUBY WILLIAMS BOGALUSA, LOUISIANA

PREP: 25 MIN. **BAKE:** 20 MIN. **MAKES:** 2 SERVINGS

- 1 medium eggplant
- ½ cup chopped onion
- 2 garlic cloves, minced
- ½ cup chopped fresh mushrooms
- ½ cup chopped zucchini
- ½ cup chopped sweet red pepper
- ¾ cup seeded chopped tomatoes
- ¼ cup toasted wheat germ
- 2 tablespoons minced fresh parsley
- ½ teaspoon dried thyme
- ¼ teaspoon salt
- ¼ teaspoon pepper
  Dash crushed red pepper flakes
- 1 tablespoon grated Parmesan cheese

1. Cut eggplant in half lengthwise; remove pulp, leaving a ¼-in.-thick shell. Cube pulp; set shells and pulp aside.
2. In a large nonstick skillet coated with cooking spray, saute onion and garlic until onion is tender. Add the mushrooms, zucchini, red pepper and eggplant pulp; saute for 4-6 minutes or until vegetables are crisp-tender. Stir in the tomatoes, wheat germ, parsley, thyme, salt, pepper and pepper flakes; cook for 1 minute.
3. Divide mixture evenly between the eggplant shells; sprinkle with Parmesan cheese. Place on a baking sheet. Bake at 400° for 20-25 minutes or until shells are tender.

Nutrition Facts: *1 stuffed eggplant half equals 186 calories, 3 g fat (1 g saturated fat), 2 mg cholesterol, 363 mg sodium, 35 g carbohydrate, 12 g fiber, 11 g protein.* **Diabetic Exchanges:** *2 starch, 1 vegetable.*

Black Bean Burgers with Chipotle Slaw M

We like to eat meatless at least one day a week, so I always keep cans of various beans in the pantry for quick meals like this.
—DEBORAH BIGGS OMAHA, NEBRASKA

PREP: 25 MIN. + CHILLING **COOK:** 10 MIN. **MAKES:** 4 SERVINGS

- 1 can (15 ounces) black beans, rinsed and drained
- 6 tablespoons panko (Japanese) bread crumbs
- ¼ cup finely chopped onion
- ¼ cup finely chopped sweet red pepper
- ¼ cup minced fresh cilantro
- 2 egg whites, lightly beaten
- 1 garlic clove, minced
- ¼ teaspoon salt
- 2 tablespoons red wine vinegar
- 1 tablespoon plus 4 teaspoons olive oil, divided
- 1 tablespoon minced chipotle pepper in adobo sauce
- 1½ teaspoons sugar
- 2¼ cups coleslaw mix
- 2 green onions, chopped
- 4 whole wheat hamburger buns, split

1. In a large bowl, mash beans. Add the panko, onion, red pepper, cilantro, egg whites, garlic and salt; mix well. Shape bean mixture into four patties; refrigerate for 30 minutes.
2. Meanwhile, in a small bowl, whisk the vinegar, 1 tablespoon oil, chipotle pepper and sugar; stir in coleslaw mix and onions. Chill until serving.
3. In a large nonstick skillet, cook burgers in remaining oil over medium heat for 3-5 minutes on each side or until a thermometer reads 160°. Serve on buns with slaw.

Nutrition Facts: *1 burger equals 327 calories, 10 g fat (1 g saturated fat), 0 cholesterol, 635 mg sodium, 48 g carbohydrate, 9 g fiber, 12 g protein.* **Diabetic Exchanges:** *3 starch, 1½ fat, 1 lean meat.*

Lentil-Tomato Soup F M

PREP: 15 MIN. **COOK:** 30 MIN. **MAKES:** 6 SERVINGS

- 4½ **cups water**
- 4 **medium carrots, sliced**
- 1 **medium onion, chopped**
- ⅔ **cup dried lentils, rinsed**
- 1 **can (6 ounces) tomato paste**
- 2 **tablespoons minced fresh parsley**
- 1 **tablespoon brown sugar**
- 1 **tablespoon white vinegar**
- 1 **teaspoon garlic salt**
- ½ **teaspoon dried thyme**
- ¼ **teaspoon dill weed**
- ¼ **teaspoon dried tarragon**
- ¼ **teaspoon pepper**

In a large saucepan, combine the water, carrots, onion and lentils; bring to a boil. Reduce heat; cover and simmer for 20-25 minutes or until vegetables and lentils are tender. Stir in the remaining ingredients; return to a boil. Reduce heat; simmer, uncovered, for 5 minutes to allow flavors to blend.

For Sausage Variation: *Stir in ½ pound chopped fully-cooked turkey sausage; heat through.* **For Kale Variation:** *Stir in 3 cups chopped fresh kale; cook, uncovered, until kale is tender.* **For Spiced Variation:** *Add ¾ teaspoon garam masala when adding other seasonings.*

Nutrition Facts: *¾ cup equals 138 calories, trace fat (trace saturated fat), 0 cholesterol, 351 mg sodium, 27 g carbohydrate, 9 g fiber, 8 g protein.* **Diabetic Exchanges:** *1 starch, 1 lean meat, 1 vegetable.*

> "Double the recipe and share this hearty soup with neighbors and loved ones on cold winter nights. I serve it with corn bread for dunking."

—**MICHELLE CURTIS** BAKER CITY, OREGON

Makeover Eggplant Parmesan M

Reader Eva McPherson in Madison, Alabama, asked if we could make over Olive Garden's Eggplant Parmesan into a healthy meal you can make at home. This version has 300 fewer calories and more than half the fat and sodium of the original.

—**HEALTHY COOKING TEST KITCHEN**

PREP: 50 MIN. **BAKE:** 30 MIN. **MAKES:** 6 SERVINGS

- 1 **medium onion, chopped**
- 1½ **teaspoons olive oil**
- 2 **garlic cloves, minced**
- 1 **can (15 ounces) crushed tomatoes**
- 1 **can (14½ ounces) diced tomatoes, undrained**
- 1 **can (8 ounces) no-salt-added tomato sauce**
- ½ **cup dry red wine**
- ¼ **cup tomato paste**
- 1¾ **teaspoons Italian seasoning, divided**
- 2 **eggs**
- 2 **tablespoons water**
- ½ **cup all-purpose flour**
- 1½ **cups dry bread crumbs**
- ½ **teaspoon salt**
- ¼ **teaspoon pepper**
- 2 **medium eggplants, peeled and cut into ¼-inch slices**
- 9 **ounces uncooked multigrain spaghetti**
- 6 **ounces fresh mozzarella cheese, halved and thinly sliced**
- ⅓ **cup shredded Parmesan cheese**
- 2 **tablespoons minced fresh parsley**

1. In a Dutch oven, saute onion in oil until tender. Add garlic; cook 1 minute longer. Add the crushed tomatoes, diced tomatoes, tomato sauce, wine, tomato paste and ¾ teaspoon Italian seasoning. Bring to a boil. Reduce heat; simmer, uncovered, for 25-30 minutes or until desired consistency, stirring occasionally.

2. Meanwhile, in shallow bowl, whisk eggs and water. Place flour in a separate shallow bowl. In another bowl, combine the bread crumbs, salt, pepper and remaining Italian seasoning. Dip eggplant slices into flour then in egg mixture; coat with crumb mixture. Place on baking sheets coated with cooking spray. Bake at 350° for 25-30 minutes or until tender and golden brown, turning once. Meanwhile, cook spaghetti according to package directions.

3. Spoon 2 cups sauce over eggplant; top with cheeses. Bake 4-5 minutes longer or until cheese is melted.

4. Drain spaghetti. Serve remaining sauce over spaghetti; top with eggplant slices. Sprinkle with parsley.

Nutrition Facts: *1 serving equals 505 calories, 13 g fat (6 g saturated fat), 96 mg cholesterol, 716 mg sodium, 74 g carbohydrate, 13 g fiber, 24 g protein.*

Harvest Vegetable Tart M

When guests lay eyes on this lightened-up veggie tart, everyone approves. I've been serving this for 30 years, and its bold taste and aroma always get a warm reception.

—**RUTH LEE** TROY, ONTARIO

PREP: 45 MIN. + CHILLING **BAKE:** 30 MIN. **MAKES:** 6 SERVINGS

- ½ cup all-purpose flour
- ¼ cup whole wheat flour
- ¼ cup cornmeal
- 2 tablespoons grated Parmesan cheese
- ½ teaspoon salt
- ⅛ teaspoon cayenne pepper
- ¼ cup cold butter, cubed
- 3 to 4 tablespoons cold water

FILLING

- ½ cup thinly sliced green onions
- 2 garlic cloves, minced
- 1 tablespoon olive oil
- 5 slices peeled eggplant (3½ inches x ¼ inch)
- 2 tablespoons grated Parmesan cheese, divided
- 1 small tomato, cut into ¼-inch slices
- 3 green pepper rings
- 3 sweet red pepper rings
- ½ cup frozen corn
- 2 eggs, lightly beaten
- ⅔ cup fat-free evaporated milk
- ¾ teaspoon salt
- ¼ teaspoon pepper

1. In a bowl, combine the first six ingredients. Cut in butter until crumbly. Gradually add water, tossing with a fork until dough forms a ball. Cover and refrigerate for at least 30 minutes.
2. Roll out pastry to fit a 9-in. tart pan with removable bottom. Transfer pastry to pan; trim even with edge of pan. Line unpricked pastry shell with a double thickness of heavy-duty foil. Bake at 450° for 8 minutes. Remove foil; bake 5 minutes longer.
3. In a large nonstick skillet coated with cooking spray, cook onions and garlic in oil for 2 minutes. Add eggplant; cook for 4-5 minutes or until softened. Cool for 5 minutes. Spoon into crust. Sprinkle with 1 tablespoon Parmesan cheese. Top with tomato slices and pepper rings. Sprinkle with corn.
4. In a small bowl, whisk the eggs, milk, salt and pepper; pour over vegetables. Sprinkle with remaining Parmesan cheese. Bake at 350° for 30-35 minutes or until a knife inserted near the center comes out clean.

Nutrition Facts: *1 piece equals 256 calories, 13 g fat (6 g saturated fat), 95 mg cholesterol, 691 mg sodium, 27 g carbohydrate, 3 g fiber, 9 g protein.* **Diabetic Exchanges:** *2 fat, 1½ starch, 1 vegetable.*

Roasted Asparagus Lasagna M

My husband is a meat-and-potatoes kind of guy, so the first time I introduced this meatless recipe, he wasn't thrilled. But once he tried it, he was hooked. Now he often asks me to prepare it!

—**CINDY MACHA** RICHMOND, TEXAS

PREP: 20 MIN.
BAKE: 45 MIN. + STANDING
MAKES: 12 SERVINGS

- 2 pounds fresh asparagus, trimmed and cut into 1-inch pieces
- 1 cup sliced fresh mushrooms
- 2 tablespoons olive oil, divided
- 2 tablespoons butter
- 3 tablespoons all-purpose flour
- ¼ teaspoon salt
- ⅛ teaspoon white pepper
  Dash ground cloves
- 1½ cups milk
- 1 cup thinly sliced red onion
- 2 garlic cloves, minced
- 12 lasagna noodles, cooked and drained
- 1½ cups (6 ounces) shredded part-skim mozzarella cheese
- ¾ cup grated Parmesan cheese

1. Place asparagus and mushrooms in a shallow roasting pan. Drizzle with 1 tablespoon oil; toss to coat. Bake at 450° for 8-10 minutes or until vegetables are browned; set aside. Reduce heat to 350°.
2. In a large saucepan, melt butter. Stir in the flour, salt, pepper and cloves until smooth. Gradually stir in milk. Bring to a boil; cook and stir for 2 minutes or until thickened. Set aside.
3. In a large skillet, saute onion in remaining oil until tender. Add garlic; cook 1 minute longer. Remove from the heat; add roasted asparagus and mushrooms.
4. In a 13-in. x 9-in. baking dish coated with cooking spray, layer four noodles, a third of the asparagus mixture, a third of the white sauce, ½ cup mozzarella cheese and ¼ cup Parmesan cheese. Repeat layers twice.
5. Cover and bake at 350° for 35 minutes. Uncover; bake 10-15 minutes longer or until heated through. Let stand for 15 minutes before cutting.

Nutrition Facts: *1 piece (prepared with reduced-fat butter, fat-free milk and part-skim mozzarella) equals 216 calories, 8 g fat (4 g saturated fat), 16 mg cholesterol, 251 mg sodium, 25 g carbohydrate, 2 g fiber, 12 g protein.* **Diabetic Exchanges:** *2 lean meat, 1½ starch.*

Lentil Soup for the Soul Ⓜ

My boyfriend and I are vegetarians, and I like to experiment with new meatless dishes. This is one of our favorites on cool fall or winter evenings. Served with warm, crusty bread, it's a rich and satisfying meal.

—**ATHENA RUSSELL** FLORENCE, SOUTH CAROLINA

PREP: 20 MIN. **COOK:** 30 MIN. **MAKES:** 3 SERVINGS

- ⅓ cup chopped peeled parsnip
- ⅓ cup diced peeled potato
- ¼ cup chopped green onions
- ¼ cup chopped leek (white portion only)
- ¼ cup chopped carrot
- ¼ cup chopped celery
- 2 teaspoons olive oil
- 1 can (14½ ounces) vegetable broth
- 1 cup no-salt-added diced tomatoes
- ⅓ cup dried lentils, rinsed
- ¼ cup dry red wine or additional vegetable broth
- 1 teaspoon Worcestershire sauce
- 1 bay leaf
- ⅓ cup minced fresh cilantro

1. In a large saucepan, saute the parsnip, potato, onions, leek, carrot and celery in oil for 3 minutes. Add the broth, tomatoes, lentils, wine, Worcestershire sauce and bay leaf. Bring to a boil. Reduce heat; cover and simmer for 25-30 minutes or until lentils are tender.

2. Just before serving, discard bay leaf; stir in cilantro.

Nutrition Facts: *1⅓ cups equals 183 calories, 4 g fat (trace saturated fat), 0 cholesterol, 631 mg sodium, 28 g carbohydrate, 9 g fiber, 9 g protein.* **Diabetic Exchanges:** *1½ starch, 1 lean meat, 1 vegetable, ½ fat.*

Impossible Garden Pie Ⓜ

The biscuit mix in this "impossible" pie settles to the bottom during baking to create a cheesy crust.

—**BARBARA GIGLIOTTI** OCALA, FLORIDA

PREP: 15 MIN. **BAKE:** 30 MIN. **MAKES:** 6 SERVINGS

- 2 cups cut fresh asparagus (1-inch pieces)
- 1½ cups chopped fresh tomatoes
- 1 medium onion, chopped
- 1 garlic clove, minced
- ¼ teaspoon dried basil
- ¼ teaspoon salt
- ¼ teaspoon pepper
- 1 cup (4 ounces) shredded part-skim mozzarella cheese
- ½ cup grated Parmesan cheese
- ¾ cup reduced-fat biscuit/baking mix
- 3 eggs
- 1½ cups fat-free milk

1. In a large bowl, combine the first seven ingredients. Transfer to an 8-in. square baking dish coated with cooking spray. Sprinkle with cheeses.

2. In another large bowl, whisk the biscuit mix, eggs and milk until smooth; pour over cheese. Bake, uncovered, at 400° for 30-35 minutes or until set and a thermometer inserted near the center reads 160°. Let stand for 5 minutes before cutting.

Nutrition Facts: *1 serving equals 221 calories, 9 g fat (4 g saturated fat), 124 mg cholesterol, 553 mg sodium, 20 g carbohydrate, 2 g fiber, 15 g protein.* **Diabetic Exchanges:** *2 lean meat, 1 starch, 1 vegetable, ½ fat.*

Garden Veggie Egg Bake C M

Looking for a healthy day-starter? Children will actually enjoy eating their veggies when they're baked into this cheesy, nutrition-packed egg dish.

—JOANNE WILSON ROSELLE PARK, NEW JERSEY

PREP: 20 MIN. **BAKE:** 45 MIN. + STANDING **MAKES:** 6 SERVINGS

- **5 eggs**
- **2 cups egg substitute**
- **½ cup 2% cottage cheese**
- **⅓ cup shredded pepper jack cheese**
- **⅓ cup shredded cheddar cheese**
- **¼ cup grated Romano cheese**
- **¼ teaspoon pepper**
- **¼ teaspoon hot pepper sauce**
- **1 medium zucchini, chopped**
- **2 cups fresh broccoli florets**
- **2 cups coarsely chopped fresh spinach**
- **½ cup shredded carrots**
- **½ cup cherry tomatoes, quartered**

1. In a large bowl, whisk the eggs, egg substitute, cheeses, pepper and pepper sauce. Stir in the vegetables. Transfer to an 11-in. x 7-in. baking dish coated with cooking spray.

2. Bake, uncovered, at 350° for 45-50 minutes or until a knife inserted near the center comes out clean. Let stand for 10 minutes before cutting.

Nutrition Facts: *1 piece equals 202 calories, 10 g fat (5 g saturated fat), 197 mg cholesterol, 478 mg sodium, 7 g carbohydrate, 2 g fiber, 22 g protein.* **Diabetic Exchanges:** *3 lean meat, 1 vegetable, ½ fat.*

Saucy Vegetable Tofu M

This is my daughter Tonya's favorite meal. Sometimes we make it with rigatoni and call it "Riga-Tonya." Either way, it's a great, quick way to prepare your kids some yummy vegetables.

—SANDRA ECKERT POTTSTOWN, PENNSYLVANIA

PREP/TOTAL TIME: 20 MIN. **MAKES:** 6 SERVINGS

- **8 ounces uncooked whole wheat spiral pasta**
- **1 large onion, coarsely chopped**
- **1 large green or sweet red pepper, coarsely chopped**
- **1 medium zucchini, halved lengthwise and sliced**
- **1 tablespoon olive oil**
- **1 package (16 ounces) firm tofu, drained and cut into ½-inch cubes**
- **2 cups meatless spaghetti sauce**

1. Cook pasta according to package directions. Meanwhile, in a large skillet, saute the onion, pepper and zucchini in oil until crisp-tender.

2. Stir in tofu and spaghetti sauce; heat through. Drain pasta; serve with tofu mixture.

Nutrition Facts: *1¼ cups tofu mixture with ⅔ cup pasta equals 274 calories, 7 g fat (1 g saturated fat), 0 cholesterol, 380 mg sodium, 41 g carbohydrate, 7 g fiber, 14 g protein.* **Diabetic Exchanges:** *2 starch, 2 lean meat, 1 vegetable, ½ fat.*

194

195

202

The Bread Basket

66It's easy for me to fix these light and tangy biscuits for my husband and I, and it's just as easy to double or triple the recipe for company.99

ANE BURKE BELLA VISTA, ARKANSAS
about her recipe, Tender Biscuits for Two, on page 201

Homemade Tortillas M

I usually have to double this recipe because we go through them quickly. Tender, chewy and simple, my homemade tortillas are so lovely you'll never use store-bought tortillas again.

—**KRISTIN VAN DYKEN** WEST RICHLAND, WASHINGTON

PREP/TOTAL TIME: 30 MIN. **MAKES:** 8 TORTILLAS

> 2   cups all-purpose flour
> ½   teaspoon salt
> ¾   cup water
> 3   tablespoons olive oil

1. In a large bowl, combine flour and salt. Stir in water and oil. Turn onto a floured surface; knead 10-12 times, adding a little flour or water if needed to achieve a smooth dough. Let rest for 10 minutes.

2. Divide dough into eight portions. On a lightly floured surface, roll each portion into a 7-in. circle.

3. In a large nonstick skillet coated with cooking spray, cook tortillas over medium heat for 1 minute on each side or until lightly browned. Keep warm.

Nutrition Facts: *1 tortilla equals 159 calories, 5 g fat (1 g saturated fat), 0 cholesterol, 148 mg sodium, 24 g carbohydrate, 1 g fiber, 3 g protein.* **Diabetic Exchanges:** *1½ starch, 1 fat.*

Tart Cranberry Quick Bread F S M

My mother loved to make this cranberry bread. I usually stock up on cranberries when they're in season and freeze them so I can make this loaf year-round.

—**KAREN CZECHOWICZ** OCALA, FLORIDA

PREP: 20 MIN. **BAKE:** 45 MIN. + COOLING
MAKES: 1 LOAF (12 SLICES)

> 1½   cups all-purpose flour
> ¾   cup sugar
> 1   teaspoon baking powder
> ¼   teaspoon salt
> ¼   teaspoon baking soda
> 1   egg
> ½   cup orange juice
> 2   tablespoons butter, melted
> 1   tablespoon water
> 1½   cups fresh or frozen cranberries, halved

1. In a large bowl, combine the first five ingredients. In a small bowl, whisk the egg, orange juice, butter and water. Stir into dry ingredients just until moistened. Fold in cranberries.

2. Transfer to an 8-in. x 4-in. loaf pan coated with cooking spray and sprinkled with flour. Bake at 350° for 45-50 minutes or until a toothpick inserted near the center comes out clean. Cool for 10 minutes before removing from pan to a wire rack.

Nutrition Facts: *1 slice equals 138 calories, 2 g fat (1 g saturated fat), 23 mg cholesterol, 129 mg sodium, 27 g carbohydrate, 1 g fiber, 2 g protein.* **Diabetic Exchange:** *2 starch.*

Ricotta-Raisin Coffee Cake F M

These few ingredients come together quickly so I can have a warm coffee cake to serve overnight guests for breakfast. If you don't have or don't like cardamom, substitute any sweet spice. I recommend ground nutmeg, cinnamon or allspice.

—**CAROL GAUS** ELK GROVE VILLAGE, ILLINOIS

PREP: 15 MIN. + RISING **BAKE:** 20 MIN. + COOLING
MAKES: 12 SERVINGS

- 1 loaf (1 pound) frozen bread dough, thawed
- 1 cup part-skim ricotta cheese
- ¼ cup honey
- ¼ teaspoon ground cardamom
- ¼ teaspoon almond extract
- 1 cup golden raisins
- ¼ cup confectioners' sugar
- 2 to 3 teaspoons fat-free milk

1. On a lightly floured surface, roll dough into a 15-in. x 9-in. rectangle. In a small bowl, combine the cheese, honey, cardamom and almond extract. Spread filling to within ½ in. of edges. Sprinkle with raisins. Roll up jelly-roll style, starting with a long side; pinch seam to seal. Pinch ends together to form a ring.
2. Place seam side down in a parchment paper-lined 9-in. round baking pan. Cover and let rise until doubled, about 30 minutes.
3. With a sharp knife, make 12 shallow slashes in top of coffee cake. Bake at 350° for 20-25 minutes or until golden brown. Cool on a wire rack. In a small bowl, combine confectioners' sugar and milk; drizzle over cake.

Nutrition Facts: *1 slice equals 203 calories, 3 g fat (1 g saturated fat), 6 mg cholesterol, 240 mg sodium, 37 g carbohydrate, 2 g fiber, 7 g protein.*

Makeover Cheddar Biscuits C M

Reader Janie Paull in Clio, Michigan, asked us to make over Red Lobster's Cheddar Bay Biscuits for her to make at home. This version has half the fat but all the garlicky goodness she loves.

—**HEALTHY COOKING TEST KITCHEN**

PREP/TOTAL TIME: 30 MIN. **MAKES:** 15 BISCUITS

- 1 cup all-purpose flour
- 1 cup cake flour
- 1½ teaspoons baking powder
- ¾ teaspoon salt
- ½ teaspoon garlic powder, divided
- ¼ teaspoon baking soda
- 4 tablespoons cold butter, divided
- ⅓ cup finely shredded cheddar cheese
- 1 cup buttermilk
- ½ teaspoon dried parsley flakes

1. In a large bowl, combine the flours, baking powder, salt, ¼ teaspoon garlic powder and baking soda. Cut in 3 tablespoons butter until mixture resembles coarse crumbs; add cheese. Stir in buttermilk just until moistened.
2. Drop by two tablespoonfuls 2 in. apart onto baking sheets coated with cooking spray. Bake at 425° for 10-12 minutes or until golden brown. Melt remaining butter; stir in parsley and remaining garlic powder. Brush over biscuits. Serve warm.

Nutrition Facts: *1 biscuit equals 106 calories, 4 g fat (3 g saturated fat), 11 mg cholesterol, 233 mg sodium, 14 g carbohydrate, trace fiber, 3 g protein.*

Cranberry-Pear Coffee Cake M

This is my favorite coffee cake to make for last-minute occasions. I also make it to give to friends because it always turns out just right, and it's made with ingredients I normally have on hand.

—BEVERLY LOVEGROVE WINNIPEG, MANITOBA

PREP: 25 MIN. **BAKE:** 40 MIN. + COOLING **MAKES:** 12 SERVINGS

 2 cups all-purpose flour
 ¾ cup plus 1 tablespoon sugar, divided
 1½ teaspoons ground cinnamon
 1 teaspoon baking powder
 ½ teaspoon salt
 ¼ teaspoon baking soda
 1 egg
 ¾ cup buttermilk
 ¼ cup butter, melted
 1 teaspoon vanilla extract
 1 large pear, peeled and coarsely chopped
 1 cup fresh or frozen cranberries, thawed and chopped
 1 teaspoon grated orange peel
 1 tablespoon brown sugar

1. In a large bowl, combine the flour, ¾ cup sugar, cinnamon, baking powder, salt and baking soda. In a small bowl, whisk the egg, buttermilk, butter and vanilla. Stir into dry ingredients just until moistened. Fold in the pear, cranberries and orange peel.
2. Transfer to a 9-in. springform pan coated with cooking spray and dusted with flour. Combine brown sugar and remaining sugar; sprinkle over batter. Bake at 350° for 40-45 minutes or until a toothpick inserted near the center comes out clean. Cool for 10 minutes before removing from pan to a wire rack. Serve warm.
Nutrition Facts: *1 slice equals 194 calories, 5 g fat (3 g saturated fat), 29 mg cholesterol, 219 mg sodium, 35 g carbohydrate, 1 g fiber, 3 g protein.* **Diabetic Exchanges:** *2 starch, 1 fat.*

Dilled Wheat Bread F M

My house smells terrific when this wonderful bread is in the oven. It makes a fantastic meal served with soup. I like to cut thick slices and eat them while they're still warm. Yum!

—BEVERLY PRESTON
FOND DU LAC, WISCONSIN

PREP: 25 MIN. + RISING
BAKE: 30 MIN.
MAKES: 1 LOAF (12 SLICES)

 2 cups all-purpose flour
 1 cup whole wheat flour
 2 tablespoons sugar
 1 tablespoon dried minced onion
 1 package (¼ ounce) active dry yeast
 2 teaspoons dill weed
 1 teaspoon salt
 1 cup (8 ounces) cream-style cottage cheese
 ½ cup water
 1 tablespoon butter
 1 egg
 2 teaspoons butter, melted
 Coarse salt, optional

1. In a large bowl, combine ¾ cup all-purpose flour, whole wheat flour, sugar, onion, yeast, dill and salt. In a small saucepan, heat the cottage cheese, water and 1 tablespoon butter to 120°-130°. Add to dry ingredients; beat just until moistened. Add egg; beat until smooth. Stir in enough remaining all-purpose flour to form a soft dough (dough will be sticky).
2. Turn onto a floured surface; knead until smooth and elastic, about 6-8 minutes. Place in a greased bowl, turning once to grease the top. Cover and let rise in a warm place until doubled, about 1 hour.
3. Punch dough down. Shape into a loaf. Place in a greased 8-in. x 4-in. loaf pan. Cover and let rise in a warm place until doubled, about 45 minutes.
4. Bake at 350° for 25-30 minutes or until golden brown. Remove to a wire rack. Brush with melted butter; sprinkle with coarse salt if desired.
Nutrition Facts: *1 slice (calculated without coarse salt) equals 160 calories, 3 g fat (2 g saturated fat), 25 mg cholesterol, 292 mg sodium, 26 g carbohydrate, 2 g fiber, 7 g protein.* **Diabetic Exchanges:** *1½ starch, 1 lean meat.*

Makeover Seven-Grain Cereal Bread F M

No longer is baking bread an all-day affair. Quick-rise yeast helps these tender, mildly sweet loaves come together in half the time.

—LAURA REESE FLAGSTAFF, ARIZONA

PREP: 35 MIN. + RISING **BAKE:** 35 MIN. + COOLING
MAKES: 2 LOAVES (16 SLICES EACH)

- ½ cup seven-grain cereal
- 2½ cups water
- ⅓ cup molasses
- ¼ cup butter, cubed
- 6 to 6¼ cups all-purpose flour
- 1 cup whole wheat flour
- ⅓ cup packed brown sugar
- 3 teaspoons salt
- 2 packages (¼ ounce each) quick-rise yeast
- 2 eggs

1. In a large microwave-safe bowl, combine cereal and water. Cover and cook on high for 4 minutes (mixture will be liquidy). Stir in molasses and butter. Let stand until mixture cools to 120°-130°, stirring occasionally.
2. In a large bowl, combine 4 cups all-purpose flour, whole wheat flour, brown sugar, salt and yeast. Add cereal mixture to dry ingredients; beat just until moistened. Add eggs; beat until smooth. Stir in enough remaining flour to form a firm dough (dough will be sticky).
3. Turn onto a floured surface; knead until smooth and elastic, about 6-8 minutes. Cover and let rest for 10 minutes. Divide dough in half. Shape into loaves. Place in two 9-in. x 5-in. loaf pans coated with cooking spray. Cover and let rise until doubled, about 45 minutes.
4. Bake at 350° for 35-40 minutes or until golden brown. Remove from pans to wire racks to cool completely.
Nutrition Facts: *1 slice equals 141 calories, 2 g fat (1 g saturated fat), 17 mg cholesterol, 239 mg sodium, 27 g carbohydrate, 1 g fiber, 4 g protein.* **Diabetic Exchange:** *1½ starch.*

Honey Wheat Rolls F S M

This is a delicious recipe for a light wheat roll that I save in my exclusive book of most-liked recipes. They're super easy to make.

—SANDY KLOCINSKI SUMMERVILLE, SOUTH CAROLINA

PREP: 40 MIN. + RISING **BAKE:** 10 MIN. **MAKES:** 2 DOZEN

- 2 packages (¼ ounce each) active dry yeast
- 1¾ cups warm fat-free milk (110°-115°)
- 2 eggs
- ½ cup honey
- ¼ cup mashed potatoes (without added milk and butter)
- ¼ cup butter, melted
- 1 teaspoon salt
- 3 cups whole wheat flour
- 2¼ to 2¾ cups all-purpose flour

1. In a small bowl, dissolve yeast in warm milk. In a large bowl, combine 1 egg, honey, mashed potatoes, butter, salt, whole wheat flour, yeast mixture and 1½ cups all-purpose flour; beat on medium speed for 3 minutes. Stir in enough remaining flour to form a soft dough (dough will be sticky).
2. Turn onto a floured surface; knead until smooth and elastic, about 6-8 minutes. Place in a bowl coated with cooking spray, turning once to coat the top. Cover with plastic wrap and let rise in a warm place until doubled, about 1 hour.
3. Turn onto a floured surface; divide into 24 balls. Roll each into a 7-in. rope. Holding one end of rope, loosely wrap dough around, forming a coil. Tuck end under; pinch to seal. Place in muffin cups coated with cooking spray. Cover and let rise until doubled, about 30 minutes.
4. Beat remaining egg; brush over rolls. Bake at 400° for 9-11 minutes or until golden brown. Remove from pans to wire racks to cool.
Nutrition Facts: *1 roll equals 146 calories, 3 g fat (1 g saturated fat), 19 mg cholesterol, 126 mg sodium, 27 g carbohydrate, 2 g fiber, 5 g protein.* **Diabetic Exchange:** *2 starch.*

Celery-Onion Popovers M

I found this handwritten recipe in a cookbook I received from my mom. With onion and celery, these pleasing popovers mimic the flavors of stuffing.

—**BARBARA CARLUCCI** ORANGE PARK, FLORIDA

PREP: 15 MIN. **BAKE:** 40 MIN. **MAKES:** 1 DOZEN

2 cups all-purpose flour
1 teaspoon onion salt
⅛ teaspoon celery salt
4 eggs
1½ cups milk
¼ cup grated onion
¼ cup grated celery
2 tablespoons butter, melted

1. In a large bowl, combine the flour, onion salt and celery salt. Combine the eggs, milk, onion, celery and butter; whisk into the dry ingredients just until blended. Grease and flour the bottom and sides of 12 popover cups; fill two-thirds full with batter.
2. Bake at 450° for 15 minutes. Reduce heat to 350° (do not open oven door). Bake 25 minutes longer or until deep golden brown (do not underbake). Immediately cut a slit in the top of each popover to allow steam to escape.
Nutrition Facts: *1 popover equals 137 calories, 5 g fat (2 g saturated fat), 79 mg cholesterol, 219 mg sodium, 18 g carbohydrate, 1 g fiber, 5 g protein.* **Diabetic Exchanges:** *1 starch, 1 fat.*

Poppy Seed-Banana Mini Loaves M

These lovely loaves are absolutely perfect for gift giving. A surprising hint of orange adds just the right touch.

—**KATHERINE STALLWOOD** KENNEWICK, WASHINGTON

PREP: 20 MIN. **BAKE:** 30 MIN. **MAKES:** 3 LOAVES (6 SLICES EACH)

⅓ cup butter, softened
¾ cup sugar
1 egg
2 medium ripe bananas, mashed

2 cups all-purpose flour
2 teaspoons baking powder
½ teaspoon salt
4½ teaspoons poppy seeds
2 teaspoons grated orange peel
TOPPING
2 tablespoons cold butter
¼ cup packed brown sugar
2 tablespoons chopped walnuts

1. In a small bowl, beat butter and sugar for 2 minutes or until crumbly. Beat in egg and bananas. Combine the flour, baking powder and salt; beat into banana mixture just until blended. Stir in poppy seeds and orange peel.
2. Transfer to three 5¾-in. x 3-in. x 2-in. loaf pans coated with cooking spray. For topping, cut butter into brown sugar until crumbly. Stir in walnuts. Sprinkle over batter.
3. Bake at 350° for 30-40 minutes or until a toothpick comes out clean. Cool for 10 minutes before removing from pans to a wire rack.
Nutrition Facts: *1 slice equals 160 calories, 6 g fat (3 g saturated fat), 24 mg cholesterol, 162 mg sodium, 25 g carbohydrate, 1 g fiber, 2 g protein.* **Diabetic Exchanges:** *1½ starch, 1 fat.*

Prosciutto Breadsticks F C

These breadsticks make a great duet with your favorite egg dish, and they're a nice substitution for ordinary breakfast toast.

—**MARIA REGAKIS** SOMERVILLE, MASSACHUSETTS

PREP/TOTAL TIME: 30 MIN. **MAKES:** 1 DOZEN

6 thin slices prosciutto or deli ham
1 tube (11 ounces) refrigerated breadsticks
1 egg, lightly beaten
¼ teaspoon fennel seed, crushed
¼ teaspoon pepper

1. Cut each slice of prosciutto into four thin strips. Unroll dough; separate into breadsticks. Top each with two strips prosciutto, pressing gently to adhere. Twist each breadstick; place on ungreased baking sheet, pressing ends down firmly. Brush with beaten egg.
2. Combine fennel and pepper; sprinkle over breadsticks. Bake at 375° for 10-13 minutes or until golden brown.
Nutrition Facts: *1 breadstick equals 86 calories, 2 g fat (1 g saturated fat), 8 mg cholesterol, 323 mg sodium, 13 g carbohydrate, trace fiber, 4 g protein.* **Diabetic Exchange:** *1 starch.*

Maple Walnut Biscotti F S C M

PREP: 30 MIN. **BAKE:** 35 MIN. + COOLING
MAKES: 28 BISCOTTI

- 2 eggs
- 1 egg white
- ⅓ cup maple syrup
- ¼ cup sugar
- 1 teaspoon vanilla extract
- 1¾ cups all-purpose flour
- ½ cup oat flour
- 1 teaspoon baking soda
- ½ cup chopped walnuts
- ½ cup dried cranberries
- ⅓ cup dark chocolate chips or white baking chips

1. In a small bowl, beat eggs, egg white, syrup, sugar and vanilla until blended. Combine flours and baking soda; gradually add to egg mixture and mix well (dough will be sticky). Stir in walnuts and cranberries.

2. With floured hands, shape into two 10-in. x 2½-in. rectangles on parchment paper-lined baking sheet. Bake at 350° for 22-26 minutes or until set.

3. Reduce heat to 325°. Place pan on a wire rack. When cool enough to handle, transfer to a cutting board; cut diagonally with a serrated knife into ½-in. slices. Place cut side down on ungreased baking sheets. Bake for 9-11 minutes on each side or until golden brown. Remove to wire racks to cool.

4. In a microwave, melt chocolate chips; stir until smooth. Place biscotti on waxed paper-lined baking sheet. Drizzle with chocolate; chill until set. Store in an airtight container.

Nutrition Facts: *1 biscotti equals 93 calories, 3 g fat (1 g saturated fat), 15 mg cholesterol, 52 mg sodium, 15 g carbohydrate, 1 g fiber, 2 g protein.* **Diabetic Exchange:** *1 starch.*

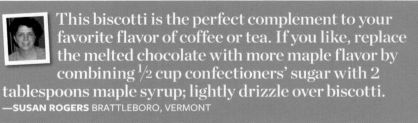

This biscotti is the perfect complement to your favorite flavor of coffee or tea. If you like, replace the melted chocolate with more maple flavor by combining ½ cup confectioners' sugar with 2 tablespoons maple syrup; lightly drizzle over biscotti.
—**SUSAN ROGERS** BRATTLEBORO, VERMONT

top tip

As a substitute for ½ cup oat flour, process ½ cup plus 2 tablespoons quick-cooking or old-fashioned oats until finely ground.
—**HEALTHY COOKING TEST KITCHEN**

Whole Wheat Pizza Dough M

Pizza, egg pockets, stromboli—this make-ahead dough has endless potential for quick and impressive breakfasts, lunches or dinners. This recipe makes three one-pound portions.

—HEALTHY COOKING TEST KITCHEN

PREP: 25 MIN. + STANDING
MAKES: 3 POUNDS (ENOUGH FOR 3 PIZZAS)

- 3 packages (¼ ounce each) quick-rise yeast
- 2 tablespoons sugar
- 1½ teaspoons salt
- 2¼ cups whole wheat flour
- 2½ cups water
- 3 tablespoons olive oil
- 3 to 3½ cups white whole wheat flour

1. In a large bowl, combine the yeast, sugar, salt and whole wheat flour; set aside. In a small saucepan, heat water and oil to 120°-130°; stir into dry ingredients. Stir in enough white whole wheat flour to form a soft dough (dough will be sticky).

2. Turn onto a floured surface; knead until smooth and elastic, about 6-8 minutes. Cover with plastic wrap and let rest for 10 minutes. Punch down dough; divide into three portions. Use immediately, refrigerate overnight or freeze for up to 1 month.

To make pizza: *Coat a 12-in. pizza pan with cooking spray; sprinkle with 1 Tbsp. cornmeal. On a floured surface, roll one portion of dough into a 13-in. circle. Transfer to prepared pan. Build up edges slightly. Top as desired. Bake at 450° for 10-12 minutes or until crust is lightly browned. If using frozen dough, thaw in the refrigerator overnight. Proceed as directed.*

Nutrition Facts: *4 ounces uncooked dough equals 229 calories, 4 g fat (1 g saturated fat), 0 cholesterol, 297 mg sodium, 43 g carbohydrate, 7 g fiber, 8 g protein.*

Tender Biscuits for Two M

It's easy for me to fix these light and tangy biscuits for my husband and I, and it's just as easy to double or triple the recipe for company.

—ANE BURKE BELLA VISTA, ARKANSAS

PREP/TOTAL TIME: 30 MIN.   **MAKES:** 2 BISCUITS

- ⅓ cup self-rising flour
- 1 tablespoon grated Parmesan cheese
- ⅛ teaspoon garlic salt
- 3 tablespoons reduced-fat cream cheese
- 3 tablespoons fat-free milk
- 1 tablespoon fat-free plain yogurt

1. In a small bowl, combine the flour, Parmesan cheese and garlic salt. Cut in cream cheese until mixture resembles coarse crumbs. Stir in milk and yogurt just until moistened.

2. Drop by scant ⅓ cupfuls 2 in. apart onto a baking sheet coated with cooking spray. Bake at 400° for 12-15 minutes or until golden brown. Serve warm.

Nutrition Facts: *1 biscuit equals 142 calories, 5 g fat (4 g saturated fat), 18 mg cholesterol, 497 mg sodium, 17 g carbohydrate, trace fiber, 6 g protein.* **Diabetic Exchanges:** *1 starch, 1 fat.*

Sesame Flatbreads M

Turn everyday dinner roll dough into an elegant gourmet flatbread with this quick and easy trick.

—HEALTHY COOKING TEST KITCHEN

PREP/TOTAL TIME: 20 MIN.   **MAKES:** 2 SERVINGS

- 2 frozen Texas-size whole wheat dinner rolls, thawed
  Cooking spray
- ⅛ teaspoon garlic powder
- ½ teaspoon sesame seeds

On a baking sheet coated with cooking spray, press dough to ¼-in. thickness. Spritz with cooking spray. Sprinkle with garlic powder and sesame seeds. Bake at 425° for 7-9 minutes or until lightly browned.

Nutrition Facts: *1 flatbread equals 146 calories, 4 g fat (0 saturated fat), 0 cholesterol, 210 mg sodium, 24 g carbohydrate, 3 g fiber, 6 g protein.* **Diabetic Exchanges:** *1½ starch, ½ fat.*

Makeover Cappuccino Muffins 🇸 🇲

These makeover muffins are perfect with a hot cup of joe. I seriously could not tell the difference between them and my original recipe—and neither could my family!

—LESLIE ROSENGARTEN MINSTER, OHIO

PREP: 20 MIN. **BAKE:** 20 MIN. **MAKES:** 15 MUFFINS

- 1 cup all-purpose flour
- 1 cup whole wheat flour
- ½ cup sugar
- ½ cup packed brown sugar
- 2 teaspoons baking powder
- 2 teaspoons instant coffee granules
- 1 teaspoon ground cinnamon
- ¼ teaspoon salt
- 1 egg
- 1 cup fat-free milk
- ¼ cup unsweetened applesauce
- ¼ cup canola oil
- 1 teaspoon vanilla extract
- ½ cup miniature semisweet chocolate chips
- ½ cup finely chopped walnuts

TOPPING
- ¼ cup packed brown sugar
- 2 tablespoons all-purpose flour
- ¼ teaspoon ground cinnamon
- 1 tablespoon canola oil

1. In a large bowl, combine the flours, sugars, baking powder, coffee granules, cinnamon and salt. In a small bowl, whisk the egg, milk, applesauce, oil and vanilla. Stir into dry ingredients just until moistened. Fold in chocolate chips and walnuts. Coat muffin cups with cooking spray or use paper liners; fill three-fourths full with batter.

2. In a small bowl, combine the brown sugar, flour and cinnamon. Stir in oil until mixture resembles coarse crumbs. Sprinkle over batter. Bake at 375° for 20-25 minutes or until a toothpick inserted in muffin comes out clean. Cool for 5 minutes before removing from pans to wire racks. Serve warm.

Nutrition Facts: *1 muffin equals 237 calories, 10 g fat (2 g saturated fat), 14 mg cholesterol, 110 mg sodium, 36 g carbohydrate, 2 g fiber, 4 g protein.*

Gluten-Free Gingerbread Loaves 🇲

I only cook and bake gluten-free foods. When I give these molasses-spiked loaves to friends, no one can tell they're gluten-free—they just know they're yummy!

—ERIN MENDELSSOHN LA QUINTA, CALIFORNIA

PREP: 20 MIN. **BAKE:** 35 MIN. + COOLING
MAKES: 3 MINI LOAVES (6 SLICES EACH)

- ¾ cup molasses
- ¾ cup boiling water
- ½ cup butter, softened
- ½ cup sugar
- 2 eggs
- 2½ cups gluten-free all-purpose baking flour
- 2½ teaspoons xanthan gum
- 2 teaspoons ground ginger
- 1 teaspoon baking powder
- ½ teaspoon baking soda
- ½ teaspoon salt

1. In small bowl, combine molasses and boiling water; set aside.

2. In large bowl, cream butter and sugar until light and fluffy. Add eggs. Gradually add molasses mixture. Combine the flour, xanthan gum, ginger, baking powder, baking soda and salt; gradually add to creamed mixture.

3. Transfer to three 5¾-in. x 3-in. x 2-in. loaf pans coated with cooking spray. Bake at 325° for 35-40 minutes or until a toothpick inserted near the center comes out clean. Cool for 10 minutes before removing from pans to wire racks.

Editor's Note: *Read all ingredient labels for possible gluten content prior to use. Ingredient formulas can change, and production facilities vary among brands. If you're concerned that your brand may contain gluten, contact the company.*

Nutrition Facts: *1 slice equals 170 calories, 6 g fat (3 g saturated fat), 37 mg cholesterol, 176 mg sodium, 28 g carbohydrate, 2 g fiber, 2 g protein.* **Diabetic Exchanges:** *2 starch, 1 fat.*

Apple-Walnut Muffin Mix M

Keep this mix on hand for small-batch baking. Each muffin comes out with a nice, rounded top, a crunchy sugar topping and hints of cinnamon, walnuts and apples.

PREP/TOTAL TIME: 15 MIN. **MAKES:** 2 MUFFINS PER BATCH

- 1 cup all-purpose flour
- 1 cup whole wheat flour
- ¾ cup sugar
- ⅓ cup chopped dried apples
- ⅓ cup chopped walnuts
- 2 teaspoons baking powder
- ½ teaspoon baking soda
- ¼ teaspoon ground cinnamon
- ⅛ teaspoon salt

ADDITIONAL INGREDIENTS

- 2 tablespoons fat-free milk
- 2 tablespoons reduced-fat plain yogurt
- 2 teaspoons canola oil
- 1 teaspoon coarse sugar

1. In a large bowl, combine the first nine ingredients. Store in an airtight container for up to 2 months. Yield: 6 batches (3 cups mix).

2. To prepare muffins: Place ½ cup muffin mix in a small bowl. Whisk the milk, yogurt and oil. Stir into dry ingredients just until moistened.

3. Coat muffin cups with cooking spray or use foil liners; fill three-fourths full with batter. Sprinkle with coarse sugar. Bake at 400° for 10-12 minutes or until a toothpick inserted near the center comes out clean. Cool for 5 minutes before removing from pan to a wire rack. Serve warm.

Nutrition Facts: *1 muffin equals 212 calories, 7 g fat (1 g saturated fat), 1 mg cholesterol, 164 mg sodium, 34 g carbohydrate, 2 g fiber, 4 g protein.* **Diabetic Exchanges:** *2 starch, 1½ fat.*

Lemon Thyme Bread S C

I created this fabulous quick bread to satisfy my love of all things lemon and to use up some fresh herbs from my garden. I was quite pleased with the results and think you will be, too.

—**DEANNA SMITH** DES MOINES, IOWA

PREP: 20 MIN. **BAKE:** 35 MIN. + COOLING
MAKES: 1 LOAF (12 SLICES)

- 1¾ cups all-purpose flour
- ¾ cup sugar
- ½ teaspoon baking soda
- ¼ teaspoon salt
- 1 egg
- 1 cup buttermilk
- ¼ cup canola oil
- 2 tablespoons minced fresh thyme or 2 teaspoons dried thyme
- 1 tablespoon lemon juice
- 2 teaspoons grated lemon peel
- ¼ cup pine nuts, optional

DRIZZLE

- ½ cup confectioners' sugar
- 1 tablespoon lemon juice

1. In a large bowl, combine the flour, sugar, baking soda and salt. In a small bowl, whisk the egg, buttermilk, oil, thyme, lemon juice and lemon peel. Stir into dry ingredients just until moistened.

2. Transfer to a greased 8-in. x 4-in. loaf pan. Sprinkle with pine nuts if desired. Bake at 350° for 35-40 minutes or until a toothpick inserted near the center comes out clean. Cool for 10 minutes before removing from pan to a wire rack.

3. In a small bowl, whisk confectioners' sugar and lemon juice; drizzle over warm bread.

Nutrition Facts: *1 slice (calculated without pine nuts) equals 191 calories, 5 g fat (1 g saturated fat), 18 mg cholesterol, 129 mg sodium, 33 g carbohydrate, 1 g fiber, 3 g protein.* **Diabetic Exchanges:** *2 starch, 1 fat.*

Nutcracker Bread M

This tender loaf has a wonderful sugar and spice flavor. Holiday turkey, ham or velvety cream cheese and jelly sandwiches always taste better on slices of this bread.

—**JACQUELINE MCCOMAS** PAOLI, PENNSYLVANIA

PREP: 20 MIN. **BAKE:** 35 MIN. + COOLING
MAKES: 1 LOAF (16 SLICES)

- 1 cup chopped walnuts, toasted and cooled
- ¾ cup packed brown sugar
- 2 cups all-purpose flour
- 1¼ teaspoons baking powder
- ½ teaspoon salt
- ¼ teaspoon baking soda
- 3 eggs
- ½ cup reduced-fat sour cream
- ½ cup fat-free milk
- 1 tablespoon cider vinegar

1. In a food processor, combine walnuts and brown sugar; cover and pulse until finely chopped. Transfer to a large bowl. Stir in the flour, baking powder, salt and baking soda.

2. In a small bowl, beat the eggs, sour cream, milk and vinegar. Stir into dry ingredients just until moistened.

3. Transfer to an 8-in. springform pan coated with cooking spray. Bake at 350° for 35-40 minutes or until a toothpick inserted near the center comes out clean.

4. Cool on a wire rack for 10 minutes. Remove sides and bottom of pan; cool completely on a wire rack.

Nutrition Facts: *1 slice equals 170 calories, 6 g fat (1 g saturated fat), 42 mg cholesterol, 150 mg sodium, 24 g carbohydrate, 1 g fiber, 5 g protein.* **Diabetic Exchanges:** *1½ starch, 1 fat.*

206

212

217

Table For 2

"This unique entree will brighten any table. Its vibrant colors draw you in while the lively blend of flavors will keep you coming back for more."

JESSICA FEIST BROOKFIELD, WISCONSIN
about her recipe, Asian Mango Chicken, on page 211

Spinach-Mushroom Scrambled Eggs C M

My husband and I enjoyed an amazing mushroom egg dish at a hotel restaurant. As soon as I got home, I made my own rendition.
—**RACHELLE MCCALLA** WAYNE, NEBRASKA

PREP/TOTAL TIME: 15 MIN. **MAKES:** 2 SERVINGS

- ½ **cup thinly sliced fresh mushrooms**
- ½ **cup fresh baby spinach, chopped**
- 1 **teaspoon butter**
- 2 **eggs, lightly beaten**
- 2 **egg whites, lightly beaten**
- ⅛ **teaspoon salt**
- ⅛ **teaspoon pepper**
- 2 **tablespoons shredded provolone cheese**

In a small nonstick skillet, saute mushrooms and spinach in butter until tender. Whisk the eggs, egg whites, salt and pepper. Add egg mixture to skillet; cook and stir until almost set. Stir in cheese. Cook and stir until completely set.

Nutrition Facts: *1 serving equals 162 calories, 11 g fat (5 g saturated fat), 226 mg cholesterol, 417 mg sodium, 2 g carbohydrate, trace fiber, 14 g protein.* **Diabetic Exchange:** *2 medium-fat meat.*

Cilantro Bean Burgers M

Seasoned with cilantro and cumin, bean patties make a tempting alternative to beef burgers. Jazz them up with a little salsa or guacamole.
—**DOROTHY ANDREWS**
GRAFTON, WISCONSIN

PREP: 15 MIN. + CHILLING
COOK: 10 MIN. **MAKES:** 2 SERVINGS

- ½ **cup canned pinto beans, rinsed and drained**
- ½ **cup canned black beans, rinsed and drained**
- ¼ **cup shredded carrots**
- 1 **tablespoon minced fresh cilantro**
- ¾ **teaspoon dried minced onion**
- ¾ **teaspoon lime juice**
- 1 **small garlic clove, minced**
- ¼ **teaspoon ground cumin**
- ⅛ **teaspoon salt**
- ⅛ **teaspoon pepper**
- ¼ **cup soft bread crumbs**
- 2 **tablespoons egg substitute**
- 1½ **teaspoons cornmeal**
- 1½ **teaspoons canola oil**
   Salsa, guacamole and tortilla chips, optional

1. In a food processor, combine the first 10 ingredients; cover and pulse until blended. Stir in bread crumbs and egg substitute; refrigerate for 30 minutes.

2. Shape bean mixture into two patties; sprinkle each side with cornmeal. In a large nonstick skillet, cook patties in oil for 4-5 minutes on each side or until lightly browned. Serve with salsa, guacamole and tortilla chips if desired.

Nutrition Facts: *1 patty equals 177 calories, 4 g fat (trace saturated fat), 0 cholesterol, 432 mg sodium, 26 g carbohydrate, 6 g fiber, 8 g protein.* **Diabetic Exchanges:** *1½ starch, 1 lean meat, ½ fat.*

---

top tip
Make Soft Bread Crumbs

It's a snap to make fresh bread crumbs. Simply tear several slices of fresh white, French or whole wheat bread into 1-in. pieces. Place in a food processor or blender; cover and push pulse button several times to make coarse crumbs. One slice of bread yields about ½ cup crumbs. —**HEALTHY COOKING TEST KITCHEN**

Tuscan Chicken for Two **C**

Have dinner on the table in no time flat! This chicken dish comes together in 15 minutes and is sized perfectly for two.
—**DEBRA LEGRAND** PORT ORCHARD, WASHINGTON

PREP/TOTAL TIME: 15 MIN. **MAKES:** 2 SERVINGS

- 2 boneless skinless chicken breast halves (5 ounces each)
- ¼ teaspoon salt
- ¼ teaspoon pepper
- 1 garlic clove, sliced
- 1 teaspoon dried rosemary, crushed
- ¼ teaspoon rubbed sage
- ¼ teaspoon dried thyme
- 1 tablespoon olive oil

1. Flatten chicken to ½-in. thickness; sprinkle with salt and pepper.
2. In a large skillet over medium heat, cook and stir the garlic, rosemary, sage and thyme in oil for 1 minute. Add chicken; cook for 5-7 minutes on each side or until chicken juices run clear.
Nutrition Facts: *1 chicken breast half equals 217 calories, 10 g fat (2 g saturated fat), 78 mg cholesterol, 364 mg sodium, 1 g carbohydrate, 1 g fiber, 29 g protein.* **Diabetic Exchanges:** *4 lean meat, 1 fat.*

Roasted Tomato Soup with Fresh Basil for 2 **C M**

Roasting fresh-picked tomatoes adds a depth of flavor like no other to this simple soup. The thyme makes it taste extra fresh.
—**MARIE FORTE** RARITAN, NEW JERSEY

PREP: 40 MIN. **COOK:** 5 MIN. **MAKES:** 2 SERVINGS

- 1¼ pounds tomatoes (about 4 medium), halved
- 1 small onion, quartered
- 1 garlic clove, peeled and halved
- 1 tablespoon olive oil
- 1 tablespoon minced fresh thyme
- ½ teaspoon salt
- ⅛ teaspoon pepper
- 4 fresh basil leaves
  Salad croutons and additional fresh basil leaves, optional

1. Place the tomatoes, onion and garlic in a greased 15-in. x 10-in. x 1-in. baking pan; drizzle with oil. Sprinkle with thyme, salt and pepper; toss to coat. Bake at 400° for 25-30 minutes or until tender, stirring once. Cool slightly.
2. In a blender, process tomato mixture and basil leaves until blended. Transfer to a large saucepan and heat through. Garnish each serving with croutons and additional basil if desired.
Nutrition Facts: *1 cup (calculated without croutons) equals 129 calories, 7 g fat (1 g saturated fat), 0 cholesterol, 606 mg sodium, 15 g carbohydrate, 4 g fiber, 3 g protein.* **Diabetic Exchanges:** *3 vegetable, 1 fat.*

Lime-Buttered Broccoli for Two C M

I grew tired of serving broccoli the same way every time, so I prepared this recipe. The simple butter sauce turns tender florets into something special.

—**DENISE ALBERS** FREEBURG, ILLINOIS

PREP/TOTAL TIME: 20 MIN. **MAKES:** 2 SERVINGS

- 2 cups fresh broccoli florets
- 1 tablespoon butter, melted
- 1 teaspoon lime juice
- ⅛ teaspoon salt
- ⅛ teaspoon pepper

1. Place broccoli in a steamer basket; place in a large saucepan over 1 in. of water. Bring to a boil; cover and steam for 3-4 minutes or until crisp-tender.
2. Meanwhile, in a small bowl, combine the remaining ingredients.
3. Drizzle butter mixture over broccoli; toss to coat.

Nutrition Facts: ¾ cup equals 71 calories, 6 g fat (4 g saturated fat), 15 mg cholesterol, 207 mg sodium, 4 g carbohydrate, 2 g fiber, 2 g protein. **Diabetic Exchanges:** 1 vegetable, 1 fat.

Peach Turkey Sandwiches

My delicious toasted sandwich gets its sweet taste from a peach and a little zip from the salad dressing. Everyone raves about it, especially my grandkids.

—**DONIE LANGSTON** WATHENA, KANSAS

PREP/TOTAL TIME: 15 MIN. **MAKES:** 2 SERVINGS

- 4 slices whole wheat bread
- 2 tablespoons Vidalia onion salad dressing
- 4 slices deli turkey
- 2 slices smoked Gouda cheese
- 1 medium peach, thinly sliced
  Cooking spray

1. Spread two bread slices with salad dressing. Layer with turkey, cheese and peach slices. Top with remaining bread. Spritz outsides of sandwiches with cooking spray.
2. In a large nonstick skillet over medium heat, toast sandwiches for 2-3 minutes on each side or until cheese is melted.

Nutrition Facts: 1 sandwich equals 357 calories, 15 g fat (4 g saturated fat), 36 mg cholesterol, 948 mg sodium, 34 g carbohydrate, 5 g fiber, 22 g protein.

Feta Frittata C M

PREP/TOTAL TIME: 25 MIN.
MAKES: 2 SERVINGS

- 1 **green onion, thinly sliced**
- 1 **small garlic clove, minced**
- 2 **eggs**
- ½ **cup egg substitute**
- 4 **tablespoons crumbled feta cheese, divided**
- ⅓ **cup chopped plum tomato**
- 4 **thin slices peeled avocado**
- 2 **tablespoons reduced-fat sour cream**

1. Heat a 6-in. nonstick skillet coated with cooking spray over medium heat. Saute onion and garlic until tender. Whisk the eggs, egg substitute and 3 tablespoons feta cheese. Add egg mixture to skillet (mixture should set immediately at edges). Cover and cook for 4-6 minutes or until nearly set.

2. Sprinkle with tomato and remaining feta cheese. Cover and cook 2-3 minutes longer or until eggs are completely set. Let stand for 5 minutes. Cut in half; serve with avocado and sour cream.

Nutrition Facts: *1 frittata half equals 203 calories, 12 g fat (4 g saturated fat), 224 mg cholesterol, 345 mg sodium, 7 g carbohydrate, 3 g fiber, 17 g protein.*
Diabetic Exchanges: *2 medium-fat meat, 1 fat.*

I tasted feta cheese for the first time a few years ago. Now my husband and I use it all the time (in small amounts) to add a nice cheese flavor to our meals.
—MARJORIE DODERO SEAL BEACH, CALIFORNIA

Did you know?

Dubbed "alligator pears" for their textured skin and oval shape, avocados are the fattiest fruit on Earth, and that's a good thing. As a concentrated source of monounsaturated fat, they can actually help lower your cholesterol. Furthermore, researchers find that replacing just 5 percent of your calories from saturated fat with monounsaturated fat could slash the risk of heart attack by more than a third. The dark-skinned California-grown variety (Hass) is fattier than the smooth-skinned, bright green Florida variety.

Asian Mango Chicken

This unique entree will brighten any table. Its vibrant colors draw you in while the lively blend of flavors will keep you coming back for more.
—**JESSICA FEIST** BROOKFIELD, WISCONSIN

PREP: 25 MIN. **COOK:** 15 MIN. **MAKES:** 2 SERVINGS

- 2 boneless skinless chicken breast halves (6 ounces each)
- 1 tablespoon sesame or canola oil
- 1 tablespoon rice vinegar
- 1 garlic clove, minced
- 1 teaspoon honey
- ½ teaspoon green curry paste
- 1 medium mango, peeled and diced
- 1 green onion, finely chopped
- 2 tablespoons diced peeled cucumber
- 2 tablespoons finely chopped sweet red pepper
- ⅛ teaspoon cayenne pepper
   Chopped dry roasted peanuts

1. In a large skillet over medium heat, cook chicken in oil for 4-5 minutes on each side or until a thermometer reads 170°. Remove and keep warm.

2. Add the vinegar, garlic, honey and curry paste to the pan; cook and stir for 1-2 minutes to allow flavors to blend. Return chicken to the pan.

3. Combine the mango, onion, cucumber, red pepper and cayenne. Serve with chicken. Sprinkle with peanuts.

Nutrition Facts: *1 chicken breast half with ½ cup salsa (calculated without peanuts) equals 342 calories, 11 g fat (2 g saturated fat), 94 mg cholesterol, 374 mg sodium, 26 g carbohydrate, 2 g fiber, 35 g protein.* **Diabetic Exchanges:** *5 lean meat, 1 fruit, 1 fat, ½ starch.*

Orange Beef Stir-Fry

Pepper flakes add a little kick to the orange sauce and tender veggies in this quick meal. Any frozen vegetable blend will do.
—**HEALTHY COOKING TEST KITCHEN**

PREP/TOTAL TIME: 25 MIN. **MAKES:** 2 SERVINGS

- 1 tablespoon cornstarch
- ¼ cup cold water
- ¼ cup orange juice
- 1 tablespoon reduced-sodium soy sauce
- ½ teaspoon sesame oil
   Dash crushed red pepper flakes
- ½ pound boneless beef sirloin steak, cut into thin strips
- 2 teaspoons canola oil, divided
- 3 cups frozen sugar snap stir-fry vegetable blend, thawed
- 1 garlic clove, minced
- 1 cup hot cooked rice

1. In a small bowl, combine the first six ingredients until smooth; set aside.

2. In a large skillet or wok, stir-fry beef in 1 teaspoon oil for 3-4 minutes or until no longer pink. Remove with a slotted spoon and keep warm.

3. Stir-fry vegetable blend and garlic in remaining oil for 3 minutes. Stir cornstarch mixture and add to the pan. Bring to a boil; cook and stir for 2 minutes or until thickened. Add beef; heat through. Serve with rice.

Nutrition Facts: *1½ cups stir-fry with ½ cup rice equals 390 calories, 11 g fat (3 g saturated fat), 64 mg cholesterol, 396 mg sodium, 41 g carbohydrate, 3 g fiber, 26 g protein.* **Diabetic Exchanges:** *3 lean meat, 2 starch, 2 vegetable, 1 fat.*

Herb Garden Vegetables ⓈⒸⓂ

PREP/TOTAL TIME: 30 MIN **MAKES:** 2 SERVINGS

- ¼ pound fresh green beans, trimmed
- ¾ cup fresh sugar snap peas
- 1 tablespoon olive oil
- ¾ cup julienned zucchini
- ¾ cup julienned yellow summer squash
- ¾ teaspoon each minced fresh rosemary, sage, basil and thyme
- ¼ teaspoon crushed red pepper flakes
- 2 tablespoons crumbled blue cheese

In a small skillet over medium heat, cook beans and peas in oil for 3 minutes. Add the zucchini, squash, herbs and pepper flakes; cook and stir 3-5 minutes longer or until vegetables are crisp-tender. Sprinkle with cheese just before serving.

Nutrition Facts: *about 1 cup equals 146 calories, 10 g fat (3 g saturated fat), 6 mg cholesterol, 129 mg sodium, 11 g carbohydrate, 5 g fiber, 6 g protein.* **Diabetic Exchanges:** *2 vegetable, 2 fat.*

> ❝I wanted to use all the wonderful vegetables and herbs growing in my garden, so I came up with this easy and tasty medley sized perfectly for two.❞

—JULIE STELLA CHAMPLIN, MINNESOTA

Small Batch Brownies ⓈⓂ

If the dessert just has to be chocolate, our rich, fudgy brownies are a perfect solution. And you can pretty them up with a slight dusting of powdered sugar.

—HEALTHY COOKING TEST KITCHEN

PREP: 15 MIN. **BAKE:** 15 MIN. + COOLING **MAKES:** 6 SERVINGS

- 2 tablespoons butter
- ½ ounce unsweetened chocolate
- 1 egg
- ¼ teaspoon vanilla extract
- ⅔ cup sugar
- ⅓ cup all-purpose flour
- ¼ cup baking cocoa
- ¼ teaspoon salt
- ¼ teaspoon confectioners' sugar, optional

1. In a microwave, melt butter and chocolate; stir until smooth. Cool slightly.

2. In a small bowl, whisk egg and vanilla; gradually whisk in sugar. Stir in chocolate mixture. Combine the flour, cocoa and salt; gradually add to chocolate mixture.

3. Transfer to a 9-in. x 5-in. loaf pan coated with cooking spray. Bake at 350° for 12-16 minutes or until a toothpick inserted near the center comes out clean. Cool on a wire rack. Cut into bars. Dust with confectioners' sugar if desired.

Nutrition Facts: *1 brownie equals 179 calories, 6 g fat (3 g saturated fat), 45 mg cholesterol, 138 mg sodium, 30 g carbohydrate, 1 g fiber, 3 g protein.* **Diabetic Exchanges:** *2 starch, 1 fat.*

Chili Potato Wedges ⒻⓂ

These potato wedges make a great side anywhere you're looking for fun flavored fries. They go especially well with burgers on the grill.

—PEGGY KEY GRANT, ALABAMA

PREP/TOTAL TIME: 30 MIN. **MAKES:** 2 SERVINGS

- 1 teaspoon chili powder
- ¼ teaspoon garlic powder
- ⅛ teaspoon salt
- 1 large baking potato
  Cooking spray

TABLE FOR 2

1. In a small bowl, combine the chili powder, garlic powder and salt. Cut potato lengthwise into eight wedges. Spray wedges with cooking spray, then coat with seasoning mixture.
2. Place in a single layer on a baking sheet coated with cooking spray. Bake, uncovered, at 450° for 25-30 minutes or until golden brown.

Nutrition Facts: *4 potato wedges equals 158 calories, 1 g fat (trace saturated fat), 0 cholesterol, 172 mg sodium, 34 g carbohydrate, 3 g fiber, 4 g protein.* **Diabetic Exchange:** *2 starch.*

Open-Faced Egg Sandwiches C M

I always experiment with different herbs on my eggs, since I eat them every morning. This one became one of my favorites!
—**VALERIE BELLEY** ST. LOUIS, MISSOURI

PREP/TOTAL TIME: 15 MIN. **MAKES:** 2 SERVINGS

- 4 **egg whites**
- 2 **eggs**
- 2 **tablespoons grated Parmesan cheese**
- 2 **teaspoons butter, softened**
- 2 **slices whole wheat bread, toasted**
- ⅛ **teaspoon dried rosemary, crushed**
- ⅛ **teaspoon pepper**

Heat a small nonstick skillet coated with cooking spray over medium-high heat. Whisk the egg whites, eggs and cheese; add to skillet. Cook and stir until set. Spread butter over toasts; top with egg mixture. Sprinkle with rosemary and pepper. Serve immediately.

Nutrition Facts: *1 sandwich equals 231 calories, 11 g fat (5 g saturated fat), 226 mg cholesterol, 416 mg sodium, 13 g carbohydrate, 2 g fiber, 19 g protein.* **Diabetic Exchanges:** *2 lean meat, 1 starch, 1 fat.*

Apricot Turkey Sandwiches

Apricot jam and Dijon mustard come together for a wonderful spread on this sandwich stacked with Swiss cheese, turkey bacon and peppered turkey slices.
—**CHARLOTTE GEHLE** BROWNSTOWN, MICHIGAN

PREP/TOTAL TIME: 15 MIN. **MAKES:** 2 SERVINGS

- 2 **turkey bacon strips**
- 4 **pieces multigrain bread, toasted**
- 2 **tablespoons apricot jam**
- 3 **ounces thinly sliced deli peppered turkey**
- 2 **slices tomato**
- 2 **slices red onion**
- 2 **pieces leaf lettuce**
- 2 **slices reduced-fat Swiss cheese**
- 4 **teaspoons Dijon mustard**

1. In a small skillet, cook bacon over medium heat until crisp. Remove to paper towels to drain.
2. Spread two toast slices with jam. Layer with turkey, bacon, tomato, onion, lettuce and cheese. Spread remaining toast with mustard; place on top.

Nutrition Facts: *1 sandwich equals 338 calories, 10 g fat (3 g saturated fat), 40 mg cholesterol, 1,109 mg sodium, 43 g carbohydrate, 4 g fiber, 23 g protein.*

top tip

Separating Eggs

A small funnel is handy for separating egg whites from the yolks. Place the funnel over a glass and break the egg over the funnel. The whites will run through the funnel, and the yolk will remain. Also, it's easier to separate eggs when they are cold. If a recipe calls for room-temperature egg whites or yolks, separate them first, then let them sit.
—**ALICE N.** REED CITY, MICHIGAN

Chicken Legs with Balsamic Vinaigrette C

Just a handful of ingredients make a tasty marinade for this light, lemony meal.

—LESLIE PALMER
SWAMPSCOTT, MASSACHUSETTS

PREP: 10 MIN. + MARINATING
BAKE: 45 MIN. **MAKES:** 2 SERVINGS

- ¼ cup balsamic vinegar
- 3 tablespoons olive oil
- 2 tablespoons lemon juice
- 2 tablespoons Dijon mustard
- 2 garlic cloves, minced
- ¼ teaspoon pepper
- 2 chicken leg quarters, skin removed

1. In a large resealable plastic bag, combine the first six ingredients. Add the chicken; seal bag and turn to coat. Refrigerate for at least 8 hours or overnight. Drain and discard marinade.
2. Place chicken in an 11-in. x 7-in. baking dish coated with cooking spray. Bake, uncovered, at 375° for 45-50 minutes or until juices run clear, basting occasionally with pan juices.
Nutrition Facts: *1 chicken leg quarter equals 261 calories, 15 g fat (3 g saturated fat), 90 mg cholesterol, 202 mg sodium, 3 g carbohydrate, trace fiber, 27 g protein.*
Diabetic Exchanges: *4 lean meat, 1 fat.*

Onion-Apple Pork Chops

You couldn't ask for a better entree to serve on a fall evening. The apple, pork and maple flavors complement each other perfectly. Rice and steamed broccoli make nice accompaniments, too.

—TRISHA KRUSE EAGLE, IDAHO

PREP: 25 MIN. **BAKE:** 15 MIN. **MAKES:** 2 SERVINGS

- 2 boneless pork loin chops (4 ounces each)
- ¼ teaspoon garlic salt
- ¼ teaspoon lemon-pepper seasoning
- 2 teaspoons olive oil
- 1 medium apple, peeled and thinly sliced
- 1 small onion, thinly sliced
- ⅓ cup reduced-sodium chicken broth
- 2 tablespoons maple syrup

1. Sprinkle chops with garlic salt and lemon-pepper. In a large ovenproof skillet, brown chops in oil. Remove and keep warm.
2. In the same skillet, saute apple and onion in drippings until tender. Stir in broth and syrup. Bring to a boil. Reduce heat; simmer, uncovered, for 5-7 minutes or until liquid is almost evaporated. Return chops to pan.
3. Cover and bake at 350° for 15-20 minutes or until a thermometer reads 145°.
Nutrition Facts: *1 pork chop with ½ cup apple mixture equals 291 calories, 11 g fat (3 g saturated fat), 55 mg cholesterol, 414 mg sodium, 25 g carbohydrate, 2 g fiber, 23 g protein.*
Diabetic Exchanges: *3 lean meat, 1 starch, 1 fat, ½ fruit.*

Watermelon-Blueberry Salad F S M

People love the unique combination of flavors in the dressing that tops the fresh fruit in this salad. It's so refreshing on a hot summer evening.

—HEALTHY COOKING TEST KITCHEN

PREP/TOTAL TIME: 5 MIN.
MAKES: 2 SERVINGS

- 1 tablespoon honey
- ¾ teaspoon lemon juice
- ½ teaspoon minced fresh mint
- 1 cup seeded chopped watermelon
- ½ cup fresh blueberries

In a small bowl, combine the honey, lemon juice and mint. Add watermelon and blueberries; toss gently to coat. Chill until serving.
Nutrition Facts: *¾ cup equals 78 calories, trace fat (trace saturated fat), 0 cholesterol, 2 mg sodium, 20 g carbohydrate, 1 g fiber, 1 g protein.* **Diabetic Exchanges:** *1 fruit, ½ starch.*

top tip Sweet Subs

Maple syrup adds a subtle sweetness to these chops, but if you don't have it, honey works, too!

Buffalo Sloppy Joes for Two 🅵

PREP/TOTAL TIME: 30 MIN.
MAKES: 2 SERVINGS

- ½ pound extra-lean ground turkey
- ¼ cup chopped celery
- 3 tablespoons chopped onion
- 2 tablespoons grated carrots
- 1 garlic clove, minced
- 3 tablespoons tomato sauce
- 2 tablespoons reduced-sodium chicken broth
- 1 tablespoon Louisiana-style hot sauce
- 1½ teaspoons brown sugar
- 1½ teaspoons red wine vinegar
- ¾ teaspoon Worcestershire sauce
  Dash pepper
- 2 hamburger buns, split
- ¼ cup crumbled blue cheese, optional

1. In a Dutch oven, cook the first five ingredients over medium heat until turkey is no longer pink. Stir in the tomato sauce, chicken broth, hot sauce, brown sugar, vinegar, Worcestershire sauce and pepper; heat through.

2. Serve on buns; sprinkle with cheese if desired.

Nutrition Facts: *1 sandwich equals 276 calories, 3 g fat (trace saturated fat), 45 mg cholesterol, 445 mg sodium, 30 g carbohydrate, 2 g fiber, 33 g protein.*
Diabetic Exchanges: *4 lean meat, 2 starch.*

Lean ground turkey makes this a lighter sloppy joe than the standard ground beef version. A hefty splash of hot sauce and optional blue cheese provide an authentic Buffalo-style flavor. —**MARIA REGAKIS** SOMERVILLE, MASSACHUSETTS

Also Try This Recipe With...

Several home cooks who have included this recipe in their dinnertime rotation use light Ranch or blue cheese salad dressing instead of crumbled blue cheese.

Meat Loaf Cake for Two

Creamy whipped potatoes atop tender beef patties are the makings of a practically perfect food—or, better yet, a perfect practical joke.
—**HEALTHY COOKING TEST KITCHEN**

PREP: 35 MIN. **GRILL:** 15 MIN. **MAKES:** 2 SERVINGS

- 1 small carrot, shredded
- 3 tablespoons quick-cooking oats
- 2 tablespoons fat-free milk
- 1 teaspoon Worcestershire sauce
- 1 garlic clove, minced
- ¼ teaspoon salt
- ⅛ teaspoon pepper
- ½ pound lean ground beef (90% lean)

TOPPINGS

- 2 medium potatoes, peeled and cubed
- 3 tablespoons fat-free milk
- ⅛ teaspoon salt
- ⅛ teaspoon white pepper
- 2 tablespoons reduced-fat cream cheese, divided
  Orange and green food coloring
- ¼ cup panko (Japanese) bread crumbs, toasted

1. In a small bowl, combine the carrot, oats, milk, Worcestershire sauce, garlic, salt and pepper. Crumble beef over mixture and mix well. Shape into two 1-in. thick patties.
2. Grill burgers, covered, over medium heat or broil 4 in. from the heat for 6-8 minutes on each side or until a thermometer reads 160° and juices run clear.
3. Meanwhile, place potatoes in a small saucepan and cover with water. Bring to a boil. Reduce heat; cover and cook for 10-15 minutes or until tender. Drain. Press through a potato ricer or strainer into a small bowl. Stir in the milk, salt and white pepper.
4. Place one burger on a serving plate. Spread ¾ cup mashed potatoes over top. Top with remaining burger. Spread remaining mashed potatoes over top and sides of cake. In a small bowl, tint 4 teaspoons cream cheese orange; pipe carrots over top of cake. Tint remaining cream cheese green; pipe tops on carrots. Press bread crumbs into sides of cake.

Nutrition Facts: *1 serving equals 421 calories, 13 g fat (6 g saturated fat), 82 mg cholesterol, 651 mg sodium, 45 g carbohydrate, 4 g fiber, 30 g protein.* **Diabetic Exchanges:** *3 starch, 3 lean meat, 1 fat.*

Pineapple Upside-Down Cake for Two ▣

Tender and sweet, these two luscious but lighter cakes are as special as the person you choose to share them with!
—**HEALTHY COOKING TEST KITCHEN**

PREP: 15 MIN. **BAKE:** 20 MIN. **MAKES:** 2 SERVINGS

- 4 teaspoons butter, melted, divided
- 4 teaspoons brown sugar
- 2 canned unsweetened pineapple slices
- 2 maraschino cherries
- ⅓ cup all-purpose flour
- 3 tablespoons sugar
- ½ teaspoon baking powder
- ⅛ teaspoon salt
  Dash ground nutmeg
- 3 tablespoons fat-free milk
- ¼ teaspoon vanilla extract

1. Pour ½ teaspoon butter into each of two 10-oz. ramekins coated with cooking spray. Sprinkle with brown sugar. Top with a pineapple slice. Place a cherry in the center of each pineapple slice; set aside.
2. In a small bowl, combine the flour, sugar, baking powder, salt and nutmeg. Beat in the milk, vanilla and remaining butter just until combined. Spoon over pineapple.
3. Bake at 350° for 20-25 minutes or until a toothpick inserted near the center comes out clean. Cool for 5 minutes. Run a knife around edges of ramekins; invert onto dessert plates. Serve warm.

Nutrition Facts: *1 serving equals 290 calories, 8 g fat (5 g saturated fat), 21 mg cholesterol, 318 mg sodium, 53 g carbohydrate, 1 g fiber, 3 g protein.*

221

224

230

Cookies, Bars & More

66This old-fashioned cookie has a pleasant honey-cinnamon flavor and a tender texture that resembles cake. It has been a family favorite for years, and I love sharing this recipe with everyone.99

ROCHELLE FRIEDMAN BROOKLYN, NEW YORK
about her recipe, Soft Honey Cookies, on page 225

Irish Cream Cupcakes M

I love to experiment with different flavors and techniques. This is the lightened-up version of my Bailey's-infused cupcakes.

—JENNY LEIGHTY WEST SALEM, OHIO

PREP: 25 MIN. **BAKE:** 20 MIN. + COOLING **MAKES:** 2 DOZEN

- ½ cup butter, softened
- 1½ cups sugar
- 2 eggs
- ¾ cup unsweetened applesauce
- 2 teaspoons vanilla extract
- 2½ cups all-purpose flour
- 3 teaspoons baking powder
- ½ teaspoon salt
- ½ cup Irish cream liqueur

FROSTING

- ⅓ cup butter, softened
- 4 ounces reduced-fat cream cheese
- 6 tablespoons Irish cream liqueur
- 4 cups confectioners' sugar

1. In a large bowl, beat butter and sugar until crumbly, about 2 minutes. Add eggs, one at a time, beating well after each one. Beat in applesauce and vanilla (mixture may appear curdled). Combine flour, baking powder and salt; add to creamed mixture alternately with liqueur, beating well after each addition.

2. Fill paper-lined muffin cups two-thirds full. Bake at 350° for 18-22 minutes or until a toothpick inserted near the center comes out clean. Cool for 10 minutes before removing from pans to wire racks to cool completely.

3. For frosting, in a large bowl, beat butter and cream cheese until fluffy. Beat in liqueur. Add confectioners' sugar; beat until smooth. Pipe over tops of cupcakes. Refrigerate leftovers.

Nutrition Facts: *1 cupcake equals 273 calories, 9 g fat (5 g saturated fat), 38 mg cholesterol, 170 mg sodium, 45 g carbohydrate, trace fiber, 2 g protein.*

Chewy Cranberry Pecan Bars S M

I've been making these for several years, as I really enjoy the combination of flavors and the relative ease of preparations. They're not only great for the holidays, but year-round if you have cranberries in your freezer.

—VIRGINIA ANTHONY JACKSONVILLE, FLORIDA

PREP: 15 MIN. **BAKE:** 40 MIN. + COOLING **MAKES:** 2 DOZEN

- 1 cup plus 2 tablespoons all-purpose flour, divided
- 2 tablespoons plus 1¼ cups sugar, divided
- ¼ cup cold butter
- ⅔ cup chopped pecans, divided
- 1 egg
- 2 egg whites
- 2 tablespoons fat-free milk
- 1 tablespoon grated orange peel
- 1 teaspoon vanilla extract
- 1 cup chopped fresh or frozen cranberries
- ⅓ cup flaked coconut

1. In a large bowl, combine 1 cup flour and 2 tablespoons sugar. Cut in butter until crumbly. Stir in ⅓ cup pecans. Press into an ungreased 13-in. x 9-in. baking pan. Bake at 350° for 15 minutes or until set.

2. Meanwhile, in a large bowl, combine the egg, egg whites, milk, orange peel, vanilla and remaining flour and sugar. Fold in the cranberries, coconut and remaining pecans. Spread over warm crust. Bake 25-30 minutes longer or until top is golden. Cool on a wire rack.

Nutrition Facts: *1 bar equals 119 calories, 5 g fat (2 g saturated fat), 14 mg cholesterol, 25 mg sodium, 18 g carbohydrate, 1 g fiber, 2 g protein.* **Diabetic Exchanges:** *1 starch, 1 fat.*

Better-Than-Fruitcake Cookies F S M

Mostly fruit and nuts, these sweet, chewy clusters make excellent gifts. They freeze well, can be shipped easily and, most important, they live up to their name.

—LILLIAN CHARVES NEW BERN, NORTH CAROLINA

PREP: 15 MIN. + STANDING **BAKE:** 15 MIN./BATCH
MAKES: 3 DOZEN

- 2 cups raisins
- ¼ cup bourbon or unsweetened apple juice
- 2 tablespoons butter, softened
- ¼ cup packed brown sugar
- 1 egg
- ¾ cup all-purpose flour
- 1 teaspoon ground cinnamon
- ¾ teaspoon baking soda
- ¼ teaspoon ground nutmeg
- ¼ teaspoon ground cloves
- 1 cup pecan halves
- ¾ cup red candied cherries, halved
- ¾ cup green candied cherries, halved

1. In a small bowl, combine raisins and bourbon. Cover and let stand for 30 minutes.

2. In a large bowl, cream butter and brown sugar until blended. Beat in egg. Combine the flour, cinnamon, baking soda, nutmeg and cloves; gradually beat into creamed mixture. Stir in the pecans, cherries and raisin mixture.

3. Drop by tablespoonfuls onto baking sheets coated with cooking spray. Bake at 325° for 12-15 minutes or until firm. Cool for 2 minutes before removing to wire racks to cool completely. Store in an airtight container.

Nutrition Facts: *1 cookie equals 93 calories, 3 g fat (1 g saturated fat), 8 mg cholesterol, 40 mg sodium, 16 g carbohydrate, 1 g fiber, 1 g protein.* **Diabetic Exchanges:** *1 starch, ½ fat.*

Light & Easy Cheesecake Bars M

These cheesecake bars are special to me because family and friends ask me to make them time and time again. Dried berries work well on the treats, too, if fresh berries are not available.

—PATRICIA NIEH PORTOLA VALLEY, CALIFORNIA

PREP: 20 MIN. **BAKE:** 30 MIN. + CHILLING **MAKES:** 1½ DOZEN

- ⅓ cup butter, softened
- 1 cup sugar, divided
- 4 tablespoons lemon juice, divided
- 1¼ cups all-purpose flour
- ½ teaspoon salt
- 1 package (8 ounces) reduced-fat cream cheese
- 1 package (8 ounces) fat-free cream cheese
- 1 egg
- 2 teaspoons grated lemon peel
- 18 fresh raspberries, halved

1. Line a 9-in. pan with foil; coat with cooking spray and set aside.

2. In a small bowl, beat butter and ¼ cup sugar until smooth, about 2 minutes. Stir in 2 tablespoons lemon juice. Add flour and salt; mix well. Press into prepared pan. Bake at 350° for 14-16 minutes or until edges are golden brown.

3. Meanwhile, in a small bowl, combine cream cheeses and remaining sugar until smooth. Add egg; beat on low speed just until combined. Stir in lemon peel and remaining lemon juice. Pour over crust. Bake 14-18 minutes longer or until filling is set.

4. Cool on a wire rack for 1 hour. Refrigerate for at least 2 hours. Using foil, lift bars out of pan. Gently peel off foil; cut into bars. Garnish with raspberries.

Nutrition Facts: *1 bar equals 153 calories, 7 g fat (4 g saturated fat), 31 mg cholesterol, 216 mg sodium, 19 g carbohydrate, trace fiber, 4 g protein.* **Diabetic Exchanges:** *1½ fat, 1 starch.*

Pistachio Pinwheels

F S C M

PREP: 40 MIN. + CHILLING
BAKE: 10 MIN./BATCH **MAKES:** 5 DOZEN

- ⅓ cup butter, softened
- ⅓ cup sugar blend
- 2 egg whites
- 3 tablespoons canola oil
- ½ teaspoon vanilla extract
- 2¾ cups cake flour
- 1 teaspoon baking powder
- ¼ teaspoon salt
  Red paste food coloring
- ½ cup pistachios, finely chopped

1. In a large bowl, cream butter and sugar until light and fluffy. Beat in the egg whites, oil and vanilla. Combine the flour, baking powder and salt; gradually add to butter mixture and mix well.

2. Divide dough in half; add food coloring to one portion. Divide red and plain doughs into two portions. Between two sheets of waxed paper, roll out one portion of plain dough into an 8-in. x 6-in. rectangle. Repeat with one portion of red dough. Remove waxed paper; place red dough over plain.

3. Roll up tightly jelly-roll style, starting with a long side. Roll the log in pistachios; wrap in plastic wrap. Repeat with remaining doughs. Refrigerate for 2 hours or until firm.

4. Unwrap logs; cut into ¼-in. slices. Place 2 in. apart on ungreased baking sheets. Bake at 375° for 7-9 minutes or until set. Remove to wire racks.

Editor's Note: *This recipe was tested with Splenda sugar blend.*

Nutrition Facts: *1 cookie equals 49 calories, 2 g fat (1 g saturated fat), 3 mg cholesterol, 33 mg sodium, 6 g carbohydrate, trace fiber, 1 g protein.* **Diabetic Exchanges:** *½ starch, ½ fat.*

Peanut Butter Crunch Cookies F S C M

The next time you're craving peanut butter cookies, try this healthy variation studded with oats and Grape-Nuts. I think it's even better than the regular cookies, which I love.
—**KATHIE AND JOHN HORST** WESTFIELD, NEW YORK

PREP: 15 MIN. **BAKE:** 10 MIN./BATCH **MAKES:** 2½ DOZEN

- ¼ cup butter, softened
- ¼ cup creamy peanut butter
- ¼ cup sugar
- ¼ cup packed brown sugar
- 1 egg
- ¼ teaspoon vanilla extract
- ½ cup all-purpose flour
- ¼ cup quick-cooking oats
- ¼ teaspoon baking soda
- ⅛ teaspoon salt
- ¼ cup Grape-Nuts

1. In a large bowl, cream the butter, peanut butter and sugars until light and fluffy. Beat in egg and vanilla. Combine the flour, oats, baking soda and salt; gradually add to creamed mixture and mix well. Stir in Grape-Nuts.

2. Drop by rounded teaspoonfuls 3 in. apart onto ungreased baking sheets. Flatten slightly with a fork dipped in flour. Bake at 350° for 9-12 minutes or until lightly browned. Cool for 5 minutes before removing from pans to wire racks.

Editor's Note: *Reduced-fat peanut butter is not recommended for this recipe.*

Nutrition Facts: *1 cookie equals 56 calories, 3 g fat (1 g saturated fat), 11 mg cholesterol, 54 mg sodium, 7 g carbohydrate, trace fiber, 1 g protein.* **Diabetic Exchanges:** *½ starch, ½ fat.*

top tip

Storing Cookies

Store soft cookies and crisp cookies in separate airtight containers. If stored together, the moisture from the soft cookies will soften the crisp cookies, making them lose their crunch. Flavors can also blend during storage, so don't store strong-flavored cookies with delicate-flavored ones.

“These whimsical treats look complex, but they're a cinch to assemble. The pistachios' nutty flavor combined with a sweet-tasting dough make them perfect for cookie exchanging.”

—HEALTHY COOKING TEST KITCHEN

Cinnamon-Cranberry Oat Bars ⓈⓂ

I'm a swim coach for kids and started making these bars for them as a snack. I wanted something that was easy for them to eat but would also give them energy. The kids loved them from the very first time I brought them. Now I bring them to every team event.

—SARAH RIVIERE PRESCOTT, ARIZONA

PREP: 15 MIN. **COOK:** 5 MIN. + COOLING **MAKES:** 16 SERVINGS

- 3 **cups quick-cooking oats**
- 1½ **cups Rice Krispies**
- 1 **cup dried cranberries**
- ½ **cup ground flaxseed**
- 1¼ **teaspoons ground cinnamon, divided**
- ½ **teaspoon ground nutmeg**
- ½ **cup packed brown sugar**
- ½ **cup light corn syrup**
- ¼ **cup canola oil**
- ¼ **cup honey**
- 1 **teaspoon vanilla extract**
- ¼ **teaspoon salt**
- 2 **teaspoons sugar**

1. In a large bowl, combine the oats, Rice Krispies, cranberries, flax, 1 teaspoon cinnamon and nutmeg.
2. In a large saucepan, combine the brown sugar, corn syrup, oil and honey; cook and stir over medium heat until sugar is dissolved. Remove from the heat; stir in vanilla and salt.
3. Stir in oat mixture; toss to coat. Press firmly into a 9-in. square pan coated with cooking spray. Combine sugar and remaining cinnamon; sprinkle over bars. Cool completely. Cut into bars.
Nutrition Facts: *1 bar equals 211 calories, 6 g fat (trace saturated fat), 0 cholesterol, 72 mg sodium, 40 g carbohydrate, 3 g fiber, 3 g protein.*

Gluten-Free Chocolate Cupcakes Ⓜ

Both my boys have food allergies and really love these cupcakes! To make my own oat flour, I grind whole oats in my blender, just pulsing until they're flour.

—DESIREE GLANZER CARPENTER, SOUTH DAKOTA

PREP: 15 MIN. **BAKE:** 20 MIN. + COOLING **MAKES:** 1 DOZEN

- 2 **cups gluten-free oat flour**
- 1 **cup sugar**
- ¼ **cup baking cocoa**
- 1 **teaspoon baking soda**
- ½ **teaspoon salt**
- 1 **cup water**
- ⅓ **cup canola oil**
- 1 **teaspoon cider vinegar**
- ½ **teaspoon vanilla extract**
- 2 **teaspoons confectioners' sugar**

1. In a large bowl, combine the flour, sugar, cocoa, baking soda and salt. In another bowl, combine the water, oil, vinegar and vanilla. Stir into dry ingredients just until moistened.
2. Fill paper-lined muffin cups three-fourths full. Bake at 350° for 20-25 minutes or until a toothpick inserted near the center comes out clean. Cool for 10 minutes before removing from pan to a wire rack to cool completely. Dust with confectioners' sugar.

Editor's Note: Read all ingredient labels for possible gluten content prior to use. Ingredient formulas can change, and production facilities vary among brands. If you're concerned that your brand may contain gluten, contact the company.

Nutrition Facts: *1 cupcake equals 187 calories, 8 g fat (1 g saturated fat), 0 cholesterol, 203 mg sodium, 29 g carbohydrate, 2 g fiber, 2 g protein.* **Diabetic Exchanges:** *2 starch, 1 fat.*

Pecan Kisses F S C M

Show someone you love a little Southern hospitality with these melt-in-your-mouth Pecan Kisses. They're especially fun to whip up with the kids, and they only require a few simple ingredients.
—**NORLENE RAZAK** KYLE, TEXAS

PREP: 15 MIN. **BAKE:** 15 MIN./BATCH **MAKES:** 4 DOZEN

- 2 **egg whites**
- 1 **teaspoon vanilla extract**
- ¼ **teaspoon vinegar**
- ⅛ **teaspoon salt**
- 2 **cups confectioners' sugar**
- 1½ **cups chopped pecans**

1. In a large bowl, beat the egg whites, vanilla, vinegar and salt on medium speed until soft peaks form. Gradually add confectioners' sugar, 1 tablespoon at a time, beating on high until stiff glossy peaks form and sugar is dissolved. Fold in pecans.
2. Drop by rounded teaspoonfuls 1 in. apart onto greased baking sheets.
3. Bake at 300° for 15-20 minutes or until firm to the touch and lightly browned. Remove to wire racks to cool. Store in an airtight container.
Nutrition Facts: *1 cookie equals 46 calories, 3 g fat (trace saturated fat), 0 cholesterol, 8 mg sodium, 6 g carbohydrate, trace fiber, trace protein.* **Diabetic Exchanges:** *½ starch, ½ fat.*

Soft Honey Cookies F S C M

This old-fashioned cookie has a pleasant honey-cinnamon flavor and a tender texture that resembles cake. It has been a family favorite for years, and I love sharing this recipe with everyone.
—**ROCHELLE FRIEDMAN** BROOKLYN, NEW YORK

PREP: 15 MIN. + CHILLING **BAKE:** 10 MIN. **MAKES:** 16 COOKIES

- ¼ **cup sugar**
- 2 **tablespoons canola oil**
- 1 **egg**
- 3 **tablespoons honey**
- ¾ **teaspoon vanilla extract**
- 1 **cup plus 2 tablespoons all-purpose flour**
- ¼ **teaspoon baking powder**
- ¼ **teaspoon ground cinnamon**
- ⅛ **teaspoon salt**

1. In a small bowl, beat sugar and oil until blended. Beat in egg; beat in honey and vanilla. Combine the flour, baking powder, cinnamon and salt; gradually add to sugar mixture and mix well (dough will be stiff). Cover and refrigerate for at least 2 hours.
2. Drop dough by tablespoonfuls 2 in. apart onto a greased baking sheet. Bake at 350° for 8-10 minutes or until bottoms are lightly browned. Cool for 1 minute before removing from pan to a wire rack. Store in an airtight container.
Nutrition Facts: *1 cookie equals 77 calories, 2 g fat (trace saturated fat), 13 mg cholesterol, 29 mg sodium, 13 g carbohydrate, trace fiber, 1 g protein.* **Diabetic Exchange:** *1 starch.*

Orange Cashew Bars S M

PREP: 20 MIN.
BAKE: 15 MIN. + COOLING
MAKES: 2½ DOZEN

- 4 ounces reduced-fat cream cheese
- ½ cup confectioners' sugar
- ¼ cup packed brown sugar
- 1 egg yolk
- 2 teaspoons vanilla extract
- 1½ cups all-purpose flour

FILLING

- 1 cup packed brown sugar
- 3 egg whites
- 1 egg
- 3 tablespoons all-purpose flour
- 2 teaspoons vanilla extract
- ½ teaspoon orange extract
- ¼ teaspoon salt
- 1½ cups salted cashews, coarsely chopped

GLAZE

- ¾ cup confectioners' sugar
- 4 teaspoons orange juice
- 1 teaspoon grated orange peel

1. In a large bowl, beat cream cheese and sugars until smooth. Beat in egg yolk and vanilla. Gradually add flour and mix well. Press dough onto the bottom and ¼ in. up the sides of a 13-in. x 9-in. baking pan coated with cooking spray. Bake at 350° for 15-20 minutes or until edges are lightly browned. Cool slightly.

2. For filling, in a large bowl, beat the brown sugar, egg whites, egg, flour, extracts and salt until smooth. Stir in cashews. Pour into crust. Bake 15-20 minutes longer or until set. Cool completely on a wire rack. Combine glaze ingredients; drizzle over bars. Refrigerate leftovers.

Nutrition Facts: *1 bar equals 145 calories, 5 g fat (1 g saturated fat), 17 mg cholesterol, 98 mg sodium, 21 g carbohydrate, trace fiber, 3 g protein.*

Two of my favorite ingredients make a fantastic combination for a holiday bar—especially when you use fresh-squeezed orange juice in the glaze. —**ANNA WOOD** CULLOWHEE, NORTH CAROLINA

top tip Freezing Bars

Most bars and brownies freeze well for up to 3 months. To freeze a pan of uncut bars, place in an airtight container or resealable plastic bag. Or wrap individual bars in plastic wrap and stack in an airtight container.
—**HEALTHY COOKING TEST KITCHEN**

Caramel Whiskey Cookies **S C M**

A bit of yogurt replaces part of the butter in this traditional cookie, but you would never know. I get a lot of requests for these and can't make a cookie tray without them.

—PRISCILLA YEE CONCORD, CALIFORNIA

PREP: 30 MIN. **BAKE:** 10 MIN./BATCH **MAKES:** 4 DOZEN

- ½ cup butter, softened
- ½ cup sugar
- ½ cup packed brown sugar
- ¼ cup plain Greek yogurt
- 2 tablespoons canola oil
- 1 teaspoon vanilla extract
- 2½ cups all-purpose flour
- 2 teaspoons baking powder
- 1 teaspoon baking soda
- ¼ teaspoon salt

TOPPING
- 24 caramels or 1 cup Kraft caramel bits
- 1 tablespoon whiskey
- 3 ounces semisweet chocolate, melted
- ½ teaspoon kosher salt, optional

1. In a large bowl, beat butter and sugars until crumbly, about 2 minutes. Beat in the yogurt, oil and vanilla. Combine the flour, baking powder, baking soda and salt; gradually add to sugar mixture and mix well.

2. Shape into 1-in. balls. Place 2 in. apart on ungreased baking sheets. Flatten with the bottom of a glass dipped in flour. Bake at 350° for 7-9 minutes or until edges are lightly browned. Cool for 2 minutes before removing to wire racks.

3. In a microwave, melt caramels with whiskey; stir until smooth. Spread over cookies. Drizzle with chocolate; sprinkle with kosher salt if desired. Let stand until set.

Nutrition Facts: *1 cookie (calculated without kosher salt) equals 93 calories, 4 g fat (2 g saturated fat), 6 mg cholesterol, 83 mg sodium, 14 g carbohydrate, trace fiber, 1 g protein.*

Pumpkin Pie Cupcakes **M**

My family always asks for these cupcakes once fall starts. We just love the flavors of cinnamon and cloves—the shining stars in this dessert.

—MELISSA STORY TREGO, WISCONSIN

PREP: 30 MIN. **BAKE:** 15 MIN. + COOLING **MAKES:** 2 DOZEN

- 1¾ cups fresh or canned pumpkin
- ¾ cup sugar
- ¾ cup packed brown sugar
- ½ cup unsweetened applesauce
- ⅓ cup canola oil
- 2 eggs
- 2 egg whites
- 2⅔ cups all-purpose flour
- 2 teaspoons baking powder
- 2 teaspoons ground cinnamon
- 1 teaspoon baking soda
- 1 teaspoon salt
- ¼ teaspoon ground nutmeg
- ¼ teaspoon ground cloves

CINNAMON-CLOVE BUTTERCREAM
- ¼ cup butter, softened
- ¼ cup shortening
- 1¾ cups confectioners' sugar
- ¼ teaspoon ground cinnamon
- ⅛ teaspoon ground cloves
- ½ cup finely chopped walnuts

1. In a large bowl, beat the pumpkin, sugars, applesauce, oil, eggs and egg whites until well blended. Combine the flour, baking powder, cinnamon, baking soda, salt, nutmeg and cloves; gradually beat into pumpkin mixture until blended.

2. Fill foil-lined muffin cups two-thirds full. Bake at 350° for 15-20 minutes or until a toothpick inserted near the center comes out clean. Cool for 10 minutes before removing from pans to wire racks to cool completely.

3. In a small bowl, beat butter and shortening until fluffy. Add the confectioners' sugar, cinnamon and cloves; beat until smooth. Spread over cupcakes; sprinkle with walnuts.

Nutrition Facts: *1 cupcake equals 229 calories, 9 g fat (2 g saturated fat), 23 mg cholesterol, 212 mg sodium, 35 g carbohydrate, 1 g fiber, 3 g protein.*

Devil's Food Snack Cake 🅜

My husband and his friends request this cake for their camping trips, but it's perfect for potlucks and entertaining, too. No frosting required.
—**JULIE DANLER** BEL AIRE, KANSAS

PREP: 30 MIN. **BAKE:** 35 MIN. + COOLING **MAKES:** 24 SERVINGS

- 1 cup quick-cooking oats
- 1¾ cups boiling water
- ¼ cup butter, softened
- ½ cup sugar
- ½ cup packed brown sugar
- 2 eggs
- ⅓ cup buttermilk
- 3 tablespoons canola oil
- 1 teaspoon vanilla extract
- ¾ cup all-purpose flour
- ¾ cup whole wheat flour
- 2 tablespoons dark baking cocoa
- 1 tablespoon instant coffee granules
- 1 teaspoon baking soda
- ⅛ teaspoon salt
- 1 cup (6 ounces) miniature semisweet chocolate chips, divided
- ¾ cup chopped pecans, divided

1. Place oats in a large bowl. Cover with boiling water; let stand for 10 minutes.

2. Meanwhile, in a large bowl, beat butter and sugars until crumbly, about 2 minutes. Add eggs, one at a time, beating well after each addition. Beat in buttermilk, oil and vanilla. Combine the flours, cocoa, coffee granules, baking soda and salt. Gradually add to creamed mixture. Stir in the oat mixture, ½ cup chocolate chips and ⅓ cup pecans.

3. Pour into a 13-in. x 9-in. baking pan coated with cooking spray. Sprinkle with remaining chips and pecans. Bake at 350°

for 35-40 minutes or until a toothpick inserted near the center comes out clean. Cool on a wire rack before cutting.

Nutrition Facts: *1 piece equals 174 calories, 9 g fat (3 g saturated fat), 23 mg cholesterol, 91 mg sodium, 22 g carbohydrate, 2 g fiber, 3 g protein.* **Diabetic Exchanges:** *1½ starch, 1 fat.*

Mint-Mallow Sandwich Cookies 🅕

My lightened-up version of whoopie pies with a peppermint twist is a favorite with kids, especially around the holidays.
—**DION FRISCHER** ANN ARBOR, MICHIGAN

PREP: 30 MIN. **BAKE:** 10 MIN./BATCH **MAKES:** 2 DOZEN

- ⅓ cup butter, softened
- 1¼ cups sugar
- 1 egg white
- 1 teaspoon vanilla extract
- 1 cup all-purpose flour
- ⅓ cup baking cocoa
- ¼ teaspoon baking soda

FILLING

- ⅓ cup marshmallow creme
- ⅛ teaspoon peppermint extract
- 1 drop red food coloring, optional

1. In a large bowl, beat butter and sugar until crumbly, about 2 minutes. Beat in egg white and vanilla. Combine the flour, cocoa and baking soda; gradually add to sugar mixture and mix well.

2. Shape into ¾-in. balls; place 2 in. apart on baking sheets coated with cooking spray. Bake at 350° for 7-9 minutes or until set. Remove to wire racks to cool completely.

3. In a small bowl, combine the marshmallow creme, extract and food coloring if desired. Spread on the bottoms of half of the cookies; top with the remaining cookies. Store in an airtight container.

Nutrition Facts: *1 sandwich cookie equals 91 calories, 3 g fat (2 g saturated fat), 7 mg cholesterol, 35 mg sodium, 16 g carbohydrate, trace fiber, 1 g protein.*

Gluten-Free Peanut Butter Blondies M

This is a recipe I converted to be gluten-free so that my family could enjoy a comforting dessert. We were really craving brownies one night, and this cakelike treat hit the spot.

—**BECKY KLOPE** LOUDONVILLE, NEW YORK

PREP: 15 MIN. **BAKE:** 20 MIN. + COOLING **MAKES:** 16 SERVINGS

- ⅔ cup creamy peanut butter
- ½ cup packed brown sugar
- ¼ cup sugar
- ¼ cup unsweetened applesauce
- 2 eggs
- 1 teaspoon vanilla extract
- 1 cup gluten-free all-purpose baking flour
- 1¼ teaspoons baking powder
- 1 teaspoon xanthan gum
- ¼ teaspoon salt
- ½ cup semisweet chocolate chips
- ¼ cup salted peanuts, chopped

1. In a large bowl, combine the peanut butter, sugars and applesauce. Beat in eggs and vanilla until blended. Combine the flour, baking powder, xanthan gum and salt; gradually add to peanut butter mixture and mix well. Stir in chocolate chips and peanuts.

2. Transfer to a 9-in. square baking pan coated with cooking spray. Bake at 350° for 20-25 minutes or until a toothpick inserted near the center comes out clean. Cool on a wire rack. Cut into squares.

Nutrition Facts: *1 bar equals 176 calories, 9 g fat (2 g saturated fat), 26 mg cholesterol, 142 mg sodium, 22 g carbohydrate, 2 g fiber, 5 g protein.* **Diabetic Exchanges:** *1½ starch, 1½ fat.*

Molasses Cookies with a Kick F S C M

This is a combination of spices that I have used for a long time. It's also one of my mother's favorite cookies. I get requests from her to make them year-round!

—**TAMARA RAU** MEDINA, NORTH DAKOTA

PREP: 40 MIN. + CHILLING **BAKE:** 10 MIN./BATCH
MAKES: 8 DOZEN

- ¾ cup butter, softened
- ½ cup sugar
- ½ cup packed brown sugar
- ¼ cup molasses
- 1 egg
- 1½ teaspoons minced fresh gingerroot
- 2¼ cups all-purpose flour
- 1 teaspoon ground cinnamon
- ¾ teaspoon baking soda
- ½ teaspoon ground cloves
- ¼ to ½ teaspoon cayenne pepper
- ¼ teaspoon salt
- ¼ teaspoon ground nutmeg
- ⅛ teaspoon each ground white pepper, cardamom and coriander
- ¾ cup turbinado (washed raw) sugar

1. In a large bowl, cream butter and sugars until light and fluffy. Beat in the molasses, egg and ginger. Combine the flour, cinnamon, baking soda, cloves, cayenne, salt, nutmeg, white pepper, cardamom and coriander; gradually add to creamed mixture and mix well. Cover and refrigerate for 1½ hours or until easy to handle.

2. Roll into ½-in. balls; roll in turbinado sugar. Place 3 in. apart on lightly greased baking sheets.

3. Bake at 350° for 8-10 minutes or until set. Cool for 2 minutes before removing from pans to wire racks. Store in an airtight container.

Nutrition Facts: *1 cookie equals 41 calories, 2 g fat (1 g saturated fat), 6 mg cholesterol, 28 mg sodium, 7 g carbohydrate, trace fiber, trace protein.* **Diabetic Exchange:** *½ starch.*

Nut-Licious Peanut Butter Bars M

My friends were astonished to find out these bars, my favorite go-to treat, are not button-busting. I nicknamed them Bamboozled Bars.

—**HANNAH WOLTERS** CULLEOKA, TENNESSEE

PREP: 45 MIN. **BAKE:** 15 MIN. + CHILLING **MAKES:** 24 SERVINGS

CRUST
- 1½ **cups reduced-fat graham cracker crumbs (about 10 whole crackers)**
- ⅓ **cup honey**
- 2 **tablespoons butter, melted**

NUT TOPPING
- ¼ **cup chopped pecans**
- ¼ **cup chopped walnuts**
- 2 **tablespoons honey**
- 1½ **teaspoons ground cinnamon**

FILLING
- 12 **ounces fat-free cream cheese**
- ⅔ **cup peanut butter**
- 3 **tablespoons butter, softened**
- ½ **cup confectioners' sugar**
- ½ **cup honey**
- 1 **egg**
- 1 **teaspoon vanilla extract**
- ¼ **teaspoon maple flavoring**
- ¼ **cup all-purpose flour**
- ¼ **teaspoon baking powder**

DRIZZLE
- ⅓ **cup semisweet chocolate chips, melted**

1. In a small bowl, combine crust ingredients. Press onto the bottom of a 13-in. x 9-in. baking pan coated with cooking spray. Bake at 350° for 8 minutes or until golden brown. Cool on a wire rack.

2. Meanwhile, combine the nuts, honey and cinnamon. Transfer to a baking sheet lined with parchment paper and coated with cooking spray. Bake at 350° for 5-7 minutes or until toasted and fragrant, stirring occasionally. Cool completely. Crumble mixture and set aside.

3. In a small bowl, beat the cream cheese, peanut butter, butter, confectioners' sugar and honey until smooth. Beat in the egg, vanilla and maple flavoring. Combine flour and baking powder; gradually add to creamed mixture. Spread over cooled crust. Bake for 14-16 minutes or until set.

4. Sprinkle nut mixture over warm filling; press in slightly. Drizzle with melted chocolate. Cool completely on a wire rack. Chill for 2 hours or until firm. Cut into bars. Refrigerate leftovers.

Nutrition Facts: *1 bar equals 189 calories, 9 g fat (3 g saturated fat), 16 mg cholesterol, 175 mg sodium, 24 g carbohydrate, 1 g fiber, 5 g protein.*

Black Bean Brownies S M

You'd never guess these rich, velvety chocolate treats contain a can of black beans.

—**KATHY HEWITT** CRANSTON, RHODE ISLAND

PREP: 15 MIN. **BAKE:** 20 MIN. + COOLING **MAKES:** 1 DOZEN

- 1 **can (15 ounces) black beans, rinsed and drained**
- ½ **cup semisweet chocolate chips, divided**
- 3 **tablespoons canola oil**
- 3 **eggs**
- ⅔ **cup packed brown sugar**
- ½ **cup baking cocoa**
- 1 **teaspoon vanilla extract**
- ½ **teaspoon baking powder**
- ⅛ **teaspoon salt**

1. Place the beans, ¼ cup chocolate chips and oil in a food processor; cover and process until blended. Add the eggs, brown sugar, cocoa, vanilla, baking powder and salt; cover and process until smooth.

2. Transfer to a 9-in. square baking pan coated with cooking spray. Sprinkle with remaining chocolate chips. Bake at 350° for 20-25 minutes or until a toothpick inserted near the center comes out clean. Cool on a wire rack. Cut into bars.

Nutrition Facts: *1 brownie equals 167 calories, 7 g fat (2 g saturated fat), 53 mg cholesterol, 131 mg sodium, 24 g carbohydrate, 2 g fiber, 4 g protein.* **Diabetic Exchanges:** *1½ starch, 1 fat.*

I usually bake these special cookies for the holidays, but my family loves them, so I bake them for their birthdays, too. The addition of ground chipotle chili pepper gives a little zing. The dough may be sticky so I dip my hands in confectioners' sugar for easier handling.
—**GLORIA BRADLEY** NAPERVILLE, ILLINOIS

Chipotle Crackle Cookies S C M

PREP: 25 MIN. + CHILLING
BAKE: 10 MIN./BATCH **MAKES:** 2½ DOZEN

- 2 **eggs**
- 1 **cup sugar**
- ¼ **cup canola oil**
- 2 **teaspoons vanilla extract**
- 2 **ounces unsweetened chocolate, melted and cooled**
- 1 **cup all-purpose flour**
- 1 **tablespoon toasted wheat germ**
- ¾ **teaspoon baking powder**
- ¼ **teaspoon salt**
- ⅛ **teaspoon ground chipotle pepper**
- ¼ **cup miniature semisweet chocolate chips**
- ⅓ **cup confectioners' sugar**

1. In a large bowl, beat the eggs, sugar, oil and vanilla until combined. Add melted chocolate. Combine the flour, wheat germ, baking powder, salt and chipotle pepper. Gradually add to egg mixture and mix well. Fold in chocolate chips. Cover and refrigerate for 2 hours.
2. Place confectioners' sugar in a small bowl. Shape dough into 1-in. balls; roll in confectioners' sugar. Place 2 in. apart on baking sheets coated with cooking spray. Bake at 350° for 8-10 minutes or until set. Remove to wire racks to cool.

Nutrition Facts: *1 cookie equals 85 calories, 4 g fat (1 g saturated fat), 14 mg cholesterol, 35 mg sodium, 13 g carbohydrate, 1 g fiber, 1 g protein.* **Diabetic Exchanges:** *1 starch, ½ fat.*

Did you know?

Chipotle peppers are red jalapeno peppers that have been slowly wood-smoked. Commonly used to add a deep smoky flavor to traditional Mexican or American Southwest cuisine, try adding ground chipotle pepper—a deep red powder—to soups, salsas, pizza, casseroles and even chocolate desserts. For soups, add ½ teaspoon per four servings.

234   242   244

Cakes & Pies

"I've always felt a special connection to my Grandmother Shirley because she was the most wonderful baker. I think she would be especially proud of my cheesecakes. This apple cheesecake has come to be a family favorite."

SARAH GILBERT HARTWELL BEAVERTON, OREGON
about her recipe, Streusel-Topped Apple Cheesecake, on page 240

Sweet Potato Cranberry Cake M

This recipe uses delicious items you have in your pantry, like sweet potatoes, cranberries, coconut and chocolate chips. The secret ingredient, however, is a bit of chili powder.
—**AMIE VALPONE** NEW YORK, NEW YORK

PREP: 15 MIN. **BAKE:** 30 MIN. + COOLING **MAKES:** 20 SERVINGS

- 1 package white cake mix (regular size)
- 2 cups mashed sweet potatoes
- ½ cup buttermilk
- 2 eggs
- 2 tablespoons canola oil
- 1 teaspoon vanilla extract
- 1 package (8 ounces) reduced-fat cream cheese
- ¾ cup confectioners' sugar
- 1 teaspoon ground cinnamon
- ¾ teaspoon chili powder
- ½ cup dried cranberries
- ⅓ cup flaked coconut, toasted
- ¼ cup dark chocolate chips

1. In a large bowl, combine the cake mix, sweet potatoes, buttermilk, eggs, oil and vanilla; beat on low speed for 30 seconds. Beat on medium for 2 minutes.
2. Pour into a 13-in. x 9-in. baking pan coated with cooking spray. Bake at 350° for 28-33 minutes or until a toothpick inserted near the center comes out clean. Cool on a wire rack.
3. In a small bowl, combine the cream cheese, confectioners' sugar, cinnamon and chili powder. Spread over cake. Sprinkle with cranberries, coconut and chocolate chips. Refrigerate leftovers.

Nutrition Facts: *1 piece equals 235 calories, 8 g fat (4 g saturated fat), 29 mg cholesterol, 250 mg sodium, 37 g carbohydrate, 1 g fiber, 4 g protein.*

Banana Chip Cake M

PREP: 25 MIN. **BAKE:** 40 MIN. + COOLING **MAKES:** 16 SERVINGS

- 1 package yellow cake mix (regular size)
- 1¼ cups water
- 3 eggs
- ½ cup unsweetened applesauce
- 2 medium bananas, mashed
- 1 cup miniature semisweet chocolate chips
- ½ cup chopped walnuts

1. In a large bowl, combine the cake mix, water, eggs and applesauce; beat on low speed for 30 seconds. Beat on medium for 2 minutes. Stir in the bananas, chips and walnuts.
2. Transfer to a 10-in. fluted tube pan coated with cooking spray and sprinkled with flour. Bake at 350° for 40-50 minutes or until a toothpick inserted near the center comes out clean. Cool for 10 minutes before removing from pan to a wire rack to cool completely.

Nutrition Facts: *1 slice equals 233 calories, 9 g fat (4 g saturated fat), 40 mg cholesterol, 225 mg sodium, 38 g carbohydrate, 1 g fiber, 3 g protein.*

❝This is my version of Ben & Jerry's Chunky Monkey ice cream (my favorite!) in a cake. The hardest part is waiting for it to cool.❞
—**BARBARA PRYOR** MILFORD, MASSACHUSETTS

Blueberry Angel Cupcakes F S M

Like angel food cake, these yummy cupcakes don't last long at my house. They're so light and airy that they melt in your mouth.

—**KATHY KITTELL** LENEXA, KANSAS

PREP: 125 MIN.
BAKE: 15 MIN. + COOLING
MAKES: 2½ DOZEN

- 11 **egg whites**
- 1 **cup plus 2 tablespoons cake flour**
- 1½ **cups sugar, divided**
- 1¼ **teaspoons cream of tartar**
- 1 **teaspoon vanilla extract**
- ½ **teaspoon salt**
- 1½ **cups fresh or frozen blueberries**
- 1 **teaspoon grated lemon peel**

GLAZE

- 1 **cup confectioners' sugar**
- 3 **tablespoons lemon juice**

1. Place egg whites in a large bowl; let stand at room temperature for 30 minutes. Sift together flour and ½ cup sugar three times; set aside.

2. Add cream of tartar, vanilla and salt to egg whites; beat on medium speed until soft peaks form. Gradually add remaining sugar, about 2 tablespoons at a time, beating on high until stiff glossy peaks form and sugar is dissolved. Gradually fold in flour mixture, about ½ cup at a time. Fold in blueberries and lemon peel.

3. Fill paper-lined muffin cups three-fourths full. Bake at 375° for 14-17 minutes or until cupcakes spring back when lightly touched. Immediately remove from pans to wire racks to cool completely.

4. In a small bowl, whisk confectioners' sugar and lemon juice until smooth. Brush over cupcakes. Let stand until set.

Editor's Note: *If using frozen blueberries, use without thawing to avoid discoloring the batter.*

Nutrition Facts: *1 cupcake equals 76 calories, trace fat (trace saturated fat), 0 cholesterol, 60 mg sodium, 18 g carbohydrate, trace fiber, 2 g protein.*
Diabetic Exchange: *1 starch.*

Moist Carrot Cupcakes Ⓜ

If your kids think they don't like carrots, just wait until these cinnamon-scented, lightly frosted little cakes hit the table.

—HEALTHY COOKING TEST KITCHEN

PREP: 20 MIN. **BAKE:** 15 MIN. + COOLING **MAKES:** 10 CUPCAKES

- ⅔ cup sugar
- 3 tablespoons canola oil
- 1 egg
- ¼ cup unsweetened applesauce
- 1 teaspoon vanilla extract
- 1 cup all-purpose flour
- ¾ teaspoon baking soda
- ¾ teaspoon ground cinnamon
- ¼ teaspoon salt
- 1½ cups shredded carrots

CREAM CHEESE FROSTING

- 6 ounces reduced-fat cream cheese
- ⅔ cup confectioners' sugar
- ¼ teaspoon vanilla extract

1. In a large bowl, beat the sugar, oil and egg until well blended. Beat in applesauce and vanilla. Combine the flour, baking soda, cinnamon and salt; gradually beat into sugar mixture until blended. Stir in carrots.

2. Fill paper-lined muffin cups half full. Bake at 350° for 15-20 minutes or until a toothpick inserted near the center comes out clean. Cool for 10 minutes before removing from pan to a wire rack to cool completely.

3. In a small bowl, combine frosting ingredients; beat until smooth. Frost cupcakes. Refrigerate leftovers.

Nutrition Facts: *1 cupcake equals 226 calories, 8 g fat (3 g saturated fat), 33 mg cholesterol, 244 mg sodium, 34 g carbohydrate, 1 g fiber, 4 g protein.*

Frosty Mocha Pie Ⓜ

This pie is so creamy and rich-tasting that no one would guess it's light. The added bonus is that you can make it a day or two ahead and keep it in the freezer until needed.

—LISA VARNER EL PASO, TEXAS

PREP: 20 MIN. + FREEZING **MAKES:** 10 SERVINGS

- 4 ounces reduced-fat cream cheese
- ¼ cup sugar
- ¼ cup baking cocoa
- 1 tablespoon instant coffee granules
- ⅓ cup fat-free milk
- 1 teaspoon vanilla extract
- 1 carton (12 ounces) frozen reduced-fat whipped topping, thawed
- 1 extra-servings-size graham cracker crust (9 inches)
   Reduced-calorie chocolate syrup, optional

1. In a large bowl, beat the cream cheese, sugar and cocoa until smooth. Dissolve coffee granules in milk. Stir coffee mixture and vanilla into cream cheese mixture; fold in whipped topping.

2. Pour into crust. Cover and freeze for at least 4 hours. Remove from the freezer 10 minutes before serving. Drizzle with chocolate syrup if desired.

Nutrition Facts: *1 piece (calculated without chocolate syrup) equals 259 calories, 13 g fat (7 g saturated fat), 8 mg cholesterol, 198 mg sodium, 31 g carbohydrate, 1 g fiber, 3 g protein.* **Diabetic Exchanges:** *2 starch, 2 fat.*

Classic Yellow Cupcakes M

Light and buttery, these golden cupcakes are made with sugar substitute and make a lovely addition to a wedding shower or brunch buffet.
—**HEALTHY COOKING TEST KITCHEN**

PREP: 15 MIN. **BAKE:** 20 MIN. + COOLING **MAKES:** 1½ DOZEN

- ⅔ **cup butter, softened**
- ¾ **cup sugar blend**
- 3 **eggs**
- 1½ **teaspoons vanilla extract**
- 2¼ **cups cake flour**
- 2 **teaspoons baking powder**
- ¼ **teaspoon salt**
- ¾ **cup fat-free milk**
  Fat-free whipped topping, optional
- 1 **teaspoon confectioners' sugar**

1. In a large bowl, cream butter and sugar substitute until light and fluffy. Add eggs, one at a time, beating well after each addition. Beat in vanilla. Combine the flour, baking powder and salt; add to creamed mixture alternately with milk, mixing well after each addition.

2. Fill paper-lined muffin cups three-fourths full. Bake at 350° for 20-25 minutes or until lightly browned and a toothpick inserted near the center comes out clean. Cool for 5 minutes before removing from pans to wire racks to cool completely.

3. Top with a dollop of whipped topping if desired, then dust with confectioners' sugar.

Editor's Note: *This recipe was tested with Splenda sugar blend.*

Nutrition Facts: *1 cupcake (calculated without whipped topping) equals 171 calories, 8 g fat (4 g saturated fat), 54 mg cholesterol, 171 mg sodium, 22 g carbohydrate, trace fiber, 3 g protein.* **Diabetic Exchanges:** *1½ starch, 1½ fat.*

Root Beer Float Pie M

This is the kind of recipe your kids will look back on and always remember. And the only appliance you need is the refrigerator.
—**CINDY REAMS** PHILIPSBURG, PENNSYLVANIA

PREP: 15 MIN. + CHILLING **MAKES:** 8 SERVINGS

- 1 **carton (8 ounces) frozen reduced-fat whipped topping, thawed, divided**
- ¾ **cup cold diet root beer**
- ½ **cup fat-free milk**
- 1 **package (1 ounce) sugar-free instant vanilla pudding mix**
- 1 **graham cracker crust (9 inches)**
  Maraschino cherries, optional

1. Set aside and refrigerate ½ cup whipped topping for garnish. In a large bowl, whisk the root beer, milk and pudding mix for 2 minutes. Fold in half of the remaining whipped topping. Spread into graham cracker crust.

2. Spread remaining whipped topping over pie. Refrigerate for at least 8 hours or overnight.

3. Dollop reserved whipped topping over each serving; top with a maraschino cherry if desired.

Nutrition Facts: *1 piece equals 185 calories, 8 g fat (4 g saturated fat), trace cholesterol, 275 mg sodium, 27 g carbohydrate, trace fiber, 1 g protein.* **Diabetic Exchanges:** *2 starch, 1 fat.*

Deconstructed Raspberry Pie S M

Here, fruit is the star. The generous portion of raspberries per serving packs in 6 grams of fiber and 35 percent of the daily value for vitamin C.

—HEALTHY COOKING TEST KITCHEN

PREP: 15 MIN.
BAKE: 5 MIN. + COOLING
MAKES: 4 SERVINGS

- 2⅔ cups fresh raspberries
- 2 teaspoons sugar
- ½ cup graham cracker crumbs
- 2 tablespoons butter, melted
- 4 tablespoons whipped cream in a can
- ¼ teaspoon baking cocoa

1. In a small bowl, combine raspberries and sugar; set aside.

2. In another small bowl, combine cracker crumbs and butter. Press into an 8-in. x 6-in. rectangle on an ungreased baking sheet. Bake at 350° for 5-6 minutes or until lightly browned. Cool completely on a wire rack. Break into large pieces.

3. To assemble, divide half of graham cracker pieces among four dessert plates; top with ⅓ cup raspberries. Repeat layers. Top each with 1 tablespoon whipped cream and dust with cocoa.

Nutrition Facts: *1 serving equals 153 calories, 8 g fat (4 g saturated fat), 18 mg cholesterol, 109 mg sodium, 20 g carbohydrate, 6 g fiber, 2 g protein.*
Diabetic Exchanges: *1½ fat, 1 fruit, ½ starch.*

Makeover Gooey Chocolate Peanut Butter Cake M

My dad made sure this dessert was on the menu for Father's Day—or else! This makeover version is great. I can't believe so much fat was cut and it still tastes like the original.

—TRISHA KRUSE EAGLE, IDAHO

PREP: 25 MIN. **BAKE:** 40 MIN. + COOLING **MAKES:** 24 SERVINGS

- 1 package chocolate cake mix (regular size)
- 1 egg
- ¼ cup canola oil
- ¼ cup unsweetened applesauce

TOPPING
- 1 package (8 ounces) reduced-fat cream cheese
- ½ cup creamy peanut butter
- ½ cup reduced-fat butter, melted
- 2 eggs
- 2 egg whites
- 1 teaspoon vanilla extract
- 2 cups confectioners' sugar

1. In a large bowl, beat the cake mix, egg, oil and applesauce on low speed until combined. Press into a 13-in. x 9-in. baking pan coated with cooking spray.

2. In a another large bowl, beat cream cheese and peanut butter until smooth. Add the butter, eggs, egg whites and vanilla; beat on low until combined. Add the confectioners' sugar; mix well. Pour over crust.

3. Bake at 350° for 40-45 minutes or until edges are golden brown. Cool on a wire rack for 20 minutes before cutting. Refrigerate leftovers.

Editor's Note: *This recipe was tested with Land O'Lakes light stick butter.*

Nutrition Facts: *1 piece equals 228 calories, 11 g fat (4 g saturated fat), 38 mg cholesterol, 255 mg sodium, 29 g carbohydrate, 1 g fiber, 4 g protein.*

top tip Buying & Storing Berries

If you're buying raspberries by the pint, remember that one pint equals 1½ to 2 cups. Leftover berries can be stored on a paper-towel-lined baking sheet covered with another paper towel for three days.

—HEALTHY COOKING TEST KITCHEN

Streusel-Topped Apple Cheesecake Ⓜ

I've always felt a special connection to my Grandmother Shirley because she was the most wonderful baker. I think she would be especially proud of my cheesecakes. This apple cheesecake has come to be a family favorite.

—SARAH GILBERT HARTWELL BEAVERTON, OREGON

PREP: 45 MIN. **BAKE:** 45 MIN. + CHILLING **MAKES:** 16 SERVINGS

1¼ cups crushed gingersnap cookies (about 25 cookies)
  3 tablespoons butter, melted

FILLING
  2 packages (8 ounces each) reduced-fat cream cheese
  1 package (8 ounces) fat-free cream cheese
  1 cup sugar
 ¼ cup fat-free milk
  2 tablespoons all-purpose flour
  1 teaspoon vanilla extract
  3 eggs, lightly beaten
  2 medium tart apples, peeled and thinly sliced
  2 tablespoons brown sugar
  1 teaspoon ground cinnamon

TOPPING
 ¼ cup all-purpose flour
 ¼ cup packed brown sugar
  2 tablespoons butter, melted

1. In a small bowl, combine crushed cookies and butter. Press onto the bottom of a 9-in. springform pan coated with cooking spray. Place pan on a baking sheet. Bake at 325° for 10 minutes. Cool on a wire rack.

2. In a large bowl, beat cream cheeses and sugar until smooth. Beat in the milk, flour and vanilla. Add eggs; beat on low speed just until combined. Pour 2 cups filling over crust. In a large bowl, toss the apples, brown sugar and cinnamon until well coated; arrange over filling to within 1 in. of edges. Pour remaining filling over apple mixture. Bake at 325° for 30 minutes.

3. In a small bowl, combine topping ingredients. Sprinkle over cheesecake. Bake 15-20 minutes longer or until center is almost set. Cool on a wire rack for 10 minutes.

4. Carefully run a knife around edge of pan to loosen; cool 1 hour longer. Refrigerate overnight. Remove sides of pan.

Nutrition Facts: *1 slice equals 262 calories, 12 g fat (7 g saturated fat), 70 mg cholesterol, 311 mg sodium, 32 g carbohydrate, 1 g fiber, 7 g protein.*

Makeover Red Velvet Cake Ⓜ

I've had a recipe for red velvet cake for over 45 years and it has become our family's favorite cake, but I would love to see it get a light makeover.

—BETTY SELCHOW
WHITE BEAR LAKE, MINNESOTA

PREP: 20 MIN.
BAKE: 15 MIN. + COOLING
MAKES: 16 SERVINGS

 ¼ cup butter, softened
  1 cup sugar
  2 eggs
 ¼ cup unsweetened applesauce
  1 bottle (1 ounce) red food coloring
  1 teaspoon white vinegar
  1 teaspoon vanilla extract
2¼ cups cake flour
  2 teaspoons baking cocoa
  1 teaspoon baking soda
  1 teaspoon salt
  1 cup buttermilk

FROSTING
4½ teaspoons all-purpose flour
 ½ cup fat-free milk
 ½ cup butter, softened
 ½ cup sugar
 ½ teaspoon vanilla extract

1. Line two 9-in. round baking pans with parchment paper; coat paper with cooking spray and sprinkle with flour. Set aside. In a large bowl, beat butter and sugar until well blended. Add eggs, one at a time, beating well after each addition. Beat in the applesauce, food coloring, vinegar and vanilla.

2. Combine the flour, cocoa, baking soda and salt. Add to butter mixture alternately with buttermilk. Pour into prepared pans. Bake at 350° for 14-18 minutes or until a toothpick inserted near the center comes out clean. Cool for 10 minutes before removing from pans to wire racks to cool completely.

3. For frosting, in a small saucepan, whisk flour and milk until smooth. Bring to a boil; cook and stir for 2 minutes. Cool to room temperature. In a small bowl, cream butter and sugar until light and fluffy. Beat in flour mixture and vanilla. Spread between layers and over top of cake.

Nutrition Facts: *1 slice equals 241 calories, 9 g fat (6 g saturated fat), 50 mg cholesterol, 315 mg sodium, 36 g carbohydrate, trace fiber, 3 g protein.*

Almond Torte S M

Reduced-fat sour cream, egg whites and applesauce lighten up this gorgeous torte, while a creamy custard filling lends richness. It's a flavor combination that never goes out of season.

—**KATHY OLSEN** MARLBOROUGH, NEW HAMPSHIRE

PREP: 45 MIN. + CHILLING **BAKE:** 25 MIN. + COOLING
MAKES: 16 SERVINGS

- ⅓ cup sugar
- 1 tablespoon cornstarch
- ½ cup reduced-fat sour cream
- 3 egg yolks
- 1 tablespoon butter
- 1 teaspoon vanilla extract
- ½ teaspoon almond extract

CAKE
- 4 egg whites
- ⅓ cup butter, softened
- 1½ cups sugar, divided
- 2 egg yolks
- ⅓ cup fat-free milk
- ¼ cup unsweetened applesauce
- 1 teaspoon vanilla extract
- 1 cup cake flour
- 1 teaspoon baking powder
- ⅛ teaspoon salt
- ½ cup sliced almonds
- ½ teaspoon ground cinnamon

1. In a double boiler or metal bowl over simmering water, constantly whisk the sugar, cornstarch, sour cream and egg yolks until mixture reaches 160° or is thick enough to coat the back of a spoon.

2. Remove from the heat; stir in butter and extracts until blended. Press waxed paper onto surface of custard. Refrigerate for several hours or overnight.

3. Place egg whites in a large bowl; let stand at room temperature for 30 minutes. Line two 8-in. round baking pans with waxed paper. Coat sides and paper with cooking spray; sprinkle with flour and set aside.

4. In a large bowl, beat butter and ½ cup sugar until blended, about 2 minutes. Add egg yolks; mix well. Beat in the milk, applesauce and vanilla (mixture may appear curdled). Combine the flour, baking powder and salt; add to butter mixture. Transfer to prepared pans; set aside.

5. Using clean beaters, beat egg whites on medium speed until soft peaks form. Gradually beat in remaining sugar, 2 tablespoons at a time, on high until stiff glossy peaks form and sugar is dissolved. Spread evenly over batter; sprinkle with almonds and cinnamon.

6. Bake at 350° for 25-30 minutes or until meringue is lightly browned. Cool in pans on wire racks for 10 minutes (meringue will crack). Loosen edges of cakes from pans with a knife. Using two large spatulas, carefully remove one cake to a serving plate, meringue side up; remove remaining cake to a wire rack, meringue side up. Cool cakes completely.

7. Carefully spread custard over cake on serving plate; top with remaining cake. Store in the refrigerator.

Nutrition Facts: 1 slice equals 215 calories, 8 g fat (4 g saturated fat), 79 mg cholesterol, 99 mg sodium, 32 g carbohydrate, 1 g fiber, 4 g protein. **Diabetic Exchanges:** 2 starch, 1 fat.

Berry Nectarine Buckle M

I found this recipe in a magazine quite a long time ago but modified it over the years. We enjoy its combination of blueberries, raspberries, blackberries and nectarines, particularly when the cake is served warm with low-fat frozen yogurt.

—**LISA SJURSEN-DARLING** SCOTTSVILLE, NEW YORK

PREP: 25 MIN. **BAKE:** 35 MIN. **MAKES:** 20 SERVINGS

- ⅓ cup all-purpose flour
- ⅓ cup packed brown sugar
- 1 teaspoon ground cinnamon
- 3 tablespoons cold butter

BATTER
- 6 tablespoons butter, softened
- ¾ cup plus 1 tablespoon sugar, divided
- 2 eggs
- 1½ teaspoons vanilla extract
- 2¼ cups all-purpose flour
- 2½ teaspoons baking powder
- ½ teaspoon salt
- ½ cup fat-free milk
- 1 cup fresh blueberries
- 1 pound medium nectarines, peeled, sliced and patted dry or 1 package (16 ounces) frozen unsweetened sliced peaches, thawed and patted dry
- ½ cup fresh raspberries
- ½ cup fresh blackberries

1. For topping, in a small bowl, combine the flour, brown sugar and cinnamon; cut in butter until crumbly. Set aside.

2. In a large bowl, cream the butter and ¾ cup sugar until light and fluffy. Add eggs, one at a time, beating well after each addition. Beat in vanilla. Combine the flour, baking powder and salt; add to creamed mixture alternately with milk, beating well after each addition. Set aside ¾ cup batter. Fold blueberries into remaining batter.

3. Spoon into a 13-in. x 9-in. baking dish coated with cooking spray. Arrange nectarines on top; sprinkle with remaining sugar. Drop reserved batter by teaspoonfuls over nectarines. Sprinkle with raspberries, blackberries and reserved topping.

4. Bake at 350° for 35-40 minutes or until a toothpick inserted near the center comes out clean. Serve warm.

Nutrition Facts: 1 piece equals 177 calories, 6 g fat (3 g saturated fat), 35 mg cholesterol, 172 mg sodium, 28 g carbohydrate, 1 g fiber, 3 g protein. **Diabetic Exchanges:** 2 starch, 1 fat.

Family-Favorite Peanut Butter Cake

PREP: 20 MIN. **BAKE:** 15 MIN. + COOLING **MAKES:** 24 SERVINGS

- ½ cup creamy peanut butter
- 6 tablespoons butter, cubed
- 1 cup water
- 2 cups all-purpose flour
- 1½ cups sugar
- ½ cup buttermilk
- ¼ cup unsweetened applesauce
- 2 eggs, lightly beaten
- 1¼ teaspoons baking powder
- 1 teaspoon vanilla extract
- ½ teaspoon salt
- ¼ teaspoon baking soda

FROSTING

- ¼ cup butter, cubed
- ¼ cup creamy peanut butter
- 2 tablespoons fat-free milk
- 1¾ cups confectioners' sugar
- 1 teaspoon vanilla extract

1. In a large saucepan, bring peanut butter, butter and water just to a boil. Immediately remove from the heat; stir in the flour, sugar, buttermilk, applesauce, eggs, baking powder, vanilla, salt and baking soda until smooth.

"My grandmother and aunts made this for family gatherings to go along with fresh homemade ice cream. I now share it with my family and friends during special gatherings."

—**KEITH GABLE** GODDARD, KANSAS

2. Pour into a 15-in. x 10-in. x 1-in. baking pan coated with cooking spray. Bake at 375° for 15-20 minutes or until golden brown and a toothpick inserted near the center comes out clean. Cool on a wire rack for 20 minutes.

3. In a small saucepan, melt butter and peanut butter over medium heat; add milk. Bring to a boil. Remove from the heat. Gradually whisk in confectioners' sugar and vanilla until smooth. Spread over warm cake. Cool completely on a wire rack. Refrigerate leftovers.

Nutrition Facts: *1 piece equals 220 calories, 9 g fat (4 g saturated fat), 30 mg cholesterol, 166 mg sodium, 31 g carbohydrate, 1 g fiber, 4 g protein.* **Diabetic Exchanges:** *2 starch, 1½ fat.*

Apple Pie Tartlets S M

Sweet and cinnamony, these apple-pie morsels are a delightful addition to a dessert buffet or snack tray. You can bake the shells a day or two in advance.

—**MARY KELLEY** MINNEAPOLIS, MINNESOTA

PREP: 35 MIN. + COOLING **MAKES:** 10 SERVINGS

- 1 sheet refrigerated pie pastry
- 1 tablespoon sugar
- Dash ground cinnamon

FILLING

- 2 teaspoons butter
- 2 cups diced peeled tart apples
- 3 tablespoons sugar
- 3 tablespoons fat-free caramel ice cream topping
- 2 tablespoons all-purpose flour
- ½ teaspoon ground cinnamon
- ½ teaspoon lemon juice
- ⅛ teaspoon salt

1. Roll out pastry on a lightly floured surface; cut into twenty 2½-in. circles. Press onto the bottom and up the sides of miniature muffin cups coated with cooking spray. Prick pastry with a fork. Spray lightly with cooking spray. Combine sugar and cinnamon; sprinkle over pastry.

2. Bake at 350° for 6-8 minutes or until golden brown. Cool for 5 minutes before removing from pans to wire racks.

3. In a large saucepan, melt butter. Add apples; cook and stir over medium heat for 4-5 minutes or until crisp-tender.

4. Stir in the sugar, caramel topping, flour, cinnamon, lemon juice and salt. Bring to a boil; cook and stir for 2 minutes or until sauce is thickened and apples are tender. Cool for 5 minutes. Spoon into tart shells.

Nutrition Facts: *One serving (2 tartlets) equals 150 calories, 6 g fat (3 g saturated fat), 6 mg cholesterol, 126 mg sodium, 22 g carbohydrate, 1 g fiber, 1 g protein.* **Diabetic Exchanges:** *1½ starch, 1 fat.*

top tip
Buttermilk Swap

If you need ½ cup of buttermilk, substitute ½ tablespoon lemon juice or white vinegar plus enough milk to measure ½ cup. Let stand for 5 minutes. Or try ½ cup plain yogurt.
—**HEALTHY COOKING TEST KITCHEN**

Maple Pumpkin Pie with a Crunch Ⓜ

PREP: 15 MIN.
BAKE: 45 MIN. + COOLING
MAKES: 8 SERVINGS

Pastry for single-crust pie (9 inches)
2 eggs, lightly beaten
1½ cups fresh or canned pumpkin
1 cup reduced-fat evaporated milk
⅓ cup packed brown sugar
⅓ cup maple syrup
1 tablespoon all-purpose flour
1 teaspoon pumpkin pie spice
½ teaspoon salt
½ cup fat-free whipped topping
11 pecan halves
Ground cinnamon, optional

1. Line a 9-in. pie plate with pastry; trim and flute edges. In a large bowl, beat the eggs, pumpkin, milk, brown sugar, syrup, flour, pie spice and salt until blended. Pour into pastry.

2. Bake at 425° for 15 minutes. Reduce heat to 350°; bake 30-35 minutes longer or until a knife inserted near the center comes out clean. Cover edges with foil during the last 30 minutes to prevent overbrowning if necessary.

3. Cool on a wire rack. Top pie with whipped topping and pecans; sprinkle with cinnamon if desired. Refrigerate leftovers.

Nutrition Facts: *1 piece equals 273 calories, 10 g fat (4 g saturated fat), 60 mg cholesterol, 310 mg sodium, 40 g carbohydrate, 2 g fiber, 6 g protein.*

Maple syrup adds a lovely flavor to the pie, but if I don't have it on hand, I use honey. If serving with whipped cream, a light sprinkling of cinnamon and nutmeg adds a nice touch. —**LORRAINE CALAND** SHUNIAH, ONTARIO

Fresh Pumpkin

Also known as sugar pumpkins, pie pumpkins are ideal for cooking and baking. One medium pie pumpkin (3 pounds) yields about 2 cups cooked pumpkin. Cooked pumpkin can be covered and refrigerated for up to 3 days or frozen for up to 3 months.

—**HEALTHY COOKING TEST KITCHEN**

Apple-Spice Angel Food Cake F M

Angel food cake mix is lower in fat and calories than regular cake mix. Apple pie spice and toasted nuts add a festive fall flavor.

—JOAN BUEHNERKEMPER TEUTOPOLIS, ILLINOIS

PREP: 10 MIN. **BAKE:** 35 MIN. + COOLING **MAKES:** 16 SERVINGS

- 1 package (16 ounces) angel food cake mix
- 1 cup water
- ⅔ cup unsweetened applesauce
- ½ cup finely chopped pecans, toasted
- 1 teaspoon apple pie spice

Reduced-fat whipped topping and/or apple slices, optional

1. In a large bowl, combine cake mix and water. Beat on low speed for 30 seconds. Beat on medium speed for 1 minute. Fold in the applesauce, pecans and pie spice.

2. Gently spoon into an ungreased 10-in. tube pan. Cut through batter with a knife to remove air pockets. Bake on the lowest oven rack at 350° for 35-45 minutes or until lightly browned and entire top appears dry. Immediately invert pan; cool completely, about 1 hour.

3. Run a knife around side and center tube of pan. Remove cake to a serving plate. Garnish with whipped topping and/or apple slices if desired.

Nutrition Facts: *1 slice (calculated without optional ingredients) equals 136 calories, 3 g fat (trace saturated fat), 0 cholesterol, 209 mg sodium, 26 g carbohydrate, 1 g fiber, 3 g protein.*
Diabetic Exchanges: *1½ starch, ½ fat.*

Makeover White Fruitcake S M

This recipe has been passed down through the generations. I remember my mother making this every holiday season, and it just wouldn't be Christmas in our home without it.

—JUDY GREBETZ RACINE, WISCONSIN

PREP: 20 MIN. + STANDING
BAKE: 1½ HOURS + COOLING **MAKES:** 20 SERVINGS

- ¾ cup red candied cherries
- ¾ cup green candied cherries
- 1¼ cups brandy, divided
- 6 eggs, separated
- 2 egg whites
- ½ cup butter, softened
- 1½ cups sugar
- 4 cups all-purpose flour
- ½ cup unsweetened applesauce
- 1½ cups sliced almonds
- 1½ cups golden raisins
- ¾ cup flaked coconut

1. In a small bowl, combine cherries and ¼ cup brandy; let stand overnight. Place egg whites in a small bowl; let stand at room temperature for 30 minutes.

2. In a large bowl, cream butter and sugar until well blended. Add egg yolks, one at a time, beating well after each addition. Beat in remaining brandy. Gradually add flour to creamed mixture alternately with applesauce.

3. With clean beaters, beat egg whites until stiff peaks form; fold into batter. Fold in the cherry mixture, almonds, raisins and coconut. Gently spoon into a 10-in. tube pan with removable bottom coated with cooking spray. Bake at 300° for 1½ to 1¾ hours or until a toothpick inserted near the center comes out clean.

4. Cool for 10 minutes before removing from pan to a wire rack to cool completely.

Nutrition Facts: *1 slice equals 352 calories, 11 g fat (5 g saturated fat), 75 mg cholesterol, 80 mg sodium, 56 g carbohydrate, 2 g fiber, 7 g protein.*

257

252

260

Treat Yourself

❝This recipe is great for those times you need to bring a dish to pass. You can make the berry sauce in advance and keep it chilled in the fridge. Then simply assemble the entire dessert a few hours before the picnic or party.❞

HEALTHY COOKING TEST KITCHEN
about the recipe, Picnic Berry Shortcakes, on page 256

Bellini Ice F S M

This ice is fashioned after the Bellini, a peach and white Italian wine sparkler. The tart white grape juice paired with ripe sweet peaches create a fantastic flavor combination. Looking for a refreshing summer dessert? I like to place some fresh peach slices in a large wine goblet, top with Bellini Ice, and garnish with a kiwi slice.

—**DEIRDRE DEE COX** KANSAS CITY, KANSAS

PREP: 10 MIN. + FREEZING   **MAKES:** 6 SERVINGS

2 medium peaches, peeled and quartered
2 cups white grape juice
1 cup lemon-lime carbonated water
¼ cup lime juice
  Fresh peach slices, optional

1. Place peaches in a food processor. Cover and process until pureed. Transfer to an 11-in. x 7-in. dish. Stir in the grape juice, carbonated water and lime juice. Freeze for 1 hour; stir with a fork.
2. Freeze 2-3 hours longer or until completely frozen, stirring every 30 minutes. Stir with a fork just before serving; spoon into dessert dishes. Garnish with peach slices if desired.

Nutrition Facts: *1 serving (calculated without garnish) equals 65 calories, trace fat (trace saturated fat), 0 cholesterol, 5 mg sodium, 16 g carbohydrate, 1 g fiber, 1 g protein.* **Diabetic Exchange:** *1 fruit.*

Slow Cooker Baked Apples S M

Coming home to this irresistible dessert on a dreary day is just wonderful. I get all the baked apple flavor without having to use my oven.

—**EVANGELINE BRADFORD** ERLANGER, KENTUCKY

PREP: 25 MIN.   **COOK:** 4 HOURS   **MAKES:** 6 SERVINGS

6 medium tart apples
½ cup raisins
⅓ cup packed brown sugar
1 tablespoon grated orange peel
1 cup water
3 tablespoons thawed orange juice concentrate
2 tablespoons butter

1. Core apples and peel top third of each if desired. Combine the raisins, brown sugar and orange peel; spoon into apples. Place in a 5-qt. slow cooker.
2. Pour water around apples. Drizzle with orange juice concentrate. Dot with butter. Cover and cook on low for 4-5 hours or until apples are tender.

Nutrition Facts: *1 stuffed apple equals 203 calories, 4 g fat (2 g saturated fat), 10 mg cholesterol, 35 mg sodium, 44 g carbohydrate, 4 g fiber, 1 g protein.*

top tip   Apples to Apples

Apples range in flavor from sweet to tart depending on the variety. They make great snacks but are also good for salads, sauces, pies and baking. The best red apples for slow cooking include Braeburn, Cortland, Empire, Jonathan, Pink Lady and Rome Beauty. —**HEALTHY COOKING TEST KITCHEN**

Baked Banana Boats S M

PREP/TOTAL TIME: 20 MIN. **MAKES:** 4 SERVINGS

- 4 **medium bananas, unpeeled**
- ½ **cup unsweetened crushed pineapple, drained**
- ¼ **cup granola without raisins**
- ¼ **cup chopped pecans**
- 4 **teaspoons miniature semisweet chocolate chips**

1. Cut each banana lengthwise about ½ in. deep, leaving ½ in. uncut at both ends. Place each banana on a 12-in. square of foil; crimp and shape foil around bananas so they sit flat. Gently pull each banana peel open, forming a pocket. Fill pockets with pineapple, granola, pecans and chocolate chips.
2. Place on a baking sheet. Bake at 350° for 10-12 minutes or until chips are softened.

Nutrition Facts: *1 serving equals 220 calories, 8 g fat (1 g saturated fat), 0 cholesterol, 4 mg sodium, 40 g carbohydrate, 5 g fiber, 4 g protein.*

❝Kids can make their own banana boats with custom toppings. We use different berries and honey or peanut butter instead of chocolate chips. They're also good topped with crushed graham crackers or granola.❞

—**REBEKAH VIERS** TAYLORS, SOUTH CAROLINA

Cranberry-Pineapple Gelatin Mold F S

This cranberry mold has become a tradition in our home during the holidays. You can use a blender to combine the cranberries and oranges if you don't have a food processor.

—**BETHANY RING** CONNEAUT, OHIO

PREP: 15 MIN. **COOK:** 5 MIN. + CHILLING **MAKES:** 10 SERVINGS

- 1 **can (20 ounces) unsweetened crushed pineapple**
- 2 **envelopes unflavored gelatin**
- 1 **package (12 ounces) fresh or frozen cranberries**
- 3 **medium navel oranges, peeled and cut into segments**
- ½ **cup honey**
   Whipped cream, optional

1. Drain pineapple, reserving juice; set pineapple aside. Place reserved juice in a small saucepan. Sprinkle with gelatin; let stand for 1 minute or until softened. Heat over low heat, stirring until gelatin is completely dissolved. Remove from the heat.
2. In a food processor, combine cranberries and oranges; cover and pulse until chunky. Add honey and pineapple; cover and pulse just until blended. Stir in juice mixture. Transfer to a 6-cup mold coated with cooking spray. Refrigerate until firm.
3. Unmold onto a serving platter. Serve with whipped cream if desired.

Nutrition Facts: *1 slice (calculated without whipped cream) equals 126 calories, trace fat (trace saturated fat), 0 cholesterol, 5 mg sodium, 32 g carbohydrate, 3 g fiber, 2 g protein.*

Makeover Sweet Kugel Ⓜ

This is a traditional recipe I make for the holidays. My close friend and I used to bake together until she moved 1,300 miles away. Now when I make this dish, I'm reminded of our time together.

—**EILEEN WOLF** ABINGTON, PENNSYLVANIA

PREP: 20 MIN.
BAKE: 55 MIN. + STANDING
MAKES: 12 SERVINGS

- 1 package (12 ounces) yolk-free noodles
- 2 tablespoons butter
- ½ medium apple, peeled and thinly sliced
- 1½ cups (12 ounces) reduced-fat sour cream
- 1 package (8 ounces) reduced-fat cream cheese, cubed
- ¾ cup sugar
- 3 eggs
- 2 egg whites
- 1½ teaspoons ground cinnamon, divided
- 1 teaspoon vanilla extract
- 2 cups fat-free milk
- 1 jar (10 ounces) apricot preserves

1. Cook noodles according to package directions; drain. Toss with butter and apple; set aside. Meanwhile, beat the sour cream, cream cheese, sugar, eggs, egg whites, 1 teaspoon cinnamon and vanilla until well blended. Beat in milk. Stir in noodle mixture.

2. In a 13-in. x 9-in. baking dish coated with cooking spray, layer half of the noodle mixture, all of the preserves and the remaining noodle mixture. Sprinkle with remaining cinnamon. Bake, uncovered, at 350° for 55-65 minutes or until a thermometer reads 160°.

3. Let stand for 10 minutes before cutting. Serve warm or cold.

Nutrition Facts: *1 serving equals 353 calories, 10 g fat (6 g saturated fat), 82 mg cholesterol, 182 mg sodium, 54 g carbohydrate, 2 g fiber, 12 g protein.*

Rhubarb-Pineapple Crisp Ⓢ Ⓜ

Treat your family to rhubarb in an irresistible new way. The fruity flavor combination is absolutely delish!

—**JUDY SCHUT** GRAND RAPIDS, MICHIGAN

PREP: 15 MIN. **BAKE:** 30 MIN. **MAKES:** 6 SERVINGS

- 2 cups sliced fresh or frozen rhubarb, thawed and drained
- 1 can (20 ounces) unsweetened pineapple tidbits, drained
- ½ cup sugar, divided
- 2 tablespoons plus ⅓ cup all-purpose flour, divided
- ⅓ cup quick-cooking oats
- ¾ teaspoon ground cinnamon
- ⅛ teaspoon salt
- ¼ cup cold butter
  Whipped cream, optional

1. In a large bowl, combine the rhubarb, pineapple, ¼ cup sugar and 2 tablespoons flour. Transfer to a 9-in. deep-dish pie plate coated with cooking spray.

2. In a small bowl, combine the oats, cinnamon, salt and remaining sugar and flour. Cut in butter until crumbly. Sprinkle over fruit. Bake, uncovered, at 350° for 30-35 minutes or until filling is bubbly and topping is golden brown. Cool for 5 minutes; serve with whipped cream if desired.

Editor's Note: *If using frozen rhubarb, measure rhubarb while still frozen, then thaw completely. Drain in a colander, but do not press liquid out.*

Nutrition Facts: *1 serving (calculated without whipped cream) equals 232 calories, 8 g fat (5 g saturated fat), 20 mg cholesterol, 106 mg sodium, 39 g carbohydrate, 2 g fiber, 2 g protein.*

Hot Cocoa Souffle

PREP: 20 MIN. **BAKE:** 40 MIN.
MAKES: 6 SERVINGS

- 5 **eggs**
- 4 **teaspoons plus ¾ cup sugar**
- ½ **cup baking cocoa**
- 6 **tablespoons all-purpose flour**
- ¼ **teaspoon salt**
- 1½ **cups fat-free milk**
- 2 **tablespoons butter**
- 1½ **teaspoons vanilla extract**

1. Separate eggs; let stand at room temperature for 30 minutes. Coat a 2-qt. souffle dish with cooking spray and lightly sprinkle with 4 teaspoons sugar; set aside.

2. In a small saucepan, combine the cocoa, flour, salt and remaining sugar. Gradually whisk in milk. Bring to a boil, stirring constantly. Cook and stir 1-2 minutes longer or until thickened. Stir in butter. Transfer to a large bowl.

3. Stir a small amount of hot mixture into egg yolks; return all to the bowl, stirring constantly. Add vanilla; cool slightly.

4. In another large bowl with clean beaters, beat egg whites until stiff peaks form. With a spatula, stir a fourth of the egg whites into chocolate mixture until no white streaks remain. Fold in remaining egg whites until combined.

5. Transfer to prepared dish. Bake at 350° for 40-45 minutes or until the top is puffed and center appears set. Serve immediately.

Nutrition Facts: *1 serving equals 272 calories, 9 g fat (4 g saturated fat), 188 mg cholesterol, 209 mg sodium, 41 g carbohydrate, 2 g fiber, 9 g protein.*

A friend invited me to go to a cooking demo at her church years ago, and one of the recipes prepared was this luscious souffle. It's so easy to prepare and tastes absolutely delicious. —**JOAN HALLFORD** NORTH RICHLAND HILLS, TEXAS

top tip On the Rise

If any fat gets in with the egg whites, they will not achieve full volume. That's why it's important to avoid getting any yolk in with the whites and to use a very clean bowl and beaters. For the most height, bake souffles immediately. You can also cover and refrigerate an unbaked souffle for up to 2 hours, but it won't rise as much.
—**HEALTHY COOKING TEST KITCHEN**

Chunky Banana Cream Freeze 🅂 🅼

PREP: 15 MIN. + FREEZING   **MAKES:** 3 CUPS

- 5 medium bananas, peeled and frozen
- ⅓ cup almond milk
- 2 tablespoons finely shredded unsweetened coconut
- 2 tablespoons creamy peanut butter
- 1 teaspoon vanilla extract
- ¼ cup chopped walnuts
- 3 tablespoons raisins

1. Place the bananas, milk, coconut, peanut butter and vanilla in a food processor; cover and process until blended.

2. Transfer to a freezer container; stir in walnuts and raisins. Freeze for 2-4 hours before serving.

Editor's Note: *Look for unsweetened coconut in the baking or health food section.*

Nutrition Facts: *½ cup equals 181 calories, 7 g fat (2 g saturated fat), 0 cholesterol, 35 mg sodium, 29 g carbohydrate, 4 g fiber, 3 g protein.* **Diabetic Exchanges:** *1 fruit, 1 fat, ½ starch.*

❝With its sweet banana-almond flavor and chunky texture, this appealing frozen dessert is a crowd-pleaser. People who ask me for the recipe can't believe how easy it is to make.❞

—**KRISTEN BLOOM** APO, AP

Amaretto Custard Berry Parfaits 🅼

As if you need a reason to assemble a parfait! This indulgent custard concoction is an attractive way to sweeten any meal.

—**SUSAN JORDAN** DENVER, COLORADO

PREP: 15 MIN.   **COOK:** 15 MIN. + CHILLING   **MAKES:** 4 SERVINGS

- ⅓ cup sugar
- 3 tablespoons cornstarch
- ⅛ teaspoon salt
- 2¾ cups 2% milk
- 4 egg yolks, beaten
- 2 teaspoons unsalted butter
- 1 teaspoon amaretto
- ½ teaspoon vanilla extract
- 1 cup sliced fresh strawberries
- 1 cup fresh raspberries
- 4 whole fresh strawberries

1. In a large heavy saucepan, combine sugar, cornstarch and salt. Stir in milk until smooth. Cook and stir over medium-high heat until thickened and bubbly. Reduce heat; cook and stir 2 minutes longer.

2. Remove from the heat. Stir a small amount of hot mixture into egg yolks; return all to the pan, stirring constantly. Bring to a gentle boil; cook and stir 2 minutes longer. Remove from the heat. Stir in the butter, amaretto and vanilla. Cool to room temperature.

3. Transfer custard to a small bowl; press waxed paper onto surface of custard. Refrigerate until chilled.

4. Just before serving, spoon ¼ cup strawberries into each of four parfait glasses. Layer each with ⅓ cup custard, ¼ cup raspberries and ⅓ cup custard. Top each with a whole strawberry.

Nutrition Facts: *1 parfait equals 279 calories, 10 g fat (5 g saturated fat), 222 mg cholesterol, 167 mg sodium, 39 g carbohydrate, 3 g fiber, 9 g protein.*

1. In a small saucepan, sprinkle gelatin over milk; let stand for 1 minute. Split vanilla bean lengthwise; using the tip of a sharp knife, scrape seeds. Add bean and seeds to gelatin mixture. Heat over low heat, stirring until gelatin is completely dissolved. Combine yogurt and sugar; gradually whisk into gelatin mixture. Cook and stir just until blended. Discard vanilla bean. Pour into four ungreased 10-oz. ramekins or custard cups. Cover and refrigerate for at least 5 hours or until set.

2. Unmold panna cotta onto dessert plates. Garnish with cranberry sauce and/or pear slices if desired.

Nutrition Facts: *1 panna cotta (calculated without optional garnishes) equals 183 calories, 3 g fat (2 g saturated fat), 12 mg cholesterol, 105 mg sodium, 31 g carbohydrate, 0 fiber, 9 g protein.* **Diabetic Exchanges:** *1 starch, 1 reduced-fat milk.*

Sweet Potato Pie Ice Cream S M

The real inspiration for this dessert was my craving for pumpkin pie. I decided to experiment, and this creamy confection was the result. You can also add cinnamon or allspice.

—**REBECCA LYNE** MEQUON, WISCONSIN

PREP: 5 MIN. + FREEZING **MAKES:** 1 QUART

- 4 **cups reduced-fat vanilla ice cream**
- 1½ **cups mashed sweet potatoes**
- 2 **tablespoons maple syrup**
- ⅛ **teaspoon ground nutmeg**
  Dash salt
- 2 **whole cinnamon graham crackers, quartered**

In a blender, combine the first five ingredients; cover and process for 30 seconds or until smooth. Transfer to a freezer container; freeze for at least 4 hours before serving. Serve in dessert dishes with graham crackers.

Nutrition Facts: *½ cup with ¼ graham cracker equals 188 calories, 4 g fat (2 g saturated fat), 18 mg cholesterol, 108 mg sodium, 35 g carbohydrate, 2 g fiber, 4 g protein.*

Vanilla Sugar F S C M

I use homemade vanilla sugar to bake angel food cake, cookies and various fillings. You can also use vanilla beans to infuse simple syrup, rice pudding and fruit sauces.

—**JACKIE TERMONT** RICHMOND, VIRGINIA

PREP: 5 MINUTES + STANDING **MAKES:** 2 CUPS

- 2 **cups sugar**
- 1 **vanilla bean**

Place sugar in an airtight container. Split vanilla bean lengthwise; using the tip of a sharp knife, scrape seeds from the center into sugar. Bury vanilla bean in sugar. Cover and let stand for at least 24 hours. Use as regular, granulated sugar, discarding bean as it loses its flavor.

Nutrition Facts: *1 teaspoon equals 16 calories, 0 fat (0 saturated fat), 0 cholesterol, 0 sodium, 4 g carbohydrate, 0 fiber, 0 protein.*

Vanilla Yogurt Panna Cotta F S

Panna Cotta always impresses, and it's so easy to prepare. It's especially stunning when garnished with cranberry sauce, sliced pears or fresh berries.

—**JAN VALDEZ** CHICAGO, ILLINOIS

PREP: 10 MIN. **COOK:** 10 MIN. + CHILLING **MAKES:** 4 SERVINGS

- 1 **envelope unflavored gelatin**
- 2 **cups 2% milk**
- ½ **vanilla bean**
- 1 **cup vanilla yogurt**
- ⅓ **cup sugar**
  Whole-berry cranberry sauce and/or pear slices, optional

Easy Lemon Berry Tartlets F S C M

These flaky, sweet treats filled with raspberries are a fun ending to a great weeknight meal. And they come together in mere minutes.

—ELIZABETH DEHART WEST JORDAN, UTAH

PREP/TOTAL TIME: 15 MIN. **MAKES:** 15 TARTLETS

- ⅔ cup frozen unsweetened raspberries, thawed and drained
- 1 teaspoon confectioners' sugar
- 1 package (1.9 ounces) frozen miniature phyllo tart shells
- 4 ounces reduced-fat cream cheese
- 2 tablespoons lemon curd
   Fresh raspberries, optional

1. In a small bowl, combine raspberries and confectioners' sugar; mash with a fork. Spoon into tart shells.
2. In a small bowl, combine cream cheese and lemon curd. Pipe or spoon over filling. Top with fresh raspberries if desired.
Nutrition Facts: *1 tartlet equals 51 calories, 3 g fat (1 g saturated fat), 7 mg cholesterol, 43 mg sodium, 5 g carbohydrate, trace fiber, 1 g protein.* **Diabetic Exchange:** *½ starch.*

Caramel Cream Crepes for 2 M

Homemade crepes are a cinch to whip up, and our special creamy caramel filling is irresistible.

—HEALTHY COOKING TEST KITCHEN

PREP: 20 MIN. + CHILLING **COOK:** 5 MIN. **MAKES:** 2 SERVINGS

- 2 tablespoons fat-free milk
- 2 tablespoons egg substitute
- ½ teaspoon butter, melted
- ¼ teaspoon vanilla extract
- 2 tablespoons all-purpose flour
- 2 ounces fat-free cream cheese
- 1 tablespoon plus 2 teaspoons fat-free caramel ice cream topping, divided
- ¾ cup reduced-fat whipped topping
- ½ cup fresh raspberries
- 2 tablespoons white wine or unsweetened apple juice
- 1 tablespoon sliced almonds, toasted

1. In a small bowl, whisk the milk, egg substitute, butter and vanilla. Whisk in flour until blended. Cover and refrigerate for 1 hour.
2. Lightly coat a 6-in. nonstick skillet with cooking spray; heat over medium heat. Pour about 2 tablespoons of batter into center of skillet; lift and tilt pan to evenly coat bottom. Cook until top appears dry and bottom is golden; turn and cook 15-20 seconds longer. Remove to a wire rack. Repeat with remaining batter.
3. In a small bowl, beat cream cheese and 1 tablespoon caramel topping until smooth. Fold in whipped topping. Spoon down the center of each crepe. Drizzle with remaining caramel topping; roll up.
4. In a small microwave-safe bowl, combine raspberries and wine. Microwave on high for 30-60 seconds or until warm. Using a slotted spoon, place berries over crepes. Sprinkle with almonds.
Nutrition Facts: *1 crepe equals 209 calories, 6 g fat (4 g saturated fat), 5 mg cholesterol, 223 mg sodium, 29 g carbohydrate, 3 g fiber, 8 g protein.* **Diabetic Exchanges:** *2 starch, 1 fat.*

Homemade Vanilla Extract F S C M

Homemade vanilla extract is a fun gift for those special friends who like to cook or bake. Pour it into decorative bottles and attach attractive labels.

—BECKY JO SMITH KETTLE FALLS, WASHINGTON

PREP: 5 MIN. + STANDING **MAKES:** 2 CUPS

- 6 vanilla beans, split lengthwise
- 2 cups vodka

Place vanilla beans in a tall jar; cover with vodka. Seal jar tightly. Let stand in a cool dark place for at least 6 weeks, gently shaking jar once a week.
Nutrition Facts: *1 teaspoon equals 11 calories, 0 fat (0 saturated fat), 0 cholesterol, trace sodium, 0 carbohydrate, 0 fiber, 0 protein.*

Cherry-Almond Streusel Tart M

Brimming with fresh cherries and topped with a crunchy streusel, this tempting tart is a great way to end dinner on a sweet note. It's fast to fix, looks elegant and tastes delicious.

—**MARION LEE** MOUNT HOPE, ONTARIO

PREP: 20 MIN. **BAKE:** 30 MIN. + COOLING **MAKES:** 8 SERVINGS

> **Pastry for single-crust pie (9 inches)**
> ⅔ **cup sugar**
> 3 **tablespoons cornstarch**
> **Dash salt**
> 4 **cups fresh tart cherries, pitted or frozen pitted tart cherries, thawed**
> ⅛ **teaspoon almond extract**
> **TOPPING**
> ¼ **cup quick-cooking oats**
> 3 **tablespoons all-purpose flour**
> 2 **tablespoons brown sugar**
> 1 **tablespoon slivered almonds**
> 2 **tablespoons cold butter**

1. Press pastry onto the bottom and up the sides of an ungreased 9-in. fluted tart pan with removable bottom; trim edges.

2. In a large saucepan, combine the sugar, cornstarch and salt. Stir in cherries; bring to a boil over medium heat, stirring constantly. Cook and stir for 1-2 minutes or until thickened. Remove from the heat; stir in extract. Pour into crust.

3. For topping, combine the oats, flour, brown sugar and almonds. Cut in butter until mixture resembles coarse crumbs. Sprinkle over filling. Bake at 350° for 30-35 minutes or until topping is golden brown. Cool on a wire rack.

Nutrition Facts: *1 piece equals 298 calories, 11 g fat (5 g saturated fat), 13 mg cholesterol, 143 mg sodium, 49 g carbohydrate, 2 g fiber, 3 g protein.*

Picnic Berry Shortcakes F S M

You can make the berry sauce in advance and keep it chilled in the fridge. Then simply assemble the entire dessert a few hours before the picnic or party.

—**HEALTHY COOKING TEST KITCHEN**

PREP: 20 MIN. + CHILLING **MAKES:** 4 SERVINGS

> 2 **tablespoons sugar**
> ½ **teaspoon cornstarch**
> 2 **tablespoons water**
> 2 **cups sliced fresh strawberries, divided**
> ½ **teaspoon grated lime peel**
> 2 **individual round sponge cakes**
> 2 **cups fresh blueberries**

1. In a small saucepan, combine sugar and cornstarch. Stir in water. Add 1 cup strawberries; mash mixture. Bring to a boil; cook and stir for 1 minute or until thickened. Remove from the heat; stir in lime peel. Transfer to a small bowl; cover and refrigerate until chilled.

2. Cut sponge cakes in half widthwise; trim each to fit in the bottom of four wide-mouth half-pint canning jars. Combine blueberries and remaining strawberries; spoon over cakes. Top with sauce.

Nutrition Facts: *1 dessert equals 124 calories, 1 g fat (trace saturated fat), 10 mg cholesterol, 67 mg sodium, 29 g carbohydrate, 3 g fiber, 2 g protein.* **Diabetic Exchanges:** *1 starch, 1 fruit.*

Slow-Cooked Bread Pudding **F M**

This warm and hearty dessert is perfect on any cold, blustery winter evening. And the slow cooker fills your kitchen with an amazing aroma. My stomach is growling just thinking about it!
—**MAIAH ALBI** CARLSBAD, CALIFORNIA

PREP: 15 MIN.   **COOK:** 3 HOURS   **MAKES:** 8 SERVINGS

- 4   whole wheat bagels, split and cut into ¾-inch pieces
- 1   large tart apple, peeled and chopped
- ½   cup dried cranberries
- ¼   cup golden raisins
- 2   cups fat-free milk
- 1   cup egg substitute
- ½   cup sugar
- 2   tablespoons butter, melted
- 1   teaspoon ground cinnamon
- 1   teaspoon vanilla extract

1. In a 3-qt. slow cooker coated with cooking spray, combine the bagels, apple, cranberries and raisins. In a large bowl, whisk the milk, egg substitute, sugar, butter, cinnamon and vanilla. Pour over bagel mixture and stir to combine; gently press bagels down into milk mixture.

2. Cover and cook on low for 3-4 hours or until a knife inserted near the center comes out clean.

Nutrition Facts: *1 serving equals 231 calories, 3 g fat (2 g saturated fat), 9 mg cholesterol, 257 mg sodium, 45 g carbohydrate, 4 g fiber, 8 g protein.*

Apricot Gelatin Mold **S**

My mother always made this for celebrations. When my husband and I were dating, he fell in love with this dish. Once we got married, he asked me to get the recipe from her. You can substitute peach or orange gelatin for a fresh summer treat.
—**SUZANNE HOLCOMB** ST. JOHNSVILLE, NEW YORK

PREP: 25 MIN.   **COOK:** 10 MIN. + CHILLING   **MAKES:** 12 SERVINGS

- 1   can (8 ounces) unsweetened crushed pineapple
- 2   packages (3 ounces each) apricot or peach gelatin
- 1   package (8 ounces) reduced-fat cream cheese
- ¾   cup grated carrots
- 1   carton (8 ounces) frozen fat-free whipped topping, thawed

1. Drain pineapple, reserving juice in a 2-cup measuring cup; add enough water to measure 2 cups. Set pineapple aside. Pour juice mixture into a small saucepan. Bring to a boil; remove from heat. Dissolve gelatin in juice mixture. Cool for 10 minutes.

2. In a large bowl, beat cream cheese until creamy. Gradually add gelatin mixture, beating until smooth. Refrigerate for 30-40 minutes or until slightly thickened.

3. Fold in pineapple and carrots, then whipped topping. Transfer to an 8-cup ring mold coated with cooking spray. Refrigerate until set. Unmold onto a serving platter.

Nutrition Facts: *½ cup equals 144 calories, 4 g fat (3 g saturated fat), 13 mg cholesterol, 128 mg sodium, 23 g carbohydrate, trace fiber, 3 g protein.* **Diabetic Exchanges:** *1½ starch, 1 fat.*

Swirled Blueberry Frozen Yogurt $\boxed{S}\boxed{M}$

PREP: 30 MIN. + FREEZING   **MAKES:** 8 SERVINGS

- 1 **cup fresh or frozen blueberries**
- ⅓ **cup sugar**
- ⅓ **cup finely chopped walnuts**
- 1 **quart fat-free frozen yogurt, softened**

DRIZZLE

- 2½ **ounces white baking chocolate, chopped**
- 1 **tablespoon fat-free milk**
- ½ **teaspoon vanilla extract**

1. In a small bowl, combine the blueberries, sugar and walnuts; let stand for 15 minutes.

2. In a large container, layer a third of the frozen yogurt and half the blueberry mixture. Repeat layers. Top with remaining frozen yogurt. Swirl mixture; freeze until firm.

3. In a small saucepan, combine the chocolate, milk and vanilla. Cook and stir over low heat until chocolate is melted. Serve with frozen yogurt.

Nutrition Facts: *½ cup frozen yogurt with 1½ teaspoons drizzle equals 221 calories, 7 g fat (2 g saturated fat), 3 mg cholesterol, 75 mg sodium, 36 g carbohydrate, 1 g fiber, 6 g protein.*

> ❝A silky homemade sauce is anything but vanilla when it comes to topping a scoop of creamy frozen yogurt. These are the touches that make celebrations extra special.❞

—**CHRISTINA SEREMETIS** ROCKLAND, MASSACHUSETTS

Mocha Pecan Balls $\boxed{F}\boxed{S}\boxed{C}\boxed{M}$

Dusted in either confectioners' sugar or cocoa, this 6-ingredient dough rolls up into truffle-like treats—no baking required.

—**LORRAINE DAROCHA** MOUNTAIN CITY, TENNESSEE

PREP/TOTAL TIME: 25 MIN.   **MAKES:** 4 DOZEN

- 2½ **cups crushed vanilla wafers (about 65 wafers)**
- 2 **cups plus ¼ cup confectioners' sugar, divided**
- ⅔ **cup finely chopped pecans, toasted**
- 2 **tablespoons baking cocoa**
- ¼ **cup reduced-fat evaporated milk**
- ¼ **cup cold strong brewed coffee**
  Additional baking cocoa, optional

1. In a large bowl, combine the wafer crumbs, 2 cups confectioners' sugar, pecans and cocoa. Stir in milk and coffee (mixture will be sticky).

2. With hands dusted in confectioners' sugar, shape dough into ¾-in. balls; roll in remaining confectioner's sugar or additional baking cocoa if desired. Store in an airtight container.

Nutrition Facts: *1 cookie equals 61 calories, 2 g fat (trace saturated fat), 1 mg cholesterol, 20 mg sodium, 10 g carbohydrate, trace fiber, trace protein.* **Diabetic Exchange:** *1 starch.*

Fresh Berries with Lemon Yogurt $\boxed{F}\boxed{S}\boxed{M}$

This is a refreshing dish that can be served for breakfast or dessert. The berries offer a powerhouse of nutrition, and the limoncello, an Italian lemon liqueur, adds a tangy burst of citrus flavor.

—**SARAH VASQUES** MILFORD, NEW HAMPSHIRE

PREP/TOTAL TIME: 15 MIN.   **MAKES:** 4 SERVINGS

- 2 **cups sliced fresh strawberries**
- 1 **medium banana, sliced**
- 1 **cup fresh blueberries**
- ¼ **cup limoncello**
- 1 **tablespoon sugar**
- ¾ **cup (6 ounces) plain yogurt**
- 3 **tablespoons lemon curd**

1. In a small bowl, combine the first five ingredients; spoon into four dessert dishes. Whisk together yogurt and lemon curd; spoon over fruit.

Nutrition Facts: *1 cup berry mixture with 3 tablespoons sauce equals 218 calories, 3 g fat (1 g saturated fat), 17 mg cholesterol, 34 mg sodium, 40 g carbohydrate, 3 g fiber, 3 g protein.*

Makeover Chocolate-Covered Strawberry Milk Shake M

Who can resist a creamy milk shake? This slimmed-down version tastes just like one straight off a Steak 'N Shake menu. One sip and you'll be slurping it down!

—HEALTHY COOKING TEST KITCHEN

PREP/TOTAL TIME: 10 MIN. **MAKES:** 1 SERVING

- ⅔ cup fat-free milk
- ⅔ cup reduced-fat strawberry ice cream
- ⅔ cup frozen unsweetened sliced strawberries
- 1 tablespoon fat-free hot fudge ice cream topping
- 2 tablespoons whipped cream in a can
- 1 maraschino cherry

In a blender, combine the milk, ice cream and strawberries; cover and process until smooth. Drizzle the inside of a chilled glass with fudge topping. Add ice cream mixture. Garnish with whipped cream and a cherry. Serve immediately.

Nutrition Facts: *1 serving equals 302 calories, 6 g fat (4 g saturated fat), 29 mg cholesterol, 173 mg sodium, 56 g carbohydrate, 3 g fiber, 11 g protein.*

Cranberry Pavlova S M

We're a family of breast cancer survivors and find baking to be thapeutic. It's wonderful knowing that desserts like this bring comfort and joy to others.

—VERONICA GANTLEY NORFOLK, VIRGINIA

PREP: 20 MIN. **BAKE:** 45 MIN. + COOLING **MAKES:** 10 SERVINGS

- 6 egg whites
- 1 teaspoon cornstarch
- 1 teaspoon white vinegar
- 1 teaspoon vanilla extract
  Dash salt
- 1½ cups sugar

TOPPING

- 2 cups fresh or frozen cranberries
- ⅔ cup confectioners' sugar, divided
- ½ cup water
- 1 tablespoon cornstarch
- 1 cup heavy whipping cream

1. Place egg whites in a large bowl; let stand at room temperature for 30 minutes. Line a baking sheet with parchment paper; set aside.
2. Add the cornstarch, vinegar, vanilla and salt to egg whites; beat on medium speed until soft peaks form. Gradually add sugar, 1 tablespoon at a time, beating on high until stiff glossy peaks form and sugar is dissolved.
3. Spread into a 9-in. circle on prepared pan, forming a shallow well in the center. Bake at 250° for 45-55 minutes or until set and dry. Turn off oven and do not open door; leave meringue in oven for 1 hour.
4. In a large saucepan, combine the cranberries, ½ cup confectioners' sugar, water and cornstarch. Cook over medium heat until berries pop, about 15 minutes. Remove from the heat.
5. In a small bowl, beat cream until it begins to thicken. Add remaining confectioners' sugar; beat until soft peaks form.
6. Spread whipped cream into center of meringue; top with cranberry sauce. Refrigerate leftovers.

Nutrition Facts: *1 slice equals 254 calories, 9 g fat (5 g saturated fat), 33 mg cholesterol, 58 mg sodium, 42 g carbohydrate, 1 g fiber, 3 g protein.*

Baklava with Honey Syrup ⑤ Ⓜ

PREP: 50 MIN.
BAKE: 35 MIN. + STANDING
MAKES: 2½ DOZEN

  Butter-flavored cooking spray
1 **package (16 ounces, 14-inch x 9-inch sheet size) frozen phyllo dough, thawed**
2 **cups finely chopped walnuts, toasted**

SYRUP

¾ **cup sugar**
¾ **cup water**
⅓ **cup honey**
¾ **teaspoon grated lemon peel**
¾ **teaspoon vanilla extract**

1. Coat a 13-in. x 9-in. baking pan with cooking spray. Unroll phyllo dough; trim to fit into pan.

2. Layer two sheets of phyllo dough in prepared pan, spritz with cooking spray. Repeat three times. (Keep remaining phyllo covered with plastic wrap and a damp towel to prevent it from drying out.) Sprinkle with 3 tablespoons nuts. Top with two sheets of phyllo and spritz with cooking spray. Repeat layering with nuts, phyllo and cooking spray 10 times. Top with remaining phyllo dough, spritzing every other sheet with cooking spray.

3. Using a sharp knife, cut into 30 triangles. Bake at 350° for 35-40 minutes or until golden brown. Meanwhile, in a small saucepan, combine syrup ingredients. Bring to a boil. Reduce heat; simmer, uncovered, for 10 minutes, stirring occasionally. Pour over warm baklava. Cool completely on a wire rack. Cover and let stand for several hours or overnight.

Nutrition Facts: *1 piece equals 136 calories, 7 g fat (trace saturated fat), 0 cholesterol, 67 mg sodium, 18 g carbohydrate, 1 g fiber, 3 g protein.*

Baklava is a sweet, buttery Greek treat. The honey syrup drizzled on top gives this classic dessert a delicious twist. —**TRISHA KRUSE** EAGLE, IDAHO

Summer Blackberry Cobbler

My husband is from Alabama, so I like to treat him to classic Southern desserts. This cobbler is a must-have!

—KIMBERLY DANEK PINKSON SAN ANSELMO, CALIFORNIA

PREP: 25 MIN. **BAKE:** 25 MIN. **MAKES:** 6 SERVINGS

- 5 cups fresh blackberries
- ⅓ cup turbinado (washed raw) sugar
- 2 tablespoons quick-cooking tapioca
- 1 tablespoon lemon juice
- 1½ teaspoons cornstarch or arrowroot flour
- 1 cup all-purpose flour
- ¼ cup sugar
- 1¼ teaspoons baking powder
- ¼ teaspoon salt
- ¼ teaspoon ground cinnamon
- 3 tablespoons cold butter
- ⅓ cup fat-free milk
  Vanilla ice cream, optional

1. In a large bowl, combine the first five ingredients. Transfer to a 2-qt. baking dish coated with cooking spray.
2. In a small bowl, combine the flour, sugar, baking powder, salt and cinnamon. Cut in butter until mixture resembles coarse crumbs. Stir in milk just until moistened. Drop by tablespoonfuls onto blackberry mixture.
3. Bake, uncovered, at 375° for 25-30 minutes or until golden brown. Serve warm with ice cream if desired.

Nutrition Facts: *1 serving (calculated without ice cream) equals 274 calories, 6 g fat (4 g saturated fat), 15 mg cholesterol, 229 mg sodium, 52 g carbohydrate, 7 g fiber, 4 g protein.*

Spiced Party Peanuts ⓈⒸⓂ

These seasoned nuts have just the right blend of spices, sugar and heat to kick up a party. They also make a great gift.

—CYNTHIA DEVOL PATASKALA, OHIO

PREP/TOTAL TIME: 30 MIN. **MAKES:** 3 CUPS

- 1 egg white
- 1 teaspoon water
- 3 cups unsalted dry roasted peanuts
- 1 tablespoon sugar
- 1 teaspoon ground cinnamon
- ½ teaspoon cayenne pepper
- ¼ teaspoon salt
- ¼ teaspoon ground cumin
- ¼ teaspoon ground coriander

1. In a large bowl, beat egg white and water until frothy. Stir in peanuts. Combine sugar and spices; add to peanut mixture, stirring gently to coat.
2. Transfer to an ungreased 15-in. x 10-in. x 1-in. baking pan. Bake at 325° for 20-25 minutes or until lightly browned, stirring twice. Cool on a wire rack. Store in an airtight container.

Nutrition Facts: *¼ cup equals 220 calories, 18 g fat (3 g saturated fat), 0 cholesterol, 56 mg sodium, 9 g carbohydrate, 3 g fiber, 9 g protein.* **Diabetic Exchange:** *3 fat.*

top tip · Quick Gift Idea

Fill festive baggies with Spiced Party Peanuts. Then use a colorful ribbon or tie to attach them to a bottle of your favorite seasonal brew. Add on a fun bottle opener to complete a custom party favor or hostess gift. Also try this recipe with a combination of unsalted roasted nuts.

—HEALTHY COOKING TEST KITCHEN

General Recipe Index

This index lists every recipe by food category, major ingredient and/or cooking method, so you can easily locate recipes that suit your needs.

• Table-ready in 30 minutes or less.

APPETIZERS & SNACKS

Cold Appetizers
•Asparagus with Horseradish Dip, 68
•Blue Cheese Stuffed Strawberries, 25
•Chicken Salad Party Sandwiches, 53
•Crab Cucumber Bites, 16
•Crisp Finger Sandwich, 23
Herbed-Goat Cheese Baguette Slices, 19
•Slim Asian Deviled Eggs, 20
•Slim Bloody Mary Deviled Eggs, 20
•Slim Buffalo Deviled Eggs, 22
•Slim Chutney Deviled Eggs, 22
•Slim Crab Cake Deviled Eggs, 20
•Slim Curried Deviled Eggs, 22
•Slim Deviled Eggs, 20
•Slim Deviled Eggs with Herbs, 22
•Slim Greek Deviled Eggs, 22
•Slim Guacamole Deviled Eggs, 20
•Slim Italian Deviled Eggs, 20
•Slim Southwest Deviled Eggs, 20

Dips
•Avocado Bean Dip, 15
•Crunchy Peanut Butter Apple Dip, 11
Southwest Hummus Dip, 26
Strawberry Corn Salsa, 8
Yogurt Dill Dip, 11

Hot Appetizers
Asian Tuna Bites with Dijon Dipping Sauce, 25
Beef and Blue Cheese Crostini, 24
•Chicken Wonton Cups, 23
Double-Nut Stuffed Figs, 24
Flank Steak Crostini, 105
Makeover Stuffed Potato Appetizers, 9
Margarita Granita with Spicy Shrimp, 16
Sausage-Stuffed Red Potatoes, 17
Southwest Egg Rolls, 13
Spinach Dip-Stuffed Mushrooms, 12
Steamed Turkey Dumplings, 26

Snack Mixes
Indian Snack Mix, 27
•Spiced Party Peanuts, 261
Spicy Almonds, 12

Spreads
•Ants On a Log Spread, 8
•Pineapple Shrimp Spread, 19

APPLES
•Apple-Beef Panini, 52
•Apple Fennel Salad, 38
Apple-Raisin Baked Oatmeal, 85
•Apple-Walnut Muffin Mix, 203
•Crunchy Peanut Butter Apple Dip, 11
•French Toast with Apple Topping, 87
Onion-Apple Pork Chops, 214
•Skillet Apple Pork Chops, 148
Slow Cooker Baked Apples, 248

Spicy Cran-Apple Sauce, 75
Streusel-Topped Apple Cheesecake, 240

APRICOTS
Apricot Gelatin Mold, 257
Apricot-Glazed Chicken Kabobs, 116
Apricot Pork Tenderloin, 156
•Apricot Turkey Sandwiches, 213

ASPARAGUS
•Asparagus and Mushrooms in Lemon-Thyme Butter, 66
•Asparagus with Horseradish Dip, 68
Roasted Asparagus Lasagna, 188
•Shrimp Asparagus Fettuccine, 169

AVOCADOS
•Avocado Bean Dip, 15
Chicken Tacos with Avocado Salsa, 124
•Slim Guacamole Deviled Eggs, 20

BANANAS
•Baked Banana Boats, 249
Banana Chip Cake, 234
Banana French Toast Bake, 87
Banana Oatmeal Pancakes, 78
Chunky Banana Cream Freeze, 253
Poppy Seed-Banana Mini Loaves, 199
•Strawberry Banana Blast, 80

BEANS (also see Lentils)
•Avocado Bean Dip, 15
Black Bean Brownies, 230
Black Bean Burgers with Chipotle Slaw, 186
Cilantro Bean Burgers, 206
Colorful Garbanzo Bean Salad, 40
Healthy Hoppin' John, 121
Makeover Mediterranean Chicken & Beans, 126
•Mustard Bean Salad, 36
Southwest Hummus Dip, 26
•Tuscan Chicken and Beans, 120

BEANS, GREEN
•Cashew Green Beans and Mushrooms, 67
•Zesty Garlic Green Beans, 72

BEEF & CORNED BEEF
(also see Ground Beef)
Appetizers
•Beef and Blue Cheese Crostini, 24
Main Dishes
•Beef and Blue Cheese Penne with Pesto, 99
Bourbon Steak Portobellos, 112
Chocolate-Chipotle Sirloin Steak, 106
Flank Steak Crostini, 105
Italian Beef Tortellini Stew, 50
Java Roast Beef, 102

•Orange Beef Stir-Fry, 211
Sassy Pot Roast, 108
•Southwest Flank Steak, 98
Steak San Marino, 111
Sweet and Sour Brisket, 112
Tender Salsa Beef, 104
Zippy Sirloin Steak, 108
Sandwiches
•Apple-Beef Panini, 52
Tex-Mex Beef Barbecues, 44
Soups & Chili
Tangy Beef Chili, 44
Sunday Herbed Pot Roast Soup, 49
Veggie Meatball Soup for 3, 59

BEVERAGES
Cold Beverages
•Cranberry Pomegranate Margaritas, 15
•Creamy Orange Smoothies, 85
•Fruity Smoothies, 78
Iced Lemon Tea, 11
•Makeover Chocolate-Covered Strawberry Milk Shake, 259
Makeover Creamy Eggnog, 27
•Strawberry Banana Blast, 80
Hot Beverage
•Sweet Pineapple Cider, 15

BISCUITS & BISCOTTI
•Makeover Cheddar Biscuits, 195
Maple Walnut Biscotti, 200
•Tender Biscuits for Two, 201

BLUEBERRIES
Blueberry Angel Cupcakes, 235
Swirled Blueberry Frozen Yogurt, 258
•Watermelon-Blueberry Salad, 214

BREADS (see Biscuits & Biscotti; Breadsticks; Coffee Cakes; French Toast & Waffles; Muffins; Pancakes; Quick Breads; Rolls & Popovers; Yeast Breads)

BREADSTICKS
•Prosciutto Breadsticks, 199

BROCCOLI
•Fresh Broccoli Salad, 34
•Honey-Orange Broccoli Slaw, 38
•Lime-Buttered Broccoli for Two, 209

BROWNIES & BARS
Black Bean Brownies, 230
Chewy Cranberry Pecan Bars, 220
Cinnamon Cranberry Oat Bars, 224
Devil's Food Snack Cake, 228
Gluten-Free Peanut Butter Blondies, 229
Light & Easy Cheesecake Bars, 221
Nut-Licious Peanut Butter Bars, 230

Alphabetical Index

This handy index lists every recipe alphabetically, so you can easily find the dishes you enjoy most.

• Table-ready in 30 minutes or less.